su

AL JUSTIFICATION: Interpretative Essays
mons (forthcoming))

APHYSICS IN KANT
tröm and H. William (forthcoming))

C000296457

Kant and Sartre

Kant and Sartre

Re-discovering Critical Ethics

Sorin Baiasu
University of Keele, UK

First published 2011 by
PALGRAVE MACMILLAN

Palgrave Macmillan in the UK is an imprint of Macmillan Publishers Limited, registered in England, company number 785998, of Houndmills, Basingstoke, Hampshire RG21 6XS.

Palgrave Macmillan in the US is a division of St Martin's Press LLC, 175 Fifth Avenue, New York, NY 10010.

Palgrave Macmillan is the global academic imprint of the above companies and has companies and representatives throughout the world.

Palgrave® and Macmillan® are registered trademarks in the United States, the United Kingdom, Europe and other countries.

ISBN 978–0–230–00150–3 hardback

This book is printed on paper suitable for recycling and made from fully managed and sustained forest sources. Logging, pulping and manufacturing processes are expected to conform to the environmental regulations of the country of origin.

A catalogue record for this book is available from the British Library.

Library of Congress Cataloging-in-Publication Data
Baiasu, Sorin.
    Kant and Sartre : re-discovering critical ethics / Sorin Baiasu.
      p.   cm.
    Summary: "This book challenges the standard view of the relationship between Kant's and Sartre's practical philosophies, making a case for regarding Kant as one of Sartre's most significant predecessors. By using an original comparative methodology, the book identifies several fundamental theses of Sartre's practical philosophy despite the common reading of Sartre as a philosopher without a practical philosophy. Furthermore, the book shows that Sartre's practical philosophy proves to be closer to Kant than dominant contemporary Kantian theories are. Starting from the similarities between Kant and Sartre, the book uncovers the project of a critical ethics which is philosophically more compelling than dominant contemporary Kantian theories"—Provided by publisher.
    Includes bibliographical references.
    ISBN 978–0–230–00150–3
    1. Kant, Immanuel, 1724–1804.   2. Ethics.   3. Sartre, Jean-Paul, 1905–1980.
    I. Title.
    B2799.E8B235 2010
    170.92′2—dc22   2010027481

10   9   8   7   6   5   4   3   2   1
20   19   18   17   16   15   14   13   12   11

Printed and bound in Great Britain by
CPI Antony Rowe, Chippenham and Eastbourne

For Roxana, Mother and grandmother Lucia, with love

Contents

Acknowledgements   xi

Abbreviations and References   xiii

Introduction   1
   §1. Historical context   2
   §2. Conceptual context   4
   §3. Kant and Sartre so far   5
   §4. Method   8
   §5. Claims and implications   10
   §6. Overview   12

Part I   Identity and Self-Choice

1. Kant   17
   §7. Two assumptions of moral accountability   17
   §8. The third paralogism   19
   §9. Numerical identity   21
   §10. The problem of the third paralogism   22
   §11. Turning the paralogism into a valid syllogism   25
   §12. Presuppositions of experience   27
   §13. Transcendental unity of apperception   29
   §14. Sensibility and the understanding   32
   §15. The understanding and objectivity   34
   §16. Character   37
   §17. Revolution in disposition   39

2. Sartre and Kant   42
   §18. Impersonal consciousness   42
   §19. Digestive philosophy   44
   §20. Intentionality   46
   §21. The Transcendence of the Ego   48
   §22. Forms of consciousness   50
   §23. Self   53
   §24. The personal   56
   §25. Deliberation   58

§26. Project 60
§27. Painting the self 62
§28. Making Kant and Sartre consistent 64
§29. Deliberation and radical change 67
§30. Problems with Sartre's account 69
§31. A Kantian solution to Sartre's problems 71
§32. Substantive similarities 73
§33. A significant difference 75
§34. Further problems 77

Part II Freedom and Normativity

3. Kant **81**
§35. Moral and psychological identity 82
§36. The third antinomy 84
§37. Solution: Theoretical freedom 86
§38. Solution: Practical freedom 89
§39. Ethical normativity 91
§40. Practical antinomy 94
§41. Solution to the practical antinomy 96
§42. Categorical imperatives 98
§43. Performing ethical actions 100
§44. Identity, freedom and moral criterion 102

4. Sartre and Kant **105**
§45. Spontaneity 106
§46. The for-itself's structure 108
§47. Reflection 110
§48. Freedom 113
§49. Freedom and determinism 115
§50. The eternal subject 118
§51. Singularity 121
§52. Ethical normativity 123
§53. Impure reflection 125
§54. Bad faith 127
§55. Being-for-others 128
§56. Self and others 131
§57. Ethics and interpersonal relations 133
§58. A framework for normativity 135
§59. Against moral codes 137
§60. Noumena and other persons 139
§61. A metaethical distinction 141
§62. Split personality 143
§63. More about critical ethics 145

Part III Authority and Progress

5. Kant   151
§64. Enlightenment   152
§65. Political emancipation   154
§66. Human emancipation   156
§67. Logical interpretation   158
§68. Practical interpretation   160
§69. The problem of justification   162
§70. The problem of practical judgement   164
§71. The standard view of practical judgement   166
§72. Problem of standard view   168
§73. Ethics and politics   170
§74. Intention and motivation   172
§75. Empirical good   174
§76. External good   176

6. Sartre and Kant   180
§77. Practical freedom and history   181
§78. The authority of the Categorical Imperative   183
§79. Ethical experience   185
§80. Values and imperatives   188
§81. Radical ethics   189
§82. The role of interpersonal relations   192
§83. Values   194
§84. Negative freedom and autonomy   195
§85. The law of freedom   198
§86. Internalization   200
§87. The fact of reason   202
§88. Universal history   204
§89. Ideas of reason   206
§90. Analytic and dialectical   208
§91. Social structures   210
§92. Freedom in the social world   213
§93. Kantian optimism   215
§94. Moral progress   217
§95. A third practical postulate   219
§96. Dialectical a priori   221
§97. If and as if   223
§98. Closing remarks   225

Conclusion   228
§99. How to account for unconditional obligations   228
§100. Kantian constructivism   230
§101. Problems for constructivism   232

§102. Kant and Sartre: Similarities   234
§103. Critical ethics   236
§104. Conflicting duties   238

Notes   241

Bibliography   275

Index   283

Acknowledgements

This book grew from the doctoral dissertation I wrote at the University of Manchester (UK), and I am most grateful to my principal supervisor, Ursula Vogel. She encouraged what seemed to be an unusual project and combined precise and detailed comments with interest in independently undertaken research. I am also grateful to the two members of my supervisory board, Geraint Parry and Hillel Steiner, for discussion and insightful suggestions. Finally, I am particularly grateful to Christina Howells, whose work has been inspiring and whose comments and support helped me considerably from the very beginning.

Turning the dissertation into a monograph has been a long and productive process, and for the latter I am indebted to many people who provided feedback, comments and suggestions concerning the book proposal or various parts of the text. I would like to thank in particular Roxana Baiasu, Howard Williams, Katrin Flikschuh, Alan Montefiore, Graham Bird, James Tartaglia, Thomas Uebel and Gary Banham.

Special thanks are also due to two of my former lecturers at the University of Bucharest, Mihaela Miroiu and Adrian Miroiu, for continuous support and advice throughout the years.

Finally, I would like to thank my editor, Pri Gibbons, for her unflinching patience and help. Additional thanks are owed to the Integra Software Services Project Manager, A. Joel Jones, for his careful attention and support at the copyediting and proof stages.

At various stages of my work, I was helped by grants and research fellowships without which this book could not have been published now. In particular, I would like to acknowledge the financial support of the University of Manchester, through their Simon Research Fund, for a three-year Research Fellowship, which enabled me, among others, to revise material and develop a successful book proposal. I am also grateful for a one-semester Research Fellowship Leave granted by the University of Keele through their Research Institute for Law, Politics and Justice Competitive Grant Scheme. This enabled me to focus work on the book at a decisive stage of the project. Finally, I would like to thank the British Academy for a Travel Grant, which allowed me to present several sections of this book to one of the APA Central Division Meetings in Chicago.

I gratefully acknowledge permission from the publishers to use material from the following papers:

"The Anxiety of Influence: Sartre's Search for an Ethics and Kant's Moral Theory", in *Sartre Studies International* 2003, 9(1): 21–53.

"Kantian Metaphysics and the Normative Force of Practical Principles", in *Ethics and Politics Review* 2007, 3(1): 37–56.

Abbreviations and References

The following abbreviations are used for frequently cited works of Kant and Sartre; all other texts referred to are listed in the Bibliography:

Kant

GMS	*Grundlegung zur Metaphysik der Sitten*
IaG	*Idee zu einer allgemeinen Geschichte in weltbürgerlicher Absicht*
KpV	*Kritik der praktischen Vernunft*
KrV	*Kritik der reinen Vernunft*
MS	*Die Metaphysik der Sitten*
RGV	*Die Religion innerhalb der Grenzen der bloßen Vernunft*
VRML	*Über ein vermeintes Recht, aus Menschenliebe zu lügen*

Sartre

TE	*La transcendence de L'Ego*
IFP	*Une idée fondamentale de la phénomènologie de Husserl: l'intentionalité*
EN	*L'Être et le néant. Essai d'ontologie phénoménologique*
CM	*Cahiers pour une morale*
CRDI	*Critique de la raison dialectiqu*e. Tome I

In references, abbreviations will be followed by the volume and page number from Kant's *Gesammelte Schriften* (1900ff.). References to the *Critique of Pure Reason* will follow the A (first edition), B (second edition) convention. For Sartre, abbreviations will be followed by page number of the French edition used. Then, for both Kant and Sartre, the page for the English translations will be given. Translations used are listed under Bibliography. Where the original year of publication is different from the date of the edition referred to, in the Bibliography the original will be introduced between square brackets, followed by the year of the edition cited. In the text, reference will be made to the edition used. For classical texts, which have a standard way of citation (for instance, through Bekker numbers for Aristotle), I will use the standard citation and will list the edition referred to in Bibliography.

Introduction

Almost ten years before having drafted the text "The Liberty of the Ancients Compared with That of the Moderns" (1988),[1] Benjamin Constant published a pamphlet entitled "Political Reactions" (1998).[2] There, he criticized a "German philosopher" for holding a view that made society impossible, namely, that truthfulness was a person's unconditional obligation (Constant 1998: 493). One year later, Kant replied to this pamphlet by arguing against the legal implications of Constant's criticism, to wit, against "a supposed right to lie from philanthropy" (*VRML*: 8:425, 611).

Constant's well-known objection is directed against the contention that "it would be a crime to lie to a murderer who asked us whether a friend of ours whom he is pursuing has taken refuge in our house" (Constant 1998: 493). Indeed, Kant does maintain that "the duty of truthfulness, which is altogether unconditional and constitutes the supreme rightful condition in statements" should not be transformed into a conditional duty since "it would directly contradict itself" (*VRML*: 8:430, 615). In other words, Kant argues that it is a crime to lie even in those circumstances.

Surprisingly, in his story "The Wall" (1969), Sartre seems to hold a similar position.[3] During the Spanish Civil War the protagonist of the story, Pablo Ibbieta, is brought before a Falangist tribunal and sentenced to death for having helped and hidden in his house an important representative of the Republican cause who is at the same time his friend. Before the execution, the judges propose to Pablo a deal: his life in exchange of Pablo's telling them where the friend is hiding at the moment.

Pablo has the information, but does not want to disclose it. Instead he wishes to make fun of the Falangists and indicates the cemetery as the place where his friend would now be, knowing that the latter is sheltered elsewhere. Nevertheless, what Pablo does not know is that, quite recently, his friend changed his hiding place and found refuge in the cemetery. Hence "The Wall" appears[4] to draw, in fact, on one of the implications of Kant's argument for the unconditional obligation to truthfulness.

1

Thus, Kant says,

> if you had lied and said that he [the potential victim] is not at home, and he has actually gone out (though you are not aware of it), so that the murderer encounters him while going away and perpetrates his deed on him, then you can by right be prosecuted as the author of his death.
>
> (*VRML*: 8:427, 612)

Merely on the basis of this text, it is, of course, a matter of speculation to decide whether Sartre did or did not think there were unconditional obligations and those who broke them were liable for the consequences. My starting point in this book will be the assumption, confirmed by Sartre's claims in other texts, that he is attracted by the idea of unconditional obligation and tries to account for it in his ethical writings.

The currency Kant's practical (ethical and political) philosophy seems to enjoy among contemporary philosophers is, I think, at least partly due to this idea, which was so important for him. More importantly, however, the success of Kant's philosophy is partly due to the challenge he sets for him to develop an account of unconditional obligation which is non-dogmatic. Clearly, many contemporary Kantians think Kant failed to respond to this challenge.[5] They are, therefore, trying to offer a better answer. This, I think, is what Sartre was also trying to do.

§1. Historical context

For Constant, societies should not be legislated by unconditional principles; laws should be adopted either by direct participation or, if a principle of direct democratic participation is not effective, by representation. In the second case, the legislator, who *represents* the citizens, issues the laws which are or would be willed by all. Clearly, the distinct aspect of Constant's position is not the principle of representation or the principle of direct participation, but a view on juridical principles as conditional. The conditional character of laws supported by Constant is a reflection of his distinct view of the nature of moral normativity.[6]

Constant's account of norms tries to steer a path between two problematic positions. There is, on the one hand, the dogmatic stance of moral realism, which claims that moral norms exist independently from moral agents. This ontological assumption presupposes an epistemological claim, namely, that we have access to these independently existing norms and can have an accurate understanding of their requirements. By contrast, on the other hand, we have the scepticism of moral non-cognitivism, for which every knowledge claim concerning moral norms can be questioned and equally convincing arguments for and against the claim can be presented. Consequently, we cannot say whether or not moral norms exist independently from us.

Contemporary constructivist accounts[7] of moral norms share this commitment to the rejection of moral realism and moral scepticism. They try to avoid the attempts of moral realism to claim knowledge of principles and values that would exist independently from us. At the same time, they hope to go beyond non-cognitivist accounts of normativity, since the implication of such a position can only be that norms are the outcome of an empirical balance of powers, the result of the decision made by the stronger party.

Constant's argument for the conception of a representative system is given a wider form in his seminal speech "The Liberty of the Ancients Compared with That of the Moderns" (1988). Twenty years after the French Revolution, Constant deems necessary to revisit a problem that preoccupied many thinkers ever since the Renaissance,[8] namely the relation between the modern values of privacy and the ancient public virtues. This is a divide between a conception of freedom as "the right to be subjected only by laws" (1988: 310), and an account of freedom as "exercising collectively, but directly, several parts of the complete sovereignty" (1988: 311).

The former, the liberty of the moderns, is the liberty of opinion, of association, of electing officials, of advancing petitions and demands, and of choosing one's religion and profession. The latter, the liberty of the ancients, is the freedom of deliberating over war and peace, of forming alliances with foreign governments, of legislating and of examining and judging the magistrates (Constant 1988: 311). Whereas the ancients strove for "the sharing of social power among the citizens of the same fatherland", the moderns aimed at "the enjoyment of security in private pleasures" (Constant 1988: 317). The liberty of the ancients is that of taking part in the political organization of society; the liberty of the moderns is that of enjoying their private lives.

Nevertheless, for Constant, even though "we live in modern times" (1988: 323), and even though "individual independence is the first need of the moderns" (1988: 321), the political liberties of the ancients are a necessary ingredient of freedom. Without political liberty we face "the danger of modern liberty", namely that of surrendering "our right to share in political power too easily" (1988: 326). However, by simply securing our share in political power at the expense of "individual rights and enjoyments" we are led to face "the danger of ancient liberty" – that of attaching "too little value to individual right and enjoyments" (Constant 1988: 326). Hence, the solution would be to "learn to combine the two [types of liberty] together" (Constant 1988: 327), and its concrete political counterpart would be "a representative system" (Constant 1988: 326).

Constant's position on the nature of political norms makes certain assumptions concerning ethical norms too. The ancient citizen's actions were mainly guided by the common good of their community. Those actions that pursued the realization of the common good were ethically valid. The modern citizen's actions are largely based on the value of the free pursuit of their singular and particular interests. An action is ethically valid when it is performed without constraining other persons' similar attempts to realize their own particular interests.

The issue of the relation between the ethical question of the right standards of action and the political question of the justice of laws is not new,[9] although Constant did not thematize it. I will elaborate on this distinction and the conceptual framework of Constant's problem of the conflict of liberties in the next section.

§2. Conceptual context

The *ethical* debate concerning the relation between the liberty of the ancients and that of the moderns refers to all interpersonal relations, whether or not they are politically constituted. In the ethical domain, Constant's problem of the conflict of liberties becomes the question of whether freedom means liberty from constraints or liberty to act ethically. Understood as self-realization, freedom cannot be reduced to the absence of constraints but implies a requirement that the action that is free from constraints be conducive to the realization of an ethically good end; thus, it compels one to make the step from a unilateral defence of liberty understood as freedom from constraints[10] (from the perspective of the modern conception of liberty) to the consideration of both types of liberty. For the realization of a good end also implies freedom from constraints.

Yet, from such a notion of freedom, no political implications emerge as necessary.[11] The (positive) freedom to choose, and to act on, an ethically good value does not by itself have any political implications unless one tries to institutionalize that value.[12] Since a person cannot arbitrarily choose an ethically valid standard of action, the positive notion of freedom *does* imply the existence of an intersubjective criterion, which is valid independently of a person's actual choice.[13] However, this notion of self-realization does not specify that the ethical criterion can or has to be institutionalized, and hence, it does *not* immediately lead to politically relevant outcomes.

Seen from the angle of *political* morality, Constant's problem of the conflict of liberties refers to politically regulated interpersonal relationships. The issue is whether freedom is to be seen as liberty from the state or liberty to act justly. Politics enters the stage when one considers the legal framework that ought to regulate a society.[14] More exactly, politics arises when one considers the question as to how a person's freedom is to be interpreted in relation to legal norms: as the right not to be interfered with beyond the restraints imposed by legitimate laws or as the collective exercise of political autonomy.

Corresponding to the notion of personal autonomy as self-realization, there is a politically relevant notion of autonomy as self-determination.[15] The idea of political self-determination presupposes the liberty to take part in political debates about the principles and laws to be enforced. Just like the notion of personal autonomy as self-realization presupposes the concept of personal freedom as liberty from constraints, political autonomy (or self-determination) presupposes a notion of political freedom as the right not to be interfered with beyond the restraints imposed by legitimate laws.

According to Constant, the problems to which the conflict between the liberties of the moderns and the liberties of the ancients gives rise can be solved by his proposal for a representative system. His solution also aims to offer a better account of political normativity than Kant's commitment to unconditional principles of justice. Thus, the idea of democratic representation presupposes that citizens have both certain rights of non-interference by the state *and* the possibility of taking part in the political process and, hence, in self-determination. What is more, the resulting laws are conditional on the views of citizens and, therefore, on their particular circumstances.

Hence, laws are neither the result of arbitrary choices nor the outcome of a search for independently existing principles or standards. The question remains, however, as to the criterion on the basis of which moral standards are then formulated. If morally valid standards are not reducible to whatever standards happen to be chosen, then some condition for their validity must be involved and a moral criterion would be required to offer precisely this condition.

Some contemporary constructivist theories start from the moral intuitions of citizens (whether or not represented by political leaders).[16] Laws would then be formulated in such a manner that they would account for these moral intuitions. Of course, not all intuitions are relevant or correct. Sometimes principles must be maintained against certain moral intuitions and the latter must be changed. At other times, principles should be changed in light of certain deeply held views about what is right or wrong.[17] The question is, however, how to decide whether to change principles or intuitions?

Contemporary constructivists do not have an answer to the question. They try to avoid postulating principles as unconditionally valid, just as they try to avoid making principles depend solely on whatever intuitions citizens happen to have. There are various solutions on offer in the literature, but I think they are not satisfactory – they oscillate between giving priority to principles and giving priority to intuitions.[18] Without a solution to this problem, Constant's question concerning the conflict between political autonomy and political freedom cannot be answered.

§3. Kant and Sartre so far

It is in the context of this philosophical predicament that I approach the comparative analysis of Kant and Sartre. While my primary concern in this book is that of making evident the significant similarities and differences between Kant and Sartre, my interest is not purely scholarly; my intention is not merely that of setting straight the record on the relationship between these two philosophers' moral theories. By bringing to light the similarities between these two philosophers, without, however, overlooking the distinctive aspects of their works, I also attempt to offer a view of Kant that is at least different from, if not more accurate than, the standard constructivist interpretation so influential today.

This difference in interpretation, I would like to claim, is important, since it enables us to answer the problem of the conflict of liberties and the related problem of the justification of moral standards. What makes it possible for us to retrieve this more accurate and more useful interpretation of Kant is precisely the comparison with Sartre. Unlike contemporary Kantian moral philosophers, Sartre, who would certainly not call himself a Kantian,[19] is less adverse to metaphysics. Although Sartre follows closely the phenomenological anti-Kantian objections to the noumenal realm of things in themselves, he can make sense without difficulty within the phenomenological tradition of the idea of constitutiveness. By this, I refer to Kant's idea that a priori intuitions and categories *constitute* the objects of our experience and, thus, make this experience possible.

In short, in this way, the comparative analysis undertaken here ultimately aims to retrieve a critical ethics that can indicate how to approach correctly the problems faced by contemporary constructivists. My approach starts from the historical fact that Sartre read, thought about, and constantly addressed, Kant's philosophy. However, I construe the two philosophers' theories from the perspective of a question of current concern: 'What can Kant's and Sartre's moral philosophies teach those who are interested today in the questions of moral normativity and justification (and, hence, also in Constant's problem of the conflict of liberties)?' In essence, the main question is: 'How can these authors account for the justification of unconditional obligations?'

Kant's advocacy of, and (what appears to be[20]) Sartre's sympathetic attitude towards, an unconditional duty to avoid untruthfulness suggests a common position that is opposed to a view of conditional fundamental moral norms. Again, it is not to the idea of representativity that Kant and Sartre object, but to the claim that this would constitute a solution to the problem Constant himself raises.

Combined with Kant's and Sartre's common response to moral realism and non-cognitivism, this suggests that far more similarities exist between the moral theories of these two philosophers than are usually acknowledged. Moreover, commentators rarely acknowledge the significance of these similarities; comparisons usually focus on issues of metaphysics, philosophy of mind and theory of knowledge, and emphasis is commonly placed on the differences, rather than the similarities, between their works.

In general, in relation to Sartre, Kant is regarded as a secondary predecessor, a major philosopher whom Sartre read and criticized, but who did not influence him as much as, say, Descartes or Husserl. Consequently, there is no book-length work on Kant's and Sartre's practical philosophies.[21] Some recent work has been done in comparing Sartre with Aristotle.[22] A few Sartrean scholars have intuited the strong influence that Kant exerted on Sartre. Some of them, especially French-speaking commentators, have also devoted a few articles to the investigation of some of the similarities and differences between Kant's and Sartre's works. But, as I will argue further, their conclusions are sometimes affected by a less than ideal methodology and by a prevailing influence of the standard interpretations.

Sartre's commentators acknowledge that existentialism should in fact be traced back to the voluntaristic tradition initiated by Kant, but they do not pursue in depth an analysis of the similarities and differences between them (see, for instance, Solomon 1989). Or, when Kant's moral and political theories are invoked and compared with existentialism, Kant's views are usually contrasted with existentialist thought (see, for instance, Olafson 1967). In a sense, this is not surprising since Sartre always distanced himself from Kant. Moreover, Sartre's emphasis on an ethics of values and Kant's insistence that an ethical system should be one of principles suggest a significant difference between their works.[23]

However, the distinction between ethical principles and legal norms, on the one hand, and values and collective goals, on the other, is far from being an indisputable divide.[24] Both Kant and Sartre thematize it, and sometimes it becomes difficult to simply characterize their positions by following the classical divide between deontology and teleology.

The choice of the terminology that I use is influenced by the need, felt by both Kant and Sartre, of going beyond the principle-value divide. I use 'criterion' to designate a higher-order principle or value, on the basis of which principles or values are tested. I use 'standard of action' to refer to both moral principles (or maxims) and values, and I distinguish between standards and 'rules of action', using the latter to refer to the action that is commanded by a standard in concrete circumstances.[25] In this way, I can use the same terminology whether I refer to Kant's or to Sartre's ethical theory.

The synchronic comparison undertaken in this book aims primarily to present the similarities between Kant and Sartre. Differences will also be made evident, but more as a by-product of the investigation of the aspects their philosophies share. I take this to be an important methodological requirement, a requirement imposed by a new, and I think more appropriate, method of comparison. Let me explain further the novelty of this method.

§4. Method

Usually, comparative studies devoted to Sartre and Kant use a standard approach. First, they begin with a presentation of several resemblances between the ways in which the two philosophers deal with a particular question or problem.[26] Between Kant and Sartre there are, however, obvious differences: their styles of writing, the contexts in which they wrote and thought, the philosophers they read, and so on. Hence, secondly, comparative studies that use the standard approach try to identify a point from which the converging thoughts of Kant and Sartre start to diverge.[27]

The comparative analysis I will present in this book draws several parallels between the ways in which Kant and Sartre deal with several issues of moral philosophy. Following the standard comparative method, it would be reasonable to expect a concluding account of the divergences between their philosophies; however, sometimes this requirement carries an urgency that may lead to hasty conclusions about where exactly Sartre and Kant part philosophical company.[28] This is only one of the problems of the standard comparative strategy.

A second important problem is specifically related to Sartre's and Kant's moral philosophies and, in particular, to their ethical thought. In general, the secondary literature on Kant and Sartre is scant, and there are several reasons for this, not the least important being Sartre's numerous disapproving references to Kant.[29] However, with regard to their ethical theories, Sartre's disparaging references to his own attempts to articulate an ethical system contribute to the suggestion that the differences are too significant to warrant further investigation. Consequently, Sartre students either deny that there is an ethics in Sartre, or, when they claim that an ethics could be found in his writings, they insist that this ethics should be understood differently, basically not as an ethical system.[30]

Therefore, a comparative study that tries, first, to find similarities between Sartre's and Kant's moral theories would not really have a starting point, or else its conclusion would always be the same and known from the beginning. Agreement in their ways of developing ethical systems would not count, since Sartre constantly discounted his own views on the topic. Correspondences between their answers to metaethical questions or to questions of 'moral psychology' would perhaps be a better place to begin a comparison but, concerning their moral systems, the conclusion about divergences in their ethical thought could be drawn from the beginning: it would have to do with the fact that Kant has a moral system, whereas Sartre does not.

An alternative comparative strategy was suggested to me by Christina Howells's remark that "Sartre's relation to Kantian ethics [...] seems to reveal what Harold Bloom would call 'an anxiety of influence'" (1989: 204 n21), a strategy that I began to develop elsewhere (2003) and that I will continue to pursue here. This alternative interpretative approach will *not* start from the similarities between Kant and Sartre, but from Sartre's criticism of Kant, hence from what he assumes distinguishes him from Kant.

Then it will try to evaluate Sartre's objections – not in order to assess their cogency and success in the attempt to undermine the position objected to (this, if appropriate, may be undertaken at a later stage) but primarily in order to see whether this position is indeed Kant's.[31] In case it is not, the subsequent move will *not* be that of drawing parallels between Kant's and Sartre's conceptions of a particular theme, as the more complex version of the standard approach will try to do;[32] instead, the further important task will be that of making clear what Sartre tries to avoid in his criticisms, and whether Kant, on an accurate interpretation, succeeds in avoiding what Sartre tries to avoid.

This alternative approach has more chances of escaping the second problem faced by the standard interpretative strategy. Thus, for instance, in the *Notebooks for an Ethics*, Sartre criticizes ethical theories that are unable to account for the singularity of the moral agents, for the normative nature of their principles and for the authority of their requirements, and he tries to formulate an alternative theory. However, it is very important to note that, although Sartre comes to reject the particular solution that he formulates in the *Notebooks*, he does *not* reject the conditions that an ethics avoid the problems of a theory unable to account for singularity, normativity and authority. Hence, the comparison has a starting point and the conclusion is informative. I will call these negative meta-ethical principles or constraints '*structural* similarities' between Sartre's and Kant's ethical thoughts.

Now, in contradistinction to the standard comparative strategy, to highlight these *structural* similarities will not subsequently require us to account for the differences between the two philosophers, and this is why the alternative comparative method overcomes also the first difficulty faced by the standard approach. To explain this, let me use an analogy.

For an architect the fact that the house he is supposed to design should not have more than three floors and less than three bedrooms does not mean that it is not possible to conceive several different plans compatible with these constraints. Similarly, the fact that Kant and Sartre share a commitment to several metaethical *constraints* concerning how a moral theory should be formulated does not mean that they would end up with the same moral theories. Therefore, for a study that adopts this alternative comparative method, the requirement to conclude its analysis with an account of the divergences between the authors compared is no longer a reasonable necessary condition.

A section on methodology cannot draw to a close before dealing with a further important issue. The issue is common to all comparative analyses and refers to the fact that, strategically interpreted, no matter how different two authors are, their views can be made to look similar. One may, for instance, interpret Plato's theory of Forms as transcendental and find several similarities between Platonism and Kantianism, despite the fundamental differences between their views (at least, as standardly interpreted).[33]

I think the issue cannot be avoided completely without a theory of interpretation.[34] Failing this, one way to mitigate the problem, in the case of a comparison between Kant and Sartre, is to state clearly from the beginning the interpretation of Kant one is going to work with. In addition, one could try to make sure that the interpretation presented is not very outlandish and includes the features most usually associated with Kant's philosophy. Only against the background of this account of Kant's position does it make sense then to claim, for instance, that, since they rely on an inaccurate interpretation of Kant, Sartre's objections miss the point.

Hence, in what follows, I will preface each comparative discussion of Kant and Sartre with a brief presentation of what I take to be Kant's position on the issues under investigation. I will then present Sartre's objections to Kant, and I will examine the extent to which we are dealing with a misunderstanding of Kant's position or with objections Sartre would himself eventually abandon or, finally, with objections which are not actually effective critiques of Kant, although they do not miss the point and do not rely on views Sartre would eventually reject.

§5. Claims and implications

My argument focuses on the structural similarities between Kant's and Sartre's moral philosophies and, against the standard view, makes a case for regarding Kant as one of Sartre's most significant predecessors. Moreover, the book shows that an investigation of the parallels between Kant's and Sartre's moral theories has surprising philosophical implications.

Given phenomenology's descriptive character, it is not surprising that most philosophers working in the Husserlian tradition recoil from approaching the issues of moral philosophy prescriptively.[35] Sartre and a few other phenomenologists who address such issues develop value-centred accounts of normativity.[36] The contrast between Sartre's value-centred ethics and Kant's principle-centred moral theory is perhaps one of the sources of the standard view of the relationship between their moral philosophies, but the significance of this contrast is exaggerated.

For, as my argument shows, in contrast to the other phenomenologists, who lean towards moral intuitionism, Sartre's ethics is structurally oriented towards a Kantian account of moral epistemology. Hence, despite its value-centred character, Sartre's ethics is fundamentally different from the value-centred ethics of intuitionism, consequentialism and virtue ethics.

The similarities between Kant's and Sartre's accounts of moral knowledge point to an even more surprising conclusion, namely, that Sartre's moral theory proves to be closer to Kant's moral theory than contemporary Kantian moral constructivism. Like contemporary constructivists, Sartre attempts to avoid the metaphysical implications of Kant's transcendental idealism, in particular his distinction between phenomena and noumena. Yet, unlike them, Sartre does not aim to eschew metaphysical considerations altogether. For him, as for Husserl, there can be no noumenal realm of things in themselves; what we perceive as phenomena are the things themselves. At the same time, however, Sartre argues against the idealistic implications of Husserlian methodology. This engagement with ontology enables Sartre to provide an account of what the fundamental criteria of moral philosophy *are* and, in this way, of how they can be *known*. By contrast, for contemporary constructivists, moral epistemology must do without a corresponding metaphysics, without even the sparse version of Sartre's ontology.

Therefore, the fact that interpreters of Kant and Sartre rarely acknowledge the significant similarities between their moral philosophies no longer appears as the outcome of a contingent oversight, but is bound up with the direction in which contemporary moral philosophy has developed (see, for instance, Darwall, Gibbard and Railton 1992).

To be sure, Sartre's numerous disapproving references to Kant and the obvious difference between Kant's principle-centred, and Sartre's value-centred, moral theories may also mislead the interpreter. However, the link between Kant's philosophy and Rawls's Kantian constructivism strongly tends to obscure the differences between the standard contemporary moral theories and Kant's view of practical knowledge. Thus, emphasis is usually placed on the opposition between a principle-centred practical philosophy and Sartre's radical scepticism about principles, rather than on the similarities between Kant's and Sartre's practical epistemologies.

Furthermore, Habermas's Kantian discourse theory mounts a concerted attack on "individualism" – perhaps the only label that Kant's and Sartre's works share in the secondary literature; Sartre's moral philosophy seems, again, to find its natural place in the camp opposed to Kant's. Nevertheless, I claim here that, despite Sartre's own efforts to distance himself from Kant's influence and despite its current reception, Sartre's moral philosophy proves to be fundamentally Kantian.

The comparative investigation of Kant's and Sartre's moral philosophies that is presented here offers, therefore, not only a reconstruction of Sartre's ethics and political morality and a defence of key aspects of Kant's moral philosophy, but also brings to light the project of a critical ethics, which is fundamentally different from, and philosophically more compelling than, contemporary constructivism.

The claim, in the title of the book, to the rediscovery of a critical ethics has to do precisely with the attempt I make to retrieve, through Sartre, the metaphysical (although non-dogmatic) aspects of Kant's philosophy and to show their significance for the questions of normativity, justification and conflict of liberties. Before I begin, a brief exposition of how the book is organized and what each of the main parts focuses on is in order.

§6. Overview

The book is organized in three parts: Identity and Self-choice (I), Freedom and Normativity (II) and Authority and Progress (III). Each part focuses on central themes of Kant's and Sartre's philosophies. Specific aspects of these themes represent starting points for Sartre's objections to Kant's moral theory. Each part has two chapters. Following the comparative method presented in the previous sections, each part starts with a chapter that offers my reading of what Kant says on the corresponding themes. The second chapter will then present Sartre's objections to Kant and will evaluate them.

I start, in Part I, with two issues, which are not so much ethical issues, but are standard topics in metaphysics – the issues of identity and self-choice. I address these themes, since they explain the extent to which we can talk about agency and moral agency in Kant and Sartre. Unless their accounts of these issues can stay non-dogmatic and relatively non-committal, the project of a critical ethics that draws on the similarities between their positions and attempts to respond to the problems of justification, normativity and the conflict of liberties will have no advantage over contemporary alternatives.

Part II moves towards more practical (in the Kantian sense of morally relevant) issues. Although the issue of freedom, which is the first topic discussed there, is again standardly placed within the remit of metaphysics, it is an issue very significant for an account of moral agency. Moreover, through the notion of freedom as autonomy, we are moving directly into the moral realm. The second issue of this part, the issue of normativity, will include questions concerning the character of the ethical theories that can be found in Kant and Sartre, as well as the nature of the justification of particular moral standards starting from ethical criteria (the Categorical Imperative and the value of authenticity) and their relevance for concrete situations.

Questions of justification, especially in relation to the ethical criteria, will be discussed also in Part III. An implication of the discussion in the previous parts concerns the authority of ethical criteria, which seems to conflict strongly with the account of the freedom of the agents that both Kant and Sartre endorse. Another important topic concerns the extent to which a non-dogmatic ethical theory is nevertheless able to put forward an account of history and moral progress that would make claims to the unity of history, the unity of its meaning and even the end towards which the course of events seems to be oriented.

In short, we can regard the three parts of this book as focusing, respectively, on the *assumptions*, *claims* and *implications* of Kant's and Sartre's ethical theories, as well as of the critical ethics that I claim can be developed starting from the similarities between the moral philosophies of these two philosophers. To be sure, some issues will be relevant across this conventional divide between assumptions, claims and implications, but the different emphases in the three parts of this monograph can be relatively accurately described in this way.

As this outline shows, the topics discussed belong to a highly selective list. Many other objections to Kant can be found both in the works I will refer to and in some of Sartre's texts, which I could not discuss here. Moreover, as we will see, the discussion presented in the next chapters is only a beginning; each of the themes approached can be explored further in much more detail. Given the limits of a monograph, discussion of several other topics, which turn out to be related to the issues discussed here, will have to be postponed for other occasions.

However, the following investigation should be sufficient for a strong case in support of the claims I am to defend in this book: that concerning the significant similarities between Kant's and Sartre's practical philosophies, that concerning an original method of comparative analysis, that concerning the existence of an ethical system in Sartre and, finally, that concerning the possibility of a critical ethics, which is closer to Kant's moral theory and able to account better for the problems of justification, normativity and the conflict of liberties than contemporary rival, even Kantian, ethical theories do.

Part I
Identity and Self-Choice

I began by noting the apparent similarity between Kant's and Sartre's responses to Constant's problem; surprisingly, they both seem to endorse the view that lying from philanthropic reasons is morally wrong and seem to support an unconditional obligation to avoid untruthfulness. As I have mentioned, contemporary moral theorists struggle to justify this degree of normative force for moral standards, given their commitment to accounts that must avoid dogmatic claims and, in particular, the claims of dogmatic metaphysics.

Kant's critical philosophy is sometimes regarded as a possible way out of this predicament, given his defence of unconditional moral standards and his objections to dogmatic metaphysics. Yet Kant also supports his own position in metaphysics, transcendental idealism, which has come to be regarded more or less automatically as a dogmatic account of what there is in the world and how we can cognize it. Radical claims against metaphysics and philosophy, such as the Rawlsian statements for a theory of justice, which is political, not metaphysical and which would stay philosophically on the surface, contribute in no way to a detailed consideration of the reasons why Kant thought his critical philosophy and metaphysics are non-dogmatic.

However, if Sartre, who joins other post-Kantian phenomenologists in criticizing Kant's doctrine of transcendental idealism, is able to offer a moral theory that can account for the unconditional account of certain values, then perhaps his approach is what contemporary moral theorists should follow in their attempts to justify moral standards with such a strong normative force. My starting point, however, is the comparative analysis of Kant's and Sartre's practical philosophies. The aim, in particular, is to show how their practical philosophies can be similar in their responses to Constant's problem. There are, however, several reasons why these similarities might be questioned. First, a response to Constant's problem involves a series of assumptions with regard to which Kant's and Sartre's theories seem quite different.

Secondly, to regard their responses to Constant's problem as similar, it would be necessary to show similarity on some key issues, such as the standard on the basis of which the actions are to be judged, the normative status of this standard and how it is to be justified. About these issues, again, there seem to be several differences between Kant's and Sartre's accounts. Thirdly, assuming that what seem to be similar responses are indeed cases of similarity, there are also implications that follow from these similarities, and Kant and Sartre might disagree with regard to them. In particular, the issue of moral progress seems to be one where Sartre and Kant part philosophical company. Let me begin with some assumptions of their similar answers, the questions of identity and self-choice.

1
Kant

In talking about methodology, in the Introduction I have argued that a comparative analysis of two philosophers, like Kant and Sartre, is best conducted by an investigation of the objections one formulates against the other. I have also anticipated then that the conclusion of this investigation will be that Sartre misinterprets Kant's moral theory and some of his most important objections miss the point; however, we can only talk about misinterpretation against the background of an interpretation that we consider accurate. This chapter, therefore, has precisely the task of making clear the interpretation of Kant's account of self with which I will be working. I will start with his view of identity and will continue with self-choice, both of which represent preconditions of moral accountability.

§7. Two assumptions of moral accountability

On Kant's account, "if you have *by a lie* prevented someone just now bent on murder from committing the deed, then you are legally accountable for all the consequences that might arise from it" (*VRML*: 8:427, 612). As we have seen, a possible consequence of a lie is that the murderer believes you, leaves your house and encounters your friend, who, in trying to flee the danger, had left the place without your knowing it. On Kant's account, then, because you have lied, you are legally accountable for the murder of your friend, although you kept your promise and you tried to protect him.

One implication of these claims is the existence of an absolute prohibition against lying. In its turn, this implication rests on some other assumptions, which seem equally difficult to defend. And, yet, they must all be supported by Kant, if his claim above is to be accepted, and they must all be implicitly supported by Sartre, if his sympathetic reaction to Kant's position is to have sense. Such a position leads to questions, like: What kind of norms can have the force to command such absolute, unconditional constraints? Can such standards be justified? Do they have any normative force in particular contexts?

17

In what follows, in this Part, I present Kant's answers to these questions, but, to begin with, in this chapter, I will not immediately be concerned with these questions, but with some of their assumptions. These are assumptions Kant seems to take for granted when he talks about this and similar cases and they seem central to his thought. One such assumption is that a person can be free to act and, hence, can be judged morally in virtue of her freely performed actions. We judge a person as legally accountable for certain actions, if the person freely performed them. Hence, in these claims about legal accountability, Kant assumes at least the possibility of freedom and, moreover, its realization in certain situations.

Even more basic is the assumption that a person who freely performs an action now can be considered as accountable later, even if she might have considerably changed since she performed the action.[1] Although claims to character reformation and even radical change of personality will probably not make the prosecutor and the court abandon or close a case, we can easily imagine situations where a person who can no longer identify herself as the author of some actions she actually performed, due, for instance, to some well-documented psychiatric problems, cannot be regarded as accountable for those actions. Hence, an assumption for attribution of legal accountability to a person is that of identity.

Both freedom and identity are important preconditions of moral judgement. Incidentally, as we will see in Chapter 2 and Chapter 4, Sartre raises objections to Kant precisely in relation to these issues. In what follows in this chapter, I will focus on Kant's account of identity and freedom. Other assumptions of Kant's claims will be discussed in Chapter 3 and Chapter 5. Once these presuppositions are clarified and justified, we will have the necessary background for both a comparison between Kant and Sartre, and a better understanding of their more startling claims.

Let me begin by exploring further the kind of identity that is at stake here. If I claim that, in trying to help his friend, Pablo proved himself to be ethically worthy, I assume that 'Pablo' refers to the same individual as that who has helped the friend. Moreover, I assume that this act of helping a friend was done by one and the same individual: Pablo was sentenced to death by the Falangist tribunal; he was offered his life in exchange for that of his friend and he lied by making up a story about his friend's whereabouts.

Are such assumptions justified? What entitles me to claim that the individual who was sentenced to death was the same as the one who was given the choice of saving his friend? In a sense, they were not at all the same. In the usual circumstances, we can say at least that the individual who, in order to save his friend, lied to the Falangist tribunal after being sentenced to death had all the experiences of the individual who was sentenced to death and some others in addition: for instance, he was offered a deal – his life in exchange for that of his friend. Two implications can be drawn here, one concerning action and one, legal accountability, and both are rooted in the problem of identity. First, how can an action be performed if every single act is performed by a person who is very likely different from the person who has performed previous acts and who will perform future acts? Secondly, assuming we can talk about actions, how can the person who performed an action in the past be considered as legally accountable for the action now? How does Kant account for this type of identity? A more detailed answer will be given in the next sections.

§8. The third paralogism

Kant discusses the problem of identity in the Third Paralogism – perhaps the most difficult and most misunderstood of all Paralogisms (Ameriks 2000: 128). In the first edition of the *Critique of Pure Reason*, he formulates the third paralogism as follows:[2]

> What is conscious of the numerical identity of itself in different times is to that extent a *person*.
> Now the soul is [conscious of the numerical identity of itself in different times].
> Therefore it is a person.
>
> (*KrV*: A362, 296)

This terminology seems strange and is in need of clarification. Kant does precisely this at the beginning of the Paralogism Chapter. First, by "soul", he means "the thinking *I*" (*KrV*: A351, 389). The use of the term "soul" reflects well on his intentions in this chapter, his aim being primarily to challenge the claims to cognition put forward by rational psychology. Rational psychology – etymologically, the rational science of the soul – aims to derive in a logical way, by using several syllogisms, properties of the soul: immateriality, incorruptibility, personality and immortality. Kant's objection is that the syllogisms of rational psychology are in fact paralogisms, that is, logical arguments based on "a fallacious inference" (this being in fact the etymological sense of 'paralogism') (*KrV*: A341/B399, 382).

Against Descartes, perhaps the clearest exponent of rational psychology (Gardner 1999: 225),[3] but also against Leibniz and Wolff, Kant shows that one cannot logically derive properties of the soul from the judgement 'I think'.[4] As we will see, the issue is more complex, since Kant does not simply dismiss the rational psychologist's claims, but thinks it necessary to accept a certain sense in which we can say that the soul has personality (or, in the case of the other paralogisms, is immaterial, incorruptible and immortal). So, his argument has both a destructive part and a reconstructive one. For the moment, however, let us focus on the more destructive part.

The rational character of the approach followed by rational psychology can more clearly be grasped by contrasting it to an empirical approach.[5] In the first case, the properties of the thinking *I* are considered as implicit in the concept of the soul. To justify these properties, the rational psychologist does not rely on particular experiences (in this case, the particular experience of her states of mind); she does not reflect on her states of mind trying to confirm that the properties of the thinking *I* are recurrent in the experience of those mental states – this is what *empirical* psychology does. By contrast, *rational* psychology tries to derive such properties a priori, independently from experience, by analysing the concept of the soul (i.e. the concept of the thinking *I*).

In this way, the rational psychologist hopes to show that, despite variation in the way the soul appears to me in experience (various states of mind, thoughts, affects, moods and similar), there is a permanent element, which is the guarantor of identity and, hence, of personality. If 'the thinking I' contains as one of its properties that of numerical identity, then, despite variation in appearance, there is an element of the soul that remains the same and gives numerical identity to the various states of mind experienced in reflection.

As an implication, we will be able to say legitimately that the individuals who performed all the acts constitutive of the helping action are one and the same person. Thus, if Pablo can reflect on his action, since his thinking *I* presupposes numerical identity throughout the various states manifested by the soul (thinking *I*) in each of the acts constitutive of the action, it will be the same person who performs these acts and, hence, the same person who performs the resulting action.[6] In a similar way, on the rationalist account, we can also explain in what sense Pablo, the person who stands in front of me, is the same as the person who tried to help his friend by a lie: we deal with the same person, since we deal with the same permanent element of the soul or thinking *I*, an element that does not change from one state of mind to the other.

Let us now go back to the syllogism. In general, Kant says that a paralogism is an invalid syllogism (*KrV*: A341/B399, 382) and that a transcendental paralogism is a paralogism that is invalid because of the "nature of the human reason", which produces "an illusion that is unavoidable although not unresolvable" (*KrV*: A341/B399, 382). The third paralogism seems to have a simple form:

All *A*s are *B*s [All beings conscious of the numerical ... are persons]
C is *A* [The soul is conscious of the ...]
C is *B* [The soul is a person]

Thus rendered, the syllogism is clearly valid. Hence, if there is a problem, this must be a problem in the way I formalized the argument. More exactly, the terms in the premises and conclusion may not mean the same thing.

A in the major premise, for instance, may mean something other than *A* in the minor.

In fact, Kant says this explicitly at A403 and B311. He thinks 'person' in the major premise is used in a way that makes it impossible to apply it to objects of experiences, whereas 'soul' in the minor premise and in the conclusion stands precisely for such an object. Hence, we must take 'person' in conclusion to mean something else than it does in the major. The major premise *defines* 'person' as the being who is conscious of its numerical identity in different times.[7] Before making any step further, the notion of numerical identity should be clarified. I will discuss this in the next section.

§9. Numerical identity

According to Kant, a being that is external to me is numerically identical if the permanent element which, as support or subject, is determined by the other, changing features remains the same. For instance, the red billiard ball on the table is the same numerically as the white ball that was in that place a few minutes ago. In the meantime, say, the ball has acquired a new colour, since I dyed it. The ball's colour is the changing feature that qualifies the permanent element (the billiard ball) by adding to it a feature or characteristic (*red* or *white* billiard ball).

Of course, the element that gives numerical identity in this case (the billiard ball) is only relatively permanent: more exactly, it is permanent relative to the change in colour. We can go further and state that, since I no longer have a billiard table and I use the ball solely as a weight for the papers on my desk, the *billiard* ball has become an object of stationery. Even then, we can say that the objects are numerically identical and their identity is given by the fact that it is the same ball with different functions.

We can claim numerical identity even when the plastic of the ball is melted and moulded into a cube. It is this substance with the same mass that represents the permanent element throughout the various transformations of the white billiard ball; various characteristics determine it as a cube or a ball, as an object of stationery or a billiard ball, and as a white or red billiard ball. Since all these determinations apply to the same mass of substance, we can say that the various objects are numerically identical.[8]

Can we determine in the same way that a person's numerical identity is given by her thinking *I*? I may try to observe my own states of mind in the way in which we observe the various states of an object;[9] I may then try to identify the permanent element beyond, or behind, the various determinations that constitute these various states of mind. Nevertheless, what I will thus obtain as numerically identical will be a thinking I *under specific conditions*, rather than merely a thinking *I*. To see this, consider again the case of external objects and the example discussed above.

When we consider the mass of plastic as the unchanging element that gives numerical identity, the permanent feature is mass, although it is abstracted from various other features of the object, like colour, function or size. I claim that the *billiard ball* is the same despite its change of colour, and I abstract in this way from its particular colour, but refer to its identical function and shape. I then claim that the same spherical object has various functions, and I abstract in this way from its function, but I refer to its identical shape as the element that gives its identity. Finally, I claim that the same lump of plastic has different shapes, and I abstract from the shape by making reference to the same mass of plastic, which is the numerically identical element.

Similarly, I may claim that, although I am sad now and happy tomorrow, there is something that remains unchanged: my optimism. My optimism gives numerical identity through the variations brought about by sadness and happiness. I can then go on and, by comparing my specific optimism with a future pessimistic state of mind, I can abstract from this type of feature by reference to the same thoughtful attitude I have throughout variations in optimism/pessimism. And, then, when faced with my thoughtlessness, I may still regard myself as numerically identical in some other specific way, which characterizes all my various states of mind I have so far considered.

So the point here is that this empirical approach will only be able to help me identify a *specific* or, as Kant puts it, a conditioned numerically identical thinking *I*, rather than the unconditioned one in the major premise. In the major premise, 'person' is defined as a being who is conscious of its numerical identity in different times. But consciousness of the numerical identity of itself in different times is a necessary condition of cognition. I cannot form a judgement and, hence, make a claim about something, if I am not conscious that the thought of that thing and the thought of the feature I attribute to it in my claim are my thoughts and, hence, are determinations of the same numerically identical being.

Hence, the major premise points to a necessary condition of cognition, a condition that must apply to any thinking I and, thus, not to some particular soul or other. Therefore, 'numerical identity' here can only refer to what is common to all my states of mind. This notion will then only be able to identify a very formal feature, one which, in fact, may well belong to all cognitive subjects rather than to my particular soul and to my particular experiences of my states of my mind. With this notion of numerical identity clarified, I can return to the question of what is wrong with the syllogisms of the rational psychologist, in particular that concerning identity. This will be the topic of the next section.

§10. The problem of the third paralogism

I have claimed that being conscious of my numerical identity over time is a necessary condition of cognition. In fact, an ever stronger claim can be made on Kant's account: consciousness of numerical identity of oneself is necessarily presupposed by the thinking *I*. The thoughts that I think over time must be my thoughts, otherwise I could not think them. But, unless I am conscious of my numerical identity over time, I cannot realize that these thoughts are my thoughts, that they are thoughts of the same person that is me.

I will come back to this,[10] but, for the moment, a first conclusion is that consciousness of the numerical identity and, therefore, the personality of the thinking I can be deduced from the notion of the thinking *I* by analysing this notion. "In my own consciousness, therefore", Kant says, "identity of the person is unfailingly to be met with" (*KrV*: A362, 397). This implies that I do not need an empirical study of my states of mind to conclude that I am conscious of the numerical identity of myself over time. Thus, the minor premise is simply an analytic judgement, a judgement that is a priori true, since it can be deduced from the analysis of concepts and without appeal to experience.

This means that the major premise points to a necessary condition that any thinking I must meet, whereas the minor premise is in fact an analytic judgement. Premises, therefore, do not refer to any *specific* element in virtue of which the thinking *I* would be numerically identical; rather, they state and make more explicit a formal condition that applies equally well to whatever subject one were to consider. One can also stress that the syllogism talks about *consciousness* of numerical identity as a condition of personality. The rational psychologist needs something more to demonstrate the soul is an entity with properties; she needs a sensible intuition similar to that one has in the case of external objects, when one is able to experience the permanent element in virtue of which only could changing features be perceived.

As a result, I can grant that the thinking *I* and the implicit consciousness of its numerical identity necessarily accompany all my states of mind; all my states of mind are thought by me and, therefore, the thinking *I* is one of their constitutive elements. Still, according to Kant, this does not entitle me to claim that there is also an entity in virtue of which the various states of my mind are numerically identical, in the manner in which the lump of plastic makes the cube and ball numerically identical.

Kant's argument is not that there might not be some element (which, together with the rational psychologist, we can call 'soul') in virtue of which a person is numerically identical throughout various states of mind. His argument is only that one cannot legitimately make this claim on the basis of the rational psychologist's syllogism, which turns out to be a paralogism.

The thinking *I* is conscious of its numerical identity over time. This consciousness is of the fact that it is the same *I* (or person) that thinks the various thoughts that occur to that person. But, contrary to the rational psychologist's claims, it does not follow that some entity or object corresponds to this *I*. As we have seen, insofar as we consider this element to correspond to the thinking *I* in general, I cannot have experience of such an element. This is because, as I have mentioned, this element is supposed to give identity to all the states of mind that I would experience in time. However, in this case, this element cannot be identified in relation to any specific empirical condition (in the manner in which, for instance, we identify the billiard ball as the element giving numerical identity to the white and red billiard balls).

If we cannot identify this element in relation to any particular sensible condition, then we cannot experience it or, as Kant says, have any sensible intuition corresponding to it. But, on Kant's account, a concept without intuition cannot provide cognition.[11] The fact that we cannot have any sensible intuition corresponding to this concept explains why Kant regards the paralogisms as possibly leading to an unavoidable, although not irresolvable, illusion (*KrV*: A399, 420). It is unavoidable, because reason tries to find a sensible intuition for this concept and, in this way, to obtain cognition. It is, however, not irresolvable, because reason itself can identify this as an illusion: for instance, an illusion brought about by the invalid syllogisms of the rational psychologist.

Therefore, the problem of the paralogism is that, in the minor premise ('The soul is conscious of its numerical identity in different times'), 'soul' has to be taken by the rational psychologist to refer to an object or an entity, rather than being regarded as a simple concept that may or may not have anything in reality corresponding to it. Without this, the rational psychologist cannot reach the intended conclusion. In fact, however, 'soul' may simply be the concept of the thinking *I*. Whether there is anything corresponding to it in reality or not, this concept includes in its meaning consciousness of numerical identity and, thus, personality. Hence, the minor premise can be asserted simply as an analytic judgement, as making explicit the empty and formal concept that can be associated with the concepts and experiences I am conscious of and that marks in this way the fact that they belong to consciousness.

By contrast, the rational psychologist aims to conclude that the thinking I exists as an entity, which gives numerical identity to my various states of mind. To obtain this as part of the conclusion, 'soul' must refer to such an object and, hence, there must be a sensible intuition corresponding to the formal *I*. As I have mentioned, therefore, 'soul' in the minor premise must stand for more than a concept. Yet, in the syllogism, 'the thinking *I*' cannot stand for such an object, since it is a formal concept used without any specific empirical condition. Because of this equivocation over 'soul', Kant regards the syllogism of personality as a paralogism.[12] Moreover, given that the root of the problem is reason's natural tendency to associate an object with an empty concept, such as that of the thinking *I*, we deal in fact with a transcendental paralogism.

I have mentioned that Kant's argument has two parts: a destructive one, where the syllogism put forward by the rational psychologist is rejected as invalid, and a reconstructive one, where the paralogism is reformulated in a way that preserves validity. In this section, I have focused on the first part of Kant's argument. In the next section, I will look at the second part.

§11. Turning the paralogism into a valid syllogism

I have started by questioning a fundamental assumption of some of the most straightforward moral judgements we make about people. This is the assumption that the individual we refer to in a judgement is the same as the individual who performed the action in virtue of which she is being judged. Even more fundamental, although related and similar, is the assumption that we can legitimately regard as identical the individuals who performed the smaller acts that constitute an action.

We have seen that Kant's rational psychologist tries to account for these assumptions by making appeal to a permanent substance, which any person has and by reference to which it can legitimately be claimed that she is numerically identical: the individual (call him 'A') who performs act ϕ is the same person as that (call him 'B') who performs act ψ, because, despite differences between A's and B's states of mind, the permanent element (the thinking *I*) is the same. Hence, they can legitimately claim that they are one and the same person and that the actions performed are that person's actions.

As we have seen, however, on Kant's account, the rational psychologist does not have a good justification for this view: his argument for the existence of an identical entity proves to be invalid. This leaves open the question of how exactly we can account for the assumption of identity we make in our most straightforward moral judgements. This is where it becomes interesting to explore further the last part of Kant's discussion of the Third Paralogism in the first edition of the *Critique of Pure Reason*.

Thus, Kant thinks there is a sense of 'person' that we can legitimately use to refer to individuals in our moral judgements. Significantly, moreover, this is a sense that "is, indeed, needed and sufficient for practical use" (*KrV*: A365: 399). In the context of the argument I presented so far, the interesting part of Kant's claim is the second: more exactly, the view that a certain sense of numerical identity and personality is *sufficient* for practical purposes. The first part of claim was precisely the starting point for the argument here.

Now, the sense in which a particular sense of personality would be sufficient for practical purposes is not immediately evident, not least because it is not yet clear what Kant takes these practical purposes to be. But consider again identity as necessary for practical purposes. If an individual acts at t and, at $t + 1$, he is no longer conscious of being the individual who so acted, then a moral judgement at $t + 1$ in virtue of the act he performed at t will be meaningless for him, since it presupposes that the person to whom the judgement refers now is the same as the individual who performed the action, whereas he is not aware of that.[13] The two individuals may have the same body, yet, since the individual whom I have in front of me at $t+1$ *cannot* acknowledge being the same individual as that who performed the action for which he is being judged, my judgement will genuinely seem to him to refer to another person.

It should, therefore, be clear in what way a legitimate sense of personality would be necessary for moral or practical purposes: it would make possible moral judgement by making possible moral accountability. Moreover, the sense of personality that Kant seems to allow in the paralogism and that would be able to meet this necessary requirement is personality as mere consciousness of identity. But note now that, on Kant's account, this is not only a necessary condition, it is also sufficient.

Thus, as soon as an individual is conscious of her identity over different times, she will accept that the action she performed at t is her action and that she can be judged for it at $t+1$. Therefore, consciousness of identity is *sufficient* for practical purposes in the sense that it is enough to enable the person to accept her accountability and, hence, the status of subject of moral judgement.[14] Of course, although sufficient for the *person's* acceptance of the status of subject of moral judgement, this consciousness of identity is *not* sufficient for the correct ascription of this status. Moreover, it is *not* sufficient for the correctness of the moral judgement.[15]

First, when a person accepts the status of subject of moral judgement, she may nevertheless disagree about the correctness of the judgement. She agrees that she can be judged for a certain action as its author, but disagrees about the judgement itself. Say, the judgement is that this is an ethically worthy action, whereas she regards it as ethically unworthy. Hence, even when a person agrees to be judged from an ethical perspective, this, by itself, is not sufficient to guarantee the correctness of the judgement.

Secondly, a person may accept the status of subject of moral judgement, but the ascription of this status to her may, nevertheless, be mistaken. Indeed, the fact that a person is conscious of her identity through different times need not imply that the way she regards herself at those times is accurate. For instance, Pablo may be conscious of being the same person as the one who helped his friend yesterday, yet this self-description may be inaccurate; we can imagine another story, according to which it was in fact Juan who helped Pablo's friend, not Pablo. Juan told Pablo the story and, say, because of extreme tiredness and stress under the scrutiny of the Falangist tribunal, Pablo now thinks that he performed the action. We may believe him and take him to be the appropriate subject of a moral judgement in virtue of an action which is allegedly *his*, in which case we mistakenly ascribe to him the status of the subject of *this* moral judgement.

This sense of personality is, therefore, sufficient only for limited practical or moral purposes. It guarantees the meaningfulness of a moral judgement, but only as far as the *subject* of that judgement is concerned. The meaningfulness of the judgement in general, as well as its correctness, are not guaranteed. Furthermore, there may be other respects in which the sense of personality is not sufficient.

Nothing has, so far, been said as to whether individuals have in fact personality in this sense, which Kant deems legitimate. It is true, insofar as we regard the minor premise in paralogism as an analytic judgement, any thinking *I* (soul) implies personality in this sense. But it is not yet clear how demanding the condition of having a thinking *I* is. For instance, it may seem that the sense of personality and identity Kant deems legitimate to preserve and assert do presuppose an actual consciousness of oneself. For recall that that person's sense of identity is given by her consciousness of her numerical identity in different times. Such a consciousness of identity implies a consciousness of oneself in different times and a consciousness of the identity of oneself at those different times. And, yet, persons are not always reflectively conscious in their actions.

I turn to the question of demandingness and of the actual possession of personality (in the legitimate sense) in the next sections.

§12. Presuppositions of experience

First of all, it must be noted that, for Kant, consciousness of one's own identity, that is, consciousness that it is me who thinks or feels something, need not always be an actual state of mind. Such a requirement would amount to the condition that, whatever the state of mind, I should not only be in that state, but be actually conscious that *I* am in that state. For example, take a melancholic state of mind; if consciousness of identity was, necessarily, an actual state of mind, I could not simply be melancholic, but I would also have to be conscious of myself as being melancholic. Yet it is quite obvious that this is not always the case.

Many a time we are absorbed in states of mind without at the same time being reflectively conscious that we are in such states. Subsequent reflection will easily bring about this consciousness, but subsequent reflection need not occur. Were the condition of being reflectively conscious of one's state of mind to be a general constraint on our conscious life, it would have to apply to our reflective consciousness of being in a certain state of mind, too, and this will lead to an infinite regress.

As Kant puts it in a very famous quote from the second edition of the *Critique of Pure Reason*, what is necessary is only the *possibility* of the appearance of self-consciousness as a presentation in the form 'I think':

> The *I think* must be *capable* of accompanying all my presentations. For otherwise something would be presented to me that could not be thought at all – which is equivalent to saying that the presentation either would be impossible, or at least would be nothing to me.
>
> (*KrV*: B131–2, 177)

Hence, according to Kant, reflecting on one's states of mind and becoming aware of them as determinations of the thinking *I* over time are *not* necessary for a person's experience. Pablo may be able to perceive his friend's predicament and to act without having to reflect on his own states of mind and without having to be reflectively aware that he is the person who is so perceiving and acting. Therefore, as we all know, one does not have to be particularly predisposed to reflection to have experience of the world and to act therein.

This implies that, for Kant, a person's experience is not premised on an *actual* consciousness of herself, that is, on an actual and reflective consciousness of her experience. Hence, it may seem that, since a person's experience does not require her actual reflective self-consciousness, then nor does experience require her *actual* consciousness of herself as numerically identical in different times (the sense of personality Kant thinks we can assert). In this case, the legitimate sense of a person seems quite demanding. Let us consider more closely how a person's experience is formed.

Something as fundamental as a particular sensation presupposes the existence in my mind of several presentations, for, unless I am able to distinguish between this sensation and other sensations, I cannot talk about *particular* sensations. To distinguish between different sensations, however, presupposes that at least one presentation be regarded as different from the others in some respect – not merely as occurring at different moments in time (since the *same* type of sensation may occur at different moments in time too), but as being different in some respect. For instance, I may recognize a sensation of red as the same as that I had before and I am able to distinguish a sensation of red from one of white, both of which I have just been having.[16]

Therefore, implicit in my sensation of red is a synthesis of presentations.[17] In addition, according to Kant, implicit in any of my presentations is the fact that they are *my* presentations. If I were not somehow aware that they are my presentations, "I would have a self as many-coloured and varied as I have presentations that I am conscious of" (*KrV*: B134, 179). I may not be explicitly aware of the fact that it is me who is having a certain sensation, but, since *I* experience that sensation, it is *my* sensation. The point here is worth dwelling on for a little longer, for it makes several assumptions that seem also to be made by Sartre.

Recall Kant's claim that a synthesis of presentations presupposes some form of self-awareness. As we have seen, on Kant's account, a presentation of red may simply be the result of being affected by a red object, but, to be able to have a particular sensation of red, I need to combine that presentation with others. However, this combination will result in the particular sensation I have only if I can combine these presentations as *my* presentations. This implies that, in the process of synthesis, there is an *actual* awareness that these presentations are mine, although I need not be reflectively aware of that. Therefore, for Kant, there must be an actual, although non-reflective, awareness of these presentations, in order for me to be able to experience something as a sensation.

This actual, but non-reflective awareness of presentations as mine is similar to what I need when I perform various activities in day-to-day life without feeling the need to reflect on myself as performing them or even to think about them. In such cases, I am working with the unquestioned assumption that this is how things should be carried out. Similarly, my experience is constituted on the basis of the unquestioned assumption that the various constitutive presentations are mine. Experience cannot imply a combination between a presentation (e.g. a sensation) of mine and a different individual's presentation (e.g. sensation), since the combination tells *me* nothing, unless I can somehow experience the other individual's presentation, in which case it becomes mine. Moreover, a synthesis or combination between two of my sensations presupposes that I am the same across the different times in which I experience the sensations. Experience, therefore, implies a combination of my presentations and, hence, at least a consciousness of identity over time.

This makes it quite clear that the condition required by the legitimate notion of a person that can be saved from the paralogism of personality is not demanding at all. That notion of a person is a necessary condition of experience and, unless we have good reasons to believe someone cannot experience the world, we can safely assume that she is a person in the sense allowed by Kant's discussion. The analysis so far, and this conclusion, is confirmed by Kant's discussion of the transcendental unity of apperception. As we will see in the next section, consciousness of identity over time (the legitimate notion of a person) is bound up with Kant's transcendental unity of apperception, which is a fundamental condition of the possibility of cognition.

§13. Transcendental unity of apperception

In the previous section we have seen that, on Kant's account, some very fundamental elements of our usual lives imply a non-reflective self-consciousness (through which I am non-reflectively aware that a sensation is mine) and an assumption that I am identical over time (which enables the implicit comparison of what I feel now with what I felt earlier on).[18] My sensations and experiences have an implicit consciousness of my identity over time, which makes possible the synthesis of various sensible affections. Hence, this identity is not a matter of reflection – I need not turn my attention to myself and compare myself with how I was before. On the contrary, reflection is only possible on the basis of this identity. For reflection implies a combination of presentations too, this time, however, of presentations of myself, of my own states of mind.

This non-reflective self-consciousness seems to be very closely related to what Kant calls the "transcendental unity of apperception" or simply "transcendental apperception":

> That unity of consciousness which precedes all data of intuitions, and by reference to which all presentation of objects is alone possible [...] I shall call *transcendental apperception*.
>
> (*KrV*: A107, 158–9)

Kant borrows the term "apperception" from Leibniz. For Leibniz, the term signifies the empirical perception of one's own states[19] (Gardner 1999: 145). For Kant, too, apperception has an empirical part, in which case it represents "consciousness of oneself in terms of determinations of one's state" (*KrV*: A107, 158).[20] But, in addition, for him, the term has also a transcendental counterpart. As we have seen, very basic and ordinary experiences presuppose a non-reflective self-consciousness, which makes possible the combination or synthesis of various presentations as my presentations. Moreover, this synthesis of various presentations also presupposes that, across these various presentations, the *I*, in virtue of which we call these presentations *mine*, is numerically identical.

Insofar as this non-reflective consciousness of oneself as numerically identical is a necessary condition that makes possible experience and is constitutive of experience, it represents the transcendental side of apperception. The transcendental character of this form of self-consciousness is also confirmed by the necessity with which we must think the identity of the *I*: "what is to be presented *necessarily* as numerical identity cannot be thought as such through empirical data" (*KrV*: A107, 158).

The reason why Kant talks also about a *unity* of apperception is that, for him, there is a close relation between the consciousness of identity and this unity. Thus, I have said that, on Kant's account, the possibility of a *particular* sensation is given by the combination of various presentations with which we are affected by the world. This combination, which of course presupposes a unity, is possible insofar as these various presentations are *my* presentations and, moreover, insofar as I am conscious of my numerical identity in the times when such presentations occur. Yet, Kant says, it is not only the case that consciousness of numerical identity makes possible the combination of various presentations into a particular sensation, the combination or synthesis of these presentations itself makes possible consciousness of numerical identity. Thus, on his account,

> only because I can combine a manifold of given presentations *in one consciousness*, is it possible for me to present the *identity itself of the consciousness in these presentations*.
>
> (*KrV*: B133, 178)[21]

The argument here relies crucially on the fact that consciousness of numerical identity refers to a formal identity, to a concept of identical *I* which, as we have seen in the discussion of the Third Paralogism, is not determined, but is formal. In principle, we could consider two specific conditions of our state of mind and compare them, at the same time trying to identify what is common to them and, hence, to identify that which remains identical across the variations of other elements that constitute the specific conditions under consideration. In this case, we can say that the comparison of the two states represents a way of combining them, but we end up with identical elements that are found empirically, by comparing determinate thoughts; therefore, those identical elements are not formal, but have a specific empirical content. In this case, an arbitrary combination makes possible consciousness of numerical identity, but this is an empirical and contingent identity, rather than that identity that is a necessary condition of cognition.

Consider now the synthetic unity of apperception, which Kant also calls pure or original apperception (*KrV*: B132, 177). This is a condition that makes possible cognition and, hence, necessarily takes place in experience.[22] For instance, a particular sensation can be formed only if the various presentations that are given by the object producing that sensation are combined as my presentations and, therefore, are unified. What I am (non-reflectively) conscious of as identical is not some specific set of features that are common to some specific states of mind on which I reflect; I am conscious of numerical identity insofar as this refers to a concept of *I* that precedes all experience of particular determined conditions of my state of mind.

Yet, to be able to become conscious of this identity I need to be also conscious of variation and differences in relation to the identical *I*. Moreover, this variation and the associated differences, although they refer to specific presentations I combine, are important only insofar as they are illustrations of a general concept of difference or variation or change. Only in this way will the numerical identity refer to a formal *I*. It does not matter through which sensible given presentations the notion of difference, variation or change is realized, it has to be realized in order to make possible consciousness of identity too.

On Kant's account, original synthetic unity of apperception, what I have called above the transcendental unity of apperception, is a fundamental condition of cognition, which makes possible even sensible intuitions or particular sensations. For him, this unity corresponds to the most fundamental contribution of understanding to cognition and illustrates the inextricable relation, in our experience, between understanding and a second important faculty or power that Kant distinguishes from understanding and calls "sensibility".

Moreover, Kant calls this unity "objective" and distinguishes it from a "*subjective* unity of consciousness" (*KrV*: B139, 182). The next section will present these distinctions in more detail. This is important for the comparative discussion of Kant and Sartre, since, as we will see in Part III, Sartre also brings in his discussion of experience, in the *Critique of Dialectical Reason*, a similar notion of unity. Moreover, he criticizes Kant generally for using such a notion – which should be genuinely formal and regulative – as constitutive of experience.

§14. Sensibility and the understanding

On Kant's account, sensibility is a purely receptive faculty that human beings have, a faculty through which we can be affected by the world in the form of a manifold of presentations, but which does not have the role of making sense of these presentations. Thus, he claims, "the [uncombined] manifold of presentations can be given in an intuition that is merely sensible, i.e., nothing but receptivity" (*KrV*: B129, 175). In the Transcendental Aesthetic (*KrV*: A19/B33-A49/B73, 71–104), he identifies two a priori forms of intuition or sensibility, that is, two ways in which the manifold with which we are affected is spontaneously presented by our epistemic power of sensibility. These forms are space and time. Hence, Kant says further, "the form of this intuition can lie a priori in our power of presentation without being anything but the way in which the subject is affected" (*KrV*: B129, 175).

The emphasis, in the case of the faculty of sensibility, on receptivity and the capacity to be affected will contrast markedly with the specific features of the faculty of the understanding, which is characterized by spontaneity and combinative power. Hence,

> A manifold's *combination (coniunctio)* as such can never come to us through the senses; nor, therefore, can it already be part of what is contained in the pure form of sensible intuition. For this combination is an act of spontaneity by the power of presentation; and this power must be called understanding, in order to be distinguished from sensibility. Hence, all combination is an act of understanding – whether or not we become conscious of such combination; whether it is a combination of the manifold of intuition or of the manifold of various concepts.
>
> (*KrV*: B129–30, 175–6)

In this relatively short quotation, Kant makes several important claims. First, he distinguishes between sensibility and understanding by contrasting the receptive and passive character of sensibility, on the one hand, and the spontaneous and combinative character of understanding, on the other. Secondly, he points out that even the most basic forms of combination, for instance those that make possible sensations, are the result of the activity of understanding. Thirdly, he notes that such combinations, as spontaneously carried out by understanding, may not even be processes of which we become conscious. Finally, he notes that such combinations will not only take place between presentations with which the world affects us directly, but also between presentations that have already been subsumed under concepts with the help of the understanding.

I have said that the understanding helps us make sense of those presentations that things in the world produce when they affect us. The understanding may help us form sensations or subsume various sensations under concepts. Yet, in addition to this, the understanding also makes possible the distinction between subject and object, between the epistemic agent who tries to obtain cognition and the objects of cognition that the agent tries to cognize. Whether these objects are of the inner or of the outer sense (i.e., perceived merely in time or also in space), they need to be distinguished from appearances, from those impressions that may turn out to be mere illusion.

To see how the understanding is supposed to do this, consider the distinction Kant draws between subjective and objective judgement. As an illustration of how subjective judgements are formulated, consider the unity obtained by my linking the word 'red' to 'cinnabar' and the unity obtained by your linking the same word to 'tulip'. Let's assume here that these unities depend for their formation on what we happen to experience. For instance, it may be that I happen to be in a field of cinnabar, whereas you are in a field of tulips. By perceiving the colour red and, then, cinnabar, I can connect these two experiences and claim that my perception of cinnabar is preceded by the sensation of red. This claim is subjective, it is a claim that describes what I am perceiving. Moreover, it is a claim that is constituted by an empirical process of synthesis. Thus, as Kant puts it,

> The empirical unity of apperception, which [...] is only derived from the original unity under given conditions *in concreto*, has only subjective validity. One person will link the presentation of a certain word with one thing, another with some other thing; and the unity of consciousness in what is empirical is not, as regards what is given, necessary and universally valid.
>
> (*KrV*: B140, 183)

Kant notes here, first, that the empirical unity by which I unite, say, 'red' and 'cinnabar' in experience is made possible by the transcendental unity of apperception. Thus, in order for me to link a presentation I now have with another one, I must be able to be aware of myself as identical over the moments when presentations occur. Hence, the empirical unity of apperception, which is given by the link I make between the sensation of red I have and the perception of cinnabar I form, depends on the transcendental unity in virtue of which I become conscious of my numerical identity across presentations.

The way it depends is clarified by Kant as a derivation "under given conditions *in concreto*" (*KrV*: B140, 183). The a priori unity through which we try to make sense of presentations may get a concrete realization simply by describing the way in which a presentation follows the other. When Kant talks here about a unity of consciousness that is not necessary and universally valid, he does not try to suggest that the transcendental unity is not necessary and universally valid, and, hence, to deny that it is a condition of experience. The claim refers only to "what is given", that is, to the way this unity is realized. When such a unity is simply the result of describing how a presentation follows the other, the presentations that are thus given are only contingently given in this way for the particular subject or epistemic agent we consider, and they may be given differently for another agent. Therefore, they are not necessary and universally valid.

Both contingency and particularity are marks of a subjective judgement, since a subjective judgement realizes the original synthetic unity of apperception by taking the contingent succession of presentations as a relationship between presentations and, hence, by making this relationship valid for me, as the particular epistemic agent who happens to experience this succession. The next question is, thus, how we get to form objective judgements. I turn to this in the next section, where I argue that, on Kant's account, only necessary relationships between presentations can establish objective judgements about the things in the world (whether of inner or outer sense) that affect us. These necessary relationships are given by the a priori concepts or categories of understanding.

§15. The understanding and objectivity

In the second edition of the *Critique*, in §19 of section II of the Deduction, Kant talks about the logical form of judgements.[23] He argues that, although judgements of the type 'Tulips are red' are empirical and contingent (and, hence, not necessary and universally valid), their validity is limited in a different sense compared to the validity of the subjective judgement 'The sensation of red follows the perception of a tulip.'

In the case of an objective judgement, like 'Tulips are red', I need a reference to an objective unity (given by transcendental apperception). Without the latter, the judgement could not be formulated, even if I would constantly perceive tulips as associated with the colour red. For, even in such a case, I could only say that 'Whenever I am seeing a tulip, I am also having a sensation of red.'[24] By contrast, in the judgement 'Tulips are red', there is no longer a reference to my perception; instead, we have a claim about an object. To be sure, a subjective judgement also makes reference to the original unity of apperception, as I have already noted. However, it does this by connecting the presentations in the way in which experience happens to tell us they are connected. This is why Kant explains this unity as a *subjective* unity of consciousness, which is a *determination of inner sense* whereby that manifold of intuition for such [objective] combination is given empirically.

(*KrV*: B139, 182)

By contrast, the objective judgement refers directly to a unity that is independent from what I perceive. 'Independent' here should not be taken in an absolute sense, as referring to separation or distinction in all possible respects, but only in a specific sense. When the unity of the sensation of red and of the perception of tulips does not refer merely to an association I happen to experience between these sensations, but to a relationship between substance and accident, I no longer merely talk about the unity given by the arbitrary succession between two sensations. The a priori concept of the understanding (substance/accident) structures experience – it does not simply copy it. I may have first the sensation of red and then the perception of a tulip or the other way around; my claim that the tulip is red is not going to be changed by the contingent order with which sensations and perceptions occur to me.

This is the case even for an object of inner sense, such as pain. While pain is not accessible to all in the way in which outer objects are, the claim that pain makes me depressed is not a simple description of a contingent succession of the sensation of pain and that of being depressed, but a relationship between cause and effect that is not affected by the way the unified presentations happen to be experienced. By contrast, the unity implied by the judgement 'I perceive the tulip and then the colour red' makes only a claim about me as the subject of sensations and, hence, a claim that cannot be necessary or universal, since it depends on the contingent and particular constitution of my perceptual apparatus.[25]

To eliminate the dependence of a judgement on my subjective states, I must say something about how the object is. The result will be an empirical judgement ('Tulips are red') because whether the colour I experience is red or black depends on the colour that tulip happens to have, rather on a conceptual truth about tulips (and, hence, the kind of objects they are). What is, however, necessary is that the tulip has a colour, something it would not be possible to claim on the basis of the subjective unity of consciousness.

A full answer to the question of the transition from subjective to objective judgements will need to make reference to Kant's *Analogies of Experience* (*KrV*: A176–219/B218–66, 247–82). It is there that Kant explains how principles of understanding enable me to distinguish between the subjective time of my presentations and the objective time of the world. While a discussion of the *Analogies* would lead too far from the topic of this chapter, the general answer is clear. What I need for an objective judgement is the possibility of identifying a certain perception I have as referring to some aspect of an object in its relationship to another aspect, whether of the same object or of some other one. Hence, what makes possible the reference of the necessary unity of apperception to the object is a category of understanding (in the case of this judgement, that of substance).

However, we can already formulate a preliminary conclusion. What the argument in this and the previous sections tries to show is that the condition of consciousness of identity is not very demanding. The process is at its basis, also at the basis of our having sensations and experiences and formulating subjective and objective judgements. This process is, for Kant, "an act of spontaneity" (*KrV*: B130, 176), which is produced, as we have already seen, by pure or "original" apperception (*KrV*: B132, 177). Of course, we may encounter cases of persons who may have sensations, experiences and formulate judgements and still not be fit to be considered moral agents. But this should not be surprising. Consciousness of identity (as actual pre-reflective self-consciousness) is only a necessary condition of accountability and only a sufficient condition of a person's acceptance of accountability; whether such a person is right in her acceptance is a different issue.

Apart from the situation I mentioned (a person wrongly accepts this due to tiredness and extreme stress, which make him believe he is the author of an action he has never performed), there are many others that may have a decisive effect on this issue. For instance, memory: an agent who forgets everything within five minutes can hardly be held responsible for her actions, unless she is taught the law, allowed to act against the law and judged within these five minutes. This may still not be enough time to formulate and apply some punishment, and anyway one may wonder whether there is any point in doing this.

However, the situation can also become complicated if we question the condition of freedom. This is the second assumption of accountability I have identified above. Without it, an agent cannot be accountable for her actions and, in fact, it is doubtful we can make much sense of the possessive 'her actions' in this context. As I have mentioned, if we presuppose that we have the standard on the basis of which to judge certain actions as right/wrong, for such a judgement to be possible the actions to be judged must have been performed freely. But to what extent can we talk about freedom?

This question will be one of the main topics of Part II of this book. For the remainder of this chapter, I will focus on a few other key elements of Kant's account of practical agency. In particular, we will see that Kant's practical philosophy is maxim- or principle-centred. What the standard of rightness is supposed to test are principles, and persons act on principles or maxims of action. On Kant's account, moreover, there is one fundamental higher-order principle in which all the other principles and actions of a person are grounded. The problem, to which, as we will see in the next chapter, Sartre objects, is precisely making sense of the idea that such a fundamental higher-order principle could be chosen, as opposed to being simply given to each of us. This is, in fact, a precondition of accountability, which is related to that of freedom. It is also a topic on which Sartre formulates one of his objections to Kant. The issue will figure prominently in Part II.

§16. Character

A very important notion of Kant's thought – a notion, however, not very much discussed in the literature – is that of character [*Charakter*]. As we will see, this notion represents perhaps the main root of a significant difference we can identify between Kant's and Sartre's philosophies. Moreover, this notion is one that plays an important role both in Kant's epistemology and metaphysics, and in his ethics and juridical philosophy. So, I will begin this section with a brief account of the notion. I will then move on to a discussion of Kant's notion of disposition. Together with the next section, these will provide the necessary background for an investigation of Sartre's second objection to Kant.

Generally, in his epistemology, Kant uses "character" to refer to the law according to which a cause determines its effect. Corresponding to the distinction between two kinds of causality (empirical and intelligible), Kant draws a distinction between empirical and intelligible characters of agents:

> In a subject of the world of sense we would have, first, an *empirical character*. Through this character the subject's actions, as appearances, would according to constant natural laws stand throughout in connection with other appearances and could be derived from these appearances as the actions' conditions [...]. Second, one would have to grant to the subject also an *intelligible character*. Through this character the subject is indeed the cause of those actions as appearances, but the character itself is not subject to any conditions of sensibility and is not itself appearance.
>
> (*KrV*: A539/B568, 539–40)

To this quotation, let me add that, on Kant's account, "any cause presupposes a rule" (*KrV*: A549/B577, 546). Hence, given a particular rule and a particular set of circumstances, from a certain cause there results a certain effect. When the conditions in which a cause takes place vary, the effects produced by the cause will vary as well; however, despite the difference in conditions and effects, these various situations manifest the same rule of causality. The rule of causality manifested by phenomena represents the *empirical* character of the cause (in this case, an agent).

Insofar as the actions, as effects of reason's causality, show a rule, reason has an empirical character. Since Kant thinks we get to cognize an agent's empirical character "through experience" (*KrV*: A540/B568, 540), the process he has in mind here must be a reflective judgement (*KU*: 5:179, 18–19). One starts from instances and tries to determine the rule in accordance with which the instances occur. Considered as appearances, all actions are determined on the basis of this rule of causality. Hence, the empirical character can be explained in terms of laws of nature. More exactly, the empirical character of actions will be explained by reference to the way a person's various sensible incentives become determining grounds of action in specific circumstances.

However, if the same actions are considered from the perspective of reason's intelligible character, that is, insofar as reason can also be a cause independent from natural laws, then the way in which actions are judged is different:

> For in that regard perhaps there *ought not to have occurred* all that according to nature's course yet *has occurred* and according to its own empirical bases inevitably had to occur.
>
> (*KrV*: A550/B578, 547)

In other words, on Kant's account, such causality will refer to other rules than the rules of natural laws. Ethical imperatives could, for instance, provide one way in which the intelligible causality of reason can be conceived of, but other normative rules may as well represent good candidates. For example, assuming that a person is committed to some aesthetic norms, her actions will also be accountable in terms of these norms, rather than simply in terms of the laws of nature. Natural laws, given existing sensible incentives a person may have, and given the specific circumstances of her situation, will be able to account for certain actions. But if the person is committed to other (ethical, aesthetic or what have you) principles, then the actions performed may also be accounted for quite differently.

At this point, one can raise a further question, namely, how an agent will get to choose between these various types of rule or principle. Kant's answer to this question requires us to cast a brief look at some aspects he introduces in his later work, *Religion Within the Limits of Reason Alone*. Moreover, it would be useful at this point to introduce a notion that occupies an important place in Kant's thought, especially in his practical philosophy, namely, that of a maxim. Discussion on this notion is ongoing in the literature, and I will present it in more detail in the second part of this book, in Chapter 4, but, for the purpose of the argument in this first part, we can define a maxim as the principle that the agent adopts in her actions.

To illustrate this, consider again Constant's example. The easiest thing for me to do might be to lie to the murderer who is at my door and, if I act on the principle that I must perform actions that are easiest for me to perform, then this is exactly what I will do: I will lie to the murderer. If, by contrast, my principle of action requires me to act in such a way that consequences that are beneficial for me obtain, then those laws of nature that show how one must act to bring about the desired consequences also become subjective grounds for my action. In both cases, the principles on which I act are my maxims. Such maxims may play a role in the unification of the laws of nature, and this is how they are presented in the first *Critique*, as maxims of reason:

> I call *maxims* of reason all subjective principles that are obtained not from the character of the object, but from reason's interest concerning a certain possible perfection of the cognition of this object.
>
> (*KrV*: A666/B694, 635–6)

However, as we have just seen, a person's character is constituted by her subjective principle of action. Hence, a maxim is the rule that governs that person's character, and we can now return to the question of how the agent decides between the various types of rule or between the various maxims that determine her actions. In *Religion*, Kant regards the various maxims of a person's actions as grounded in a more fundamental principle, which he calls "disposition" and which represents the only basis for a person's choice of a maxim:

> The disposition, *i.e.* the first subjective ground of the adoption of the maxims, can only be a single one, and it applies to the entire use of freedom universally.
>
> (*RGV*: 6:26, 74)

Therefore, on Kant's account, there is a second-order maxim, "the first" subjective ground for the adoption of maxims, which, in specific circumstances, can determine the agent to choose one particular maxim of action over another one. This then provides the answer to the question above. Moreover, on Kant's account, this second-order maxim is one that is going to be applied by the agent to all her actions. I concluded the previous section by mentioning that Sartre, among others, points to a certain difficulty that Kant's account of practical agency will face, because of his notion of disposition. The next section, which will also conclude this chapter, will present this problem. A detailed discussion of this problem will occupy us in Chapter 2.

§17. Revolution in disposition

Kant's claim that maxims of action are further grounded in a disposition has implications that lead to some interesting objections. If agents are to be responsible for their actions and if actions are ultimately derived from the agents' dispositions, then agents must be also responsible for their dispositions. Hence, an agent's disposition, as the ultimate ground of her actions, must be chosen by the agent, for, as Kant puts it, "otherwise it could not be imputed" (*RGV*: 6:25, 74).

This requirement leads to a first problem, with which, however, Kant deals in an arguably satisfactory manner. Thus, talking about the ground for the adoption of a disposition, he says:

> But there cannot be any further cognition of the subjective ground or the cause of this adoption [...], for otherwise we would have to adduce still another maxim into which the disposition would have to be incorporated, and this maxim must in turn have its ground.
>
> (*RGV*: 6:25, 74)

As suggested by Kant here, his account of practical agency risks leading to an infinite regress. If the disposition has to be chosen in order for actions to be imputable, then we can raise the question of the grounds for the choice of the disposition. Furthermore, we can raise the question of the grounds of the grounds of such a choice and so on ad infinitum. Kant proposes to stop this infinite regress by the claim that we cannot know the grounds of the adoption of a disposition. He refers to this adoption by calling it a "revolution" in the person's "disposition" (*RGV*: 6:47, 92).

Kant talks about two dispositions, an ethical disposition and an evil disposition. He suggests that the status of these dispositions is not that of some fundamental grounds of maxims, which are given independently from the person in the noumenal realm; dispositions are not similar to Platonic Ideas, which await to be discovered and adopted by the person. Rather, dispositions cannot be separated from a person. He suggests this by talking about *pre*dispositions, rather than simply dispositions. Thus, the ethical disposition is an original disposition, or what Kant calls a "predisposition": "The predisposition to *personality* is the susceptibility to respect for the moral law *as of itself a sufficient incentive to the power of choice*" (*RGV*: 6:27, 76).

Even though Kant considers a good or ethical disposition to be a *pre*disposition, he does not maintain that ethical actions simply follow from a kind of natural tendency of human beings to observe the moral law. It is for this reason that Kant talks about the necessary revolution in disposition that will lead to ethical actions. Without this revolution, our actions are evil, since Kant thinks that we start with a predisposition to evil.

The change of disposition is the result of the adoption by the agent of the ethical disposition. What then is the relation between a person's intelligible character as the rule that legislates the person's causality, and the good disposition as the ground of the person's maxims? For Kant, the revolution in disposition brings about

> the recovery of the *purity* of the law, as the supreme ground of all our maxims, according to which the law itself is to be incorporated into the power of choice, not merely bound to other incentives, nor indeed subordinated

to them (to inclinations) as conditions, but rather in its full purity, as the self-*sufficient* incentive of that power.

(RGV: 6:46, 91)

The good disposition is then a person's determination to be moved only by the moral law as an incentive for action. A morally good person's maxims will be justified in virtue of being grounded in the moral law. Hence I interpret Kant's intelligible character as the source of the "revolution", which makes possible the adoption of a good disposition. By contrast, the person's disposition establishes a relation between the agent's intelligible character and her maxims. In this way, Kant can account for the fact that the disposition, maxims and actions of the practical agent are imputable.

Therefore, the good disposition places the moral law as supreme incentive in the choice of maxims and actions. Similarly, the evil disposition takes sensible incentives to be prior to the moral law. In general, a disposition is a determination to establish a relationship of priority between the moral law and other incentives for action. A person's empirical character can be identified by the formulation of the rules that govern her actions, when these are regarded as consequences of certain sensible incentives. By contrast, a person's intelligible character refers to the laws of the person's intelligible causality.

For instance, situations in which a person's actions are accompanied by fear may suggest that the person is a coward and her actions are determined by fear and, hence, cowardly. This is her empirical character. By contrast, the same actions, if they happen to be the result of a determination to act ethically and, hence, to act on an ethically valid maxim, manifest an intelligible character governed by the moral law. To be sure, an intelligible character governed by the moral law is likely to bring about a change in the types of incentive that will accompany a person's actions, but the actions can also be regarded as determined by sensible incentives; such sensible incentives always accompany actions, but they need not be the determining grounds of those actions.

Now the objection Sartre raises at this point does not have to do with Kant's solution to the threat of the infinite regress. More interestingly, Sartre suggests that Kant makes appeal here to an idea of choice that goes beyond the world of phenomena and is a non-temporal choice made by an intelligible character. Needless to say, if correct, this objection would in fact point to a serious problem in Kant's account of practical agency, since it goes against the very principles of Kant's critical philosophy, according to which there is no way in which we can have cognition without experience and we can have no experience beyond phenomena. A discussion of Sartre's alternative notion of original choice and an evaluation of Sartre's objection will be one of the tasks of the next chapter.

2
Sartre and Kant

For methodological reasons, I have started, in Chapter 1, with a presentation of Kant's account of self, in particular the conditions of identity and self-choice that seem to be required by moral accountability and the possibility of moral judgement. Structural similarities, as I have mentioned, are identified when Sartre's objections to Kant turn out to rely on a mistaken reading of Kant and when it can be shown that Kant, too, argues against the claims Sartre objects to. Now that we have a fairly detailed view of what Kant says about identity and self-choice, we can move on to a consideration of the Sartrean objections and to an evaluation of their merits. This chapter will consider two objections, both of which target Kant's account of self. Chapters 4 and 6 will continue the comparative discussion with particular emphasis on freedom and moral normativity.

§18. Impersonal consciousness

In *The Transcendence of the Ego*, Sartre offers a subtle interpretation of Kant's account of the *I*.[1] He starts by quoting, approvingly, Kant's famous claim concerning the necessity of the possibility of 'I think', a quote I already discussed in Chapter 1. He then claims to follow in Kant's footsteps by separating the possibility and the actuality of the *I*: Kant is talking about the possibility of the 'I think', he says, not about its *de facto* existence (*TE*: 13–14, 2). Moreover, on this account, Kant is interested in the necessity of this possibility, as a condition that makes experience possible.

The agreement with Kant persists even after Sartre indicates that his questions are different from Kant's. For the latter, the main question has a *de jure*, not a *de facto*, character – it refers to what must be, not what is, the case. Kant is, therefore, interested in the *necessary* conditions of experience. Sartre agrees that what is necessary is for the 'I think' to be able to accompany all our presentations.[2] But he is also interested in two further *de facto* questions. First, he asks whether a presentation that is not accompanied by the 'I think' undergoes any change when it becomes so accompanied and also whether presentations are unified by the 'I think', rather than by an already existing unity of presentations (*TE*: 15–16, 3–4).

In other words, Sartre seems simply interested in exploring further new questions inspired by Kant's answers to more fundamental problems, answers that Sartre seems to take for granted. He does not seem engaged in a polemic with Kant. But the impression is misleading. Shortly afterwards, it becomes evident that the stakes are much higher. For Sartre, Kant regards the *I* as a *formal* structure of consciousness, yet, he adds, "an I is never purely formal" (*TE*: 37, 16–17). For Sartre, "the I ever appears on the occasion of a reflective act" (*TE*: 36, 16). Since not all experience is reflective, but all experience is conscious, it follows that the *I* need not be in the consciousness. If consciousness constructs an *I* as part of the world, then there is, in fact, no *I* in the consciousness. Consciousness is only an impersonal transcendental field, in a certain sense, a "*nothing*" (*TE*: 74, 43).

To be sure, as we have seen in the previous chapter, Kant takes the *I* to be in consciousness, because he thinks the *I* is purely formal. Yet Sartre denies precisely this. Here, Sartre assumes that Kant holds the *I* to be a formal structure of consciousness and he argues that, in fact, consciousness is impersonal until the moment it constructs or it posits an *I* as part of the world. As necessary for experience that is independently from such a posited *I* (which, following Kant, Sartre acknowledges to be only a possibility), consciousness is impersonal.

So, here, we do not simply have a confusion on Sartre's part between an *I* and an ego (the transcendental unity of apperception and the reflective 'I think'), which are in fact kept distinct by Kant. Sartre is well aware that Kant wants to keep these distinct, but he thinks that, insofar as there is no purely formal *I*, the *I* of the transcendental apperception is the result of reflection and, hence, must be placed outside consciousness. As prereflective, consciousness becomes *I*-less and, therefore, impersonal. That Sartre is aware of Kant's distinction between the *I* of transcendental unity of apperception and the *I* of the reflective 'I think' is clear from his account of Kant's argument. He stresses, for instance, that Kant raises a *de jure* question concerning the necessary conditions of experience. At the same time, he explicitly acknowledges the possibility of experience without the reflective *I*. So, he cannot simply confuse this *I* with that of the transcendental unity of apperception.

Several questions emerge at this point: How does Sartre get to this view of transcendental consciousness as impersonal? Is his interpretation of Kant correct? If it is correct, does his objection hold? There seems to be little point in comparing further aspects of Kant's and Sartre's works were they to disagree on such fundamental issues. So let me turn now to these questions and examine them in some detail.

§19. Digestive philosophy

How does Sartre derive the conclusion that transcendental consciousness is impersonal? To answer this, a short presentation of the general epistemological framework of Sartre's thought is in order. For this purpose, Sartre's short essay, "Intentionality: A Fundamental Idea of Husserl's Phenomenology", is not only the first point of reference, but perhaps the best too (*IFP*: 9, 4). In this text, Sartre presents phenomenology as the method able to avoid the problems generated by those approaches to knowledge that rely on realist and idealist metaphysics. Moreover, the "digestive" epistemology of the realist and idealist is precisely what, in Sartre's reading, Husserl's phenomenology seems able to overcome:

> "He devoured her with his eyes". This expression and many other signs point to the illusion common to both realism and idealism: to know is to eat. [...] We have all believed that the spidery mind trapped things in its web, covered them with a white spit and slowly swallowed them, reducing them to its own substance. What is a table, a rock, a house? A certain assemblage of "contents of *consciousness*", a class of such contents. O digestive philosophy!
>
> (*IFP*: 9, 4)

The metaphor of a digestive philosophy is not clear at this point. It is clear perhaps that idealists reduce reality to ideas, but realists seem to militate precisely against a digestive philosophy that would reduce the being of things to that of ideas. What exactly is Sartre arguing against here?

To the idealist view that things in the world are reducible to contents of consciousness (for instance, as given by perception), Sartre opposes Husserl's contention that "one cannot dissolve things in consciousness" (*IFP*: 9, 4). He makes haste to add, however, that this should not be regarded as a realist claim. What I perceive of, say, a tree standing in front of me is not the tree as an entity existing completely independently from my consciousness; to have such a perception would presuppose a process of communication between me and the tree, a process which, however, should not guarantee that what I perceive would correspond to the way the tree is, independently from my perception of it.

But how could I ever know how the tree is, independently of my perception of it? To be able to do something like this, I would need a way of having access to it as it is in itself,[3] and this seems contradictory. After all, to have a view of something as it is in itself is to have a view of it as it is independently from the way I or any other epistemic agent conceives it. How can I have a view of something as it is, independently from my view of it? My view of something, no matter how I try to conceive of it, cannot be independent from my view of it.

In addition to all this, if both realism and idealism subscribe to the epistemology of this so-called "digestive" philosophy, then the opposition between realism and idealism cannot offer any insight into what is characteristic for the digestive way of thinking. So, when Sartre claims, following Husserl, that "one cannot dissolve things in consciousness", the way Sartre sees the independence of things from consciousness must be quite distinct from the realist claim. From within the phenomenological perspective, when we talk about things or about the world we must not imagine them as a picture of how things exist in themselves. As I have just suggested, it is doubtful that such an idea would be coherent anyway. In fact, in Sartre's view, "consciousness and the world are given at one stroke: essentially external to consciousness, the world is nevertheless essentially relative to consciousness" (*IFP*: 9, 4).

The discussion so far seems to complicate matters further. It is now unclear not only what Sartre has in view when he criticizes the so-called digestive philosophy, but also how the phenomenological approach he endorses offers a view of the relation between consciousness and the world that is distinct from the realist one. To deal with the first question first, whereas traditional idealists are committed to the view that things in the world ultimately consist of ideas, realists claim that there is something independent from consciousness, a reality that constitutes the things in the world. Therefore, in order to acquire knowledge of the world, consciousness has to get to know this reality. The assumption here for both realists and idealists, in addition to a correspondence theory of truth, is that we can have ideas about the world, ideas that correspond to the way things in the world really are.

The claim that the world is really nothing apart from our ideas is a claim that does not depend for its truth on our perception of the world or on what we can know about the world; it is a claim that requires that we go beyond our ideas and see whether there is anything else of the world apart from them. Similarly, for the realist, the claim that our ideas correspond to the way the world really is, independently from us, presupposes a perspective that is independent from any of the perspectives from which we usually form ideas. However, this means that the assimilation of the objects of experience by consciousness need not be the reduction of their *being* to the being of consciousness. This may further suggest that there is no place for Sartre's metaphor of a digestive philosophy.

Still, the metaphor remains apt, for, through its ideas and claims, consciousness seems able to assimilate the properties of the world or the ways in which the world really is. In this manner, consciousness *understands* the world as the world is, independently from consciousness. Consciousness does not reduce the being of the world to ideas, but captures the way the world really is in its ideas. This applies equally well to realism and idealism, but, as we will see, not to the phenomenological standpoint.

In short, the realist and idealist positions share a belief in the possibility of determining the relationship of ontological dependence between consciousness and the world. Yet the question of whether or not the world is ontologically dependent on consciousness implies that we have access to the world and consciousness independently from each other and that we are then able to determine the direction of this relationship. This implies, in its turn, the assumption that we can know the world in two distinct ways: through our consciousness and in some other way, independently from consciousness.

This, of course, is only the beginning of a new problem; if we do not accept as absurd the suggestion of an additional epistemic access to the world, independently from that given by our consciousness, then an account of this would be required. Yet, for us, there can be a world only insofar as we can at least think of it and, hence, be conscious of it. The plausibility of this claim provides at least some reasons to go along with Sartre's suggestion and accept the phenomenological approach. He emphasizes the relationship of mutual dependence between consciousness and the world, but this is not taken to be a claim about the way the world and consciousness really are, independently from our cognition of them. On the contrary, assuming that what we say about the world depends on the particular way we cognize the world, the claim of mutual dependence is an implication of the general features of our cognition.

The discussion in this section should be able to offer a clear view of what Sartre has in mind when he talks about and criticizes a digestive approach in philosophy. This is then able to answer the first of the two questions mentioned above (in what sense Sartre rejects idealism and realism as illustrative of the digestive approach and how the phenomenological approach he puts forward is distinct from the realist account). The answer to the second question is the focus of the next section.

§20. Intentionality

From the discussion in the previous section, we can see that Sartre is committed neither to a problematic distinction between epistemological and ontological perspectives[4] nor to their problematic identification through reduction; he is interested in bringing to light the distinction's complexities and, in particular, he attempts to map out the relationship between these two perspectives. Thus, it seems clear from his account that a metaphysical commitment to idealism or realism leads to an epistemological commitment to the possibility of saying something accurate about the world independently from the way consciousness presents it. To claim with the idealist that things in the world ultimately are nothing beyond ideas in consciousness, or with the realist that ultimately they are independent from ideas, is to assume access to a realm beyond that of consciousness and in a way that does not involve consciousness.

In response to realism and idealism, Sartre adopts Husserl's thesis that "all consciousness is consciousness *of* something" (*IFP*: 11, 5). This formula seems able to bridge the gap between subject and object, person and world, and leads to Sartre's view that a person's specific way of being is that of "being-in-the-world" (*IFP*: 11, 5). "Being-in" is to be understood as a *movement* of consciousness towards something that is different from it, that is, towards the world. The idea here is not that there is an already constituted world, which includes persons who have the property of being-in-the-world. On the contrary, this movement of being-in constitutes the world for a person. Following Husserl, Sartre calls this necessary feature of consciousness (namely, that of existing as consciousness of something other than itself) "intentionality".

By the end of Sartre's "Intentionality", an even broader meaning is associated with the concept in the title: 'intentionality' covers more than merely the epistemic relationship of the person to the world. Hating or loving a person, for instance, is also one possible form that my consciousness "of" that person can take. In general, whether epistemic, simply ethical, aesthetic or affective, all such claims about things and persons in the world imply a consciousness *of* the things or persons, that is, they imply intentionality.

In this way, the "of" no longer stands for assimilation or representation, but for relation. The colour of the sky, the feelings towards the loved ones, the beauty of a piece of music and the demands of a particular situation are not representations *in my consciousness* of the way things are. Instead, they are particular instances of the various relationships I have to the world, relationships that constitute my experience.[5]

Two important consequences follow: first, my presentations no longer can stand for the way in which various things (from objects in the world to affection towards other beings) are independently from my consciousness, since they are in fact relationships between me and my world; secondly, consciousness is emptied not only of the things of the world that the idealist reduces to ideas, it is also emptied of any mental entities that may seem to bear properties specific for a person's consciousness. A melancholic state of mind presupposes consciousness of oneself as melancholic and, hence, a relationship between consciousness and something distinct from consciousness, something towards which consciousness transcends itself.

In general, to cognize the world (in a broad sense of cognition, which includes relationships to the world and oneself of an affective, aesthetic and moral kind) is to experience the world or oneself, and the only way to do this is if consciousness transcends itself towards the object of experience. To realize this radical transcendence of the world is, according to Sartre, Husserl's most important achievement (*IFP*: 12, 5).

However, it is not only my representations of things and my feelings towards others that should be considered as directed towards the mundane realm, even my own reflective *I* has its place outside consciousness, a claim this time directed *against* Husserl's later philosophy.[6] Sartre criticizes Husserl for what he takes to be the latter's relapse into a rationalist position concerning the *I*. According to the rationalist position, there is a "transcendental" ego or *I*, which is not subject to the contingent and irrelevant changes that a person's empirical self undergoes. Hence, as we have also seen in the previous chapter in the discussion of the third paralogism, this *I*, which constitutes one pole in a person's relationship to the world, has features that can, in principle, be determined through rational analysis, and that must therefore be a priori.

To this view of identity, Sartre opposes the claim that the relationship between consciousness and ego is not one of immanence, that is, the ego does not dwell in consciousness but transcends it. The relationship between consciousness and ego is the same as that between consciousness and an object in the world. It is in this sense that Sartre reassigns the ego to the mundane realm, as an implication of his commitment to phenomenology and of his critical reaction to the traditional philosophy of assimilation.

I have started this section with the question of the distinction between the phenomenological view of the independence of the world from consciousness, and the realist view. An answer can now be offered, following the discussion of Sartre's conception of intentionality. The world is independent from consciousness not as a thing in itself, but as a thing that transcends consciousness and makes consciousness possible. Hence, the phenomenologist is not committed to the realist claim of the existence of a realm of things in themselves, nor is she committed to an idealist denial of this realm. She only asserts the irreducibility of the world to consciousness and is content to attribute the objectivity of the world to this distinctive feature the world has, as an object of the consciousness' intentionality.

We can now also answer one of the three questions raised at the beginning of this chapter. Recall that, there, the following problems remained open: why Sartre thinks consciousness is impersonal, whether his critique of Kant relies on an accurate interpretation of Kant, and, finally, whether the critique has any force. It should now be clearer why Sartre thinks that the *I* in the 'I think' must be relegated to the mundane realm. Moreover, it seems obvious that, if the *I* is the mark of the personal, then Sartre is right to claim that, since the *I* is in the world consciousness must be impersonal. To address the other two questions will be the task of the next sections.

§21. The Transcendence of the Ego

In the previous section, we have seen that Sartre objects to Kant's attempt to retain a personal element that is immanent in relation to consciousness. What, in Sartre's account, Kant says to justify this place for personality is that this is a formal structure of consciousness, rather than a contentful element to which consciousness could relate and which would thus be necessarily outside consciousness, would transcend it. Yet, on Sartre's account, the *I* is never purely formal – it is a structure which transcends me (my consciousness) and even this *me*, which is still a personal element, need not be immanent to consciousness.

As we have seen in Chapter 1, it is correct to say, with Sartre, that Kant thinks there is a formal structure of consciousness, which makes possible experience and which has a personal character. Thus, for Kant, the personal character is given by consciousness of numerical identity, and the *I* that stands for this identity is only legitimate as a concept without concrete determinations, an empty concept that accompanies my various conscious states. This formal structure, I have said, is the *I* of transcendental apperception and is closely related to what Kant calls the original synthetic unity of apperception.

If Sartre is right and no personal element is purely formal, then even the *I* of transcendental apperception must have some specific content, which consciousness could posit, thus expelling it from consciousness. In this case, Sartre's objection to Kant would be correct: consciousness would have to be only an impersonal transcendental field and there would be no *I* or trace of an *I* immanent to it.

It is true that Sartre seems to use the notion of an *I* in various ways, in particular, in his interpretation of the Kantian *I*. For instance, he correctly acknowledges that, for Kant, what is necessary is the possibility of the 'I think' (*TE*: 13–14, 2). In other words, he agrees that a necessary condition of experience is that we *can* reflect on experience and make it explicit that it is our experience. However, in places, he also regards the 'I think', rather than its possibility, as a necessary condition of experience (*TE*: 26, 9). Moreover, he does not take transcendental apperception (which explains how the possibility of the 'I think' has a necessary character) to be the formal structure of consciousness, but the *I* itself (*TE*: 36–7, 16).

We can explain the apparent inconsistencies between these various uses. For instance, we may regard the second use of 'I think' as a necessary condition of experience as given by a *pre-reflective* cogito (to use Sartre's terminology in *Being and Nothingness*). I will explain in more detail shortly what this means, but, for the moment, the point is that we can regard this 'I think' or cogito as non-reflective and, hence, similar to Kant's notion of transcendental apperception. The latter, as we have seen, is a genuine condition that makes experience possible. We can consider here in addition that, as I have just noted, there is nothing inconsistent in regarding both transcendental apperception and the *I* as formal structures of consciousness.

This is confirmed by the fact that Sartre is clearly aware of Kant's distinction between the reflective 'I think' or cogito and the possibility of the 'I think', and he clearly acknowledges that only the latter has a necessary character. So I do not think that the major problem here is Sartre's interpretation of Kant; rather, the problem seems to be introduced by two other claims that Sartre makes: first, that there is no purely formal structure of consciousness and, secondly, that what has no *I* is impersonal.

Sartre maintains the thesis of the transcendence of the ego throughout his writings, from "Intentionality" through *Being and Nothingness* to the *Critique of Dialectical Reason*.[7] Yet, there is an important shift from *The Transcendence* to *Being and Nothingness*. Although extremely relevant, this shift is rarely considered by those who examine Kant's and Sartre's views. Thus, in *Being and Nothingness*, the personal is no longer seen as bound up with reflective consciousness. The pre-reflective consciousness which, in *The Transcendence of the Ego*, was thought to be impersonal and, hence, to go beyond freedom and everyday morality, becomes personal there.[8]

As it might be evident by now, the significance of this change for the comparison with Kant and the idea of a critical ethics is considerable.[9] However, some more steps have to be taken before I will be able to spell this out adequately. Besides, in this section I have used several of Sartre's technical terms and assumed that they are clear enough. For instance, I have talked about consciousness' positing content and about pre-reflective cogito. Such notions must, however, be properly introduced and clarified. For the moment, the importance of Sartre's change of view about personality in *Being and Nothingness* can be briefly explained by noting that, if the personal is no longer bound up with the reflective *I*, on Sartre's new account, the fact that a reflective *I* is outside the fundamental field of consciousness no longer implies immediately that this Sartrean transcendental field of consciousness is impersonal. How does Sartre account for the distinct view of *Being and Nothingness*?

§22. Forms of consciousness

In the Introduction to *Being and Nothingness*, Sartre distinguishes several forms of consciousness. Thus, we have first a distinction between an immediate or non-positional consciousness and a positional consciousness. When I am perceiving something, I may be conscious of that thing in virtue of an *immediate* consciousness that I have with regard to it. This immediate consciousness is not positional – it will not present its object as situated in a determinate place or as bearing particular properties. Hence, immediate consciousness is not able to make *judgements* with regard to the world, because it does not posit the object that it perceives. It may, however, subsequently focus on the object and posit it.[10]

Consider now the situation when I am judging something, such as the quality of a piece of paper that lies in front of my eyes. Although, in this instance, I am positing the piece of paper and I am involved in the activity of judging its quality, I may not be reflectively conscious of doing this; on the contrary, I may be absorbed by my activity to the point of forgetting about myself. The focus of my activity is, therefore, the transcendent object of my attention (the piece of paper), not my activities, what I am doing. This leads to the second important distinction Sartre draws between types of consciousness, namely, that between consciousness and self-consciousness. Self-consciousness, as the name indicates, takes itself as an object. When I am positing my own conscious activities, I am self-conscious and, moreover, I am reflecting on myself. By contrast, when I am positing an object distinct from myself without also positing myself as doing this, I am simply conscious of that object.

A further distinction drawn by Sartre is that between reflective and pre-reflective self-consciousness. Thus, although in the example above, I am trying to establish the quality of the paper in front of me, I am not reflectively aware of doing this. Yet, I cannot say that I am not conscious of myself as doing this. In my mind the thought that it is me who is doing such-and-such a thing does not occur, but I can always explain what I am doing to someone who asked me to. However, I can only explain now what I have just done, if what I have done is inscribed somehow in my memory as having been done by me. But this is not possible, if I have not been somehow aware of myself as having done such-and-such a thing while doing it.[11]

Hence, one can be reflectively or pre-reflectively aware of oneself as doing something. According to Sartre, any form of consciousness is at the same time pre-reflectively conscious of itself. Hence, my positional consciousness of the piece of paper in front of me is also pre-reflectively conscious of itself as such a consciousness. This pre-reflective self-consciousness is distinct from reflective consciousness (consciousness of self) and, to mark this difference, Sartre calls it "consciousness (of)[12] self".[13]

Reflective self-consciousness presupposes a positional consciousness of oneself, whereby one's self is posited as an object (an "I" or ego). By contrast, pre-reflective self-consciousness or consciousness (of) self, as pre-reflective, cannot be posited, since it would then have to become an object for a positional consciousness and, hence, simply part of a reflective process. To be sure, consciousness (of) self is bound up with the immediate consciousness of something or with the positional consciousness of something and can only undertake a subsequent reflection by turning into a different type of consciousness. Thus, to use one of Sartre's examples, consciousness (of) belief is bound up with belief and they form one being; by focusing on belief as consciousness that such-and-such is the case, consciousness posits this belief and pre-reflective consciousness refers now to the positional consciousness of belief, rather than to belief itself.[14]

Moreover, for Sartre, I cannot say that I have a cognition of something, if I am not at the same time conscious of this fact (*EN*: lii–liii, 18–19). However, he rejects the hypothesis that the condition of cognition is that of having a cognizing positional consciousness of cognizing,[15] for this will lead to an infinite regress.[16] He suggests, therefore, that it is sufficient for the cognizing consciousness of an object that it be at the same time conscious (of) itself. Hence, this pre-reflective self-consciousness is a necessary condition of the knowing consciousness. By implication, Sartre regards this necessary condition as an absolute.

Consciousness has nothing substantial, it is pure "appearance" in the sense that it exists only to the degree to which it appears. However, it is precisely because consciousness is pure appearance, because it is total emptiness (since the entire world is outside it) that it can be considered as the absolute (*EN*: lii, 18–19).

What is the argument here? First, why does Sartre regard this pre-reflective, that is, non-positional self-consciousness, as absolute? Recall that, on Sartre's account, every consciousness is at the same time conscious (of) itself, which means that this pre-reflective level of consciousness is always at work within human experience. But, then, as a necessary condition of cognition, pre-reflective consciousness cannot become the object of cognizing consciousness and, hence, relative to the way it is cognized. Thus, the reason why it is absolute is that

> it is not subject to the famous objection according to which a known absolute is no longer an absolute because it becomes relative to the knowledge which one has of it.
>
> (*EN*: lvi, 23)

Secondly, however, we must ask why Sartre regards pre-reflective self-consciousness or consciousness (of) self as pure "appearance" with nothing substantial. The answer can be seen from the fact that pre-reflective self-consciousness is non-positional. Hence, although it is an accompanying consciousness for every positional consciousness, it cannot posit itself and, therefore, cannot specify any particular determination for what appears. Without any particular determination, it is empty, no content can be specified and it is pure appearance. This implies that such a level of consciousness is in fact absolute in a twofold sense. First, without a specific content, it cannot be challenged in the way in which specific claims usually are, namely, by having a certain feature or other contested. Secondly, as a particular, even if empty, form of consciousness, one can in principle object to its status as a necessary condition of cognition, but every objection would reinforce it, since every objection is a cognition claim that involves a positional consciousness and, hence, the very condition that is objected to.[17]

Pre-reflective self-consciousness makes possible the other levels of consciousness. It simply implies a movement of separation of itself from itself, in order to enable consciousness to appear to itself – to make possible both positional (knowing) and non-positional consciousness of the world, as well as reflective consciousness. This kind of appearance to itself makes a person exist or be *for* herself and leads Sartre to the characterization of a person as "being-for-itself" (*EN*: lxiii, 31). Accordingly, persons can be defined as conscious beings.[18]

The notion of the self occurs frequently in *Being and Nothingness* and in various contexts. We have two types of self-consciousness, but, as we will see, we also have the two regions of being, being-for-itself and being-in-itself. On this account, there is a pre-reflective self-consciousness, which is consciousness (of) self. Hence, if a self is present in pre-reflective consciousness and if pre-reflective self-consciousness is a condition for all consciousness – whether reflective or non-reflective – then it becomes conceivable that this condition of experience be after all personal, in the same sense of 'personal' as that defined by Kant. More on the Sartrean notion of the self will be presented in the next section.

§23. Self

We have seen that, according to Sartre, pre-reflective self-consciousness is a necessary condition for the other forms of consciousness. Since it is a non-positional relation to itself, pre-reflective self-consciousness cannot reflect on itself in the manner of reflective self-consciousness; however, as consciousness (of) self, pre-reflective consciousness manifests an attempt to reveal itself. There is, therefore, a structural similarity between reflective consciousness and self-consciousness, and, in order to underscore it, Sartre calls pre-reflective self-consciousness "pre-reflective cogito":

> This *cogito*, to be sure, does not posit an object; it remains within consciousness. But it is nonetheless homologous with the reflective *cogito* since it appears as the first necessity for non-reflective consciousness to be seen by itself. Originally then the *cogito* includes this nullifying characteristic of existing for a witness, although the witness for which consciousness exists is itself.
>
> (*EN*: 74, 117)

The pre-reflective cogito represents a first attempt on the part of consciousness to appear to itself, without, however, being reducible to other forms of consciousness (whether immediate, positional or reflective), which it makes possible. This first movement of self-identification on the part of consciousness, the movement of pre-reflective cogito, I will call *reflexivity*. Reflexivity represents, therefore, the constitutive process of the pre-reflective cogito and, hence, a condition for the possibility of all forms of consciousness, of consciousness in general. As a condition of possibility of consciousness, reflexivity is implicit in every experience. This has far-reaching implications for identity. As Sartre puts it for the case of belief, by the sole fact that my belief is apprehended as belief, it is *no longer only belief*; that is, it is already no longer belief, it is troubled belief. Thus, the ontological judgement "belief is consciousness (of) belief" can under no circumstances be taken as a statement of identity; the subject and the attribute are radically different though still within the indissoluble unity of one and the same being.

(EN: 74–5, 118)

The very fact of believing implies being conscious (of) believing. The latter, the non-positional consciousness of self as believing presupposes, however, a duality and "a game of reflections", which are specific for the pre-reflective cogito (*EN*: 75, 118). The self who experiences the belief under discussion is not identical with the self who is conscious of itself as believing, although they "are one and the same being" (*EN*: 75, 118). The reflexive process, although immanent to consciousness, implies a movement of separation within the person who believes, a movement that introduces a duality in the unity of consciousness, a duality of the believing self and of the reflexive self, which is pre-reflective, conscious of oneself as believing.

We have seen that a person's mode of being is being-for-itself. Given the implication that the reflexive movement of pre-reflective self-consciousness has for identity, Sartre suggests that we talk about the unity between the moment of conscious life (say, a belief) and the consciousness (of) this moment. Reflexivity, however, carries implications also for the other fundamental type of being Sartre mentions at this point. Thus, for him, non-conscious beings in the world are beings-in-themselves. For such beings, the unity between consciousness and consciousness (of) self is reduced radically until reflexivity disappears, the separation within the pre-reflective cogito vanishes and we end up with a being identical with itself.

Without the immanent separation of the self, this being can in no way reflect itself; it simply is. Since only beings that are in-itself are identical and since a person is for-itself, Sartre regards personal identity as an ideal.[19] This is the reason why, for Sartre, the very term "in-itself" (*en-soi*) is contradictory, since it associates a self (*soi*) with a type of being which, as identical, cannot be self-conscious and cannot have a self.[20]

Thus, Sartre notes that, grammatically, the word "self" functions as reflexive, that is, it refers back to the grammatical subject of a sentence, and indicates a relationship of the subject to itself, as in the phrase "She dresses her*self* up" (*EN*: 76, 118–19).[21] When one dresses oneself up, 'one', the person who performs the required acts of dressing-up, is not different from the person who is dressed up as a result. The relationship established by the "self" is a duality, and excludes the identity of the in-itself. However, although this relationship is a relationship between two distinct beings, it is not an external relationship, that is, it does not emerge from a negation (this being is different, it is *not* that being) that leaves the two beings untouched; rather, it affects the subject *in* its being:

> In fact the self cannot be apprehended as a real existent [...]. But neither can it *not be* itself since the self is an indication of the subject himself. The *self* therefore represents an ideal distance within the immanence of the subject in relation to himself.
>
> (*EN*: 76–7, 119)

Hence, to talk about a person's self-identity is an ideal in a specific sense. If we take identity as a lack of the immanent separation introduced by reflexivity, then self-identity is a contradiction and a person's self cannot be identical. All that Sartre asserts is unity, a unity established as a negation of identity. Thus, personal identity is an ideal, insofar as it is impossible to realize such a concept, when what is personal is given by the pre-reflective cogito. And, yet, a personal pre-reflective cogito is exactly what Sartre rejected in *The Transcendence*, and the reason why he criticizes Kant. For the moment, therefore, we can simply say that the self cannot be identical in the way in which a non-conscious being is. The reflexive movement of consciousness is primarily a unity.

Imagine now that this unity, which, Sartre thinks, allows a certain identity (belief and consciousness (of) belief are "within the indissoluble unity of one and the *same* being"), were to be turned into an identical thing by positing certain features as features of the same thing. In this case, in Sartre's account in *Being and Nothingness*, such a thing would have to be expelled from consciousness as no longer having the reflexivity specific for pre-reflective cogito and for a person. Hence, the rationalist mistake is also rejected by Sartre.

By contrast, were the distinct moments implied by reflexivity to be considered as no longer united by the fact that they belong to the same consciousness, we would in fact end up with two persons, each with her own consciousness. Hence, Sartre's account would in this way also reject the empiricist mistake concerning personal identity. In conclusion, Sartre will claim that the self or the reflexive movement will disappear when we have in mind a specific moment of consciousness with specific features, which is either regarded as an object or as a distinct consciousness. Hence, the self is

> a way of *not being his own coincidence*, of escaping identity while positing it as unity – in short, of being in a perpetually unstable equilibrium between identity as absolute cohesion without a trace of diversity and unity as a synthesis of multiplicity.
>
> (*EN*: 77, 119)[22]

At this point we have almost all the elements necessary for the evaluation of Sartre's objection to Kant in *The Transcendence*. The next section will focus precisely on this evaluation.

§24. The personal

Even though Sartre rejects the idea of self-identity, he cannot reject the fact that people in general talk about personal identity and try to find criteria on which to identify a person. However, for Sartre, this belongs to a different level of consciousness, namely reflective consciousness. At this level, our states, qualities and acts are psychologically constituted as things, as beings with the ontological structure of the in-itself.[23] These states, qualities and acts are unified under the umbrella of an ego, and, Sartre claims, in this way, we become persons with a certain identity for others and subject to the judgement of others.[24]

As we have seen, in *The Transcendence of the Ego*, the reflective ego is taken as the mark of personality. Since the reflective ego appears on the reflective level, pre-reflective consciousness is considered as impersonal. This view is amended in *Being and Nothingness* where the sign of personality becomes the self, which is constitutive of pre-reflective consciousness and makes possible reflectivity and the 'I' (*EN*: 162, 209). As the being of the person, self-consciousness makes itself personal from the very moment[25] when it transforms itself from an in-itself into a for-itself.[26]

Hence, in *Being and Nothingness*, Sartre changes his view of consciousness. What, in the *Transcendence*, he used to call the "unreflected act of reflection" (*TE*: 36, 16) becomes, in *Being and Nothingness*, a consciousness (of) self; moreover, the self is an indication of a unity of the subject in relation to himself, since "consciousness comes from consciousness itself" (*EN*: 11, 22) and, thus, presupposes identity. This unity is quite similar to Kant's transcendental unity of apperception – it represents a condition of the possibility of experience and, although it cannot be experienced independently from the particular experiences it is a condition of, it is experienced *through* these particular experiences.

Moreover, in *Being and Nothingness*, the self is located within the immanence of the subject. It is therefore clear that Sartre no longer regards it as transcending consciousness, but as an important part of consciousness. Finally, through its reflexivity, the self destroys the identity of the being-in-itself and raises a new question of identity, the identity that enables us to talk about reflexive consciousness as consciousness (of) self. Reflexive consciousness must be conscious in a pre-reflective way of something, which must in some sense be distinct from itself (as object) and identical with itself and, thus, lead to consciousness (of) self.

Hence, the self makes possible this new question of identity and answers it by affirming identity through unity. I am conscious of being the same at different times, if I can unify the various consciousnesses as my conscious states. As Sartre notes, without the multiplicity introduced by reflexivity, we cannot make sense of the unity presupposed by the attempt to reveal ourselves reflexively and form presentations of ourselves and the world. On this reading, through his comments on the ideal of identity, Sartre seems to reassert the Kantian claim that unity and multiplicity are mutually dependent conditions, which make identity possible (as consciousness of numerical identity).

Not surprisingly, therefore, Sartre claims that "from its first arising, consciousness by the pure nihilating movement of reflection makes itself *personal*" (*EN*: 143, 127). This may seem more or less the same as the claim in the *Transcendence*, since, one may object, reflection brings about the *I* or the ego, which even there had a personal character. And, yet, Sartre adds that "what confers personal existence on a being is not possession of an Ego" (*EN*: 143, 127). This makes it clear that, in the quotation above, by the pure nihilating movement of "reflection", Sartre means the reflexive movement of pre-reflective consciousness, which can now be regarded as personal.

It is time to return to the objection Sartre raises to Kant's transcendental apperception. Recall that, on Kant's account, self-consciousness, insofar as it enables the 'I think', is a necessary condition of experience. Yet, the *I*, as the formal concept that stands for the identity of which persons are conscious in different times, must, according to Sartre's objection, be expelled from consciousness, since nothing can be purely formal, everything will have determinations from which consciousness, in its free, spontaneous reflexivity can separate. But, if this *I* belongs to the world, rather than to consciousness, then consciousness is impersonal or pre-personal, even in Kant's definition of a person in the Third Paralogism.

In the previous sections, apart from introducing the main elements of Sartre's conceptual framework, I have also considered whether his objection to Kant stems from an inaccurate interpretation or relies on some invalid or unsound argument. We have seen that Sartre's account of Kant is sufficiently subtle and, if the assumption concerning the inexistence of purely formal elements turns out to be true, Sartre's objection is quite strong.

Yet, be that as it may, at the beginning of this section I have shown that Sartre changes his mind and is happy to allow, in *Being and Nothingness*, that reflexivity gives personal character to consciousness. Hence, like Kant, he allows as legitimate the existence of a necessary condition of experience, which, since it is constitutive of consciousness, cannot be expelled from consciousness and, moreover, relative to possible determinations of conscious states, is purely formal.

This first Sartrean critique seems to rely on an accurate interpretation of Kant, but starts from an assumption and an argument that Sartre eventually abandons. The situation, in fact, leads to a stronger similarity than perhaps we would have expected, since Kant and Sartre turn out to support the same position. This also leads to a structural similarity, since they argued against the contradictory view. Indeed, they both argue against an impersonal transcendental field of consciousness and for a fundamental personal reflexive consciousness. This is the move that brings Sartre closer to Kant and further away from Hegel.[27]

One may try, of course, to speculate further on the similarities and differences between these forms of self-consciousness.[28] Yet, by following again the methodological discussion in the Introduction, I think that the best way to explore further the comparison between Kant and Sartre is by moving on to the next objection to Kant that Sartre raises and by trying to evaluate its relevance for this comparison. So let me now move on to the second objection Sartre formulates against Kant.

§25. Deliberation

The second objection I would like to consider at this point is related both to the previous one, concerning the personal character of transcendental apperception, and the next one, in Chapter 4, which centres around freedom. It therefore constitutes a good bridge between the first and second parts of this book. I have already mentioned the nature of this objection at the end of Chapter 1. It is now time to present it further. The objection is formulated by Sartre in *Being and Nothingness*, more exactly in chapter 1 ("Being and Doing: Freedom") of part 4 ("Having, Doing and Being"). Here, in section I ("Freedom: The First Condition of Action"), Sartre says:

> The fundamental project which I am is a project concerning not my relations with this or that particular object in the world, but my total being-in-the-world; since the world itself is revealed only in the light of an end, this project posits for its end a certain type of relation to being which the for-itself wills to adopt. This project is not instantaneous, for it can not be "in" time. Neither is it non-temporal in order to "give time to itself" afterwards. That is why we reject Kant's "choice of intelligible character". The structure of choice necessarily implies that it be a choice in the world. A choice which would be a choice *in terms of nothing*, a choice *against nothing* would be a choice of nothing and would be annihilated as choice.
>
> (*EN*: 536, 501–2)

Sartre refers here to Kant's revolution in disposition, a notion that I have introduced in the previous chapter. One interesting point to note is the parallel Sartre draws between Kant's notion of disposition (which he calls "intelligible character") and his own concept of a fundamental project.[29] I will discuss this Sartrean notion shortly; for the moment, I would like to summarize Sartre's objection and to clarify its status by distinguishing it from two other related problems. Thus, Sartre claims that Kant should not regard the choice of intelligible character as a non-temporal choice that gives time to itself afterwards. By contrast, he goes on to say that choices are always "phenomenal". The choice of the fundamental project is the choice of the phenomenal in general, and, "in its very upsurge, the choice is temporalised" (*EN*: 536, 502).

If we start with the question of the possibility of moral judgement, one condition for passing such a judgement on a person's actions is that those actions be imputable to the person. Actions will not be imputable if they derive from a disposition that was simply given to, rather than changed by, the person. Now, the assumption that both Kant and Sartre make, and that I will not try to defend here but rather take for granted, is that the requirement that an action be imputable to a person (and, hence, the person be accountable for that action) implies that the action be performed freely by that person.[30]

In order to explain how actions can be imputed to the agent when they are all rooted in the same disposition/fundamental project, we can say that the disposition/fundamental project itself is imputable, since it is adopted or freely chosen by the agent. At this point, there are at least three issues that can be raised. The first one is the general problem of freedom, which will be discussed in Part II of this book. The second one is the problem of accounting for the very notion of adopting or freely choosing the disposition/fundamental project. This will be discussed later on in this chapter. These problems will be faced by both Kant and Sartre.

The third issue is the objection raised by Sartre. Assuming there is freedom, and that the idea of a free choice of disposition makes sense or at least it is not contradictory, how does such a choice take place? Sartre attributes to Kant the view that this choice is non-temporal, and Sartre himself rejects this view. In what follows, I will first focus on this objection and, then, I will look at the second issue of whether the idea of a choice of disposition is contradictory.

First, let me distinguish Sartre's view of original choice from deliberation. The notion of choice implies the existence of alternatives between which one must decide. If the decision is not arbitrary, then the alternatives must be evaluated on the basis of some standards. It may therefore seem that Sartre regards the choice of a fundamental project as the result of deliberation, understood as a reflective process of weighing up various alternatives.

Yet, on Sartre's account, the case of the choice of a fundamental project (the case of original choice) must be kept distinct from deliberation. For voluntary deliberation is not some privileged mode of making a choice; there are alternative candidates for the role of a process of decision-making with regard to fundamental projects. Given the existence of alternatives, we should be able to identify those various decision-making processes as part of distinct fundamental projects:

> If I am brought to the point of deliberating, this is simply because it is part of my original project to realise motives by means of *deliberation* rather than by some other form of discovery (by passion, for example, or simply by action, which reveals to me the organised ensemble of causes and of ends as my language informs me of my thought). There is therefore a choice of deliberation as a procedure which will make known to me what I project and consequently what I am.
>
> *(EN: 506, 473)*

Sartre mentions here that we have a choice between deliberation, passion and action, as decision-making procedures for the realization of motives and for action. Moreover, he does not give primacy to any of them over the others. Instead of acting on the result of deliberation, I might have chosen to act in whatever way the most powerful passion dictated.

The choice of an action based on the most powerful passion will lead me to one action, whereas the choice that the action be determined by an evaluation of the various incentives for the available courses of action will lead to a different action, of course, under the assumption that the choice is between the same alternatives. The point is, therefore, that deliberation cannot help me to choose my fundamental project, since such a procedure already points to a fundamental project or to a set of fundamental projects, commitment to which is already presupposed.

As we will see in Part II, this feature has also important implications for freedom. For the moment, however, let me return to Sartre's objection. We have just seen that, in his criticism of Kant, Sartre does not mean to suggest that, instead of the Kantian non-temporal original choice that he rejects, we should embrace as alternative the deliberative procedure. Therefore, he must have had in mind a distinct account of how one commits oneself to a fundamental project. The objection to Kant suggests this process will not be non-temporal and will not be beyond time and phenomena. In the next section, this distinct Sartrean account will be further clarified through a discussion of its key conceptual components.

§26. Project

If deliberation is viewed as an evaluation of the reasons for and against various possible alternative actions in order to decide which course of action is the most appropriate, then, since every evaluation presupposes a standard of evaluation, which is used for some reason, there is no evaluation of courses of action, which could be undertaken from a standpoint, which would not already be normatively committed. This is how Sartre articulates this thought: on his account, every action has an end, which can be seen as the instantiation of a more general project. For instance, if I plan to run a marathon, I must also plan to run a few miles every day, and this was the end or purpose of my running this morning. Moreover, for Sartre, even this more general project of running a marathon can be understood on the basis of a more profound project:

> The problem indeed is to disengage the meanings implied by an act – by every act – and to proceed from there to the richer and more profound meanings until we encounter the meaning which does not imply any other meaning and which refers only to itself. This ascending dialectic is practiced spontaneously by most people; it can even be established that in knowledge of oneself or of another there is given a spontaneous comprehension of this hierarchy of interpretations.
>
> (*EN*: 457, 535)

To see this more clearly, consider the following example that Sartre discusses in *Being and Nothingness*: I start out on a hike and after several hours my fatigue increases until it becomes painful; I may then either try to resist it and go on walking, or I may give up and let myself fall down beside my knapsack.[31] Here and in general, each of my acts is comprehensible in terms of its end: "I place my knapsack down *in order to* rest for a moment" (*EN*: 460, 537). The importance of resting at that point is comprehensible from the perspective of a more general end – perhaps that of wanting to have enough energy left to enjoy the evening properly, where enjoyment is one of the more general ends of my actions.[32] Alternatively, I could go on walking in order to overcome this limit, as part of a general project of undertaking physical training, where enjoying an evening, rather than going directly to bed, is no longer part of my end.

In this sense, for Sartre, every particular project is a way of specifying a person's ultimate project or possibility, and each person has her own ultimate project (*EN*: 464, 542). It is on the basis of this fundamental project that I may choose to act only after deliberation, and to give in to fatigue in order to contemplate the scenery in a relaxed manner. Moreover, it is this project that defines me and my relation to the world and which, Sartre says, is the result of a renewed act of freedom:

> Thus the fundamental act of freedom is discovered; and it is this which gives meaning to the particular action which I can be brought to consider. This constantly renewed act is not distinct from my being; it is a choice of myself in the world and by the same token it is a discovery of the world.
>
> (*EN*: 461, 539)

Insofar as it underlies all my particular choices, this fundamental project is renewed by every one of the actions that result from my choices. Most importantly, at this stage, is Sartre's claim that the original choice is a choice of myself in the world and a discovery of the world. If this choice is what makes the world possible for me and also what makes possible my particular existence in the world, then it becomes difficult to understand how the original choice can be otherwise than non-temporal, a choice that takes place beyond the world.

For recall that, in Sartre's account, Kant takes the original choice of the fundamental project to be "non-temporal in order to 'give time to itself' afterwards"; by contrast, he claims that "there is only phenomenal choice, provided that we understand that the phenomenon is here [that is, in the case of the choice of a fundamental project] the absolute" (*EN*: 536, 501–2). But, one may ask, will such a choice not be non-temporal, if it were indeed a choice of the absolute phenomenon, and thus also of time?

While Sartre acknowledges that such a choice cannot be in time, obviously he does not take it to be non-temporal either, since he clearly attributes this view to Kant and rejects it. The alternative, he seems to suggest, is that, "in its very upsurge, the choice is temporalised" (*EN*: 536, 502). However, I think problems remain. Why should we not class a process which is temporalized in its upsurge as non-temporal? After all, without this project, Sartre claims, there is no person and no world, and therefore no time either. This suggests that the emphasis in Sartre's objection must be not only on the claim of non-temporality, but also on the claim that, once the non-temporal choice is made, for Kant, it gives time to itself afterwards.

What exactly then is the relationship between Kant's and Sartre's views of the original choice? One interesting suggestion can be found in Thomas Baldwin's "The Original Choice in Sartre and Kant" (1980). In the next two sections, I will present and evaluate this suggestion.

§27. Painting the self

Baldwin focuses on several similarities that seem to exist between Sartre's view of the original choice in *Being and Nothingness* and Kant's view of the revolution in the disposition in *Religion Within the Limits of Reason Alone*. One of his aims is to show that Kant's philosophy marks "a tradition into which Sartre's thought fits" (1980: 31). In itself, this is a very important task, for, as noted in the Introduction, Sartre's philosophy is most often compared with that of Descartes, Nietzsche, Hegel, Heidegger or Freud, but not with Kant's. For this task, the similarities Baldwin identifies, if correct, should suffice.

However, he also aims to illustrate "one way in which some of the tensions in Kant's philosophy lead to the development of something altogether unKantian" (Baldwin 1980: 31). The tensions Baldwin has in mind here stem from one of the claims he thinks Kant and Sartre share. This is the view that no transformation of a person's disposition/fundamental project can be voluntary.[33] Baldwin formulates the implications of this view – implications that he thinks are in tension – and offers a particular account of the original choice as a possible solution to the tension. This account is the unKantian view mentioned in the quotation above.

Two questions immediately spring to mind at this juncture. First, is it accurate to attribute such a claim to Kant and Sartre? And, secondly, assuming such an interpretation is accurate, how cogent is Baldwin's alternative view of self-choice?

I will begin with the second question and will first present the problem Baldwin is trying to solve. As I have mentioned, he notes that his account solves the inconsistencies that plague Kant's and Sartre's conceptions of original choice/revolution in disposition. The charge of inconsistency rests on the way two notions are understood. First, the voluntary transformation of a person's fundamental project is regarded as a reasoned process – a process that relies on the existence of some reason(s) for change. Secondly, a person's project is understood as a source of reasons for actions. For instance, to use one of Sartre's examples, the project of creating a counterweight to Rome gave Emperor Constantine a reason to establish himself at Byzantium (*EN*: 487–8, 455).

If every project is a source of reasons, the original or fundamental project, as the most general project towards which all the other projects and actions are directed, is the final source of reasons. Hence, a change of the original or fundamental project could not be reasoned or voluntary. There would be no further reason on which to rely for a voluntary transformation of the fundamental project. Therefore, no change of a person's fundamental project can be voluntary. And, yet, both Kant and Sartre also claim that a person should be able to choose her original project or to bring about a revolution in her disposition. Otherwise, her original project or disposition would be regarded as given, imposed upon her. In Kant's and Sartre's accounts, a person's actions are not and cannot be merely imposed, because they cannot be seen as merely deriving from an imposed disposition or fundamental project; at least some actions must be imputable to the agent, if the agent is to be an appropriate subject of moral judgement.

Apparently, the solution could not be to point to the status of the choice of fundamental project, as *original* choice, although one may argue that, unlike our everyday choices, the *original* choice is *not* voluntary and, moreover, grounds the fundamental project simply on freedom. Yet, this does not seem to be a solution, because any choice presupposes (at least) two alternatives between which a decision must be made and, hence, presupposes some reason(s) for making the decision, if not also for taking precisely these, rather than other, alternatives into consideration.[34]

To bring consistency to the argument, Baldwin proposes the following conception of the original project (1980: 41).[35] He draws on one of Sartre's analogies to view the fundamental project as a painting and the actions a person performs as brush strokes.[36] He also mentions a second analogy: the fundamental project is similar to Husserl's concept of a physical object and individual actions are similar to the physical object's sensible aspects. While both analogies suggest that the meanings of individual actions are given by the meaning of the fundamental project (Baldwin 1980: 40), it is also in principle possible that an individual action changes the meaning of the fundamental project. This, for instance, is what happens when a brush stroke changes suddenly the theme of the painting in the making or when an aspect makes you realize that the object is not what you thought it was up to that point. Therefore, the fundamental project is indeterminate and can be changed at any moment with the appropriate individual action.

Accordingly, self-choice is potentially instantiated with every individual action. From the perspective of the fundamental project, we do not have a radical distinction between two types of choice – original and ordinary; even ordinary choices can be choices of self (Baldwin 1980: 41). Recall that the starting point of the argument was the assumption that, unless we explain how the fundamental project can be changed voluntarily, we cannot explain how it is imputable to the agent and, hence, we cannot explain how moral judgement of her actions is possible. Even more fundamentally, we cannot account for the fundamental project as a result of a choice.

Now, if we follow Baldwin and regard the project as indeterminate, then we cannot talk about its change, unless, of course, by this we simply mean the fact that new features are added to it, in which case we can say that it is becoming more determinate. An action which changes the 'theme' of the project will be an action that can be seen as relying on the project as existing now to add an element that will bring about a new project. There will, therefore, no longer be any problem with the lack of reason for action. We no longer deal with an action that changes the whole project; actions now add elements to projects and many even change the projects' themes. Since they can change the theme of the fundamental project, they can be seen as imputable. Moreover, since such actions can be seen as relying on the existing project, they can be regarded as the result of choices, perhaps even voluntary choices.

How convincing is this account as a solution to the tensions Baldwin identifies in Kant and Sartre?

§28. Making Kant and Sartre consistent

We know that this new conception of original choice is supposed to make Kant's and Sartre's accounts consistent. Yet, in fact, it is unclear whether much is achieved by way of consistency. Recall that the initial problem was that a disposition or fundamental project could not be changed voluntarily, since a voluntary change implied a reasoned transformation, a transformation for which there is some reason, and the disposition or fundamental project was the condition that made reasons possible in general.

As we have seen, in Baldwin's model, individual actions are still comprehensible from the perspective of the disposition or fundamental project; but, now, the disposition or fundamental project are indeterminate. Hence, every individual action will either add an aspect to, or simply reiterate an existing feature of, the disposition/fundamental project. An indeterminate fundamental project does not *change*, but acquires new aspects and features. New reasons and actions can always emerge from the fundamental project, and, since they are performed by the agent, rather than being imposed upon her by an already given fundamental project, they can be imputed to her.

Yet we end up with problems concerning the comprehensibility of such reasons and actions. If the fundamental project is still a reference for the understanding of reasons and actions, then its indeterminate character implies that our understanding of such reasons and actions will always be indeterminate. Therefore, reasons and actions will in fact be incomprehensible, as far as the comprehensibility offered by disposition/fundamental project is concerned. Baldwin's account of original choice seems therefore unable to resolve the tensions he identifies in Kant and Sartre.[37] What can we do about them in this case?

An argument like Baldwin's relies on an understanding of choice as the result of deliberation. This view of the notion of choice is also the source of the claim that there are inconsistencies in Kant and Sartre.[38] Put simply, the premise of the objection to Kant and Sartre is that, if they want to maintain the claim that a person's deeper project is chosen, then they have to accept that the deeper project is the result of voluntary deliberation.

Baldwin claims that, if we do not understand a deeper project as the result of voluntary deliberation, the particular choices a person makes of maxims or ends do not represent "real choices" (1980: 42). Yet, as we have seen, according to Sartre, what the notion of choice implies are alternatives. Moreover, Sartre acknowledges explicitly that the deliberative model of agency is only one possible model of agency. Finally, for Sartre, an action that involves a choice of the fundamental project does not precede the project in order to bring it forth afterwards, but cannot be separated from the project. Hence, the reason for the actions can be seen as given by the fundamental project presupposed by this very action, a project that this very action creates.

The idea that we must have several projects, at least one reason for each project and a process of evaluation that provides the reason for the choice of fundamental project relies clearly on the deliberative model of agency. After all, we make choices in our everyday life without deliberation. We decide to do this, rather than that, because we have no reason to doubt that this is an effective action to our purpose, although there might be no explicit consideration of this lack of doubt.[39] Moreover, as I have already pointed out, if actions are comprehensible in terms of a deeper project, deliberation cannot lead to a change of a fundamental project/disposition. This is because deliberation presupposes a choice between at least two alternatives on the basis of some process of evaluation. Ultimately, if these alternatives must be comprehensible, then they can only be comprehensible in terms of the fundamental project/disposition.

Therefore, the course of action chosen after deliberation cannot modify the fundamental project/disposition, since it is one of the alternatives that only makes sense within the framework of the fundamental project/disposition. Moreover, if the action had some unexpected consequences, which led to the change of the fundamental project, then one could not say that it was due to voluntary deliberation that the project had been changed. By supposing that it is possible to voluntarily change the deeper project, the person appears as a transcendent deliberative observer, an observer who can make sense of the world independently from a fundamental project/disposition or, rather, from within the neutral, objective fundamental project/disposition (whatever that would mean). It is this type of observer that both Kant and Sartre reject.[40]

As we have seen, on Sartre's account, choice of the deliberative model already presupposes a fundamental project from the perspective of which not only is deliberation chosen, but the incentives and reasons for various courses of action are also constituted. Both Kant and Sartre can be seen as subscribing to an implication of this, namely, to the view that action on voluntary deliberation is inefficacious as a way of changing the fundamental project or disposition. This is what Sartre means by the inefficacy of voluntary decisions – although voluntary decisions can be made and we can build our being and character to only act voluntarily, they cannot help us change ourselves deeply, since they cannot change the very project on which they rely:

> It amounts to saying that by means of the will, we can *construct* ourselves entirely, but that the will which presides over this construction finds its meaning in the original project which it can appear to deny, that consequently this construction has a function wholly different from that which it advertises, and that finally it can reach only details of structures and will never modify the original project from which it has issued any more than the conclusion of a theorem turn back against it and change it.
>
> (*EN*: 476, 555)[41]

While this seems fairly conclusive, it remains to be seen whether we can attribute equally easily a similar position to Kant. This will be one of the questions in the next section.

§29. Deliberation and radical change

It seems that Baldwin's view of original choice is not only unKantian, as he acknowledges from the very beginning, but also unSartrean. For his view is based on a deliberative model of choice and so are his objections. However, Sartre argues precisely against the claims of this model. Whether we can say the same about Kant is the issue to which I now turn.

Kant argues similarly about the change of a person's disposition; moreover, he does not simply have in view the attempt to change a disposition through voluntary deliberation, but, in general, any attempt to change a disposition from within that disposition:

> A human being's moral education must begin, not with an improvement of mores, but with the transformation of his attitude of mind and in the establishment of a character, although it is customary to proceed otherwise and to fight vices individually, while leaving their universal root undisturbed.
>
> (*RGV*: 6:48, 92)

To try to change a disposition by different actions and maxims cannot yield the expected result. What one needs, Kant says, is a more fundamental change, a change of disposition, which is the ground of character. But, of course, this transformation of a person's cast of mind is the revolution in the disposition required by Kant. It follows, therefore, that, for both Kant and Sartre, a change of disposition/fundamental project requires more than deliberative choice. Deliberative choice can only take place within the fundamental project/disposition.

Moreover, Baldwin's suggestion that a rejection of the possibility of self-choice commits one to a view of future choices as determined by the disposition/fundamental project relies precisely on a view of choice as a fixed process similar to that of solving mathematical problems. Both Kant and Sartre explicitly argue against such a view.

Thus, for Kant and Sartre, each action is a choice that presupposes that the person take as end of her action one of her possibilities and denies the others. If the action is performed within the framework of a fundamental project/disposition, then it will of course manifest this deeper project. Nevertheless, this would not amount to being determined to follow a particular course of action. The deeper project is the framework within which a person's possibilities are constituted and made comprehensible; it is a 'primary structure' within which various 'secondary structures' can exist and need to be selected to ensue in actions.

This implies that, even if we assumed that the fundamental project/disposition were given and unchanging, we could not conclude that actions would be predetermined. For the fundamental project/disposition constrains the range of possibilities a person has, it does not determine the maxim on which the agent acts. It might still be possible to impute actions to persons. Or, if we talk about freedom, persons would still exercise a certain degree of freedom.

There is yet another objection we can raise to Baldwin's account at this point. Thus, while it remains the case that a new action might change a person's fundamental project or disposition, on Kant's and Sartre's accounts this is not because this deeper project would be indeterminate. For Sartre, the method by means of which one could get to know one's fundamental project is called existential psychoanalysis. For Kant, one can acquire cognition of one's disposition by means of the critique of practical reason. Interestingly, both Kant and Sartre place these methods in the domain of morality. For Sartre, existential psychoanalysis is a "moral description" (*EN*: 574, 662) of the person's behaviour and aims at enabling the person to discover his original choice: "it is a method destined to bring to light, in a strictly objective form, the subjective choice by which each living person makes himself a person" (*BN*: 574, 662). It is by uncovering this original choice that the person becomes aware that his values and ends are the result of a choice.

Similarly, for Kant the critique of practical reason has the task of showing that a person's actions are not solely determined by incentives that are causally determined, but that reason is able to provide the necessary incentives for action. By showing that the categorical imperative can determine practical reason to act, Kant also shows how a good disposition can ground a person's actions. In the Introduction to the *Critique of Practical Reason*, entitled "On the idea of a critique of practical reason", Kant sets the goal of this *Critique*:

> Here, therefore, the first question is whether pure reason is sufficient by itself alone to determine the will, or whether reason can be a determining basis of the will only as empirically conditioned.
>
> (*KpV*: 5:15, 23)

Of the three issues concerning original choice, which I formulated in §8 (the issues of freedom, the consistency of original choice and its feasibility), I have said that only the last two questions will be the focus of this chapter. Sections 10 and 11 discussed the second issue and, in particular, an account of original choice that claims (as we have seen, unsuccessfully) to be more consistent than Kant's and Sartre's account. But the claim of inconsistency was undermined as relying on the deliberative model of choice, a model, I have argued, that both Kant and Sartre reject as appropriate for original choice.

In the next section, I turn to the third issue, the issue of how the original choice is carried out; this will take us back to the objection to Kant that Sartre formulates in *Being and Nothingness*, which represents the second Sartrean objection I will consider in this Part.

§30. Problems with Sartre's account

Recall again Sartre's objection:[42] Kant's revolution in disposition or transformation of a person's cast of mind (what Sartre calls, a "choice of intelligible character") is non-temporal in order to "give time to itself" afterwards. Sartre would agree that this choice cannot be in time, but, for him, choice is nevertheless phenomenal and must be so if the notion of choice is to be properly used. Yet, he notes that the phenomenon here is the "absolute". He also claims that, if we are to use "choice" appropriately, we must accept that other choices will be possible (*EN*: 536, 502). Moreover, reinforcing his rejection of the deliberative model, these other choices are neither made explicit, nor posited; they are "lived in the feeling of unjustifiability" (*EN*: 536–7, 502).

Kant talks indeed about "intelligible character", and he emphasizes that a human being should become not merely *legally* good, but also *ethically* so, "i.e., virtuous according to the intelligible character (*virtus noumenon*)" (*RGV*: 6:47, 91–2). He also agrees that the revolution in one's disposition, the choice whereby one may get a disposition according to the intelligible character, is not comprehensible to us (*RGV*: 6:50, 94). Hence, this new disposition is also lived in the feeling of unjustifiability.

Kant does claim that the transformation of a person's cast of mind is non-temporal, but he does not make this claim without qualification. What Kant says is that such a transformation can be seen as non-temporal only by God, not by us, human beings:

> for the judgement of human beings, however, who can assess themselves and the strength of their maxims only by the upper hand they gain over the senses in time, then change is to be regarded only as an ever-continuing striving for the better, hence a gradual reformation...
>
> (*RGV*: 6:48, 92)

Therefore, Kant only claims that the revolution in disposition is non-temporal from a perspective that goes beyond time, for a being like God who can penetrate "to the intelligible ground of the heart" (*RGV*: 6:48, 92). This claim is almost a tautology, one that can hardly be a ground for rejecting Kant's position. Sartre must have interpreted Kant's position as claiming much more than that to see here a reason for objecting to Kant's view.

Perhaps here we can again connect this objection to the different ontological commitments of Kant and Sartre. If, as I have already mentioned, Sartre rejects the idea of a noumenal part of the world, then he will be reluctant to accept any discussion of a "*virtus noumenon*" or of some "intelligible ground of the heart". Yet, it is not clear that this is not precisely what Sartre eventually, too, does at the end of the section on "Freedom: The First Condition of Action", namely, make room for some noumenal realm.

Thus, in talking about the fundamental project, Sartre explains that it is a project that concerns my relation to my total being-in-the-world, not only with this or that particular object in the world; moreover, the fundamental project "posits for its end a certain type of relation to being which the for-itself wills to adopt" (*EN*: 536, 501). It is for this reason that, as we have seen, he then claims that the choice of this fundamental project is phenomenal insofar as the phenomenon is here absolute (*EN*: 537, 502).

Furthermore, at this point, Sartre claims that the fundamental project is not coextensive with the entire life of the for-itself, rather it "must be constantly renewed"; in this way, "I choose myself perpetually" (502). Since there are other possible choices, I may choose a different project and, hence, "the for-itself can confer on itself a new existence" (*EN*: 537, 502).

As we have seen, these claims are necessary to explain the moral accountability of the person, for, unless the person can change her fundamental project, it is not clear to what extent actions can be imputed to her. But, now, Sartre introduces the idea of an all-encompassing "global project": "Our particular projects, aimed at the realisation in the world of a particular end, are united in the global project which we are" (*EN*: 537, 502). Moreover, Sartre says,

> but precisely because we are wholly choice and act, these partial projects are not determined by the global project. They must themselves be choices; and a certain margin of contingency, of unpredictability, and of the absurd is allowed to each of them although each project as it is projected is the specification of the global project on the occasion of particular elements in the situation and so is always understood in relation to the totality of my being-in-the-world.
>
> (*EN*: 537, 502)

At first sight, what we may seem to be dealing with here is precisely the view of the fundamental project in Baldwin's interpretation. If you recall the painting analogy, each project may change the profile of the global project, since there is this margin of unpredictability and absurdity related to my choices. The global project does not specify my choice, rather my choices contribute to the construction of my global project. However, if we follow the painting analogy, the global project must play the role of the fundamental project in the example, the role of the painting, which can be changed by a brush stroke.

Yet this is clearly not a construal Sartre intended, since he regards the global project as consisting of several fundamental projects. The notion of the global project seems also to attribute a moment in time to each fundamental project, something Sartre rejects. Recall that, for Sartre, by choosing a fundamental project, I temporalize myself; time does not precede the fundamental project.

Moreover, it seems clear that, by "global project", Sartre does not simply mean a fundamental project, for, to begin with, he acknowledges that a person may have more than one fundamental project, but has only one global project. Moreover, the global project seems to be coextensive with the entire life of the for-itself, whereas Sartre explicitly says that this is not the case for the fundamental project. If the global project is not the fundamental project, but it is coextensive with the life of the for-itself, and if particular projects, including fundamental ones, are united in the global project, then they will each have a moment in time when they begin, something Sartre seemed to deny. Unless we make a distinction between the time of the global project and the time that is the result of the for-itself temporalizing itself through the choice of a fundamental project, it is not clear what Sartre actually wants to claim.

In the next section, I will present a possible way out suggested by Kant's account, and I will formulate some preliminary conclusions.

§31. A Kantian solution to Sartre's problems

One way of understanding the notion of a fundamental project is along Kantian lines. Kant explicitly rejects the possibility of cognizing anything about the revolution in disposition, but accepts that we can think about such a project, and we can draw certain implications. For instance, we can draw some implications from the fact that we usually take a person to be free and responsible for the actions she performs. One such implication, Kant claims, is that we adopt the disposition through a revolution in our cast of mind; how we do this, however, cannot be cognized further. So perhaps Sartre, too, is engaged in a similar enterprise, when he talks about the global project.

Maybe he only thinks about the fundamental project and tries to make sense of certain aspects to which we do not actually have access. Yet, as I have already mentioned, the problem with reading Sartre in this way is that he rejects the idea of a noumenal part of the world to which we have no access or about which we can form no cognition. This may suggest an inner tension in Sartre's account, but exploring this would lead too far away from the starting point of the argument here; the main issue for discussion here is the objection Sartre raises in relation to Kant's notion of a revolution in disposition.

As we have seen, Sartre's interpretation of Kant here is not entirely accurate, for Kant makes no claim about a non-temporal choice that would be in any way similar to phenomenal choices. In fact, Kant talks about the *adoption* of a disposition, not about a *choice* of disposition. What Kant claims at this point, is that, in order to conceive of persons as accountable agents, it should be possible to regard them as able to adopt actions, maxims and dispositions, rather than necessarily having to follow them. How this process is supposed to take place is something, Kant says, we cannot cognize.

Perhaps one source of additional complexity is that Kant talks about the revolution in disposition in the context of his practical philosophy. By contrast, Sartre's discussion is placed in the context of his phenomenological analysis. For Kant, practical philosophy enables us to acquire a form of cognition of the noumenal realm to which we have no access outside the practical domain. Hence, some of Kant's claims can be regarded as cognitively stronger than the results of thinking about possible concepts. However, I will say more about Kant's and Sartre's ethical theories in Parts II and III of this book.

I have argued, in the Introduction, that one important problem for a comparative analysis of Kant and Sartre is methodological, and this problem is sometimes noticeable in the discussion in the literature. Baldwin, for instance, is right to take the notions of self-choice, identity and fundamental project/dispositions as starting points for his analysis, but this is because Sartre raises objections to Kant's view of identity, in *The Transcendence of the Ego*, and to Kant's view of the revolution in disposition, in *Being and Nothingness*. Since Sartre felt these were topics of debate with Kant, he must have assumed that there is a common understanding of the basic notions and of the main aims of the arguments.

By contrast, the attempt to identify affinities between two authors starting from what look like similar positions cannot go very far, since there is no indication that the authors even intended to engage with the same problems. In addition, many claims, which are only superficially distinct, will wrongly be considered as manifesting significant differences of philosophical views.

The comparative analysis so far followed the methodology presented in the Introduction and started from Sartre's objections to Kant. We have seen that, ultimately, these objections are directed against views of identity and self-choice that are not Kant's, since Kant himself rejects the positions Sartre challenges. This has constituted the appropriate ground for presenting several *structural* similarities between their accounts of identity and self-choice. Yet, as I have argued in the Introduction, once such similarities are identified, we also acquire the necessary ground for pursuing a comparative analysis even with regard to topics where Sartre did not engage explicitly or directly with Kant.

In this way, some more *substantive* similarities between their views can be identified in addition to the structural similarities. Although this enterprise is already more speculative than that concerning structural similarities, it has a basis in the latter. Spelling out some of these substantive similarities is the task of the next sections. The discussion of the common aspects of Kant's and Sartre's philosophies will also make possible the identification of a central difference between their accounts, a difference that will also have an implication for their ethical and political theories.

§32. Substantive similarities

The first issue, discussed in these two chapters has been that of identity. We have seen that, in his account of the self, Sartre emphasizes the elusive character of the ideal of self-identity. A person always tries to achieve self-identity, but she is always separated from that identity by the nihilating movement of consciousness. Any attempt to define the person's identity in terms of objective characteristics cannot be more than a definition of a person's ends, which are not given but perpetually chosen by the person.

Psychology's attempt to transform these ends into given objects, and to unify them as an ego is the result of an impure reflection by means of which the possibilities of the person are reflected as being ontologically in-itself. At the very moment when the ego is posited as an object of consciousness, the possibilities synthesized by the ego are no longer that person's possibilities; they are objective characteristics that the person can choose or can reject.

Hence, a person's identity is not a set of objective characteristics. To talk about identity one needs a first-person, not a third-person perspective, and this holds even if the person himself tries to grasp his identity. The first-person perspective would thus never yield an identity in terms of objective characteristics, but an identity as the underlying unity of potentially always changing objective characteristics and possibilities. The unity of the person is made possible by the unity of self-consciousness. Self-consciousness is thus the condition of identity and ontological freedom.

By criticizing rational psychology, Kant also objects to a conception of the person defined in terms of a substance. His doctrine of the unity of pure apperception makes it clear that the identity of the person is not given in terms of objective characteristics. The very attempt to define the identity of the person in terms of objective characteristics transforms those characteristics into presentations that need to be unified by self-consciousness as the identity of the person. Even if I try to grasp the elements that are essential for my personality in terms of objective characteristics, I need to appeal to the synthesizing activity of pure apperception in order to obtain the presentation of my identity.

If this identity is given in empirical terms, then it can be contradicted by further experiences. If it is given in a priori terms, then, according to Kant's third paralogism of pure reason, it can only yield the experience of a formal identity, as the consciousness of the numerical identity of the person. Hence, a person's identity requires a first-person perspective, since it represents a presupposition of my consciousness of the underlying unity of my experiences.

The second issue investigated has been that of self-choice. We have seen that, according to Kant and Sartre, a person's actions are comprehensible only as part of a totality that represents the life of the person. This totality has a threefold structure starting from particular actions and going through secondary structures, which in turn can finally be seen as grounded in a fundamental project or intelligible character. The life of the agent, or her global project, is the totality of these fundamental projects or characters, although the conclusion has been that the status of this global project in Sartre remains unclear and would repay further investigation.

Kant sees a person's action as the effect of the incentive she incorporates in her maxim. The maxim is defined as the subjective principle of action and represents the higher-order rule according to which incentives bring about actions as effects. In turn, each maxim is grounded in a person's intelligible character. For instance, moral actions will be grounded in a good disposition.

The intelligible character is also a rule that governs the causality that brings about actions, but it is a rule that does not start from empirical incentives in order to arrive at actions, but from a person's pure reason, which is not empirically affected. The causality of pure reason as a cause without other causes represents pure reason's spontaneity. However, depending on the rule adopted as a sufficient ground for action, a person's intelligible character may change. By analogy with the interpretation formulated above for Sartre's notion of a global project, we can say that, in Kant, too, the synthetic unity of these various characters constitutes the life of the person as an agent.

Particular actions are comprehensible, so Sartre says, only in the light of their more general projects. Each project represents a person's particular end as the possibility towards which the person projects himself. The end is given as an ideal situation that does not yet exist but which the person tries to realize by his action. Particular projects are, however, only secondary structures of the agent's global project. They are elements of a third structure, which represents the person's fundamental project.

The fundamental project of an agent is also centred around an end, more precisely around the person's sum of possibilities or values. This sum is the in-itself-for-itself or the self of the person, and it is an ideal projected by the for-itself with its first reflexive movement. As we will see, it, too, can be interpreted in an authentic way or in bad faith. The fundamental or original project establishes the most basic relations between the for-itself and the world.

Since without the world there is no person, the fundamental project provides the framework within which the reasons for the person's actions are constituted. Therefore, as a result of a radical self-choice, the change of the fundamental project cannot be accounted for except within the framework of the new fundamental project. The synthetic unity thus obtained forms the global project of a person.

These affinities have becomes evident in the process of investigating, in Chapter 2, the two Sartrean objections to Kant. They point to further possible affinities in their moral theories, and I will discuss these in the next two Parts of the book. But we can already raise a question now concerning significant differences between Kant and Sartre, differences, that is, which are not simply terminological or due to distinct philosophical styles, but are of philosophical substance. I will conclude this chapter and this part of the book by making a suggestion concerning such a difference.

§33. A significant difference

Baldwin's argument for the similarities between Kant and Sartre excludes any pretension of uncovering a hidden Kantian source in Sartre.[43] It is, however, possible to include this topic into a comparative analysis of the two philosophers' accounts of human agency. Thus, in an article (written 15 years after Baldwin's study), which evaluates the influence exerted by the works of Plato and Kant on Sartre's philosophy, Pierre Verstraeten also provides the biographical information concerning Sartre's interest in Kant's *Religion Within the Limits of Reason Alone* (Verstraeten 1995).

Namely, Sartre had not only read Kant's *Religion* quite early – before 1928 – but one of his friends, Raymond Aron, reports on the discussions on the choice of the intelligible character in Kant that he had had with Sartre at the time (Verstraeten 1995: 215). Aron had prepared his undergraduate dissertation on the problem of non-temporality in Kant's philosophy and Sartre read it.

Moreover, despite Sartre's explicit critique of Kant's idea of "the choice of intelligible character" in *Being and Nothingness*, Aron remained convinced of a significant similarity between Kant and Sartre on this question.[44] In spite of this clear evidence concerning the influence exerted by Kant's philosophy on Sartre, Verstraeten puts more emphasis on the differences between them; however, I think this comparative analysis would have benefited from the method introduced and used here. I will give two examples.

The first one concerns the status of Kant's and Sartre's accounts of self-choice; thus Kant's doctrine of the revolution in disposition is clearly part of Kant's moral theory, whereas Sartre's account of original choice is set in non-moral terms, even if it is underpinned by the intention of elaborating a moral theory (Verstraeten 1995: 219); however, as we have seen, it is very difficult to separate Sartre's account of self-choice from the moral connotations of terms like bad faith or authenticity. It would be sufficient to regard the fundamental project of a person as centred around the ideal of the in-itself-for-itself, rather than as some specification of this formal ideal, and also to anticipate Sartre's argument in *Being and Nothingness* and *Notebooks for an Ethics* that such a project can be lived either in authentic way or in bad faith, in order to see, beyond apparent differences, the affinities with Kant's project.

In Verstraeten's view, another difference between Kant and Sartre refers to the possibility of acting after the conversion, given that the authentic person is aware of the inauthenticity of the belief that the redemptive goal has been realized by conversion (Verstraeten 1995: 220). This is the second example I would like to consider. According to Verstraeten, this is not a problem for Kant, since he makes appeal to God as a guarantor of the legitimacy of this hope (1995: 220); for Sartre, on the other hand, "the liberating endeavour" is "an incessant struggle" (1995: 221).

I think, however, that the contrast suggested by Verstraeten does not hold. It is true that for Kant, "in the light of that purity of the principle which he has adopted as the supreme maxim of his will", the person can hope to be redeemed, since "for God, this amounts to his being actually a good man (pleasing to Him)" (*RGV*: 6:46, 91). However, redemption is here conditioned by Kant with the observance of the moral law, and as regards the person's certainty of being moral Kant is sceptical.[45]

But, if we place the comparison in the domain of morality, then we can conclude that, for Kant, moral action is a matter of continuous struggle in the attempt not merely to act in conformity with the moral law, but also for the sake of the moral law. By contrast, Sartre seems to maintain that it is possible to escape bad faith, and become authentic:

> If it is indifferent whether one is in good faith or in bad faith, because bad faith reapprehends good faith and slides to the very origin of the project of good faith, that does not mean that *we can not radically escape bad faith*. But this supposes a self-recovery of being which was previously corrupted. This self-recovery we shall call authenticity, the description of which has no place here [in *Being and Nothingness*].
>
> (*EN*: 70 n9, 111 n)[46]

In fact, Sartre's claim is not different from Kant's insofar as Sartre, like Kant, is claiming that it is *possible* to act in good faith – this by no means implies that one actually acts in good faith and escapes bad faith.[47]

I think that our discussion of the structural similarities between Kant and Sartre, as guided by the comparative methodology outlined above, can already help us to find a more significant difference between their accounts of identity and self-choice. This difference is briefly noted by Baldwin, for whom, Sartre's "theory differs, of course, from Kant's in respect of its intimate connections with the teleological account of self-consciousness and the account of consciousness as a nihilation" (1980: 42). Baldwin does not come back to this point, but I think he is right to see a difference between Kant and Sartre in this respect. This difference stems from the dissimilarities between Kant's and Sartre's accounts of freedom. Even though they distinguish in a similar manner two types of freedom, they account for these two types of freedom in a different way, as we will see in the next part.

For the moment, however, we can note that this significant difference can already be noticed between the emphasis Sartre puts on concepts, such as end, project and original choice, on the one hand, and the way Kant gives pride of place to rules of action, maxims and the higher-order principle represented by disposition. Further implications of this difference will easily be noticed not only between their accounts of freedom, but also between their moral theories. This will become more evident in Chapters 4 and 6.

§34. Further problems

I have started with several questions suggested by the notion of an absolute prohibition against lying: What kind of norms can there be that have the force to command such absolute constraints? Can such standards be justified? Do they have any normative force in particular contexts? I have, however, focused mainly on some fundamental assumptions of these questions, in particular, how a person who freely performs a right or wrong action now can be considered as accountable later, even if she might have considerably changed since she performed the action.

I have concluded that the sense of person as a being conscious of her identity over time is sufficient for her acceptance of the status of moral subject, although I have shown that the attribution of this status to her, as well as the moral judgement formulated about her actions, may rightly be questioned. I have claimed that, on Kant's account, the notion of a person one can legitimately preserve is that of a being conscious of its numerical identity over time. I have shown that this notion is sufficient for the acceptance by the person of the status of moral agent and that it is in fact a relatively weak assumption, insofar as it is presupposed even by the experience of a particular sensation.

One problem, which can now be raised, is that, precisely because of the undemanding character of this notion, it will be too easy to satisfy its condition and, hence, it will become implausible. For, in many situations, persons cannot legitimately accept the status of moral agents. Related to this is another problem: even if the condition of weak identity turns out somehow not to be too weak, it is still necessary to account for the freedom of the action. As I have just said, the problem from which I started was how a person, who *freely* performs an action, can be considered as accountable later, when she may well have changed in certain respects.

Finally, I have mentioned the question of the unconditionality of Kant's prohibition against lying, which gives rise to several issues worth pursuing further. For instance, if such a standard exists, what is its status? Assuming such standards do exist, can they be justified? Assuming they can be justified, do they have normative force in specific contexts? Such questions will occupy us in the next two Parts of the book.

Part II
Freedom and Normativity

I have started, in the Introduction, by noting the apparent similarity between Kant's and Sartre's responses to Constant's problem. I have mentioned what I take to be the importance of this observation. First, it suggests a similarity between Kant and Sartre where perhaps nobody would have expected it. The standard interpretation of Sartre is that of an author without a 'moral theory' in the usual sense of the word, as proposing a set of values or standards to be followed, or as formulating a criterion on the basis of which such values or principles should be justified. On this standard account, Sartre's practical philosophy is either a set of objections to traditional theories or, at most, a moral theory that does not endorse as absolute any particular value or principle, but advocates the free creation of values by each individual.

Secondly, if Sartre does have a moral theory (a set of standards – values or principles – which are endorsed as morally valid and to be pursued) or a moral system (a criterion on the basis of which the validity of moral standards can be justified), then it is very significant to find him advocating or suggesting the possibility of unconditional standards, such as the obligation to truthfulness or the prohibition against lying. For, as I have argued, contemporary moral theorists struggle to justify this degree of normative force for moral standards.

I have suggested that, given Sartre's objections to Kant's doctrine of transcendental idealism, perhaps his approach is what contemporary moral theorists should follow in their attempts to justify moral standards with such a strong normative force. This conclusion, however, assuming even that Kant's and Sartre's practical philosophies turn out to be similar in respect of the normative force of moral standards they are prepared to defend, is only tentative and has a guiding intention; accepting it without caution would be hasty. For, in spite of the standard interpretations, several alternatives might still turn out to provide a more accurate reading of Kant and Sartre.

First, it may well be that Sartre's practical philosophy makes, in fact, metaphysically stronger claims than Kant's theory, in spite of his objections to transcendental idealism. One may regard, for instance, Sartre's argument against the existence of God in *Being and Nothingness* as much stronger than Kant's claims that, as far as our usual cognition is concerned (i.e., cognition in the Kantian sense, which presupposes experience), we cannot decide whether or not God exists.

Secondly, it may be the case that Kant and Sartre make claims that are metaphysically equally strong, but are nevertheless still considered to be too strong by contemporary moral theorists. Sometimes, commentators consider that, after all, Sartre also proposes a version of transcendental idealism, in spite of his criticism of Kantian metaphysics. If contemporary moral theorists rightly object to this type of metaphysics as dogmatic for the purpose of formulating a moral theory in conditions of moral and political pluralism, then they should look elsewhere for an appropriate account of moral unconditionality.

Thirdly, it may turn out that Sartre indeed supports a position that is metaphysically weaker than Kant's and that, within the framework of such a position, he cannot actually account properly for unconditionality and would need something closer to the view Kant defends. One would then need a further argument to show that Kant's view is not metaphysical in a dogmatic sense and can be developed further into an appropriate account of moral necessitation.

While I think these debates are highly relevant and significant, dwelling on them sufficiently in order to be able to adjudicate between these various alternatives would take the argument too far away from the task with which I have started, namely, providing a comparison of Kant's and Sartre's practical philosophies. In Part I, I have focused on the issues of identity and self-governance. In this Part, I will look at freedom and normativity. The final Part will deal with some implications concerning normativity, but also moral progress.

So, how similar are Kant's and Sartre's accounts of freedom and normativity, especially given Sartre's objections to these aspects of Kant's account?

3
Kant

The previous chapters go some way towards explaining Kant's radical view concerning the principle of truthfulness and Sartre's surprisingly sympathetic reaction to Kant's position. True, the preconditions of identity and self-choice explored there do not yet clarify on what basis such an unconditional commitment can be justified; they are necessary assumptions of such a commitment, but very far from being sufficient. If anything, Kant's and Sartre's radical views concerning unconditionality still suggest an idealized view of human beings, as Constant pointed out.

Nevertheless, and paradoxically, the discussion of their accounts of identity and self-choice show that their premises are not very strong; in general, they avoid the radical claims of realists and idealists, as well as those of rationalists and empiricists. In particular, they postulate neither some identical entity existing beyond the various states of consciousness nor some neutral perspective from which free choices can be guaranteed.

Additional necessary conditions for the justification of an unconditional commitment to truthfulness are required, conditions such as freedom or the existence of a basis of justification. We need, for instance, at least a starting criterion from which to be able to identify the principle of truthfulness as right. And one condition for the acceptability of such a criterion is that the view of human beings it presupposes does not place unrealistic constraints on us. One way in which such a criterion can be expressed is that the criterion be able to account for human persons as *both* rational and sentient beings.

Finally, some indication of how it is possible to move from such a criterion to a justified principle or standard would be required in order to obtain the main elements of an account of an ethics of unconditional standards. The claim that such an ethics can be found in Sartre will come as a surprise, at least with regard to the early Sartre of the *Transcendence* and *Being and Nothingness*, since, as already noted, usually, despite the *Notebooks for an Ethics*, commentators either regard him as a moralist without a moral theory or think that there is a coherent and well-supported ethics in the early

Sartre, although this is by no means regarded as an ethics of unconditional standards.[1]

Before looking comparatively at Kant and Sartre, let me first present my reading of those elements of Kant's ethics that I take to be necessary for this comparison. I will start with Kant's account of freedom, will continue with his view of moral goodness and the criterion of his moral theory (the Categorical Imperative), and will conclude with a brief look at the application of the moral criterion to the justification of moral standards. It is with regard to these aspects that I will then present, in Chapter 4, several objections raised by Sartre. Following the methodology presented in the Introduction, the aim will be to identify the similarities and differences between Kant's and Sartre's practical philosophy and to evaluate their significance for the more conceptual or systematic aim of accounting appropriately for moral normativity in conditions of pluralism.

In particular, one important and perhaps decisive factor that Kant introduces with his practical philosophy is the possibility of a particular form of cognition of things in themselves. This suggests that, metaphysically, Kant's practical philosophy is very demanding. Consequently, my hypothesis of a critical ethical theory, which would start from Kant's and Sartre's practical philosophies, and would be able to account non-dogmatically for unconditional obligation in conditions of pluralism, seems to have little chance of confirmation.

These, however, are considerations that are of more distant concern, and I will return to them later in the book. For the moment, in this chapter, the focus will be mainly on Kant's moral philosophy and on the three topics already mentioned, freedom, moral goodness and the application of the Categorical Imperative. If Kant must be able to account appropriately for an unconditional obligation, in particular the obligation not to lie, then he must also be able to account for these three issues. Similarly, if we understand Sartre as defending a similar position, then these three issues must also be considered in relation to his ethical theory. These will be the tasks of the next sections in this part of the book.

§35. Moral and psychological identity

In Chapter 1, I have claimed that the notion of a person one can legitimately preserve is that of a being conscious of its numerical identity over time. This does not necessarily presuppose the existence of an identical entity by reference to which I become conscious of my identity in different times. As Kant says,

> proving this [stronger sense of] identity could not be accomplished by merely analysing the proposition *I think*, but would require various

synthetic judgements based on the given intuition [of the subject as object].

(KrV: B408, 426)

In fact, for limited beings like us, it turned out to be impossible to support this stronger notion and its employment proved thus to be illegitimate. By contrast, I showed that there is a legitimate notion of identity, which is sufficient for the acceptance, by the person, of the status of moral agent. Moreover, I showed that this is a relatively weak assumption, insofar as it is presupposed even by the experience of a particular sensation. Thus, for Kant, the presentation *I think* is an a priori judgement (*KrV*: A341/B399, 382) that "makes even all transcendental concepts possible" (*KrV*: A343/B401, 383).

As I have mentioned at the end of Part I, the problem that can be raised now is that, precisely because of the undemanding character of the condition, it will become very easy to satisfy it and, hence, the notion will become implausible. Consider now Kant's claim, in the *Metaphysics of Morals*, that:

> A person is a subject whose actions can be *imputed* to him. *Moral* personality is therefore nothing other than the freedom of a rational being under moral laws (whereas psychological personality is merely the ability to be conscious of one's identity in different conditions of one's existence).

(MS: 6:223, 378)

By distinguishing between moral and psychological personality, Kant goes some way towards answering this objection, because, although necessary for practical purposes, psychological personality is not yet sufficient for making actions imputable. To be sure, when he uses the term "psychological identity", Kant seems to have in view an empirical notion of identity. This is because, while the notion of personality in the Third Paralogism refers to an *unconditional I*, of which we are conscious as numerically identical, here Kant talks about being conscious of one's identity in different *conditions* of one's existence.

Be that as it may, for the purpose of providing an answer to the objection of implausibility, suffice it to pay heed to Kant's reference to freedom in the definition of moral personality. Thus, apart from being conscious of one's identity in different times, one must also be free to act in the way one acted, if one is to be held responsible for the action. This shows also how the two problems formulated at the end of Part I, namely, this problem of implausibility and the problem of freedom, are related. For the latter is raised by a condition that shows why the condition of identity can be relatively weak without making the notion of accountability implausible.

Kant is very much aware that the question of attributing freedom to a person is in a sense a very complicated one, for, to begin with, even the very basic claim that freedom is possible requires a serious argument against determinism, an argument with far-reaching implications. Once this is established, to determine whether a person acted freely in a particular situation raises additional difficulties, which are also far from simple.

But let me focus now on the first claim and see how Kant deals with it in the Third Antinomy of the *Critique of Pure Reason*. In the next section, I will present the antinomy and explain why Kant regards it as setting forth a problem, which puts into question our status of rational beings. The next few sections will present Kant's solution to this problem and, hence, his attempt to rescue our rational nature.

§36. The third antinomy

Recall that, in discussing the paralogisms of pure reason, Kant's argument was that these syllogisms are, in fact, invalid. They represent attempts made by the rational psychologist to justify claims concerning the identity or unity or simple nature of the soul as a priori true. Kant's argument was, therefore, that, in such instances, the rational psychologist relies too much on the knowing power of reason. In this respect, Kant's argument in the Antinomies is similar. Thus, he argues precisely against the claims made by rational cosmology, which attempts to derive knowledge about an empirical object from reason. To the extent that, in the antinomies, reason tries to achieve knowledge about the totality of appearances, reason is based on what Kant calls "world concepts" or the idea of a "world whole" (*KrV*: A408/B434, 444). Hence the name of this enterprise: "rational *cosmology*" (from the Greek *cosmos* – world whole and *logos*).

In the paralogisms, reason starts from an a priori concept of subject and tries to derive cognition without reference to an empirical object. In the antinomies, reason tries to think an empirical object as conditioned appearance and hopes to attain an "absolute totality in the synthesis of appearance" (*KrV*: A408/B434, 444). Then, it draws a conclusion concerning this totality which, as a sum of all conditioned appearance, is itself "unconditioned" (*KrV*: A408/B434, 444). Since cognition can only be of conditioned appearances, rational cosmology can only achieve "an ideal of pure reason" (*KrV*: A408/B435, 444).

All these claims sound very abstract, and they are. So let me focus on the argument of the Third Antinomy to illustrate them. Here, the arguments of rational cosmology are proved by Kant as invalid by following a different method than the one deployed in the sections on paralogisms. In the latter case, he shows that the syllogisms put forward by rational psychology are fallacious; in the former case, he shows that rational cosmology is rationally led to two conflicting, antinomic conclusions – hence the name "antinomies". The two conflicting conclusions drawn by rational cosmology as regards freedom are:

THESIS	ANTITHESIS
The causality according to laws of nature is not the only causality, from which the appearances of the world can thus one and all be derived. In order to explain these appearances, it is necessary to assume also a causality through freedom. (*KrV*: A444/B472, 473)	There is no freedom, but everything in the world occurs solely according to laws of nature. (*KrV*: A445/B473, 473)

This is the Third Antinomy as presented by Kant in the first *Critique*. Appearances or phenomena are the result of the way in which sensible input is ordered and synthesized according to the pure intuitions of sensibility (space and time) and pure categories of the understanding. One of these categories is that of causality. Hence, every phenomenon can be seen as the effect of some other phenomenon, which is its cause. Appearance will necessarily stand under the law of causality; however, this type of causality concerns only appearances, not things in themselves (*KrV*: A538/B566, 539).

By definition, things in themselves stand for appearances as they are, independently from the way they appear to an observer through sensation. For such a sentient observer, everything is conditioned, in the sense of being brought about by certain causes. In this sense, the actions of a person can be understood as consisting of a series of movements caused by muscular tensions and distensions, as well as external causes. In turn, these tensions and distensions are also caused by other factors in the person's environment or mind.

We can further argue that the latter factors are also caused by other factors, which have their own causes too. Hence, appearances stand connected under the law of causality. Yet, if everything in the world occurred solely in accordance with the laws of nature (as the Antithesis states), the link to the previous causes that determined my actions would be infinite. And, yet, an infinite link of causes could never produce a current event, since to cause an event to happen requires that the cause take place at some moment in time while an infinite string of causes and events would never end, would require an infinite time and, hence, would never actually get to take place at some point in time.

To counter this first problem, which goes against the fact that events do take place in the world and actions are being performed, we can try to identify a first cause, a prime mover, which, by definition, could no longer be caused by further factors. Yet, this prime mover, which is supposed to exist without being caused, must therefore have existed even before the link of causal connections with which we are familiar in our world began and which now led to current events, like your reading my book now. The usual notion of cause that we employ refers to something that happens *at one point* to produce an effect *afterwards*; a prime mover is not a cause in this sense, since a prime mover exists before all causes and effects exist. We cannot explain the prime mover's first move by reference to some other event, which would have determined this first move, unless we turned the prime mover into a standard, usual cause, which, in its turn, would be an effect caused by some other event.

Hence, Kant argues that the causality of the prime mover must be a different type of causality – one that triggers the succession of what we usually call causes and effects. To mark its *sui generis* character, Kant calls it "causality through freedom". This is what the Thesis states in a much more condensed way. The problem with such a causality is generated by the fact that a prime mover is supposed to act also as a cause in the usual sense of the term, as a physical cause, in order to trigger the string of causes and effects with which we are familiar. This implies that, before its first move, the prime mover (which then is not yet moving) must be in a state that is distinct from its state at the moment of its first move.

Now, unless we regard these states as distinct as far as the emergence of the first move is concerned, we turn the first move into an effect brought about by the previous state of the prime mover. This would mean that the prime mover would no longer be an uncaused cause and, hence, by definition, would no longer be a prime mover. But, if the prime mover cannot be determined to make the move, it must have "the power to begin a state *on one's own*" (*KrV*: A533/B561, 535). According to this characterization, therefore, and as we have seen from the discussion above, as free, the prime mover is not subject to another cause and, therefore, does not belong to phenomena, but "is a purely transcendental idea" (*KrV*: A533/B561, 535).

This discussion provides the necessary material for grasping in what sense the Third Antinomy raises a problem for reason and may question the assumption that we are rational. I will elaborate further on this challenge and present Kant's solution to the antinomy in the next section.

§37. Solution: Theoretical freedom

For Kant, the two characteristics of a transcendental idea are given by its a priori status and by its regulative role in experience. The first characteristic concerns the independence of the idea from experience, whereas the second refers to the role that it plays in our knowledge of phenomena. Thus, although the pure intuitions of sensibility (space and time) and the concepts of understanding (e.g. the concept of cause) are a priori, they are not regulative. They are constitutive of phenomena or appearances. The ideas of pure reason are a priori, but they do not constitute phenomena. When they are used to refer to phenomena (Kant calls this their "transcendent use" – *KrV*: A643/B671, 618), for instance in the case of the antinomies, they lead to contradictions and misunderstandings. The correct use of transcendental ideas should be that of giving unity to the concepts of understanding:

Just as the understanding unites the manifold in the object by means of concepts, so reason in its turn unites the manifold of concepts by means of ideas – viz., by setting a certain collective unity as the goal of the understanding's acts, which otherwise deal only with distributive unity.

(*KrV*: A644/B672, 618–19)

Thus, freedom as an idea of reason cannot be constitutive of phenomena in the world in the way causality is. This is why phenomena are determined by physical causality, whereas the causality of freedom seems to act from outside the world of appearances. Because the series of phenomenal causes and effects cannot be totalized, since this would lead to an infinite regress, reason creates the idea of freedom as a spontaneous cause of phenomena, which can thus stop the infinite regress.[2]

To resolve the Third Antinomy, Kant aims to steer a path between the empiricism of the antithesis and the dogmatism of the thesis (*KrV*: A465–6/B494–5, 488–9). His solution is well-known and subject to much controversy.[3] On Kant's account, dogmatism has on its side a *"practical interest"*, namely, it wants to prove that the self is, "in its voluntary actions, free and raised above the constraint of nature", and this is one of the "foundation stones of morality and religion" (*KrV*: A466/B494, 489).[4] Mere empiricism does not have any such corresponding practical interest. To the contrary, empiricism "seems, rather, to deprive both of these [morality and religion] of all force and influence" (*KrV*: A468/B496, 490).[5]

Kant tries to reconcile the contradiction between the claims of the empiricist and dogmatist by discarding those aspects that lead these views to contradictions. Once this is done, there remain aspects of the dogmatic and empiricist position that are worth preserving.[6] Given the distinction between phenomena and things in themselves, the subject can be regarded both as a phenomenon in the world and as a free being. As a phenomenon, he is determined according to the causality of nature, but, as a free being, he is the cause of his own actions.

Following this distinction, Kant can claim that the empiricist's and dogmatist's arguments are compatible. This is because the actions of the agent can be regarded as phenomena that are in causal relationships with other phenomena in the world. Yet, as a thing in itself and, more exactly, as a cause that is not in its turn caused by some phenomenon, the agent can also be regarded as an uncaused cause of his actions. The empiricist position is therefore correct as an account of why the idea of an uncaused cause is empty, in the sense that no possible experience corresponds to it, but it cannot show that the notion of an uncaused cause is impossible and must be rejected.[7]

Likewise, the dogmatist view can be regarded as an account of why the knowing power of understanding must be limited to the domain of phenomena, but not as a view that rejects the absolute validity of physical causality in that realm. Hence, in his critical theoretical philosophy, Kant's solution to the antinomy does not attempt to offer a proof that there is freedom, but only to show that there *can* be freedom, or in other words, that freedom is not impossible. As Kant puts it:

> To show that this antinomy rests on a mere illusion and that nature at least does *not conflict* with the causality from freedom – this was the only goal that we were able to accomplish, and it was, moreover, our one and only concern.
>
> (*KrV*: A558/B587, 552–3)

It is in his critical practical philosophy that Kant tries to show that there is freedom. Yet, already in the first *Critique*, Kant foreshadows a 'proof' of the second *Critique* with the following 'argument'. For him, it is "evident" that reason has the power of causality, because of the "*imperatives* which, in all that is practical, we impose as rules on the performative powers" (*KrV*: A547/B575, 545). Let me first present here Kant's distinction between a descriptive and a prescriptive account of action; in the next section, I will discuss further this second 'proof' Kant offers in relation to the Third Antinomy.

The characteristic of an imperative is the *ought*, which expresses the requirement that a particular action be performed even when some other action has actually been, or is likely to be, performed. Kant contrasts here the way in which actions as appearances take place as merely a matter of fact, with the way in which actions are conceived from the perspective of an imperative.

What we can ask, Kant says, is what properties a circle has, not what properties it ought to have (*KrV*: A547/B575, 545). 'Circle' here refers to the correctly constructed geometrical object that represents the two-dimensional set of points that are placed at an equal distance from a fixed centre. The properties of the circle define it and, hence, the circle has these properties. It would be misleading to say that a circle ought to have them, since without them we do not have a circle.

Similarly, an action that has just been performed has a series of properties that describe it. If 'action' refers to the action that has just been performed, then its properties *describe* this action. If we say that the action ought to have had such-and-such properties, then by 'action' one means something else, namely, the obligatory action. The action that has just been performed may be, but is not necessarily, the action we ought to have performed; hence, the properties in virtue of which we say that an action is morally right and, hence, ought to be performed are different from the properties that describe the action that has been performed and constitute a prescriptive account of action. With this distinction between the obligatory and the actual action we can move on to the 'proof', which will also introduce elements of a different notion of freedom – practical freedom – that Kant distinguishes from theoretical freedom. These will be discussed in the next section.

§38. Solution: Practical freedom

According to Kant, in the order of appearances, we explain an action by regarding it as an effect produced by sensible causes. These sensible causes condition my power of choice (*Willkühr*) to act in a certain way. For instance, my desire to eat chocolate may be seen as a cause that prompts me to eat some chocolate; however, we have also seen that it is in principle possible for me to act in a particular way because I think this to be the right thing to do independently of whether, in this way, I am satisfying any sensible incentive.

The assumption here is that I have at my disposal an imperative or standard, with which I can evaluate whether the actions to which I am prompted by my incentives are worth performing. Hence, Kant says, the imperatives of reason presuppose an authority that goes against "this conditioned willing with measure and goal" (*KrV*: A548/B576, 545).[8] In other words, the unconditional nature of the 'ought' of imperatives has a check on the conditioned sensible incentives and can determine a person to act freely, that is, independently from them. To be sure, the fact that we talk in this way about imperatives and that we are able to resist certain sensible incentives and to act according to what we consider to be the right thing does not yet demonstrate that we are free and act freely. Hence, my cautious attitude in presenting this as a 'proof' of, or 'argument' for, freedom.

In this sense, Kant's conclusion is not that reason actually brings about free actions, but that it is "at least possible that reason actually has causality with regard to appearances" (*KrV*: A548–9/B576–7, 546). In this way, he shows that reason *can* be a cause of free actions. Yet it remains to be proven that this intelligible causality is compatible with the order of nature (the empirical causality of appearances), and that reason not only can, but also does cause free actions. At this point, Kant is still on the side of the dogmatist and reason "must yet show itself as having an empirical character" (*KrV*: A549/B577, 546). I will focus on this argument in the next section.

One can see now the basis of the relationship that Kant establishes between freedom and obligatory laws in the quotation on moral personality from the *Metaphysics of Morals* and in the 'argument' for freedom in the *Critique of Practical Reason*: laws are universal principles, which do not describe what happens, but prescribe what ought to happen; obligatory laws, therefore, are laws of freedom. Given Kant's view of freedom as causality and given his concept of causality as character (rule-based relationship between causes and effects[9]), freedom, at least insofar as we do not simply talk about a purely negative notion of freedom (as independence from the laws of nature), is indissolubly connected to the obligatory character of laws.[10]

Kant's account of the empirical character of the power of choice would suggest that the power of choice is determined by phenomena according to the law of natural causality; however, the power of choice has a corresponding freedom, called "practical" freedom. This can, in the first instance, be distinguished from theoretical or transcendental freedom (the freedom Kant showed to be possible in the Third Antinomy), because practical freedom is actually based on transcendental freedom.

On Kant's account, we can talk about the *freedom* of the power of choice, although a person's power of choice is affected by sensible stimuli. This is possible because, although affected, the power of choice is not completely necessitated by such stimuli.[11] As Kant puts it, *"freedom in the practical meaning* of the term is the independence of the power of choice from coercion by impulses of sensibility" (*KrV*: A533–4/B561–2, 536). The question is how it is possible that the power of choice, on the one hand, be not completely dependent on sensible impulses and, on the other hand, be determined by a subjective principle of action that excludes freedom.

As we have seen, the empirical character of the power of choice represents the rule according to which the actions, as effects, follow other appearances, which are usually called 'causes'.[12] Yet, as the Third Antinomy means to establish, there can be an alternative account of how phenomena take place in the world. Thus, phenomena can be determined to happen by a causality we bring on our own, through which a series of events can follow. Let me quote Kant here at some length:

> practical freedom presupposes that although something did not occur, it yet *ought* to have occurred, and that hence the cause of something in [the realm of] appearance was not completely determinative: not so determinative, viz., that there did not lie in our power of choice a causality for producing, independently of those natural causes and even against their force and influence, something that in the time order is determined according to empirical laws – and hence a causality whereby we can begin a series of events *entirely on our own.*
>
> (*KrV*: A534/B562, 536–7)

By now it is probably clearer in what way practical freedom is based on transcendental freedom, and how the power of choice can be determined both by an empirical character and by an intelligible character. Practical freedom, as the independence of the power of choice from the coercion of sensible impulses, refers to a particular aspect of the distinction between things in themselves and phenomena. Thus, in the case of actions, we usually say that obligatory actions ought to be performed, whether or not they actually are performed. This suggests a distinction between natural necessity and practical necessity.

Natural necessity is given by natural laws, which determine the effects of certain phenomena we regard as causes. Practical necessity is given by obligatory laws, which determine a person's will or practical reason. While a person may choose what is (practically) rational to do, she may also choose differently, given that the power of choice is also affected by sensible impulses. Yet, the power of choice must be able to choose against sensible impulses and in accordance with what the will (or practical reason) dictates, otherwise the necessity of obligatory laws, although in principle normatively valid, will be an empty word. Practical freedom is, therefore, transcendental freedom applied to the agent's actions.[13]

This concludes the brief presentation of Kant's Third Antinomy and of the solution he offers. As could be seen, the solution relies crucially on transcendental idealism, more exactly, the distinction between things in themselves and phenomena, as well as the constitutive role that the a priori structure of the mind (or reason in the general sense[14]) plays in experience. Since this is the assumption on the basis of which a solution to the contradiction of the antinomy is presented, if we grant the rational nature of human beings, then the solution to the Third Antinomy, which explains how our rational nature is possible (because free from contradictions), represents also an indirect argument for transcendental idealism. In the next section, I will begin with a few concluding remarks on the Third Antinomy of pure reason and will then move on to the Antinomy of Practical Reason.

§39. Ethical normativity

The Third Antinomy shows that, although always accompanied by them, a person's will can be independent from sensible incentives, since natural necessity simply refers to the way things are ordered by the understanding's concept of causality. By contrast, transcendental freedom, as independence from the order of natural necessity, is possible if we talk about things as they are in themselves, independently from our way of experiencing them.[15] At least two assumptions are required to resolve the Third Antinomy in this way: first, we need the distinction between things in themselves and phenomena, and, secondly, we need to accept that freedom as independence from natural necessity refers to things in themselves.

Therefore, although the Third Antinomy can only show the *possibility* of transcendental freedom, and not that there is freedom, in a certain sense we can conclude that there must be such freedom, for otherwise we end up with contradictions. The possibility of transcendental freedom explains also the possibility of practical freedom. In addition, the possibility of practical freedom gets some (limited) support from the distinction people make in ordinary speech between what happens in the world and what ought to happen. This distinction is also reflected by what is usually called the

Incorporation Thesis, according to which an incentive can only determine an action if I choose it as an incentive, if I make it the ground of my acting on the maxim or, in other words, if I incorporate it in this way in my maxim.[16] This suggests that the agent can, in principle, choose a different maxim of action. Indeed, our day-to-day lives suggest precisely this: we sometimes refrain from acting on incentives which, although very powerful, prompt us to act in ways we think are wrong; we may choose a different maxim and action than those incentives prompt us to adopt.

This may seem to reaffirm the traditional view concerning the crucial importance of duty for Kant's ethics. It has, however, been some time since Kant scholars have pointed out the mistake of regarding duty as the starting point of Kant's account of ethical normativity.[17] The appropriate starting point for Kant, it has been argued, is not duty, but the idea of unconditional goodness (Höffe 1994: 141).[18] Although this is certainly true as far as certain aspects of Kant's ethical theory are concerned, and Section 75 and 76 below raise some further questions in this respect, in what follows I will focus on a different important aspect of Kant's moral theory. As shown in his discussion of Practical Antinomy, Kant's starting point is the person as a limited rational individual who is guided by an idea of unconditional goodness, but who also needs to account for the fact that her rationality is limited by sensibility. An ethical theory will, therefore, have to account for both these aspects of a person.

The account of ethical goodness presented by Kant as the solution to the problem raised by the antinomy of pure practical reason does precisely this (*KpV*: 5:114–19, 145–52). Thus, the contradiction of the antinomy stems from the attempt to combine, on the one hand, virtue, as a reflection on the agent's rationality, and, on the other, happiness, as an expression of the agent's sentient nature. A coherent combination would represent the complete good or *summum bonum* (*KpV*: 5:112–13, 144). Virtue and happiness are the standards that rationality and sensibility, respectively, try to follow. Reconciling these despite all the conceptual difficulties represents Kant's attempt to offer an ethical theory that does not rely on an idealized view of the person.[19] And here we have one place where, despite the standard reading of Kant, his ethics comes very close to Aristotle's.[20]

Let me start by presenting the Practical Antinomy. I will begin, in the remainder of this section, with two important Kantian distinctions that directly concern the antinomy: first, that between the good and the pleasant, and, secondly, that between autonomy and heteronomy.

In the "Analytic of Pure Practical Reason", more precisely in the chapter "Of the Concept of an Object of Pure Practical Reason" (*KpV*: 5:57–71, 77–94), Kant claims that the notion of the good, as the only object of pure practical reason (*KpV*: 5:58, 78), cannot be defined as starting from what is pleasant (*KpV*: 5:63, 84–5). For, if it were so defined, the notion of the good would be dependent on the feeling of pleasure and, therefore, in order to define the notion of the good it would be necessary to make appeal to experience (*KpV*: 5:58, 78–9). The object of an action that had as purpose the good would in that case only be good relatively to the way in which the subject experienced it; it would not be unconditionally good or good in itself (*KpV*: 5:58–9, 79).

Moreover, Kant says, even in the ordinary usage of language *pleasant* is distinguished from *good*. We do not immediately assume that what is pleasant is necessarily good and, hence, has to be followed. Perhaps the best illustration at this point is that you are reading this book on, which means I kept writing it, although, probably for both of us and most certainly for you, at certain moments, there were things we could have done that promised to be more pleasant. The notion of an unconditional good must, therefore, be defined as starting from an ethical standard that is a priori, independent for its validity from experience and which, as such, is unconditionally valid. Hence, according to Kant, the good is to be defined as starting from the moral law, rather than from what is pleasant. But, then, this means that one has first to determine the moral law, and only after that and by means of it should one define the concept of the good (*KpV*: 5:62–3, 84).

According to Kant, ethicists usually commit the conceptual fallacy of defining first the good and then deriving the determining principle of the will from this notion of the good (*KpV*: 5:64, 85). They place the good either in happiness or in perfection or in moral feeling or in the will of God. As a result, Kant says, the principle of action derived from this value is heteronomous (*KpV*: 5:64–5, 86). Such a principle is heteronomous in the sense that its normative authority (*nomos*) is given by something other (*heteras*) than the person's will or practical reason; it is given by a normative authority that is not that of the person herself. For instance, one may rely on sensible feelings (which depend on circumstances, given physiological constitution of the perceptive apparatus, upbringing and similar contingent factors) or on some idea of perfection given by moral intuitions handed down perhaps by tradition or on some idea concerning the will of God.

Since, as far as we can say, on the basis of our experience, the sources of our claims regarding what is good are ultimately two, namely, sensible feelings and reason, all attempts to define a notion of the unconditioned good will either be based on sensible feelings or on reason.[21] In the latter case, since (practical) reason is regarded as structured by the moral law, the good would be defined autonomously, the source of normativity being reason itself. A person's good would be that good that is given by her own reason. In short, as self-legislating, the person would be autonomous (*auto* – self, *nomos* – norm, law). And, yet, as we will see in the next section, such a notion of the good would still be far from the *summum bonum*. We will see that, on Kant's account, the additional element we would need to account for the *summum bonum* will, however, bring about contradictions, which will lead to another Antinomy, this time an antinomy of practical reason.

§40. Practical antinomy

I have just said that a notion of the good that is defined starting from the moral law is an interesting candidate for the role of *summum bonum*. Yet, the good thus defined is incomplete, since it relies on reason (more exactly, the moral law that structures practical reason) and human beings are essentially also sentient beings, not merely rational beings. In fact, Kant calls it "supreme" good and distinguishes it from the complete good. But we do not make much progress either, if we start from sensible feelings. In that case, two distinct notions are confused: that of the good, as unconditioned good, and that of the pleasant. Thus, defining the good on the basis of sensible feeling would mean turning the notion into a subjective one that depends on contingent factors. Here the problem would not yet be incompleteness, but the inappropriateness of such an account of a notion of the unconditioned good. What we end up with in this case is an account of what is pleasant.

The distinction between the pleasant and the unconditioned good is also the reason why, in fact, in "The Antinomy of Practical Reason", Kant excludes at the outset the hypothesis of a relationship between virtue and happiness, according to which one is part of the other and can be reduced to the other. This part-whole relationship is what Kant calls an analytic relation between virtue and happiness. In general, an analytic relation between *A* and *B* would imply that simply by analysing one of these notions (A) we would obtain the second (B), as part of the first. The analytic connection between happiness and virtue would, therefore, imply either that it is sufficient to be happy in order to also be virtuous or that it is enough to be virtuous in order to be happy. On Kant's view, the first claim points to the Epicurean position, whereas the second, to the Stoic view (*KpV*: 5:115–16, 146–8).

Both of these views of happiness and virtue miss the distinctive features of happiness and virtue. Hence, a more appropriate view would be that virtue and happiness are two distinct elements of the whole, or perfect, good (*summum bonum*). As the value that guides the human being's action, the *summum bonum* should contain both happiness and virtue. Happiness is necessary since human beings are sentient beings with wants (*KpV*: 5:61, 83). Virtue is also an essential element of the *summum bonum*, because human beings are also rational beings and, as such, are also prompted to act by reason. Therefore, Kant concludes that:

> happiness and morality are two *elements* of the highest good which are entirely *different* in kind, and that therefore one cannot cognise their linkage *analytically* (that, say, someone who seeks his happiness will in this [very] conduct of his find himself virtuous by merely resolving his concepts; or that someone who follows virtue will in the very consciousness

of such conduct *ipso facto* find himself happy); rather, this linkage is a *synthesis* of concepts.

(KpV: 5:112–13, 144)

At least the significant difference between sensible incentives and reasons should enable Kant to exclude an analytic relation between virtue and happiness. This leaves him with the alternative of a synthetic relation. A synthetic relation is a relation between two concepts where the link is not established in virtue of the fact that one concept is part of the other, but through a connection of a non-conceptual nature, for instance, by experience. The link between 'book' and 'yellow' is synthetic, because some books are not yellow and, hence, 'yellow' is not necessarily part of the concept of 'book'. When I happen to see a yellow book in front of my eyes, the link between these concepts is made through experience.

To sum up, in the quotation above, Kant excludes the idea of an analytic relationship between virtue and happiness, and, hence, the relation must be synthetic. The antinomy of practical reason represents the result of an argument that shows the impossibility of conceiving of a synthetic relation between virtue and happiness. As we have seen, a synthetic relationship can be simply defined negatively by reference to the analytic one: it is a relationship between concepts, none of which is entirely part of the other, although overlaps are possible. Since the question is how the complete good or *summum bonum* can be brought about, Kant focuses on a relationship of causality between virtue and happiness. For, obviously, if virtue caused happiness to appear or happiness caused virtue to appear, this would by itself bring about the complete good (*KpV*: 5:113, 145).

However, on the one hand, to see happiness as the cause of virtue is absolutely impossible, Kant says, since an action produced by the determination of the faculty of desire is not moral but only pleasant (even when it happens to conform to the moral law). On the other hand, however, it seems also impossible to conceive of virtue as the cause of happiness: a causal relationship between virtue and happiness would imply that virtue, as cause, necessarily brings about happiness, as an effect. Yet happiness is the satisfaction of that set of interests (needs, desires, inclinations, cravings and so on) which will lead to the maximum amount of pleasure. Hence, it is true that happiness can necessarily be produced, yet it cannot be produced necessarily by virtuous actions, but only by efficacious ones (those that represent the best means to the given end). To be sure, performing the ethically right actions to the end of virtue may bring about happiness, but only contingently. This is why the relationship between virtue and happiness cannot be simply taken as one of causality, as a relationship of the *necessary* connection between cause and effect (*KpV*: 5:113–14, 145).

Without an account of a necessary synthetic relation between virtue and happiness, we cannot account for the *summum bonum* and, hence, for an ethical theory that is fitting for the two essential aspects of human beings: the sentient and the rational aspects. In the next section, I will present Kant's solution to the Antinomy of Practical Reason.

§41. Solution to the practical antinomy

Kant's solution starts from the claim that, whereas it is absolutely impossible to conceive of happiness as the cause of virtue, it is not absolutely impossible to imagine virtue as a cause of happiness (*KpV*: 5:114, 146). By seeking happiness, a person chooses sensible incentives as the grounds or determining bases of her actions. While the actions may have legality, that is, may conform to the moral law, they necessarily lack morality, that is, conformity for the right reason. By seeking happiness, the agent performs the actions because they make her happy, not because they are right. Hence, in such cases, the agent's actions cannot be ethically worthy.

As I have suggested, in Kant, ethically worthy actions not only conform to the moral law and, thus, are actions of a specific kind, but they are also performed for the sake of the moral law, rather than for that of happiness. The difference between virtue as a cause of happiness and happiness as a cause of virtue is that happiness cannot produce virtue, whereas virtue can produce happiness, even if only contingently. Yet, for a relationship of causality between virtue and happiness we need more than contingency here, we need necessity.

The *summum bonum*, as the necessary supreme end of an ethically determined will, is possible from a practical standpoint insofar as the relation between virtue and happiness can be considered as one of causality. In order for this to happen, actions that were performed for the sake of the moral law would have to satisfy that set of interests that would produce the maximum of pleasure (*KpV*: 5:114–15, 146).

I have briefly mentioned above that, according to Kant, Stoicism and Epicureanism failed to account appropriately for the *summum bonum*, for, to begin with, by regarding the relation between virtue and happiness as analytic they were unable to properly account for the antinomy of pure practical reason. Epicureans considered that actions performed because they produced pleasure were also virtuous actions. For them, a virtuous disposition is manifested by a person's consciousness of happiness. Hence, the person who acts from the motive of pleasure is also virtuous. There is no place for an antinomy here.

Stoics considered that actions performed out of duty, simply because they were virtuous, were actions directed to happiness and the most efficient ones at that. Hence, for them, happiness was already contained in the consciousness of virtue. For them, happiness could genuinely be obtained only by performing virtuous actions. Again, on this account, we cannot have an antinomy related to the *summum bonum*, for the *summum bonum* is pursued as soon as virtue is.

On Kant's account, both Stoics and Epicureans reduced the complete good to one of its elements and presupposed that the second element was merely the consciousness of possessing the first. Kant's response to the Stoics is that, although virtue is the supreme good, it is not the complete good, the *summum bonum*. A virtuous person acts in accordance with, and for the sake of, the supreme ethical principle, the Categorical Imperative.

As part of the *summum bonum*, happiness must be the effect of acting virtuously, but not in the sense that happiness represents the mere consciousness of being virtuous. Moreover, there is another sense in which, in our world, happiness is not the effect of acting virtuously: this is the usual sense in which a physical cause (say, a moving ball) produces an effect (say, the movement of a second ball, hit by the first). Virtuous actions are not directed towards the satisfaction of sensible interests, but towards conformity to the supreme ethical principle for the sake of its rightness. Hence, virtuous action will only contingently bring about happiness. In our world, virtue is not a direct cause of happiness or is not sufficient to produce happiness.

What is needed, in addition, is something that can turn the contingent occurrence of happiness from virtue into a necessary occurrence. The person who acts virtuously is worthy of being happy, but she is not necessarily happy. To make this a necessary result – that is, an effect of virtue – we need certain conditions in which happiness is distributed necessarily to those worthy of happiness and in proportion to how worthy they are. This, however, is not something that can be done by limited persons like us; such a task involves a power that outruns whatever force persons, as a group, let alone individually, can summon up.

Moreover, such a task cannot be restricted to the phenomenal world, since, here, one cannot be sure of the ethical character of actions, which depend on individual motivation. What is more, in order for all virtuous actions to be necessarily rewarded by happiness, one needs a complete control over the world as a whole. As we have seen in the discussion of the third antinomy and as we will see in Part III of this book, the idea of the world as a whole goes beyond our experience, which is always limited to specific aspects of the world or to specific sequences of aspects, as given by the limited span of our life and, hence, by the limited span of our experience.

For all these reasons, the solution to the antinomy of pure practical reason, like that to the third antinomy of pure theoretical reason, will point to the noumenal realm. What is impossible for limited beings like us (the idea of the world as a whole, control over the world's causal chains, absolute knowledge) may be possible for a perfect being, like God. If a solution to the antinomy of practical reason is found, then the *summum bonum* can be taken to stand for the goal of all ethical ends. At the basis of the *summum bonum*, however, Kant places the supreme good of the ethical action, namely, virtue. Virtuous action is based on good maxims, maxims justified by the Categorical Imperative. The next section will present in more detail the nature of categorical imperatives.

§42. Categorical imperatives

We have seen that, for Kant, we can account for the complete good of human beings only if we start from the supreme good of virtue, which is given by actions performed in accordance with, and for the sake of, the fundamental ethical principle, the Categorical Imperative. For Kant, practical *principles* are propositions that contain a general determination of the will.

Principles are personal policies, specific ways of acting in similar situations; in other words, they determine certain patterns of action for various ranges of circumstances. Principles can be maxims or laws. Whereas *maxims* are practical principles in which the condition for the determination of the will is regarded by the subject as valid for himself, *laws* are practical principles that have a condition for the determination of the will that is valid for all subjects, that is, laws have an objectively valid determination condition (*KpV*: 5:19, 29).

For Kant every general determination of the will, which is contained in a practical principle, has under it several practical *rules*. Every rule describes an action as a specific way of enacting the general determination of the will. For a purely rational being, practical reason determines directly the will, and the action is spontaneously rational. Yet, for a finite rational being, that is, for human beings, the will may also be determined by inclinations and sensible drives. Ethical rules are then followed only if the will is determined by reason. Thus, for human beings, ethical rules are commanded by reason as rational determinations of the will against pathological affections of the will (by inclinations and sensible drives). Ethical rules are in that case *imperatives* (*KpV*: 5:20, 30–1).

Imperatives may determine the will conditionally on certain effects being produced, in which case we deal with *hypothetical* imperatives, since the determination of the will is adopted on the assumption or by making the hypothesis that these effects will be achieved. When the imperative determines the will without reference to an effect, but simply because the imperative is taken to be the right thing to do, then the imperative is *categorical*. A hypothetical imperative cannot be an objectively valid principle, that is, an ethical law, since the way in which it determines the will holds only for those persons who take the expected effects to be of real value and worth pursuing.

The validity of hypothetical imperatives is relative to the subjective condition which determines a person to value certain effects or consequences. This is a direct implication of its conditional, hypothetical nature. By contrast, categorical imperatives can function as laws and, as such, they are objectively and universally valid. Whereas hypothetical imperatives prescribe the means by which the will can bring about certain consequences, categorical imperatives determine the will unconditionally, without reference to any subjective condition, on the basis of which certain consequences, rather than others, would acquire value.

Therefore, categorical imperatives can determine a priori only the will, and not the effect of the action. Even though, for Kant, there is a clear-cut distinction between laws and maxims as practical principles, a maxim *can* function as a practical law for a human being when it determines the will not by its matter, but by its form (*KpV*: 5:27, 40). To be sure, certain maxims are formulated in such a way that they seem to make no reference to a "matter", that is, to a subjective condition or to some significance being placed on the value of the action's effects.

For instance, 'Open the window' is a command which does not seem to depend for its value on any consequences of the action thus formulated. Nevertheless, if we do not take into consideration its possible consequences, by itself the action does not have any particular value either. Once we consider its consequences, the action may acquire significance: I open the window in order to get fresh air or because I want to see who is at the door in order to avoid the murderer or because I want to see whether the window's hinges function properly. Despite more complex cases, on Kant's account, to distinguish between maxims whose adoption depends on their matter and maxims whose adoption is only dependent on their form represents a task that can be performed by the "commonest understanding" (*KpV*: 5:27, 40).

Now, a will which adopts a maxim in virtue of its form only is a free will. This is because it adopts the maxim without reference to empirical elements, such as the consequences of the action and my sensible interests in relation to these consequences. Even the satisfaction of the particular interests I may have for a certain action (rather than for its consequences) is to be seen as a consequence of performing the action.

For instance, I may enjoy dancing, but not care about its consequences (good physical condition, making new friends and similar). Alternatively, I may enjoy helping, but not care about its consequences (gratitude of those I helped, their own happiness and other similar consequences). In other words, the inclination to follow this maxim or other is becoming part of the maxim's matter when I perform actions on that maxim out of that inclination.

Nevertheless, although the performance of an action may be something I am naturally inclined to do, it does not mean that performing that action will necessarily happen in my case on a maxim which includes this inclination as the motive, the ground or reason for action. I may help because it is the right thing to do, rather than because I am inclined to, despite the fact that I am also inclined to help.

Thus, the action may be valued a priori, rather than on the basis of experience. As such, the adoption of the maxim is independent from experience and the natural law of phenomena. In other words, the maxim is taken to hold unconditionally. This indicates that freedom and morality are connected. More exactly, Kant says, "freedom and unconditional practical law reciprocally refer to each other" (*KpV*: 5:29, 43).[22]

Now, one question which will be relevant to consider in relation to the comparative discussion of Kant and Sartre in the next chapter is how the agent is supposed to act ethically – how to find the maxims for the rules of action, how to find the rules of actions and how to perform the appropriate actions. This topic will be discussed next.

§43. Performing ethical actions

In "Kants kategorischer Imperativ als Kriterium des Sittlichen", Otfried Höffe offers an account of Kant's Categorical Imperative in which he makes clear the kind of role Kant expects the agent to play in her moral life (Höffe 1977).[23] Particularly important in this context is Kant's notion of a maxim. If we look at this notion from the perspective of the criterion on the basis of which ethical judgement is supposed to take place, that is, from the perspective of the Categorical Imperative, a maxim is "the object of the generalisation" presupposed by the Categorical Imperative (Höffe 1977: 356).

As Höffe notes elsewhere, this is a notion to which Kant did not pay much attention, mainly because, in his practical philosophy, he was primarily concerned to refute ethical empiricism and scepticism (1994: 150). Yet, as Höffe shows, maxims are extremely important for Kant's ethics, since, in order to decide whether a particular action is morally permitted or forbidden, one has first to find a maxim for it.

While maxims are central for Kant's ethics, actions are obviously important too, and the next problem is to determine the relation between maxims and actions. An action which is described by a rule of action, Höffe notes, may be subsumed, in Kant, under different maxims, depending on the context in which the action is performed (Höffe 1977: 356). Consider Höffe's example of the rule of action which prescribes that one should sing a song every evening. Depending on whether one lives in a house with many tenants and with the walls poorly soundproofed or one lives in a house only with one's family and sings to entertain or whether one sings in order to improve one's voice, we have different attitudes with regard to the same practical rule, since each action is assessed as being under a different maxim.

Some actions will be ethical, whereas others, unethical, depending on circumstances, purposes or abilities, all of these determining the maxim under which the action is to be performed. Singing, for some purpose or other, in a house with the walls poorly soundproofed will most likely manifest an inconsiderate attitude towards the neighbours, whereas singing to entertain one's family in a detached house can be regarded as an attitude of care and love. In the former case, the rule of action will be assessed under the maxim of being inconsiderate, in the latter, under the maxim of being caring. Singing to improve one's voice can be regarded as a way of discharging one's duty to oneself, and will be assessed under the maxim of self-improvement. At the same time, when one has a sore throat, it may be assessed under the maxim of caring for oneself.

Hence, even when the same rule of action is subsumed under the same maxim, the rule can be followed differently depending on the situation in which a person finds himself (Höffe 1977: 363). Höffe concludes that, in Kant, a maxim provides neither a precise description of a concrete action, nor a way of prioritizing sensible incentives. Precisely which action is to be performed can be established neither simply on the basis of the maxim, nor according to inclinations (Höffe 1977: 363).[24]

On Höffe's reading, in Kant's moral theory "one asks the agent himself to invent [*erfinden*] through a corresponding process of judgement the individual structure of moral action and to realise it by his own actions" (1977: 364). The power of judgement has the task of interpreting and estimating in order to make possible the connection between the concrete situation and the corresponding maxim, and eventually to obtain practical rules.

The general framework of Kant's argument can be summarized as a two-step process (Höffe 1977: 365). First, and less important for our purposes here, Kant needs to justify, to expose and legitimize the Categorical Imperative as a moral criterion. This will be discussed in more detail in Chapter 5. The second step, however, refers to the application of the Categorical Imperative. In the first instance, different maxims are legitimized or disqualified through the test put forward by the Categorical Imperative. Then, moral maxims are applied in concrete situations with the help of the moral faculty of judgement. As it has already been mentioned, Kant was not so much interested in this second step, even though in the chapters on "Casuistical questions" in the *Metaphysics of Morals*, he offers some hints with regard to the applicability of his moral philosophy (Höffe 1977: 365).[25]

Here, as well as in the preceding discussion of maxims, laws and imperatives, the distinction between an action which is conditionally good from an ethical perspective and an action which ethically is unconditionally good is crucial. Hence, the next question I will consider is Kant's question concerning our cognition of the unconditionally ethical or more generally of the unconditionally practical (*KpV*: 5:29, 43). The starting point of this cognition cannot be freedom, he answers, since the only concept of freedom which we have at this stage is a negative concept – freedom as required by the solution of the third antinomy of pure reason in the *Critique of Pure Reason*. As we have seen earlier in this chapter, this is the transcendental freedom as independent *from* the law of causality, which governs the mechanism of nature.[26]

According to Kant, the unconditional ethical validity of the moral law presupposes independence from all matter (sensible incentives and interests) (*KpV*: 5:33, 48–9). Hence, it is indeed the case that the ethically unconditional makes reference to transcendental freedom. But, to cognize this unconditional, we need a different starting point. This, Kant says, will be given by the moral itself, more exactly, by the consciousness of the moral law.[27] We get to know freedom through the moral law, but the moral law cannot exist without freedom.[28]

Thus, for Kant, the moral law "*first* offers itself to us, and [...] leads straight to the concept of freedom" (*KpV*: 5:29, 43). Consciousness of the moral law is possible in the same way in which consciousness of theoretical laws is possible, namely, by taking into account the necessity with which reason prescribes them. Between the concept of pure will and that of moral law there is the same relationship as between the concept of the understanding and that of theoretical law (*KpV*: 5:30, 43).

At this point, the relevant issues start to move from those pertaining to the first important part of a discussion of the Categorical Imperative, namely its application, to those related to the normatively more fundamental part, its justification and the authority the Categorical Imperative can legitimately have on this basis. This will be one of the important themes in Part III and will be discussed in more detail in Chapter 5.

In the next chapter, however, we will see that Sartre formulates a few objections to some of the important aspects of Kant's account of the application of the moral criterion, the Categorical Imperative. I will argue that, compared to what Kant says, these are quite strong objections, in which Sartre relies on imaginative and subtle interpretations of Kant. Before I move on to this comparative analysis, a brief summary of the main claims introduced is in order.

§44. Identity, freedom and moral criterion

In this chapter, I have presented my reading of several additional important aspects of Kant's philosophy, in particular, the issue of freedom and the issue of normativity. I have discussed his Third Antinomy of Pure Reason and the Antinomy of Practical Reason together with their solutions. I have also introduced an outline of the way in which the Categorical Imperative is supposed to function in the attempt to justify maxims as moral laws. These aspects of Kant's thought will be discussed in more detail in Chapter 4, where they will represent the background against which I will evaluate some more objections formulated by Sartre.

The starting point of the discussion here has been Kant's distinction between moral and psychological personality. He links the notion of personality with those of action and accountability for action. Furthermore, he links moral personality to freedom and psychological personality to identity. I have shown that, although the notion of identity Kant is willing to support at the end of the Third Paralogism is relatively weak, it does not suffice to make moral judgement possible, since a person must also be free in order to be accountable. But the freedom Kant associates with moral personality, the freedom of a rational being under moral laws, is a complex issue, which needs more time and further discussion to be clarified properly.

I have discussed two of the three main forms of freedom that Kant distinguishes in his work. The first type of freedom, theoretical (or transcendental or negative) freedom is part of his theoretical philosophy and is closely linked to his metaphysics and epistemology. The second, practical (or empirical) freedom, is part of his practical (or moral) philosophy and is grounded in negative freedom. I introduced the third type of freedom, freedom under moral laws or autonomy, in §5, and I will discuss it further in Part III. Although I think theoretical and practical freedom are sufficient for a person's accountability for her action, I think Kant defines moral personality by reference also to autonomy, since only autonomy introduces the idea of a standard or criterion by reference to which actions for which the agent is accountable can be judged as right or wrong.

Kant's criterion of rightness, the Categorical Imperative, guides virtuous persons in their actions. The focus of this criterion is on the type of action that is right, rather than on the possible consequences of the actions. Irrespective of whether an action is regarded as bringing about some favoured consequences or as manifesting a person's inclinations or as satisfying a person's desires or as presenting conformity with some already established rules, Kant claims that the action cannot be right, since all these aspects of actions are contingent – on circumstances, on the constitution of the agent or on what the agent happens to take as authoritative.

But this leads to the problem of the Antinomy of Practical Reason, since only actions directed to specific consequences can necessarily bring about happiness, whereas virtuous actions are only contingently actions which bring about the agent's happiness. And, yet, as a sentient being, an agent should consider seriously her happiness too. I have, therefore, discussed Kant's solution to the Antinomy of Practical Reason, a solution which makes reference to two Postulates of Practical Reason, that concerning the existence of God and the immortality of the soul. Although there is a third Postulate of Practical Reason, this is not directly related to the Antinomy and I will introduce it later on in Part III of this monograph.

Finally, I have noted that Kant's main focus in his practical philosophy has been the clarification, formulation and justification of the Categorical Imperative, rather than its application. I have, therefore, discussed in more detail the conceptual framework within which the Categorical Imperative is presented and I have explored the way in which it is supposed to be applied as a guide for actions. To be sure, the clarification, formulation and justi-fication of this Kantian moral criterion are very important too, but for the purpose of the comparative discussion in Chapter 4, a discussion of these aspects of Kant's philosophy (freedom, moral goodness for human beings and the application of the Categorical Imperative) will suffice.

I will come back to the Categorical Imperative and to the third Postulate of Practical Reason in Part III, where I will discuss Kant's views on the authority of the moral criterion and the moral progress of human beings. In particular, one important aspect is the status of the moral criterion: Is it an entity which exists independently from our minds and to which we must gain access in order to cognize how to act rightly? How can we cognize this criterion and how can we formulate it? Once formulated, is this not a criterion which is too strong to be compatible with our freedom? And while we may agree that this is the imperative that we ought to follow in our actions, how do we know that this is not too difficult a requirement and will never be achieved?

I will consider some of these questions in Chapters 5 and 6; for the moment, I will move on to the comparative discussion of Kant and Sartre.

4
Sartre and Kant

Two objections, or rather sets of objections, to Kant that Sartre formulates in *Being and Nothingness* and *Notebooks for an Ethics* seem to deny any similarities between their views. First, according to Sartre, Kant offers an inappropriate account of freedom, more exactly, one which seems to contain a contradiction in terms. For, on Sartre's reading, Kant's account of freedom in the Third Antinomy suggests that a free agent is free from all constraints, whereas his account of the free agent as spontaneous suggests that there are certain constraints the agent cannot overcome.

As we have seen, a response to Constant's problem, such as Kant's and Sartre's, importantly involves an appeal to a standard on the basis of which actions are to be judged, in particular, the action of lying. Sartre advances some objections to Kant's moral theory in this respect too. More exactly, he thinks Kant's moral theory and the moral standards which it formulates are unable to give guidance in concrete and specific cases. Moreover, he thinks the standards of an ethical theory must necessarily involve interpersonal relations, whereas, on his reading, Kant only grounds moral standards in the autonomy of the agent.

Several aspects of these objections must be considered for the purpose of the comparative analysis of Kant and Sartre. Thus, it might be the case that Sartre objects to claims and arguments which are not in fact Kant's. In other words, as turned out to be the case for the second objection in Chapter 2, Sartre may start from an inaccurate reading of Kant and his objections might in fact be directed to claims or arguments Kant himself would disagree with. In this situation, it is likely we will have a structural similarity between Kant's and Sartre's practical philosophies.

In case Sartre's reading is correct, it might still be the case that his objection to Kant does not hold. Since it is likely this disagreement is related to other aspects of his work, we can look in this case for a genuine difference between their views. In case Sartre's account is accurate and his objection has force against Kant's argument, it can still be the case that Sartre comes to change his view and, from the perspective of the new account, the earlier objection can no longer be raised. This was the case for the first objection discussed in Chapter 2. In such a case, the result of the comparative analysis is again most likely a structural similarity.

Even when Kant and Sartre clearly disagree and their views are distinct in a particular respect, the comparison is still worth undertaking. One line of inquiry that I would like to pursue here is the extent to which any of their views would be better able to solve the contemporary predicament of finding an ethical approach able to adjudicate in situations of conflict, but without appeal to dogmatic claims of a metaphysical, more generally philosophical or of some other nature. So let me begin with the issue of freedom.

§45. Spontaneity

In the second part of *Being and Nothingness*, entitled "Being-for-Itself", Sartre discusses freedom in the context of a section devoted more generally to "Temporality"; there, in part B ("The dynamics of temporality") of the sub-section "The Ontology of Temporality", he contrasts his view of the for-itself's freedom with Kant's account of the spontaneity of a person. He makes reference to Kant's Third Antinomy and objects to Kant's appeal to a non-temporal spontaneity as a way of explaining away the contradiction between Thesis and Antithesis. Thus, he claims:

> It would be useless to remind us of the passages in the *Critique* where Kant shows that a non-temporal spontaneity is inconceivable, but not contradictory. It seems to us, on the contrary, that a spontaneity which would not escape from itself and which would not escape from that very escape, of which we could say, "It is this", and which would allow itself to be enclosed in an unchangeable denomination – it seems that such a spontaneity would be precisely a contradiction and that it would ultimately be the equivalent of a particular affirmative essence, the eternal subject which is never a predicate.
>
> (*EN*: 188, 171)

The issue at stake is quite complex, especially since Sartre formulates it without providing the details of Kant's argument. Moreover, he states this objection from within his own conceptual framework, rather than attempting to start from the context of Kant's thought. Nevertheless, the main elements of the Third Antinomy have been presented in Chapter 3 in some detail. Moreover, Sartre's account of freedom will be discussed in the following sections; what is more, we can already grasp the gist of Sartre's criticism: the general objection is that, by his solution to the Third Antinomy, Kant provides an inappropriate account of freedom as non-temporal spontaneity.

The suggestion in the quotation is that, since change presupposes time, a non-temporal spontaneity can only be unchanging. Yet, there is a contradiction in the idea of an unchanging spontaneity, since the very idea of spontaneity goes against that of a fixed, unchanging element. Hence, on Sartre's account, Kant would congeal the person in an "unchangeable denomination", that of "the eternal subject which is never a predicate". As such, we do not really have a genuine spontaneity, a person who is really free.

It seems clear that Sartre refers here to Kant's account of transcendental freedom (freedom from the constraints of causal determination), which he regards as an account of spontaneity. He does not suggest that such an account should be rejected altogether. He seems to suggest that freedom is correctly viewed by Kant in terms of spontaneity. What must be changed is *Kant's* account of spontaneity. Therefore, Sartre only reacts critically to some aspects of Kant's account and to its implications, in particular to the non-temporality of spontaneity and the logical consequences of adopting this account.

According to Sartre, what an appropriate view of this type of freedom must avoid is the mistake of fixing the spontaneity of the for-itself in the guise of an in-itself. In fact, Sartre advocates a sort of autonomy of spontaneous being:

> *This* spontaneity should be allowed to define itself; this means both that it is the foundation not only of its nothingness of being, but also of its being and that simultaneously being recaptures it to fix it in the given.
>
> (*EN*: 188, 171)

The view of spontaneous being as autonomous suggests that Sartre accepts Kant's conception of an uncaused, *sui generis* cause which initiates freely a chain of further causes and effects. Yet, on Sartre's reading, Kant claims, first, that this unchanging, non-temporal spontaneity is not contradictory, secondly, that it is nevertheless inconceivable, and, thirdly, that it is fixed, congealed in an essence – that of the eternal subject without a predicate. Sartre's assertion that Kant would enclose spontaneity in an unchangeable denomination (while he should have allowed spontaneity to escape from itself and, furthermore, from every determination which attempts to identify its essence) follows naturally from this third claim.

There are here several presuppositions that Sartre must defend in order to support his objection. There is, first, a claim concerning the type of spontaneity which belongs to the for-itself. There is, then, a claim concerning the appropriate way in which this spontaneity can be accounted for, in particular, by avoiding the Kantian idea of a non-temporal freedom.

As mentioned above, the objection is stated within the conceptual framework of Sartre's thought and needs further discussion of the elements of this framework. These will be presented in the next three sections, which focus on Sartre's conceptions of the for-itself, freedom and the solution to the debate between free will theory and determinism. An appropriate account of freedom is essential for the possibility of moral judgement, and it is required by both Kant's and Sartre's responses to the problem raised by Constant.

More generally, I have claimed that, through the comparative analysis of Kant's and Sartre's practical philosophies, we begin to discover elements of a critical ethical theory. I have also said that this critical ethical theory is able to account for the unconditional nature of an obligation, like the obligation to be truthful, while at the same time avoiding dogmatic metaphysics. Obviously, for such a critical ethics, an appropriate account of freedom is essential.

§46. The for-itself's structure

For Sartre, there is a constitutive similarity between self and value (*EN*: 131, 117). The self is for the for-itself, what a value is for our actions. We act in pursuit of certain values – some more distant, such as long-term projects and ideals, some more quickly achievable, such as more immediate goals or the satisfaction of certain desires or needs. Pursuing a value implies bringing about states of affairs which are valued and which are perceived as lacking. Similarly, the for-itself lacks something in relation to the self and constantly attempts to eliminate this lack and achieve the fullness of the self.

Consequently, for Sartre, in relation to the self, the for-itself is a lack, and what the for-itself lacks in order to be self is called the for-itself's possibility (*EN*: 135, 120). An important distinction here is that between the for-itself's possibilities and its mere wishes. Possibilities represent courses of action, which can be physically performed by the for-itself and through which the for-itself attempts to achieve its self. So, possibilities must be physically realizable and, in addition, must be regarded as important by the person whose possibilities they are. Through these possibilities she regards herself as realizing her self, and it is to the realization of the self's fullness that the for-itself aims. By contrast, a wish may have in common with a person's possibility the fact that what the person intends to achieve is valued by her, yet a wish need not refer to a physically realizable action.

An important point here is that the relationship between person, world and possibilities is not one in which a person wakes up in a world already constituted and tries to discern her possibilities, as these are already inscribed in the nature of things. A person's relationship to the world is not prior to her possibilities. As we have seen, for Sartre, a person cannot be conceived outside of the world and indeed is already in a relationship to the world. Moreover, her possibilities are constituted in the process through which person and world constitute each other in their relations of mutual dependence.

This, however, does not mean that a person can project her possibilities in an arbitrary way, since a person's relation to the world presupposes a world which is not created by the person (even though it is not constituted independently from the person either). It is in this sense that a person is not simply a nihilating being, a being that can radically question and evaluate herself, but she is also similar to the world:

> The for-itself *is*, in the manner of an event, in the sense in which I can say that Philip II *has been*, that my friend Pierre is, exists. The for-itself *is*, in so far as it appears in a condition which it has not chosen, as Pierre *is* a French bourgeois in 1942, as Schmitt *was* a Berlin worker in 1870 [...]. It [the for-itself] *is* in so far as there is in it something of which it is not the foundation – its *presence to the world*.
>
> (*EN:* 117–18, 103)

On Sartre's account, therefore, a person's relation to the world involves certain conditions, which are associated with the person's place in the world and which frame the person's situation. These conditions constitute her presence to the world. Even though they are not determined by her presence to the world, a person's possibilities are nevertheless *conditioned* by the world. The world is not entirely the result of the for-itself's choice – for instance, the for-itself's birthplace is not chosen by the for-itself, but the for-itself can refer to it in various ways and attribute to this fact various meanings.

The difference between a project and a mere wish makes apparent the fact that a person's projects start to emerge with the same reflexive movement which institutes her presence to the world. A mere wish need not be physically realizable in order to remain a wish; by contrast, as I have mentioned, a project or possibility has to be physically performable. What is more, although a person needs to act in order to realize her projects, what she can realize is always conditioned by the situation which she is already in.[1] Hence, the world conditions her.

Sartre calls this conditioning aspect of my presence to the world "facticity" (*EN:* 121, 107). Like the presence to self, value and possibility, facticity is an element of the structure of the for-itself, an element which arises at the pre-reflective level of consciousness.[2] For Sartre, the world is always given from the perspective of a self as the for-itself's value. My possibility, as the missing for-itself in my quest for the self, is absent or yet to be achieved. Nevertheless, to the extent that my possibility arises at the level of the presence to self, it is present.

This is what Sartre calls the "absent-presence" of my possibility.[3] My possibilities are non-positionally and non-reflectively present to consciousness: the world appears to me as a complex of entities, and my perception of the world has meaning because it is in a certain relation to my possibilities; nonetheless what I perceive positionally is the complex of things, not my possibilities.[4] Reflective consciousness makes my possibilities explicit by self-reflection. Reflective consciousness tries to determine what I am lacking, what I need to achieve in order to obtain the fullness of self. Hence, reflective consciousness comes as a further attempt on the part of the for-itself to acquire identity.[5] If the for-itself lacks its possibilities in order to achieve the fullness of the self, reflection is one further way in which it can determine itself, its possibilities and how to bring itself from the stage of a lacking for-itself to that of self-sufficiency.

Self-sufficiency is the stage where the for-itself achieves independence, since it becomes its own foundation: it becomes at the same time an in-itself, which is not lacking, since it simply is, and a for-itself, which alone is able to make sense of things, such as lack, sufficiency and value. This is why Sartre sometimes calls this ideal of a self-sufficient, full self, the "in-itself-for-itself"; since it is an ideal, to achieve it will necessarily be an unsuccessful attempt.[6] Thus, for Sartre, "this effort to be itself its own foundation, to recover and to dominate within itself its own flight [...] – this effort inevitably results in failure; and it is precisely this failure which is reflection" (*EN*: 193, 176–7).

So, at this point, we have the main constitutive elements of the for-itself: possibility, facticity and reflection. In the next section, I will focus specifically on reflection, before moving on to discuss Sartre's account of freedom.

§47. Reflection

I have mentioned that, on Sartre's account, reflection is a further attempt on the part of the for-itself to achieve identity, in the form of a full self or as the ideal of an in-itself-for-itself. Through reflection, the for-itself transforms its possibilities into a consciousness reflected-on and transforms itself into a reflecting consciousness. This immediate reflecting consciousness will then be a reflection of its own possibilities. But, as reflecting consciousness, the for-itself needs to posit its reflected possibilities as objects of reflection and, thus, becomes distinct from them. There is a necessary negation in the reflective process, since, in order to reflect its possibilities, consciousness must distance itself from these possibilities.[7]

As a result, reflection introduces in the for-itself a deeper separation than the one brought about by the pre-reflective cogito. The *reflective* process brings about a consciousness reflected-on and a reflective consciousness, each of them being conscious (of) itself. Hence reflection separates the person in two types of consciousness, each having the structure of a person's consciousness. As Sartre notes, this situation "may be best compared to a man who is writing, bent over a table, and who while writing knows that he is observed by somebody who stands behind him" (*EN*: 191–2, 175).

Of course, reflection cannot actually yield interpersonal relations, since it is a process which takes place in one consciousness and which is triggered by a for-itself. But it is a step forward towards the interpersonal (as we will see, an ontological dimension that Sartre calls "being-for-others") from the level of the pre-reflective cogito:

> Thus reflection (reflexion) as an effort of a for-itself to recover a for-itself which it is in the mode of non-being is a stage of nihilation intermediate between the pure and simple existence of the for-itself and the existence of *for-others* [...].
>
> (*EN*: 194, 177)

Even though they are reflected on as distinct objects, the person's possibilities do not have the ontological status of being-in-itself, but that of being-for-itself. Hence, the process of reflection does not simply amount to an epistemic process, whereby an object is perceived in the world; the possibilities of the for-itself are *recognized* by reflective consciousness: "Reflection is limited to making this revelation exist for-itself; the revealed being is not revealed as a given but with the character of the 'already revealed'. Reflection is a recognition rather than knowledge" (*EN*: 195, 178).

Hence, on Sartre's account, possibilities are foreshadowed at the stage of the original project, they become known or, at least, the for-itself becomes familiar with them given its pre-reflective cogito, and they are also recognized and more specifically determined through reflection. If the consciousness reflected-on represents the for-itself as lacking or (if we go back to the discussion of value in Section 46 above) as perceiving its situation as lacking and to be improved, then among the objects of reflection we will also find the for-itself's possibilities. When these possibilities are reflected on, they are synthesized.

As we have seen in Part I, the numerical identity which constitutes the person makes possible the synthesis, which creates the possibility of the person, that is, the possible courses of action that the person can pursue towards the realization of her values. In the interaction between persons, not only do we regard these possibilities as possibilities, but sometimes we also take them to stand for objective requirements transcending us and given to us. Similarly, we turn the actions of others into "acts": not expressions of their possibilities, but transcending requirements which we perceive as obstacles in the realization of our projects.

Thus, on Sartre's account, such acts are the level on which "concrete relations between men are established – claims, jealousies, grudges, suggestions, struggles, ruses, etc" (*EN*: 198, 181). Each of these presupposes a representation of "our person as a transcendent psychic unity" (*EN*: 201, 185). A person's transcendent psychic unity represents an important aspect of the for-itself.[8]

Although this is not an "essential" aspect of a person, since it is derived from the other personalizing outlooks (for instance, from that of the self[9]), it is significant for issues concerning freedom and moral deliberation. Most importantly, the reduction of a person to such a psychic unity leads to a consideration of this person as devoid of freedom and, hence, also as inappropriate for consideration as a moral agent. On Sartre's account, such a reductive move takes place through a certain type of reflection.

Reflection is, for Sartre, of two types. Impure reflection posits the consciousness reflected-on as an object having the ontological structure of an in-itself. This, however, is not a legitimate process, since the consciousness reflected-on is at the same time self-consciousness. Impure reflection attempts to cognize the consciousness reflected-on, and not simply to recognize it as already revealed.

The consciousness reflected on by impure reflection is thus transformed into an object of psychic life. For instance, actions are the result of a synthesis, since each action requires time in order to be realized, and it has various stages corresponding to various non-reflective consciousnesses. Impure reflective consciousness focuses on these consciousnesses and not only apprehends the action as a unity, but posits it as a transcendent unity.

The unification performed by impure reflective consciousness posits a particular end of the action as given. Every act is the result of a synthesis of different consciousnesses reflected-on. Acts are the result of impure reflection and since they are not only the results of a synthesis of various consciousnesses reflected-on, impure reflective consciousness also turns them into transcending units.

> By acts we must understand all synthetic activity of the person, that is, every disposition of means with a view to ends, not as the for-itself is its own possibilities but as the act represents a transcendent psychic synthesis which the for-itself must live. For example, the boxer's training is an act because it transcends and supports the for-itself, which, moreover, realizes itself in and through this training.
>
> (*EN*: 202, 185)

Hence, impure reflection synthesizes and objectifies the result, losing sight of the for-itself, whose possibilities are in this way turned into necessities. Therefore, on the level of the act constituted as an object by impure reflective consciousness, my freedom is simply that of realizing the already given ends. On the level of impure consciousness the person's sensible desires, emotions and beliefs are objects that are causally determined by other objects. Hence, one does not actually realize an end, or does not attempt to realize it, but is determined (causally led) to attempt to realize it. Therefore, whether one talks about a free action or about an action determined by certain causes, it *seems* to be the same.

It is by its reaction to the constraining effects of impure reflection that existentialism has acquired the reputation of a philosophy of absolute freedom. The next sections will attempt to offer a more balanced view of the role of freedom in Sartre's thought. This will complement the conceptual background necessary for the understanding of Sartre's objection to Kant's view of spontaneity, from which we started in this Chapter.

§48. Freedom

'Existentialism' is sometimes used as a label standing for the affirmation of absolute freedom.[10] If this were correct, Sartre's existentialist account would not only be implausible,[11] but also quite different from Kant's. In the following sections, I will investigate Sartre's view of freedom and probe the standard interpretation of existentialism. One question mark which can already be raised about the standard interpretation of existentialism is offered by Sartre's comment that what he means when he claims that a prisoner is free is not that he could walk out of prison as he wishes at whatever moment. In this sense, Sartre adds, a person is not free.

The sense of 'freedom' presupposed in this context, that is, the sense in which it is correct to say the prisoner is not free, is that of freedom as the successful realization of one's purposes. In other words, the sign of a person's being free is the realization of the goals of her action(s); she is not free when she cannot bring to fruition whatever her actions aim to realize. This is problematic, however, since a person's goals are sometimes realized by chance, whether or not she is free and whether or not she can act to bring about their realization. Given that this sense of freedom is implausible and is rejected by Sartre anyway, perhaps what he has in view when he talks about freedom is the setting of purposes, rather than their realization.

But the mere setting of a purpose cannot be freedom either. For we are not free simply when we wish that something happened; an action seems to be required in addition to the intention to act. An action represents the attempt to change a situation, and is performed by taking into account the circumstances of the situation. As we have seen, in §6, where we have distinguished between wishes and possibilities, a wish is simply a longing for something and may not be accompanied by an attempt to devise a possible course of action that would be able to fulfil the wish. In fact, a wish may even be unrealizable. So this sense of freedom seems also implausible and seems to be implicitly rejected by Sartre.

Indeed, on his account, 'freedom' applies to actions, not to imagination:

> Thus we shall not say that a prisoner is always free to go out of prison, which would be absurd, nor that he is always free to long for release, which would be an irrelevant truism, but that he is always free to try to escape (or get himself liberated); that is, that whatever his condition may be, he can project his escape and learn the value of his project by undertaking some action.
>
> (*EN*: 540, 505)

So, Sartre suggests here that neither success nor the mere capacity to wish is a sufficient condition of freedom. Moreover, even devising a project is not sufficient as a manifestation of a person's freedom – a concrete project is not very different from a dream or a wish until it is put into practice. This is why, although for Sartre freedom is "the autonomy of choice", it is not simply a capacity or power to choose; choice, "being identical with acting, supposes a commencement of realisation in order that the choice may be distinguished from the dream and the wish" (*EN*: 540, 505).

To define freedom as a capacity to choose would be to separate it from the action, namely to say that that person who had that capacity would be free – whether or not she would make use of it. By contrast, on Sartre's account, "freedom [...] determines itself by its very upsurge as a 'doing'" (*EN*: 542, 507). In short, a person's freedom is not simply success, desire to realize a certain goal or even the capacity to realize it.

Freedom refers to an action a person undertakes in order to realize some goal. But, if acting is necessary for freedom, so must be the capacity to act and, in a sense, also success. Without success, either the person was hindered in her action and could not realize its goal, in which case she was not free, or she did not set that goal as her goal to begin with, in which case the question of freedom does not arise. At the same time, as we have seen, for Sartre, success, capacity to act and even action are not sufficient conditions of freedom either.

In the last part of *Being and Nothingness*, Sartre emphasizes that he is not interested in the concept of freedom advanced by "common sense", namely, "the popular concept of freedom" (*EN*: 540, 505) and "the practical concept of freedom" (*EN*: 542, 507). We have seen that he rejects as irrelevant the concept of freedom as "the ability to obtain the ends chosen" (*EN*: 540, 505), which I take to be what he means by the popular notion. He also rejects the "wholly negative" notion whereby "we can be free only in relation to a state of things and in spite of this state of things", probably the practical notion (*EN*: 542, 507). This is, in fact, also what Sartre calls, in the first part of *Being and Nothingness*, "empirical" freedom. More exactly, he defines it as "the nihilation of man in the heart of temporality and [...] the necessary condition for the transcending apprehension of *négatités*" (*EN*: 80, 68).

Some of the terms used here need further explanation. Thus, let us assume that the situation in which freedom seems most obviously involved is that in which a person acts against circumstances, against the interests, desires, inclinations that are prompted by current circumstances and against the facts which favour the realization of certain goals and hinder the realization of others. But the intention to act in this way can appear to a person only if she can detach herself from her present and past, which determine such inclinations, interests or needs, and constitute a future situation as a *desideratum* (*EN*: 488, 456), that is, regard a situation which does not exist yet as desirable in some sense.

It is only because the person transcends her present situation towards the desideratum that she can apprehend the former as *lacking*, as *not* being satisfactory in relation to the desirable situation. This is the reason why the current situation regarded from the perspective of the *desideratum* is perceived as lacking, as unsatisfactory. The term *"négatité"* stands for that situation, which has negative features, for instance, an unsatisfying state of affairs which appears as lacking.[12]

The freedom to stand out from the current situation and from past experiences is only "empirical", because, after all, even the desirable end, the *desideratum*, may be an expression of a constraint when the end is imposed or already set. To the extent that freedom is confined to this empirical form of acting against circumstances, freedom is easily replaceable with causality. For desires can be read as psychic objects caused by various circumstances, hence, the *desideratum* may well be an effect of circumstances.

Consequently, empirical freedom can only be understood as freedom by presupposing a freedom which goes beyond the fact of having an end as a *desideratum*. Sartre needs, therefore, to take on a new task, that of "found[ing] this empirical freedom" (*EN*: 80, 68). As a form of freedom, empirical freedom needs a grounding, which I will call 'ontological' freedom. The next section will focus on this form of freedom and on the task Sartre sets for himself, of founding empirical freedom on ontological freedom.

§49. Freedom and determinism

On Sartre's account, freedom is indissolubly related to constraint.[13] If correct, this view offers additional ammunition against the popular view of freedom (as the realization of, perhaps, even the ability to obtain the chosen ends), for any constraint that would limit such an ability or actual realization would be seen as a constraint on the person's freedom (in the popular sense). Hence, on this account, freedom and constraint would be mutually exclusive, rather than indissolubly related.

In contrast to popular freedom, empirical freedom suggests the indissoluble relation between freedom and constraints. Empirical freedom depends on the apprehension of the present situation and past conditions as *négatités*. The very notion of *desideratum*, which, as we have seen, is presupposed by that of *négatité*, only makes sense in the context of constraints. If there are no obstacles or constraints in reaching what is desirable, then we no longer have an object of desire but are already enjoying its possession and no desire is appropriate at that point. This shows again that empirical freedom can be a genuine form of freedom, although, as I have shown, it needs to be grounded in ontological freedom.

If constraints, *per se*, are not an obstacle to freedom, then there is no point in trying to show freedom exists by identifying a situation where there are no constraints. In fact, for Sartre, it is precisely this attempt which keeps alive the spurious dispute between the advocates of determinism and those of free will. This dispute is quite similar to that between the dogmatist and empiricist in Kant's Third Antinomy:

> Thus at the outset we can see what is lacking in those tedious discussions between determinists and the proponents of free will. The latter are concerned to find cases of decision for which there exists no prior cause, or deliberations concerning two opposed acts which are equally possible and possess causes (and motives) of exactly the same weight. To which the determinists may easily reply that there is no action without a *cause* and that the most insignificant gesture (raising the right hand rather than the left hand, *etc.*) refers to causes and motives which confer its meaning upon it.
>
> (*EN*: 490–1, 458)

Sartre approaches this debate by showing that it is an illusion to try to look for an uncaused cause and also that it is an illusion to think that an action with its associated commitment can be physically determined. Neither the free-will theorist nor the determinist has any chances of demonstrating their respective view. To see Sartre's response to this "antinomy" between determinism and free-will, consider first his conception of action already foreshadowed by the earlier discussion of empirical freedom.[14]

A consciously performed action tries to bring about a change in the world. On Sartre's account, the action is *motivated* by the desire or, in general, willingness to bring about that change.[15] The intention to make a change stems from the dissatisfaction with the current situation of the world. This dissatisfaction with the current arrangement of the world felt as intolerable,[16] which prompts the agent to act, is the *cause* of action;[17] however, as we have seen, when a certain situation becomes intolerable, it is felt in this way against the backdrop of an ideal situation, a situation which appears as the most desirable. The action tries to bring about a change in the current situation so as to bring it closer to the projected ideal situation.[18]

We could say that the ideal situation is the end towards which the action is directed; from the perspective of the person's project of realizing the end, the current situation is apprehended as having to be changed, and this constitutes the cause of his action. The unsatisfactory character of the present situation offers the person the motive of action – this is the ground for the choice of acting in that particular way, rather than in another one. The project, the end, the cause and the motive represent for Sartre the constitutive elements of action.[19]

Thus defined, the cause of an action cannot determine the action; on the contrary, the cause is possible only insofar as there is a project of an action from the perspective of which the current state of the world is perceived as intolerable and as having-to-be-changed. We can see, therefore, why, on

Sartre's account, "the cause, far from determining the action, appears only in and through the project of an action" (*EN*: 503, 470). We can take subjective incentives as factors which determine an action only if we posit them as transcendent objects having the same ontological status as the non-conscious things in the world (in-itself). Yet, even when conceived as objects, subjective incentives can be seen as constraints which are compatible with freedom.

For, if the motive is transcendent, then it can have no necessarily occurring effect on the agent, since the agent is separated from it and may or may not choose to adopt it. The motive has the necessary force of producing a certain effect only to the extent that the for-itself projects itself as willing to act on the basis of that motive. The motive

> can act only if it is *recovered*; in itself it is without force. It is therefore by the very thrust of the engaged consciousness that a value and weight will be conferred on motives and on prior causes. What they have been does not depend on consciousness, but consciousness has the duty of maintaining them in their existence in the past.
>
> (*EN*: 505, 472)

The point is, therefore, that *actions cannot be determined*: if something is an action, then we should be able to talk about its end, cause and motive. And yet, cause and motive only exist if the agent is committed to their corresponding end; an action cannot be determined by a physical cause either, since it must be performed by an agent who must be committed to the end which constitutes the action's cause and motive.

To be sure, this view of freedom accommodates a situation where, against her will, an agent may be determined to act in a particular way. If I am forced to hold a gun in my hand, for instance, to point it to an innocent bystander and to pull the trigger, I am determined to act in a way which I find reprehensible, to say the least, and which assumes a motive I have no intention of committing myself to. The case of the agent who makes certain physical movements, because she is forced to make them, movements which resemble a particular action, is not the case of a person performing an action, but of an agent being determined to move in a particular way.

Moreover, this view of freedom does not deny that, sometimes, an agent may act in ways she herself finds reprehensible even when there is no external force which moves her directly to perform those actions. Although nobody forces me directly to hold a gun in my hand and shoot, I might do this if I know this will save my life or if, under special circumstances, only in this way I am able to avoid a deeply miserable life. What Sartre says does not even deny situations where I act in ways which I used to consider reprehensible, but which I no longer see as such, because I have a short memory.

Having clarified his view of action and of free action, we can briefly return to Sartre's critique of the positions adopted by free-will theorists and determinists in their dispute over freedom. His claim is that freedom of action cannot be proven by finding an uncaused cause or an uncaused commitment; nor can our lack of freedom be demonstrated by showing that all actions have causes. The mental experiment of imagining an action performed for no reason or performed after a decision which picked out one action at random, out of several alternatives supported by equally strong reasons, cannot be used to prove freedom. An action done for no reason is no action, but perhaps a movement; an action performed on purpose at random is an action done with the intention of illustrating something or for the sake of acting.

These cases can be used to show the importance of commitment in action. Hence, if freedom is sought, then it must be sought as a particular type of commitment, not as the absence of commitment. But what kind of commitment does freedom require? This will be a topic to which I will return shortly. For the moment, the more important question concerns Sartre's objection to Kant's account of freedom and the implications we can draw from it for the comparison between them. This will be the theme of the next section.

§50. The eternal subject

Let us now return to Sartre's objection, according to which Kant's account of freedom is inappropriate, since it remains contradictory in spite of Kant's claim to the contrary. The discussion of freedom and of the structure of the for-itself in the previous sections have made clear several respects in which Kant's and Sartre's accounts of freedom are similar. If we go back to Chapter 3, where Kant's view of the Third Antinomy and his account of freedom were presented, we can see that both philosophers distinguish between two main types of freedom (practical and transcendental/'ontological'), they both take one of these to be more fundamental than, and to ground, the other, and they both question the assumptions on the basis of which the classical debate between free-will theory and determinism emerges.

As we have seen, in the Third Antinomy, Kant starts by giving the dogmatist and the empiricist the benefit of the doubt. Since the conclusions of their arguments are contradictory, however, we have to explain away this contradiction somehow. Kant's solution starts from the distinction between things in themselves and phenomena. A contradiction only emerges, Kant claims, when this distinction is blurred. Once we identify clearly when we are talking about things in themselves and when about phenomena, and once we keep this distinction in place, the contradiction evaporates.

Yet, Sartre maintains that a contradiction can still be identified in Kant's account of freedom. As we have seen in the previous chapter, on

Kant's account, transcendental freedom is possible as a *sui generis* causality operating at the level of things in themselves. This means that, as Sartre suggests, Kant does indeed allow a non-temporal spontaneity in his account of freedom. Yet, this non-temporal spontaneity must also be unchangeable and impossible to be identified and cognized (since it is beyond phenomena), and, as a result, it appears as an eternal subject, which cannot be identified and cannot become a determination (a predicate) or some other thing (the subject).

Such a spontaneity becomes similar to an affirmative essence. Yet, the idea of an unchanging, eternal essence contradicts the open-ended character of spontaneity, which should in principle be able to escape any fixed account and to express freedom. As we have seen in Chapter 2 and in the previous sections of this chapter, Sartre's objection is formulated from the perspective of his account of consciousness (of) self or reflexivity, which makes possible a person's separation from her situation and conditioning factors. To assume that there is some feature of the person which is immune to change means to deny precisely the person's freedom or at least part of her freedom and also to deny her spontaneity.

In fact, however, Kant's account would not suffer from Sartre's objection; if anything, Kant himself would formulate such an objection to appropriate targets. As we have seen in Chapter 3, Kant's account of practical freedom is precisely the account of freedom as enabling the person to act against conditioning factors. More generally, when Kant talks about transcendental freedom, as we have seen in the previous chapter, he offers only a negative account of freedom as independence from the constraints of natural causality and also offers a mode of *thinking* about the agent that is free in this sense as a *sui generis* form of causality. However, Kant is equally clear that this form of causality is quite distinct from the natural causality with which we are familiar, and he says explicitly that we cannot cognize this type of free agent. Hence, our thoughts about the free agent and her spontaneity do not and cannot claim to identify some features which would characterize the agent beyond the realm of phenomena.

Kant would agree with Sartre that the spontaneity of the agent should not be congealed in a fixed denomination, such as that of an eternal subject that is never a predicate. This, for Kant, would also be a contradiction, since it would amount to using a priori categories of the understanding (substance/accident is what Sartre's subject/predicate pair stands for) to characterize a thing in itself.

Now, Sartre is right: Kant does talk about the free agent as a cause bringing about a series of causes and effects in the phenomenal world. Yet Kant talks in terms of causes without making any claim to cognition. The use of the notion of cause only has the purpose of making sense of the free agency of the person; it is a way of *thinking* about freedom while at the same time denying the possibility of any *cognition* of spontaneity or free agency.

It is possible, however, to introduce a further complication, which enables an even more generous interpretation of Sartre's objection and, hence, a reading which is more challenging for Kant's account. As we have seen, like Kant, Sartre acknowledges that the reply of the determinist, according to which every action can be accounted for through the principle of causality, mistakenly leads to the challenge of finding an action which is performed in the absence of causes and constraints. This supports, for Kant, the view that freedom, in this sense, can only have its source in the transphenomenal realm.

Now, Sartre does not reject the idea of a transphenomenal realm, yet, following Husserl and Heidegger, he thinks such a realm is epistemically not different from the phenomenal realm. For them, things in themselves are the things themselves.[20] Whereas the being of phenomena is transphenomenal, in the sense that it is not reducible to the being of conscious states, yet, whatever cognition we have of phenomena, it is also going to be cognition of these phenomena as they are in themselves.

The implication of this epistemological assumption is that to talk about things in themselves in terms which are appropriate for phenomena is not a categorical mistake, as it is for Kant. Hence, on this assumption, to regard the spontaneous agent as an eternal subject which cannot be a predicate can no longer be rejected as an inappropriate use of the categories of the understanding.

Let me put this in a different way: Sartre may acknowledge that Kant's aim is to defend transcendental idealism and to suggest the importance of the distinction between things in themselves and phenomena. He may also acknowledge that Kant's intention is to say that thinking about things in themselves in terms appropriate for phenomena is only an attempt to make sense of very significant concepts, such as that of freedom, but involves no claim to cognition. Yet Sartre can still argue that Kant fails to realize his aim and intention, and that by talking about spontaneity in terms of an eternal subject which cannot be a predicate he simply provides an inappropriate account of spontaneity, rather than merely offering us a way of making sense of spontaneity.

Even if this interpretation were correct, the result of Kant's and Sartre's accounts of freedom would be the same: they argue that spontaneity requires freedom from all phenomenal determinations and they both argue against an attempt to account for freedom in terms which would in fact limit the agent's scope of decision and choice. The disagreement is therefore moved from the metaphysical and moral questions of freedom to the epistemological question of the cognition of things in themselves.

Thus, as far as Sartre's objection to Kant's account of freedom is concerned, we have another structural similarity between their accounts or, more exactly, between their views of freedom. The issue of the possibility of cognizing things in themselves is a problem which, as I have already mentioned, goes beyond the scope of this book. So, it is now time to focus on the second Sartrean objection. Presenting and evaluating this will be the tasks of the next sections, as well as some sections of Chapter 6.[21]

§51. Singularity

So let us now move on to the second objection or, more exactly, to the second set of objections Sartre formulates against Kant in the *Notebooks for an Ethics* (*CM*). This book is the result of Sartre's work on the project of an ethical theory announced at the end of *Being and Nothingness*. The project was never completed and it was only published posthumously. Moreover, as we will see, Sartre changed his view of the type of ethical theory he wanted to formulate by the time he finished the *Critique of Dialectical Reason* (*CRDI*). Nevertheless, his objections to Kant that I have discussed so far and that I will discuss in what follows continue to be relevant even from the perspective of Sartre's later ethical thought.

For Sartre, Kant's ethical system has several features that are characteristic for an "analytic" ethics (*CM*: 95, 88). From the very beginning this claim may be confusing, especially given the discussion in the previous chapter of Kant's claim that the notion of the complete good is not the result of an analytic relation between the concepts of virtue and happiness. Yet "analytic" here stands for something else.

Sartre traces the origins of analytic morality back to the second half of the eighteenth century and the beginning of the nineteenth century, when people became increasingly separated from their concrete community and projected themselves towards a universal human community, in which all individuals were the same abstract person. In this way, the totality of a concrete community was denied to the benefit of individual units that nevertheless sought to realize another communal totality (*CM*: 95, 88).

On this new model, ethics becomes universal and abstract precisely because the abstract community that a person came to relate himself to is nothing but an infinite repetition of himself; ethical imperatives are transformed into precepts addressed to the same abstract persons. Because persons are deemed the same, actions and circumstances are regarded as the same, and analytic ethics asks questions in an inappropriate form, namely: what ought one to do in that particular situation? (*CM*: 52, 46). This type of question makes the assumption that human conduct is a reaction to events that are already invested with meaning, independently of the person's fundamental projects. Circumstances of the situation are selected from among those which, in order to be equally applicable to all, tend to be abstract, separated from specific details.

In this way, devoid of particular features, the situation becomes equally applicable to all, but also equally irrelevant for all. Thus morality is transformed into a set of precepts, imperatives that command particular actions;

it becomes a code, a morality (understood as a code) of imperatives (*CM*: 52, 46–7). Hence, insofar as imperatival rules of action are formulated for abstract persons and situations, Kant's categorical imperatives are not useful when concrete situations and the singularity of the persons concerned are considered (*CM*: 441–2, 426).

This understanding of Sartre's objection to Kant implicitly attributes to Sartre a certain reading of Kant. The assumption is that Sartre regards Kant's ethics as a set of rules, which prescribe for each type of situation the action which ought to be performed; however, Sartre could also be interpreted here differently. We can read him as objecting to a conception of ethics which is more sophisticated than the rule-based construal I have just presented.

The idea, in this case, is that Kantian ethics does not do so much as to formulate *rules* which dictate how one ought to perform every particular action, but devises a set of *principles* for each significant situation, principles starting from which a person would deduce rules of action for his singular circumstances. On this second construal, Kant's moral theory would still reflect an analytic character,[22] since it would still regard morality as a matter of devising rules for each morally relevant situation. However, the account which emerges is less abstract and better able to guide action and, in this way, Sartre's reading is closer to Kant's texts and his objection, more interesting.

Thus, on this reading, we can still assume that Kant formulated categorical imperatives in order to determine, for *paradigmatic* situations, the purpose or goal to be pursued by a person. Moreover, we can accept that, for Kant, rules of action had to be deduced by each person, starting from the imperative, which would correspond to her situation, and paying attention to her singular circumstances.

But, even in this case, for Sartre, the ethical demand made by an imperative would pertain to an abstract universalism and, for this reason, would be deprived of any practical force. In this case, Kant's ethics would be an ethics which could not guide concrete actions and, because these are the actions that we perform, "Kantianism does not teach us anything" (*CM*: 14, 7).

An ethical imperative represents an ethical demand. The object of the demand is the purpose, the realization of which is commanded by the imperative. But, Sartre adds, this purpose is posited unconditionally with the stipulation that no actual circumstance may be an excuse for not realizing it (*CM*: 146, 138). The person, however, Sartre says, cannot be separated from the actual circumstances in which she lives, and therefore the categorical imperative posits the goal as essential, whereas the concrete person is deemed inessential. On Sartre's reading, this contrast is intensified in Kant, since an imperative does not only command against the circumstances in which a person is, it also commands against the sensible characteristics of the person (sentiments, sensible desires, feelings).

In fact, the categorical imperative expressing the ethical demand presupposes the freedom of an abstract individual from his situation and addresses itself to freedom. Yet, Sartre says, the freedom addressed is not freedom as generosity, which "penetrates" the circumstances of the concrete situation, but a "purely negative freedom that affirms itself against the concrete man I am" (*CM*: 146, 138). Further points of apparent disagreement between Kant and Sartre will be presented in the next section.

§52. Ethical normativity

We have seen that, even on the more sophisticated interpretation, the Kantian analytic ethics would still be conceived of as a code; it would, however, be one of particular principles and not of more specific rules of action. The freedom affirmed by such a moral code would be based on the destruction of a person's concreteness and singularity, since it would rely on the assumption that the features of persons and their situations are reducible to a set of paradigmatic cases for which the principles belonging to the code can appropriately regulate from an ethical point of view. What remains of the concrete individual, Sartre continues, is his pure, universal freedom, which is the same in him as in all the others (*CM*: 147, 139).

In *Being and Nothingness*, Sartre claims that Kant's ethical system is the first great ethical system of doing (*EN*: 485, 453–4). From the perspective of the *Notebooks*, this claim is one of appreciation, since here Sartre defines ethics as a theory of action. But he immediately adds that "action is abstract if it is not work and struggle" (*CM*: 24, 17), by which he means that the action needs to incorporate the particular social and historical circumstances which give its concreteness and of which it is an expression. For Sartre, Kant's ethical theory accurately focuses on action, as the proper *topos* of ethics, but fails to direct its focus further towards concrete practical contexts.

Perhaps Kant can escape this objection, perhaps his ethical system is able to account for the singular, or at least particular, character of concrete persons, circumstances and situations. This would still leave his account of normativity open to at least another objection that Sartre formulates in the *Notebooks*. Thus, for Sartre, a demand is expressed by a morally valid imperative,[23] and he identifies as a necessary aspect of the demand its interpersonal character (*CM*: 263, 256). In Kant's ethics, however, valid imperatives are understood as those imperatives which enable individuals to be free.

The sense of freedom appropriate here is of a third type, distinct from the practical and transcendental/'ontological' notions. Freedom in this third sense is the notion of autonomy or self-legislation. This implies that ethically valid imperatives are self-imposed rules which have the source of normativity in the person herself. In addition, this suggests that Kant overlooks the interpersonal character of demand and tries to replace it with a sort of intrapersonal test (the moral law as an expression of a person's autonomy).

If Sartre were right, Kant's account of imperatives would seem to be a form of bad faith or, more exactly, a form of a person's impure reflection

(*EN*: 192–4, 175–7). This further objection seems to offer more serious grounds for criticism. In the next sections, I will present in more detail Sartre's account of bad faith and an example of conduct in bad faith. At this point, suffice it to say that, on Sartre's account, in Kant, we are dealing with an illicit reduction of an interpersonal relationship to an intrapersonal connection between two parts of the same reflecting consciousness. This will obviously mean that Kant will not only have an inappropriate account of interpersonal relations, but also of imperatives.

Given all this, it is not surprising that Sartre subscribes to the standard accusation that Kant is an individualist. Yet, surprisingly, Sartre seems to object to this view, given his superficial reading of this aspect of Kant. Moreover, individualism seems to be one of the few common aspects between Kant's moral theory and Sartre's existentialism. To show that the ethical demand represented by an imperative presupposes an interpersonal relationship, Sartre contrasts the normative force of an imperative with the ideal character of a value.

According to Sartre, there are two features of a demand that cannot be accounted for in terms of the defining characteristics of values. First, a demand involves a claim that I obey the corresponding imperative, which subjects me to a command that I realize the imperative's end or purpose. Secondly, a demand imposes on me a duty to realize an end without, however, requiring that I make it "*be* as an end"; in other words, whether or not I adopt this end, I am under an obligation to realize it (*CM*: 261, 250).

Here it may be useful to clarify the second characteristic by distinguishing it from the standard view that juridical imperative or norms can be obeyed without the person's being motivated to act by the imperative's rightness. What Sartre says here about ethical imperatives is different. He does not say that ethical imperatives can be followed without the agent's making their rightness the reason for her actions. He only says that the normative force of the ethical imperative does not depend on the norm's being adopted by the agent: the imperative has the same normative force even when the agent does not adopt it as maxim of her action; she is still under the obligation of this maxim, even if she, say, chooses to ignore it.

By contrast, the projection of a value is in fact the choice of one of my possibilities as an end to be realized. From the perspective of my end, the world is revealed as a set of tools for the realization of the end, and the perception of the world as a set of tools, which are necessary for the realization of my end, reveals my end as valuable (*CM*: 250–1, 240). The end is not a purpose to which I am a means, but it is my possibility, in the pursuit of which I can realize myself by means of, and against, the world (*CM*: 256, 246). As soon as my possibility is no longer revealed to me as an ideal (either because it appears as impossible, or because it is overshadowed by another ideal), it disappears as an end for my action (*CM*: 258–9, 248).

On the contrary, the purpose established by a demand exists independently from my choices and transforms me into a means for its realization. A duty or an obligation is my duty or obligation even if I fail to recognize it as such. Hence, according to Sartre, the demand of an imperative cannot be grounded in the individual person, but can only emerge through the other person (*CM*: 261, 250).

We now have a general view of Sartre's objections to Kant's account of normativity. For an evaluation of these objections, we need, however, a deeper understanding of these objections. As I have mentioned above, starting with the next section, I will present in more detail some of the fundamental concepts Sartre uses in his criticism of Kant.

§53. Impure reflection

The normative source of demand, Sartre states, is not duty as universal and unconditional; on the contrary, it is in the demand of a person vis-à-vis another that duty finds its origin (*CM*: 248, 238). Kant may reply that a categorical imperative is not necessarily dependent for its validity on an interpersonal relation. He can argue for this validity as grounded in the freedom (autonomy) of the person. We have seen that, in the performance of an ethically worthy action, a person's will is determined by the lawgiving form of a universalizable maxim. In this sense, the will is beyond the sensible world of experience and can find a determining ground only in its own law. Sartre acknowledges this argument, but claims that:

> The freedom that for Kant upholds the categorical imperative is noumenal therefore the freedom of another. It is separated by that slight stream of nothingness which suffices so that I *am not it*. It is the projection of the Other in the noumenal world. There is a demand only through another freedom.
>
> (*CM*: 147, 139)

Sartre's claim here connects the discussion with the comments (in §50) on his view of transphenomenality and the difference one can note in this respect from Kant; however, my emphasis here is not so much on the distinct aspects of Kant's and Sartre's positions, but on Sartre's view of transphenomenality. I will discuss this issue in relation to the alleged interpersonal character of ethical imperatives in §60. For the moment, let me begin a more detailed presentation of Sartre's account of impure reflection and interpersonal relations.

If one does not have the degree of consciousness necessary to acknowledge the contingency of one's fundamental project, that is, the fact that the original project is the result of a free choice, then one is in bad faith. For

Sartre, a person is initially in bad faith, because she judges her actions, ends and states of mind on the basis of impure reflection. He draws the distinction between pure and impure reflection on the plane of reflective consciousness, which is, as we have seen in Chapter 2, the third important aspect of the for-itself's consciousness.

I have briefly presented Sartre's distinction between pure and impure reflection at the beginning of this chapter.[24] We have seen that, by impure reflection, a person does not simply posit her possibilities as a conscious-ness reflected-on, but she regards them as ontologically in-itself, as objects enmeshed in the causal determination of the non-conscious objects of the world. By contrast, pure reflection is a condition of impure reflection; it is "the original form of reflection and its ideal form", and "must be won by a sort of catharsis", since even though it is the original form of reflection, it "is never first *given*" (*EN*: 194, 177–8).

Thus, impure reflective consciousness posits the consciousness reflected-on, which constitutes psychic states, qualities and acts, and, as posited forms of consciousness, these become transcendent. By the same stroke, the Ego as the unifying synthesis of these psychic elements appears also as an object. Even though they are seen as having the ontological status of an in-itself, the psychic elements share in the ontological characteristic of consciousness, which is for-itself. As Sartre puts it:

> Thus participating simultaneously in the in-itself and in the for-itself, psy-chic temporality conceals a contradiction which is never overcome. This should not surprise us. Since psychic temporality is the product of impure reflection, it is natural that it *is made-to-be* [*soi étée*] what it is not and that it is not what it *is made-to-be* [*est-étée*].
>
> (*EN*: 207, 190)

For Sartre, on the level of impure reflection, psychic states and actions are made to be objects whereas ontologically they are not in-itself and, con-sequently, as ontologically for-itself, they are not what they are made to be. This ambiguity pertaining to the psychic states and actions of the indi-vidual invites misinterpretation, in particular it makes easier a determinist construal which underscores the aspect of states and actions, which has the character of being-in-itself. This is because the ambiguity leads to an under-standing of that aspect of the person, which has the status of being-for-itself, as at best a useful way of talking about a person in certain situations.

For instance, to see a desire as caused by other desires or an action as determined by other actions is to deny the freedom of the person and to regard an action as an in-itself caused by another in-itself. A person's freedom becomes then the name ascribed to the fact that a particular set of effects in the world is brought about by that person, and not by another one; at best, it describes a situation in which a person causes an event without being 'externally' constrained. This way of looking at desires or of conceiving of freedom reflects what Sartre calls "bad faith", to which I turn in the next section.

§54. Bad faith

Impure reflection and bad faith are very closely related. Impure reflection is reflection in bad faith and bad faith is an attitude brought about by impure reflection. In other words, impure reflection and bad faith are mutually constitutive. Sartre explicitly denies the deterministic interpretation of the person on the level of impure reflection. The very idea of transforming a psychological state into an object of reflection presupposes the freedom of the for-itself to modify reflectively a consciousness (of) acting into the object of positional consciousness.

Hence, by making use of freedom in order to present an account of agency as devoid of freedom, "this reflection is in bad faith" (*EN*: 201, 187). Sartre makes unrestricted use of his terminology in the following comment about reflection in bad faith:

> To be sure, it appears to cut the bond which unites the reflected-on to the reflective, and it seems to declare that the reflective *is not* the reflected-on in the mode of not being what one is not, at a time when in the original reflective upsurge, the reflective is not the reflected-on in the mode of what one is. But this is only *in order to* recover subsequently the affirmation of identity and to affirm concerning this in-itself that "I am *it*". In a word reflection is in bad faith in so far as it constitutes itself as the revelation of *the object which I make to be me*. But in the second place this more radical nihilation is not a real, metaphysical event. The real event, the third process of nihilation is the *for-others*. Impure reflection is an abortive effort on the part of the for-itself *to be another* while *remaining itself*.
>
> (*EN*: 201, 184)

Sartre starts here from the obvious and undisputed fact that we can have both a difference between two aspects of the same being (the reflective and the reflected-on of the same consciousness) and a difference between two beings (the consciousnesses of two persons). His claim is that impure reflection starts from the first and illicitly assumes the second. The genuine process of transition from an intrapersonal relation of a person to an interpersonal relation to another person, he says at the end, is that which leads the being-for-itself to become the being-for-others. Being-for-others is the third fundamental ontological category introduced by Sartre in *Being and Nothingness*, together with being-for-itself and being-in-itself. I will present this third ontological dimension of Sartre's philosophy in the next section.

For the moment, let us note that, as against impure reflection, existential psychoanalysis reveals "the *ideal* meaning of all human attitudes", and the fact that this ideal meaning – as a particular value – is ultimately contingent (*EN*: 690, 646). It must be noted here, however, in light of the discussion of original choice in Chapter 2, that the sense of "contingent" is a peculiar one. We have seen that, for both Kant and Sartre, the meaning of human attitudes and actions is given by a fundamental project or disposition, which must be freely chosen. This meaning is contingent from the perspective of free choice, since a necessary meaning would seem to exclude the freedom of choice.

In another sense, however, this project is necessary in order for meaning even to exist, and meaning is necessary for a person and her world to exist as person and world. Nevertheless, a person's particular ideal meaning is contingent. In other words, while any person necessarily presupposes *some* fundamental project, that the person has chosen this, rather than the other project is contingent on her free choice. The role of existential psychoanalysis is to reveal this contingency. Sartre claims that existential psychoanalysis is in fact practised by "many men" even before they have learned "its principles".[25] It is, in other words, a practice which need not have its method explicitly presented in order for a person to engage in it. Since it is a means of escaping bad faith, Sartre also calls it a "moral description" (*EN*: 690, 645).

Existential psychoanalysis aims to realize that catharsis which transforms impure reflection into pure reflective consciousness, since existential psychoanalysis attempts to provide the person with that degree of self-consciousness which enables her to become aware of her fundamental project. The free choice underlying this fundamental project shows that an action or a psychic state is not determined but is only conditioned by the world.

Hence, a preliminary conclusion we can draw here is that not any values which a person adopts can be considered as ethically good. If such values are not regarded as grounded in the person's freedom (ultimately, the ontological freedom which makes possible the free choice of the fundamental project), then the value is not ethically good. Yet, as we have seen, on Sartre's account, the source of ethical claims is in the interpersonal relations. So, in the next section, I turn to Sartre's view of the third fundamental ontological category, being-for-others. I will come back to the issue of the moral criterion for the evaluation of actions shortly.

§55. Being-for-others

When I introduced Sartre's objection to Kant's account of normativity, I mentioned that Sartre rejects a view of a person as an isolated individual, and that he aims to replace it with a conception where interpersonal relations play a more significant role and are essential for commands. In Chapter 2, §22, I have pointed out that Sartre relates the third aspect of the person (reflective consciousness) with this ontological structure of for-others. This does not mean that interpersonal relations can only emerge on the level of reflective consciousness. The suggestion is rather that actions performed in bad faith presuppose an impure reflection, which tends to divide a person into two beings.

Moreover, another manifestation of bad faith that Sartre mentions is the attempt of impure reflection to posit the consciousness reflected-on as an object. However, since consciousness reflected-on is self-consciousness, the most impure reflection can achieve is to regard consciousness reflected-on as another person. To be sure, the result is not a genuine relation between two persons and, hence, the for-itself is not yet a for-others. The person's relation to the others presupposes a third type of nihilation; it is neither the nihilation of the pre-reflective cogito nor that of the immediate consciousness,[26] which is also essentially of the same type as reflection; rather, the third type of nihilation is a transformation of the person's relation to the world.

This type of nihilation takes place on the level of non-reflective consciousness, since it is there that the relation between person and world is constituted. When another person appears explicitly, the world is no longer simply the result of the person's upsurge produced by the reflexive negation of the in-itself. The relation between person and world becomes more complex, since the person herself becomes an object in a world in which the other constitutes the world by his self-choice. This type of nihilation is presented by Sartre in the third part of *Being and Nothingness*, more exactly in the fourth section "The Look" (*EN*: 298–349, 276–326) of the first chapter, "The Existence of Others" (*EN*: 265–349, 245–326).

Sartre uses the example of a person who "moved by jealousy, curiosity, or vice" looks through a keyhole and tries to hear a conversation which takes place in another room (*EN*: 305, 282–3). Let us suppose that I am that person and the objects which surround me are arranged in accordance with my projects, that is, things represent potentialities which reveal my possibilities. If I am on the level of non-reflective consciousness, the situation appears to me as follows:

I am a pure consciousness of things, and things [...] offer me their potentialities as the proof of my non-thetic consciousness (of) my own possibilities. This means that behind that door a spectacle is presented as "to be seen", a conversation as "to be heard". The door, the keyhole are at once both instruments and obstacles; they are presented as "to be handled with care"; the key-hole is given as "to be looked through close by and a little to one side", *etc.*

(*EN*: 305, 283)

At this level, I do not have a *cognition* of my particular project since I am on the level of non-positional consciousness: "Jealousy, as the possibility which I *am*, organizes this instrumental complex by transcending it toward itself. But I *am* this jealousy, I do not *know* it" (*EN*: 305, 283). Thus jealousy is constituted by the very acts that make the keyhole appear as to be looked through or the conversation as to be heard. This is the reason why, for Sartre, this situation reflects my freedom and facticity. I am free, since jealousy, as *the project* to be accomplished by action, is *my* project and breaks down in several particular "tasks to be freely done" (*EN*: 306, 283); the facticity of my situation appears in the form of the various obstacles to be overcome in order to realize the project.

Thus I am in fact in a situation, that is, in the middle of a complex of objects which are organized by my project, however, I cannot define myself "as *being* in a situation" (*EN*: 306, 283). This is not only because a definition would presuppose reflection, but also because, on the level of non-reflective consciousness, the person escapes any definition, since on that level his possibilities are simple possibilities, that is, they are projections of a person's ends and they are negated by the non-reflective cogito.

As pure possibilities, the person is in a process of acting which is continually negated by reflexive consciousness, and hence definition, which presupposes a limitation of myself and the appearance of an *I* as the active aspect of the Ego, is not possible. A definition of the person could still be possible if the person's possibilities could be limited by a "Me", that is, the passive aspect of the Ego. But this aspect is not available when the person is her possibilities.[27] This describes a first stage, where the person is in the same relation to the others as she is to the world and the objects in the world.

This state of non-reflective consciousness in which I act changes as soon as I hear footsteps in the hall. However, for Sartre, the change does not bring about a reflective consciousness; what happens is a phenomenon that Sartre thinks specific for interpersonal relations, namely the appearance on the level of non-reflective consciousness of a me:

> So long as we considered the for-itself in its isolation, we were able to maintain that the unreflective consciousness cannot be inhabited by a me; the me was given in the form of an object and only for the reflective consciousness. But here the me comes to haunt the unreflective consciousness. Now the unreflective consciousness is a consciousness *of* the world. Therefore for the unreflective consciousness the me exists on the level of objects in the world.
>
> (*EN*: 306, 284)

The process Sartre describes here is the following: under the look of another person I cannot be regarded as the series of my possibilities and, therefore, I become an object in the world. However, my consciousness cannot apprehend this new object as *its* object, since it is still a *non*-reflective consciousness, but what this new non-reflective consciousness perceives now, under the potential gaze of the other, is the world, including the new object as an object for the other. Since this *me* arises on the level of non-reflective consciousness where I am my possibilities, I am this *me*.

This recognition (rather than cognition) of the fact that I am the object which the other is judging defines what Sartre calls "shame" (*EN*: 307, 285). This attitude is authentic but lies at the basis of those conducts in bad faith by which I try to transform myself into an object. So being-for-others is a way of being (and, hence, of being in the world), which brings about a way of relating to the world that is quite distinct from the way I usually relate to the world in isolation. So far, the analysis Sartre has provided has mainly focused on the emergence of the particular type of being the for-itself is, in the presence of another person. In the next section, the analysis of this type of being will be further pursued and developed.

§56. Self and others

We have seen that the type of being in the world that I am in isolation is quite different from that which emerges once other persons manifest their presence. We have also seen that, even the potential presence of the other can bring about my being-for-others and, hence, the new meaning things in the world have for me. The new meaning is that attributed by the other, a meaning I do not know. At that point, my relation with myself (the *me*) is one of being, not of knowing, namely, I am what Sartre calls "shame".

In that situation, my actions lose their original meaning conferred by my fundamental project and I become a *me* in "a world which the Other has made alien to me, for the Other's look embraces my being and correlatively the walls, the door, the keyhole" (*EN*: 307, 285). The world is alienated by the other, since all the instruments which surrounded me in a certain order are now constituting the other's situation, which is arranged in another order.

At that moment, I do not know what the meanings are that are attributed by the other to all the instruments which used to populate my situation. And, even if I knew it, the other person could always change that meaning since she is free: "The Other's freedom is revealed to me across the uneasy indetermination of the being which I am for him" (*EN*: 308, 285). This indetermination, however, does not stem from my freedom, from the fact that I am always transcending my *me*, my *I* or my Ego. In fact as an object for the other, I disappear as transcendence, and I acquire a nature, an essence which depends on the other's freedom:

> This is because my transcendence becomes for whoever makes himself a witness of it [...] a purely established transcendence, a given-transcendence. This is accomplished, not by any distortion on my

transcendence through his categories, but by his very being. If there is an Other, whatever or whoever he may be, whatever may be his relations with me, and without his acting upon me in any way except by the pure upsurge of his being – then I have an outside, I have a *nature*.

(*EN*: 309, 286)

My transcendence acquires a fixed character to the extent that the instruments of my situation are alienated from me. My possibility of using an object escapes me, since it is affected by the other's look. Since I am in the middle of the world as an object for another person, I apprehend my possibilities through that person. Thus Sartre says, changing the example,

> my possibilities are present to my unreflective consciousness in so far as the Other *is watching me*. If I see him ready for anything, his hand in his pocket where he has a weapon [...], I apprehend my possibilities from outside and through him at the same time that I *am* my possibilities, somewhat as we objectively apprehend our thought through language at the same time that we think it *in order to* express it in language.

(*EN*: 310, 287–8)

Hence, my way of being, as affected by the perceived presence of the other person, constitutes an interpersonal relation, which deprives me of my freedom. My possibilities become first mere probabilities; they depend for their character on the freedom of the other person who at once posits them and posits *me* as an object. Clearly, inasmuch as I remain on the level of non-reflective consciousness, the other cannot be cognized by me, since, as we have seen in the previous chapter, for Sartre, cognition implies the positing of an object, and the positional consciousness of the other would destroy my positional consciousness of the *me*. However, this *me* is not an object for me, since this would presuppose that I am reflectively consciousness of myself. Rather, Sartre says, I am the *me* as an object for the other.

What is more, "the *Other's look* as the necessary condition of my objectivity is the destruction of all objectivity for me" (*EN*: 316, 293). Hence, it is not only the other or the *me* who cannot be an object for me, but I cannot even perceive the world as an object, since my possibilities are alienated; before my encountering the other person, my possibilities were reflected by the world posited as an object, now the world is the object of the other person's look. Since my possibilities are determined by the other person, what I experience, in fact, is the other person's freedom: "Thus in the look the death of my possibilities causes me to experience the Other's freedom" (*EN*: 317, 294–5).

This experience reflects the status of the other person in relation to *me*. Thus, the other person is a subject, whereas I am an object. The appearance of the other-as-subject presupposes the negation which constitutes shame, namely the negation implied in the transformation of my possibilities into dead possibilities, into a "nature" (*EN*: 309, 287). This negation does not come from me, but from the other person.

But there is also a second negation which I effect by a re-apprehension of myself as free. Insofar as I experience the other-as-subject, I am immediately, but not reflectively, conscious of myself as a *me* which has the possibilities of the other. However, to the extent that I am also self-consciousness, I can effect a second negation, which denies that my possibilities are the possibilities of the other person:

> Thus at first I must grasp only that one of the two negations for which I am not responsible, the one which does not come to me through myself. But in the very apprehension of this negation there arises the consciousness (of) myself as myself; that is, I can obtain an explicit self-consciousness inasmuch as I am also responsible for a negation of the Other which is my own possibility. This is the process of making explicit the second negation, the one which proceeds from me to the Other.
>
> (*EN*: 334, 311)

It is this second negation which lies at the basis of the "Other-as-Object" (*EN*: 336, 313), and which transforms shame into self-pride (*orgueil*)[28] (*EN*: 337, 314). Self-pride is the result of a second nihilation, which makes possible the reappearance of my freedom.[29]

In the last two sections, I followed Sartre's presentation of the transformation of a person's mode of being from a for-itself in isolation in the world, to a for-others and, back again, to a mode of being in the world where, among the objects in the world, we also perceive the others. In the next section, I will explore the ethical importance of these various stages, before going back to Sartre's objections to Kant.

§57. Ethics and interpersonal relations

So far we have seen that a person may transform himself into an object as a consequence of a relation to the others, a relation in which he is not able to recuperate his freedom. Moreover, we have seen that the attempt to regain his freedom may lead a person to perceive the other as an object. These two non-reflective and authentic attitudes of a person in his relation to the others may, however, lead to inauthentic conduct.[30]

As we have seen, for Sartre, the two authentic conducts in my relation to another person are shame and self-pride.[31] Both of these authentic moments may be transformed further by the for-itself into attitudes of bad faith. Shame may be transformed into pride or fear; self-pride may become pride, for instance, when we get to an attitude which transforms the other person into an object which is no longer perceived as a "transcendence transcending", that is, as a being who projects his own possibilities. By contrast, the other becomes a "transcendence transcended", that is, an object in the world (*EN*: 338, 315).

Sartre's analysis of the bad faith which develops from pride makes evident the connection between the patterns of bad faith manifested in interpersonal relations and those patterns which are specific for the for-itself's relation to itself. Hence, the analysis of the being-for-others makes manifest the way in which morality and interpersonal relations are related for Sartre; however, there is no moral priority given by Sartre to any of these fundamental ontological categories.

It is important to note that self-pride, shame, fear or pride are not seen by Sartre as psychological states of a person; they are ontological structures of the for-itself in relation to another for-itself.[32] Now, in contrast to self-pride, pride is a structure of the for-itself which tries to overcome shame but ends up in a reaction of bad faith. Pride starts from ontological shame, but modifies the structure of shame. Thus, in pride, I recognize the other person as the origin of my object-state, but I also effect the second negation by which I come to apprehend myself as the origin of my object-state.

However, in pride, this second negation does not lead to an awareness of my freedom, since I am trying to affect the other person with objectivity not by transforming myself into a subject and the other person into an object, but by inconsistently considering the other person as an objectified subject.[33] Thus pride is a contradictory attempt to transform the other into an object. In the case of my relation to myself, impure reflection tries to turn my possibilities into an object by constituting the consciousness reflected-on into another person.

In pride, I am already in relation to another person and I try to see that person at once as, on the one hand, a subject who freely reveals my possibilities (beauty, strength, intelligence), and, on the other, an object that reflects my possibilities. But here the contradiction is more subtle than in the first case. In the case of the impure reflection of myself, it is obvious that I cannot consider myself as an other objectified subject, since I am my possibilities. In the case of pride, impure reflection considers the other person, and not my possibilities, as an object.

It is for this reason that Sartre sees the person's conversion from the "natural" attitude of bad faith to the "original" conduct in good faith as the key in the constitution of authentic, that is, ethically valid interpersonal relations. The *Notebooks* represent Sartre's attempt to put forward an ethical theory in which interpersonal relations are developed in good faith. Thus the *Notebooks* describes two ways in which one could relate to the other's freedom; the relation between one and the other could be a relation of demand, by which one demands something from a free person, or a relation of pure proposal, by which one submits something to the judgement of a free person (*CM*: 146, 138).

According to Sartre, true freedom gives – that is, proposes – its projects and recognizes the other's freedom through the recognition of the other's projects (*CM*: 146–7, 139). By contrast, by demand, one's free consciousness informs the other's free consciousness about a duty. By demand, Sartre adds, I communicate to the other a categorical imperative (*CM*: 248, 237). Like in *Being and Nothingness*, in the *Notebooks*, Sartre sees the categorical imperative as a particular maxim or rule of action which is imposed upon a person from without her projects and ends.

However, this attitude is in bad faith to the extent that this external limit is not in fact given, since it requires the freedom of a person in order to be adopted and followed. Hence, since an imperative is seen as based on an external authority, while it is in fact freely chosen, and since this external authority is considered as an absolute authority, while it is in fact based on the freedom of another person, a moral theory formulated in terms of such imperatives is inauthentic.

I will come back to Sartre's ethical theory in Chapter 6, where I will discuss his conception of the relation between imperative and value. I will look at how he views this relation in the *Notebooks*, and I will then consider his view of values and imperatives in the ethics elaborated as a sequel to the *Critique of Dialectical Reason*. While in his later ethics Sartre sees the imperative as manifesting more fully a person's freedom, he still does not propose a morality of imperatives.

My general view in this respect is that Sartre's interpretation of imperatives has not changed considerably; there is a shift in his view of the relation between imperative and value, but this is mainly due to a change in Sartre's interpretation of values. Thus, values are no longer seen as expressing freedom, since Sartre realizes that particular values also alienate freedom. This does not mean that Sartre also gives up on his "teleological" conception of human agency, and it is for this reason that, even though it could be seen as formulating a criterion for the evaluation of values and even though there are other structural similarities one can note, his later "radical ethics" is quite different from Kant's.

Before I get to these issues, however, I would like to continue the exploration of the similarities and differences between Kant and Sartre by returning to Sartre's objections to Kant's account of normativity.

§58. A framework for normativity

The second set of objections considered in this chapter concern the account of normativity offered by Kant and, in particular, his view of the ontological status of ethical standards and his account of the source of this ontological status. I have already formulated these objections in §51 and §52, and, against the background of Sartre's account of impure reflection, bad faith, for-others and the ethics of interpersonal relations (presented in §53–§57), they can now be understood more fully.

As we have seen, for Sartre, the context of the action is crucial – both the situation in which the agent finds herself and her own character traits are very important for an understanding of the appropriate ethically valid action. Hence, from this perspective, for Sartre, an ethics consisting of a code of rules or principles is not well-focused; the focus should be on determining the rules and principles of actions which are appropriate for the particular case under consideration.

Secondly, we have seen that, for Sartre, ethical standards require as a condition of their existence the interpersonal ontological dimension given by being-for-others. The authentic attitude towards the other – that of pure proposal – presupposes an interpersonal relation, rather than constituting it on the basis of the autonomous decisions of individuals. Now, although Sartre's main aim seems to be to clarify the differences between his ethics and Kant's practical philosophy in these respects and to defend his own account, these objections seem to represent serious challenges to Kant's ethical theory.

So, let us have another brief look at Kant's conceptual framework, as presented in Chapter 3, and the use he makes thereof when articulating his ethics. As we have seen, Kant defines a practical principle as a proposition that contains a general determination of the will. For instance, a principle, like 'Help those in need', tells me what to do and, in this sense, once I adopt it, determines my will to act in a particular way. Recall also that Kant distinguishes two kinds of practical principles. First, a maxim is a practical principle which determines the will through a condition the agent regards as valid only for her; by contrast, laws are principles which determine the will through conditions which are cognized as valid for all rational beings (*KpV*: 5:19, 153).

We have seen that, on Kant's account, a maxim, as a general determination of the will, has under it several practical rules. Every rule prescribes an action as a specification of a principle for the particular circumstances which define the concrete situation under consideration (*KpV*: 5:20, 154). For instance, to use one of Sartre's examples, the rule "Don't give away this information" can be a specification of a principle of non-collaboration with the Nazis in 1940[34] or, to add other examples of specific contexts, with the Communists in the 1950s or with the would-be murderer who is pursuing your friend.

When we deal with a purely rational will, a law of pure practical reason spontaneously determines the will; there is no need for a demand or an imperative for a purely rational will, just as there is no need, for a finite rational will like ours, to formulate laws of nature in the form of imperatives – we follow them spontaneously. Nevertheless, in our case, where rational faculties coexist with the sensible powers (powers of inclinations and sensible drives), practical laws cannot determine the will spontaneously, since they have to counteract the influence of the faculty of sensible desire. Hence, reason in this case is not the only determining ground for the will, and the rules it devises contain an "ought" – the sign of imperatives (*KpV*: 5:20, 154).

As we have seen, for Kant, imperatives may be hypothetical or categorical. When the purpose of a rule of action is adopted because it is a means to some other end, the imperative is hypothetical. Therefore, a hypothetical imperative cannot be a practical law since its validity is conditioned by a further end. By contrast, when the purpose is adopted because it is right, the imperative is no longer conditioned by the validity of a further purpose – it is an unconditional or categorical imperative (*KpV*: 5:21, 154–5).[35]

For instance, if the principle 'Help those in need' is adopted *merely* because I happen to desire to help those in need or because I get some pleasure out of this, then the purpose of helping those in need will be realized only when I happen to be inclined to help or to enjoy helping. However, if I adopt that principle because it is right, then its validity does not depend on my contingent sensible incentives; the principle is in this sense unconditional or categorical, it ought to be applied whether or not it is desired.

Moreover, I have already mentioned that, on Kant's account, when the will is determined by a practical principle in virtue of the fact that its purpose is desired, then it is determined by the matter of the principle. When the principle determines the will because its purpose is right, then the purpose does not primarily count as an object of desire, and Kant says that the will is determined not by the matter, but by the form of the principle. Hence, despite the distinction between maxims and practical laws, a maxim can function as a practical law for a limited rational person (more exactly, as a categorical imperative), when it determines the will by its form (*KpV*: 5:27, 160).

Having rehearsed the main aspects of Kant's conceptual framework for normativity, in the next sections I will explore the extent to which Sartre's objections are in fact based on an accurate reading of Kant and whether Kant can answer them.

§59. Against moral codes

Now, it seems that Kant's ethics has the conceptual resources to respond to the problems raised by Sartre's first set of objections. In the harsher interpretation, he claims that two aspects of Kant's ethics reflect an inappropriate view of normativity: the formulation of practical rules and the formulation of practical principles. Moreover, he claims that Kant's ethics is abstract in two senses: it cannot account for the concrete circumstances a person is in, and it cannot account for the concrete characteristics of a person. Sartre regards the process of the formulation of both practical rules and principles in Kant's ethics as a process guided by the ideal of working out codes of rules and principles applicable to all situations.[36]

Kant tries to find unconditional imperatives on the basis of which practical rules of action can be justified, for instance, the imperative of truthfulness which justifies the action in his solution to Constant's problem. Sartre construes this attempt as aiming at drawing a code of imperatives, which cannot appropriately take into account the particular characteristics of a person, and which aims to reduce every situation a person is in to some paradigmatic cases. The ensuing ethical principles and rules of action will not be able to consider *concrete*, singular persons and situations. Accurately interpreted, however, Kant's moral theory proves to have the guiding force that Sartre requires.

As we have seen in Chapter 3, Kant does not develop this aspect of his moral theory very much. His focus is primarily on the justification of the criterion of moral judgement, the Categorical Imperative, rather than on its application and the derivation of principles and the rules of action. We have looked, however, at the careful discussion and elaboration on these issues that Höffe offers and have mentioned some of the most important aspects of Kant's position in the previous section. It remains to evaluate Sartre's objections.

First, he claims that, in deriving rules of action from maxims, Kant does not take into account the circumstances of the concrete situation a person is in, and the particularities of the concrete person himself; secondly, that, in deriving maxims of action by means of the moral criterion (the Categorical Imperative), Kant does not take into account the concrete situation that is being judged. Hence, he concludes that Kant's account of normativity is out of joint with the concrete situations and characteristics that constitute the moral context of any action in reality.[37]

In fact, we have seen that, when he formulates rules of action, Kant is not guided by the idea of a code of norms that ought to be applied in every situation. First, in order to decide which rule of action ought to be applied in a certain situation, Kant considers as necessary a study of the person's circumstances and characteristics. Secondly, since circumstances and characteristics change, one has to take them into account each time a moral problem arises. As the example provided by Höffe shows, a person should not follow the same rule of action independently of the relevant circumstances or the relevant characteristics of the agent and situation.[38]

Moreover, when he formulates maxims for certain actions, a person has to *invent* the maxim, and the exact formulation of the maxim will depend again on the singular circumstances of the situation the person is in, as well as on that person's characteristics. Hence, once more, Kant does not hope to be able to provide a code of valid maxims that should be applied in every context, let alone to choose an appropriate maxim without the knowledge of the context.[39] For Kant, devising maxims and rules of action on the basis of the Categorical Imperative is not like deriving a conclusion from the premises of a syllogism in logic. Moreover, to choose the right action requires judgemental effort on the part of the agent.

Although Kant seems to agree to Sartre's objection to an account of normativity conceived in terms of a code of rules or principles of action, he still needs to respond to a further objection concerning the ontological source of those rules and principles. For Sartre may claim that, although Kant can perhaps readily agree that rules of action and second-order standards or principles do not exist independently from the person and her world,[40] Kant still errs in his view of the ontological source of these standards and rules, and ultimately also of the criterion of moral judgement, the Categorical Imperative. Thus, whereas Kant seems to place these standards in the human beings' faculty of reason, Sartre regards it as essentially grounded in the interpersonal relations between individuals.

In addition, as we have seen, contrary to Kant, for Sartre the transcendent realm is no longer beyond our experience as sensible beings. Following one of the main ontological presuppositions of phenomenology, Sartre denies the epistemological distinction between the phenomenal and the noumenal worlds. When he claims that Kant's categorical imperative is based upon a noumenal freedom, he hints at the distinction between phenomena and things in themselves, a distinction I have presented in Chapter 3, in relation to the Third Antinomy.

Kant's distinction between phenomena and noumena is, in fact, a mark of his transcendental idealism and can be found throughout his critical writings.[41] This distinction suggests further support for Sartre's objection that Kant's view of the source of normativity needs a proper account of interpersonal relations. I will discuss this objection in the next section.

§60. Noumena and other persons

When applied to a person, the distinction between phenomena and noumena yields a further distinction between two points of view from which the person can regard himself:

> *first*, insofar as he belongs to the world of sense, under laws of nature (heteronomy); *second*, as he belongs to the intelligible world under laws which, being independent of nature, are not empirical but grounded merely in reason.
>
> (*GMS*: 4:452, 99)

The power which distinguishes human beings from other sensible beings is reason. However, what is more, Kant claims that reason does not distinguish human beings only from other sensible beings. He claims that reason actually distinguishes a human being "even from himself insofar as he is affected by objects" (*GMS*: 4:452, 99; see also *MS*: 6:417–18, 543). Sartre alludes then to this distinction and identifies a further problem in Kant's account of normativity.

The problem is that the self-legislative reason which grounds the consciousness of the moral law and which belongs to a person as an intelligible being is introduced in Kant, according to Sartre's reading, in order to substitute for the missing interpersonal relation. The self-legislating reason is, in fact, the other person projected in the noumenal realm as an aspect of the agent. Hence, we get a relation between the self-legislating aspect of the person and the legislated aspect, instead of a relation between two persons. Thus, on Sartre's account, Kant had to create a duality sufficiently strong to suggest an interpersonal relationship without completely compromising a person's unity. This, according to Sartre, is a "sleight of hand" which tries to maintain the appearance of freedom without the anxiety of free choice (*CM*: 265–6, 255).

In other words, Sartre offers the following picture of normativity (more exactly, of the ontological source of normativity) and of Kant's account of normativity. For him, interpersonal relations are a necessary ontological source for normative standards. In other words, without a person who proposes or imposes a standard and a person who commits herself to that standard, we have no normativity.[42]

On Kant's account, however, Sartre notes, a person may follow a moral standard in isolation from the others, since her reason provides the standard which can guide the person in the attempt to act morally. This radical separation between reason and sensible incentives, Sartre suggests, is meant to precisely replace the distinction between two persons and the interpersonal relation, which is required for the existence of moral standards.

To draw this conclusion, Sartre relies on a further assumption, namely, that there is no moral standard existing independently from a person's consciousness and waiting to be discovered and followed. In other words, whatever standard is taken as action-guiding, it is so taken because the person freely adopts it, and not because it is already given as to be followed and the person has to conform to it. Along these lines, Sartre contrasts a standard which corresponds to a person's values as reflected by her possibilities and an absolute value.

Thus, when I exercise my freedom in concrete situations, "I exist my unconditional freedom and I am my own project in its autonomy" (*CM*: 267, 257). On this level, I choose ends which are in fact my possibilities of realizing a fundamental project. However, if I try to anchor my ends in something beyond my free choice and I make appeal to an "absolute" purpose, the value of my ends gets transformed, it becomes "an objectified and transcendent value that passes through my subjectivity" (*CM*: 267–8, 257). The role I play changes from that of a person who *creates* ends and grounds them in his free choice, to a person who *participates* in the realization of ends that are grounded independently of his choices.

My appeal to an "absolute" purpose is an attempt to ground my choices in something more objective. For Sartre, it is sufficient that the "absolute" purpose be based on freedom, but on the freedom of another person. However, in Kant's account, I take this freedom to be my freedom, something I can only do, Sartre thinks, through a conduct in bad faith. This conduct, however, finds a justification and, in this way, appears more plausible:

> In exchange for this mystification I do have one advantage: my freedom is safe from anxiety. Indeed it is discharged of any anxiety by that freedom in back of freedom that takes it upon itself to decide on my ends.
>
> (*CM*: 268, 257)

So, Sartre's objection here is that, on Kant's account, the Categorical Imperative, as an a priori law of reason, is taken to be absolute through an impure reflection, which attributes to the for-itself reflected-on an objective role. This role should have been performed by another person, but is now attributed, through bad faith, to a law of reason claiming to provide cognition (although, admittedly, only *practical* cognition) of the things in themselves. Through this conduct in bad faith, the guiding moral criterion is regarded as absolute and, in the end, the choice that the for-itself must make appears as already made; hence the for-itself bears no responsibility for this choice.

This interpretation of Kant is quite subtle and convincing. It connects important issues in Kant's philosophy, such as that of unconditionality, intersubjectivity and transcendental idealism.[43] If correct, since in Kant's ethical system categorical imperatives are justified as based on the autonomy of the person, it follows that his practical philosophy can only be grounded in the forms of mystification and bad faith identified by Sartre. But is this correct? I will address this issue in the next section.

§61. A metaethical distinction

Sartre offers here an original reading of Kant and, implicitly, also an original challenge to his account of normativity.[44] He retains Kant's notion of "transcendence", which refers to the noumenal realm of things in themselves, but he makes it refer to the phenomenal world (as that which is beyond a person's consciousness). Moreover, Sartre is in agreement with Kant that the ground of a demand's imperative is "another" than the person on whom the demand is imposed; Sartre even acknowledges that "in Kantian freedom there is a duality of the atemporal and the temporal that does a good job of depicting the structure of obligation" (*CM*: 264, 253).[45]

However, unlike Kant, for whom the 'other' (the source of the demand) refers to the same person regarded from a different standpoint, Sartre takes this 'other' to refer to another person. Sartre wants, thus, to retain key terms of Kant's philosophy, but he thinks that they should be invested with another meaning.[46] An important part of Sartre's objection to Kant and of his alternative account of normativity rests on the distinction Sartre draws between imperatives and values.[47] More exactly, the key distinguishing feature that Sartre identifies in the comparison between imperatives and values is their normative force.[48] In order for a value to determine my will to act, I have to choose its end as my possibility. This end is normative ("to be realized") insofar as I chose it; otherwise it does not determine my will and cannot motivate me.

By contrast, in order for an imperative to be a moral imperative, and hence to be normative, an actual choice of its purpose as my possibility is not required. In short, values require actual choice, whereas imperatives do not. What is more, as Sartre acknowledges, even if I tried to choose an imperative, I could still not *choose* its purpose as my possibility, since its normative force goes beyond my *actual* choice of a purpose: "even if all our desires were *conformed* to our obligation and as a consequence *served* the pure Will, there would still remain an underlying duality that is the source and ground of all the others" (*CM*: 267, 256).[49]

Nevertheless, what Sartre identifies here as a distinction between imperatives and values, and between his account and Kant's account is not so much a difference between two moral theories and type of norms, as a metaethical distinction between a purpose (or a principle), as regarded by a descriptive account of action, and a purpose (or a principle), as presented by a prescriptive account of action. Hence, in order to distinguish between values and imperatives, Sartre makes use of the distinction between a descriptive and a prescriptive account of action.

Thus, when he claims that the end represented by a value is "to be realized", if I actually choose it as my possibility, he formulates the necessary and sufficient condition for a person *to act* in order to reach, against certain adverse circumstances, an end. This is because, when I choose an end, I regard the end as to be realized and, hence, I act to bring it about. By contrast, when he asserts that the purpose of an imperative is "to be realized" independently of, and even against, my actual choice of it as my possibility, he formulates a condition for how a person *ought to act*.

We have seen that, for Kant, whether or not a person has adopted a certain principle for the determination of the will and has acted on that principle in a certain situation cannot conclusively help us determine whether the action ought to have been performed. We only learn that the action has been possible, in the sense of being physically possible, but this feasibility is, of course, a necessary condition for both permissible and impermissible principles.

According to Sartre's account, which I think is incomplete here, in order to determine whether the end of a value is "to be realized" by a person, we should simply determine whether or not the person has chosen that end;

actual choice is in this case both a necessary and a sufficient condition for the normativity of an end. Yet, again on Sartre's account, actual choice is no longer either a necessary or a sufficient condition for the purposes of the normativity of categorical imperatives.

A categorical imperative formulates an obligation and can even claim to obligate a person who chooses to do precisely the opposite of what the categorical imperative commands. The problem with this, however, is that a value or purpose or end will only have normative force if it can still impose an obligation, when they have not actually been chosen as ends of actions. Without such a distinction, whatever value a person happens to adopt, it must be accepted as morally valid.

Yet, it is not the case that whatever end we adopt, as an end of our action, is also a morally valid end. As Sartre himself acknowledges, values which are chosen in bad faith cannot be morally valid. But, since a value which has actually been chosen may not be morally valid, then actual choice cannot be the sufficient condition of moral normativity. And since a value which has not actually been chosen may be morally valid, then actual choice is not even a necessary condition of moral normativity.

This is exactly the situation with Kant's categorical imperatives: the morally valid imperatives impose an obligation the person ought to follow, but cannot determine the person to actually choose it and follow it. For Kant, it is important that this standard be chosen by the person freely because it is the right thing to do. This, however, seems to be also Sartre's requirement – that the standard proposed be followed freely by the person to whom it is proposed, and, hence, be chosen because it is considered to be right.

In this section, we have seen that Sartre draws a problematic distinction between values and imperatives. But it is still unclear how this relates to his objection to Kant's view of, what I have called, the ontological source of normativity. I will suggest a possible answer to this in the next section.

§62. Split personality

The next question, then, concerns the condition of intersubjectivity or the requirement that another person propose the standard the agent can choose as right. Why does Sartre need this condition and how does it relate to the problematic distinction between values and imperatives presented above?[50]

Let us assume that Sartre's account of the normativity of values is correct: someone proposes a value that I freely choose and this value is, therefore, morally valid and represents one of my possibilities. If, as we have assumed, Sartre is correct to claim that actual choice is sufficient to make a value morally good or valid, then we seem to have a problem when someone is challenged to explain how she knows that the actions she performs are still pursuing the value she initially chose to pursue.

The problem here is given by the fact that, on this reading of Sartre's account, values are normative simply in virtue of having been chosen. Thus, consider the person who performs certain actions; these actions are directed towards specific ends. These ends are normative and, hence, values, since we assumed that the only conditions for the validity of value is the fact that they are actually chosen by a person. Yet, since actual choice is not in its turn premised on any other condition, there is no way in which we can distinguish between the end she is pursuing now and the value she initially chose and pursued.

A person may adopt and pursue the same value at different moments in time, but, unless she chooses this value in virtue of some feature which makes it morally good, she cannot know whether later on she still pursues the same value or some other one. By contrast, if her choice of a value takes place in virtue of some feature the value has, then it is not simply actual choice that makes a value normative – a value that is chosen, but does not have the appropriate feature is not normative. Hence, the distinction we said we would take for granted between values and imperatives collapses.

Sartre's idea of a second person and an interpersonal relation is meant to provide an answer to the question of the identity of the values a person pursues without recourse to moral realism. As we have seen, Sartre rejects the view of values given independently from the person's consciousness.[51] But, if the value I choose is a value another person has proposed, then questions concerning the identity of any values over time can be answered by imagining that the second person acts as a witness. It is difficult to see what other answer Sartre can give, if he wants to avoid Kant's solution of a distinction between two aspects of the person.

Interestingly, however, what this shows is that Sartre's claim concerning the requirement of interpersonal relations for normativity does not refer to the issue of the validity of norms, but to that of their identity. Yet Kant himself offers an answer to this question and one which avoids, as Sartre's does too, moral realism (or at least that version of moral realism corresponding to the definition I offered in the Introduction). However, it is in no way immediately evident that Sartre's answer to the question of identity of normative standards (values or imperatives) is better than Kant's answer. The only obvious problem may be the split Kant introduces in the person through his transcendental idealism.

This split, however, can also be found in Sartre. We have, in Sartre, a distinction between being-for-itself and being-in-itself, which are the two main regions of being. But he points out that a person is not simply in the mode of for-itself, rather she is in an ambiguous position between these two modes. A person's past is in-itself and so are the circumstances in which she finds herself. Her freedom is a manifestation of the being-for-itself, but, as we have seen, it is directed towards the attempt to retrieve her possibilities and achieve the identity of an in-itself. The ideal which is followed by a person, Sartre claims, is that of an in-itself-for-itself. In fact, as presented in §46, a person can only detach herself from her current situation, evaluate it and attempt to act in order to achieve a better state of affairs only from the perspective of this ideal.

So, in Sartre too, there is a split between two ways in which a person is, a split which makes possible ethical questioning, evaluation and action. It is this state of ambiguity in a person that led Simone de Beauvoir to formulate an ethics of ambiguity, as a possible ethics of existentialism. Francis Jeanson, too, in an interpretation of Sartre's existentialism highly praised by Sartre for its accuracy and for its attempt to draw out the ethical implications of existentialism, puts emphasis on this ambiguity as a condition which makes possible ethical thought. By following this avenue, we seem to arrive at another structural similarity between Kant and Sartre, which is expressed as a critical reaction to merely monist or dualist philosophies.[52]

The issue needs, however, further discussion. For it might be argued that the split Sartre introduces is not between two persons (a phenomenal and a noumenal one), but between two regions of being (in-itself and for-itself). Further investigation will lead us too far for the purposes of the argument here, especially since there are two other objections to Kant that Sartre formulates and that must be considered. This will be the task of Chapter 6, in Part III. Before moving on to Part III, I will conclude, in the next section, with a summary of the main results in this part.

§63. More about critical ethics

I began this chapter with Sartre's critique of Kant's account of freedom, in particular with his view that freedom, understood in terms of spontaneous agency should not be presented as limited by any specific characteristics. I explored then the background from which Sartre advances his critique, in particular, his account of the structure of the for-itself and his view of freedom in response to the classical debate between free-will theorists and supporters of determinism.

Drawing on Kant's treatment of the Third Antinomy, as presented in Chapter 3, I concluded that Kant would join Sartre in objecting to any theory that would present freedom in terms which would attribute it a specific nature and, hence, features which could not be overcome. By contrast, Kant's account of this type of freedom (transcendental freedom) is cast in negative terms, as independence from the constraints of the laws of nature and is quite similar to Sartre's account of spontaneity as the ('ontological') freedom of the agent to question and transcend determinations specific for the realm of phenomena.

I have then considered a set of objections to Kant's account of normativity, in particular Sartre's view that Kant's moral theory cannot guide actions in concrete situations and that Kant lacks an appropriate account of interpersonal relations, although such relations are a condition for the possibility of moral standards. Having explored further the background of Sartre's critical comments, through a discussion of impure reflection, bad faith and interpersonal relations, I have then evaluated his objections.

References back to the discussion of Kant in Chapter 3 have clearly shown that Kant would also object to an ethical theory which tries to find a code of standards for paradigmatic situations. Such an ethical theory, Kant could also claim, is unable to give specific guidance in concrete situations. Concerning the objection on the ontological source of moral standards and the fact that Kant cannot provide an appropriate account, we have seen that Sartre's objection seems to be based on a peculiar distinction between values and imperatives, which leads to a view of ethical validity as premised only on actual choice.

In this respect, we seem to deal with a genuine disagreement between Kant and Sartre. Yet, on this point, Sartre changes his view considerably in his later ethics, and this may lead again to a structural similarity with Kant's practical philosophy. Discussion of this aspect, however, must be postponed until Chapter 6, which mainly considers Sartre's later practical philosophy. Before moving on to Chapters 5 and 6 in Part III, I should mention that several other similarities between Kant and Sartre emerged through the discussion of the two main objections.

Concerning freedom, as I have noted, it is extremely interesting to see that two important notions of freedom in Kant and Sartre are quite similar. The first notion of freedom refers to our capacity in concrete situations to evaluate various impulses and incentives to act and to choose the end of the action. This "practical" freedom, however, may simply be the result of the fact that the agent has a more powerful incentive or desire, which outweighs the others and leads the agent to act in a particular way. So both Kant and Sartre think that it is necessary to have a second type of freedom to ground practical freedom and vindicate its status as expression of genuine freedom.

This second type of freedom is the idea of independence from the constraints of natural laws, the idea of the capacity to act spontaneously. This can be contrasted with a situation where actions are prompted by contingent factors in the world. For both Kant and Sartre, agents are free in this fundamental sense and this freedom is also grounded in practical freedom. Whereas every action may be seen as a phenomenon involved in the world and conditioned by various factors, it can also be seen as a free action.

Recall that, in Chapter 2, I noted a similarity between Kant's and Sartre's accounts of action. Thus, for both of them, actions can be described by rules and have ends which represent the projects people have when they act. These projects can also be understood as general policies of action or maxims. Projects and maxims have several rules of action under them and they guide action, hence they are second-order rules. In turn, these second-order rules seem to be regulated by third-order rules (the Categorical Imperative, for instance, or the value of authenticity). Moreover, there seems to be an even higher-order rule, which represents the sum of the person's ethical attitudes and which Sartre calls the global project and Kant, the disposition.

The discussion in this chapter indicates that Kant and Sartre also agree that ethically valid projects and maxims are not exhaustively describable as a code, but are to be formulated depending on the situation and the features of the person who is in that situation. The only thing which is supposed to be valid for all situations and all agents is what I have called the criterion of morality, the value of authenticity, for Sartre, and the Categorical Imperative, for Kant.

Finally, a couple of notes on the ethical theory, which gradually takes shape on the basis of the similarities between Kant's and Sartre's philosophies, and which I have called 'critical ethics': whereas Kant's views of freedom and normativity are based on his doctrine of transcendental idealism, Sartre's views are not. Sartre subscribes to the idea that what we are conscious of are phenomena, to the constitution of which the structures of our consciousness or reason (in the general sense) contribute. The implication would be that, in practical philosophy too, moral judgements are constituted by reference to a fundamental structure of our consciousness or practical reason, a position which goes against ethical realism.

Yet, even to those who would claim that transcendental idealism, although metaphysically less committed than moral realism, still has dogmatic elements, we can reply by pointing to Sartre's theory. This theory is even less metaphysically committed than Kant's ethical theory; hence, it shows that critical ethics need not rest on the premises of transcendental idealism.

At this point, among the various important questions which can be raised, we can raise the question of the major difference between Kant and Sartre, a difference which has its root in the contrast between Kant's rule-centred and Sartre's purpose-centred views of actions, as presented in Chapter 2. This difference continues to survive in spite of the various similarities identified in this chapter. So will critical ethics be a principle- or value-centred theory? An answer to this will be given at the end of the third part of this book, to which I now turn.

Part III
Authority and Progress

Having examined some of the assumptions of Kant's and Sartre's ethical theories (identity, self-choice and freedom) and some of their significant aspects related to normativity, in this part, I would like to focus on further aspects of normativity and some implications. First, insofar as Kant's and Sartre's accounts of freedom and normativity are similar, they need to explain how it is possible to advocate the absolute negative freedom of the spontaneous agent and, at the same time, an absolute moral constraint on moral agents. Both Kant and Sartre suggest we can do this, but Sartre seems unhappy with Kant's account.

Secondly, however, we need to understand to what extent such a view of ethics can be compatible with the idea of a meaning of history that both Kant and Sartre think can be identified. Not only does this seem to contradict again their accounts of freedom, but Sartre seems to be in disagreement with Kant in this respect too. It remains to be seen whether the objections raised by Sartre turn out to reveal structural similarities with Kant, – as was the case for the objections related to identity, self-choice, freedom and normativity – or genuine differences, as the comparison concerning the interpersonal basis of morality seemed to suggest.

I will begin, in the next chapter, with a discussion of those aspects of Kant's moral philosophy that are required for an understanding and evaluation of Sartre's objections. I will then continue the comparative analysis of Kant and Sartre with an examination of Sartre's objections and an evaluation of their import. We will move, in this way, to a discussion of aspects of Sartre's later philosophy, both in the *Critique of Dialectical Reason* (first volume, published in 1960), and in the lectures he was invited to give to Cornell University and which he prepared in 1965. It is, in fact, Sartre's discussion of the relation between imperatives and values in the Cornell Lectures that will suggest a distinct understanding of his objection to Kant's account of the ontological basis of the criterion of ethics, and will show that that objection, too, reveals, in fact, a structural similarity between Kant and Sartre.

We have seen in the first two parts of this book that the assumptions of Kant's and Sartre's ethical theories, at least with regard to those aspects examined, are not metaphysical in a dogmatic sense. They are justified on the basis of plausible arguments and by reference to elements of experience. To be sure, one of the most controversial aspects in this sense is Kant's transcendental idealism, which is present throughout in his arguments, whether in relation to identity, self-choice, freedom or normativity. But, if Sartre defends similar views on these issues, then we have at our disposal an alternative theory, which makes similar points but without recourse to transcendental idealism.

To be sure, as I have mentioned, it remains to be seen to what extent Sartre can make the points he wants to make without assuming transcendental idealism and also how far his ontology is from Kant's critical metaphysics. These are issues which cannot be discussed here. My assumption throughout has been that Sartre can make good on the claim that the phenomenological method can properly account for, say, freedom, without any commitment to a realm of things which cannot be cognized.

The worry of substantive assumptions will, however, have to be raised again in relation to the issues discussed in this third part, since both the strong authority of a moral criterion and the claims of moral progress throughout history towards a cosmopolitan end suggest the need for assumptions which are even stronger than transcendental idealism. I will return to this issue in the Conclusion to this book.

5
Kant

The idea of an ethical criterion that has absolute validity over agents, their circumstances and their particular characteristics makes a very strong normative commitment. This is particularly worrying if we recall that, for Kant, the ethical criterion is supposed to be constitutive of practical reason, which has normative priority over theoretical reason.[1] Another claim which seems to imply a strong metaphysical commitment is that concerning the cosmopolitan end of history and the moral progress of human beings.

To alleviate these worries, in this chapter, I will begin with a discussion of Kant's ideal of enlightenment, understood as the person's use of her own understanding for the evaluation of existing norms and the vindication of standards of action. Although this ideal suggests that Kant's commitment to critical evaluation is not as strong as it might seem at the beginning and that the emancipatory function of enlightenment is limited, I will show that, in fact, Kant's view in this respect is quite radical.

The idea of emancipation through the use of one's own understanding is bound up with the idea of justification, for what one tries to achieve in the questioning of existing authorities is a separation of those which have justification and can be freely pursued from those which do not have justification and must be taken for granted or accepted under threat. Hence, I will then focus on the question of justification starting from the issue of the justification of practical principles on the basis of the Categorical Imperative. I will argue that the only way in which we can understand this process of justification is by analogy to the argument Kant employs in his theoretical philosophy to justify a priori concepts and principles. This analogy will suggest an approach to the question of the justification of moral norms.

Although I am using the expressions 'moral standard (or norm, principle, value, end)' and 'ethical standards (or norm, principle, etc.)' interchangeably, especially in this third part of the book, I only do this in the appropriate contexts, where the claims apply equally well to ethical and juridical (or political) standards. Next in this chapter, I make this distinction and some associated distinctions explicit, in order to show the extent to which the claims I make are politically relevant even when the context is explicitly ethical.

As I have mentioned, in his later writing Sartre started to question his own view of the relationship between imperatives and values. Not only did he claim that, in certain respects, imperatives are to be preferred to values, but he also suggested that imperatives and values are in fact different ways of expressing the same normative content. To anticipate the comparative discussion on this topic, in the final part of this chapter I will present Kant's view of the relation between the moral law and the good. I will argue that the normative priority Kant ascribes to the moral law over the good is not justified and can productively be questioned.

Let me begin with the emancipatory role of enlightenment.

§64. Enlightenment

Kant's "What is Enlightenment?" opens with the exposition[2] of the idea of enlightenment:

> *Enlightenment is man's emergence from his self-incurred immaturity. Immaturity* is the inability to use one's own understanding without the guidance of another. This immaturity is *self-incurred* if its cause is not lack of understanding, but lack of resolution and courage to use it without the guidance of another. The motto of enlightenment is therefore: [...] Have courage to use your *own* understanding!
>
> (Kant 1970: 8:35, 54)

The elaboration of the idea of enlightenment follows the traditional manner of clarifying the parts of the exposition, proceeding from the notion of immaturity to that of self-incurred immaturity, and, finally, to the way in which man's emergence from the state of immaturity is to be conceived: by his *own* understanding. First of all, the motto of the enlightenment represents an invitation to have the *courage* to use one's own understanding. The reasons which lie behind Kant's claim that one needs courage for enlightenment are further spelled out:

> Laziness and cowardice are the reasons why such a large proportion of men, even when nature has long emancipated them from alien guidance [...], nevertheless gladly remain immature for life. For the same reasons, it is all too easy for others to set themselves up as their guardians. [...] The guardians who have kindly taken upon themselves the work of supervision will soon see to it that by far the largest part of mankind [...] should consider the step forward to maturity not only as difficult but also as highly dangerous.
>
> (Kant 1970: 8:35, 54)

Though only implicitly at this stage, the passage sheds light upon the social interplay which causes the "dangers" that only enlightenment can overcome. Thus, political immaturity is a consequence of the individual's conformism and lack of courage ("cowardice"), on the one hand, and, on the other, of the authority's ("guardians") arrogated task of ruling by using "threats" and "intimidation" as means of legitimation:

> Having first infatuated their domesticated animals, and carefully prevented the docile creatures from daring to take a single step without the leading-strings to which they are tied, they next show them the danger which threatens them if they try to walk unaided.
>
> (Kant 1970: 8:35, 54)

The metaphorical language presents freedom as the distinctive attribute of human beings. For what distinguishes human beings from animals is that the former do not "pursue their aims purely by instinct" (Kant 1970: 8:17, 41). However, since they do not "act in accordance with any integral, pre-arranged plan" (Kant 1970: 8:17, 41), they are bound to face the danger of emancipation on their own. Moreover, even their nature stands against enlightenment:

> Thus it is difficult for each separate individual to work his way out of the immaturity which has become almost second nature to him. He has even grown fond of it and is really incapable for the time being of using his own understanding, because he has never been allowed to make the attempt.
>
> (Kant 1970: 8:36, 54)

Neither some external, absolutely valid authority, nor some internal, pure capacity – unaffected by long immaturity – is able to offer guidance to the person who wants to take the path of Enlightenment. For Kant, human beings are distinguished negatively from other beings by their freedom to act independently from instincts; positively, however, human beings are rational, and "only a rational being has the capacity to act *in accordance with the representation* of laws" (*GMS*: 4:412, 66). Thus, the positive sense of freedom – what Kant calls the individual's autonomy – represents one's ability to rule oneself. For Kant, this does not only mean the individual's capacity to observe, rather than disobey, certain rules dictated by "an alien guidance", but to follow one's own rules. These laws of actions are the laws of reason (*GMS*: 4:396–7, 52).[3]

At first glance it seems that the only way out of the predicament that afflicts the person in search of maturity is to use the practical power of reason. Nevertheless, although every human being is endowed with reason, and although reason has the power to guide his actions, it seems that it is not

enough to offer him even the lowest degree of certainty on the way towards
self-emancipation:

> Dogmas and formulas, those mechanical instruments for rational use (or
> rather misuse) of his natural endowments, are the ball and chain of his
> permanent immaturity. And if anyone did throw them off, he would still
> be uncertain about jumping over even the narrowest trenches, for he
> would be unaccustomed to free movement of this kind.
>
> (Kant 1970: 8:36, 54–5)

What Kant has in view when he doubts the capacity of the individual to act
in the situation in which he is left free to think for himself is the paramount
role played by experience in a person's life. Thus, even though the ideas of
reason (in its theoretical as well as practical use) and the concepts of the
understanding are a priori, independent of any possible experience, reason
and the understanding need something upon which to act. Thus, the ideas of
reason can be determined only when they apply to the experience structured
by the concepts of understanding.

Moreover, on Kant's account, although the a priori structures of the
mind are not reducible to experience, we do begin our cognitive life with
experience.[4] But, if a person has no acquaintance with autonomous life, then
she cannot have much cognition of it either. Finally, the critique of (pure or
practical) reason represents the investigations which seek to determine the
ideas of reason. But if a person's reason has been "misused" rather than edu-
cated, how can it offer guidance? What does Kant suggest in this situation?
An answer to these questions and a possible objection will be discussed in
the next section.

§65. Political emancipation

Recall the problem: Without finding instruction either in external rules or in
inner powers, after "throwing off" the authoritative "dogmas and formulas",
the person seeking enlightenment seems rather condemned to darkness.
Kant has more confidence in the human species and tries to reassure those
determined to reach maturity despite their unavoidable reluctance that:

> This danger is not in fact so very great, for they would certainly learn
> to walk eventually after a few falls. But an example of this kind is
> intimidating, and usually frightens them off from further attempts.
>
> (Kant 1970: 8:35–6, 54)

Up to this point, what Kant seems to suggest to those willing to emanci-
pate themselves from the allegedly valid authority of dogmas, guardians
and self-incurred prejudices is to throw all of these constraints off and to

have the courage to make their own choices. However, one may envisage two alternatives: either Kant has forgotten to mention some other capacity of human beings by which they could rationally decide the way in which to take their further steps; or he simply invites them, at least for a while, to lead an irrational, or purely instinctual, life. If listening to deceptive imperatives has become their "second nature", and if they misused their reason, which eventually became "the ball and chain" of their "permanent immaturity", the only road to enlightenment seems to pass through irrationality.

This would be to overstate the problem. Kant's philosophy can answer this; thus, although Kant advocates the questioning of all authorities and the attempt to act autonomously even on the basis of a reason which has been misused to the point of adopting deceptive imperatives as a second nature, he does not advocate irrationality. Since, as we have seen in Chapter 3, in order for the moral law to provide guidance one only needs to use one's own understanding, that is, to freely judge a situation; a person can find guidance in the practical power of reason. Moreover, for Kant, enlightenment has more chances to succeed when it is pursued by an entire public.[5] Apart from freedom, this public also needs the help of those few who think for themselves, and, Kant claims, the latter may belong to the group of the "guardians of the common mass" (Kant 1970: 8:36, 55).

In Chapters 1 and 3, I confined the argument mainly to the exposition of my reading of Kant and I did not try to defend it otherwise than as a coherent account of the various topics under consideration. At this point, however, it would be useful to consider an objection to Kant's account of the emancipation he hopes Enlightenment can bring about. This objection will be helpful not only as an illustration of a standard critical approach to Kant's work (an approach sometimes adopted also by Sartre), but also for understanding Sartre's objection to the authoritarianism of Kant's theory.

The objection I would like to consider is formulated by Jürgen Habermas, according to whom, in Kant's philosophy, there is an extension of the liberal fiction which conflates political and human emancipation; in other words, he assumes that Kant's notion of enlightenment represents a form of political emancipation of the bourgeois public of private persons from the authority of the state. The implication is that Kant's notion of enlightenment, as a process of emancipation from unvindicated authorities, is a concealed form of political emancipation. Instead of defending a genuine process of human emancipation, Habermas notes, Kant supports political emancipation and justifies it by presenting its scope as much broader, perhaps as broad as that of general human emancipation.

As Habermas tells us, the distinction between political and human emancipation belongs to the young Marx (Habermas 1989: 56). In "On the Jewish Question" (1979), Marx draws the distinction, and indicates the relationships, between these two forms of emancipation. Marx's text is a review of Bruno Bauer's essays on the Jewish Question (Marx 1979: 85). The problem approached in Bauer's essays is that of the emancipation of the German Jews who were living in a Christian state (Marx 1979: 86). Marx deems Bauer's solution to the Jewish Question incomplete. Thus, whereas Bauer contends that the emancipation of Jews could be realized by a critique of the Christian state, and by a transformation of religion into a purely private matter, Marx identifies in Bauer's solution "an uncritical confusion of political and universal human emancipation" (Marx 1979: 88–9).

The confusion between human and political emancipation becomes apparent when Bauer claims that, by relegating religion to the private sphere, "religion no longer exists"; and he concludes: "Take from religion its power of exclusion and it ceases to exist."[6] For Marx, religion exists even when the state is secular (Marx 1979: 90). Moreover, for him the secular state is based in fact upon religion as a presupposition. Marx deems the secularization of the state as merely political emancipation, and he claims that: "Political emancipation is not the completed and consistent form of religious emancipation, because political emancipation is not the completed and consistent form of human emancipation" (Marx 1979: 91).

Therefore, for Marx, the annulment of the rights based on contingent attributes, like holding Christian religious beliefs or property-owning, represents by no means a complete form of human emancipation. According to Marx, the state, as the authority which protects private property, is based upon property even if property-owners no longer enjoy political privileges: "Is private property not abolished ideally speaking when the non-owner has become the law giver for the owner?" asks Marx rhetorically. And he answers: "The political annulment of private property has not only not abolished private property, it actually presupposes it" (Marx 1979: 93).

Thus, the redistribution of the rights which define citizenship by no means implies the questioning of those rights. Marx considers political emancipation as the process whereby all persons living in a society eventually acquire personal freedom, that is, a set of rights which protect them from the state. But this by no means implies the citizen's freedom as self-determination, that is, the freedom of the citizen to question those very rights which define her personal freedom. Self-determination requires, according to Marx, human emancipation.

In the next section, I will raise an objection to Marx's solution and will consider a possible answer Kant can give to Habermas.

§66. Human emancipation

On Marx's account, the solution to the Jewish Question and to the problem of human emancipation in general is the critique of the secular state and the disentanglement of the "sophism" of the political state (Marx 1979: 94). The concrete form of criticism that shapes the transformation of the secular state is, in Marx's view, the critique of the private rights enforced by the state, because those rights are incompatible with a complete human emancipation (Marx 1979: 104). More precisely, human emancipation should proceed as a critique of the separation between human beings as members of civil society and as moral persons in the public sphere, that is, a critique of the separation between the private and public spheres (Marx 1979: 108).

However, if what Marx advocates is the annulment of private rights, then he fails to acknowledge that the citizen's political autonomy as the freedom to participate in the formulation and sanctioning of legal norms is not possible without the private rights which form an important part of the citizen's personal freedom. The force of Marx's criticism consists in having realized that a redistribution of rights does not actually lead to the person's freedom, since it only grants him a limited freedom, namely the freedom defined politically by the state.

Yet, coming back to Kant's notion of enlightenment, one can see that membership in the "entire public" cannot be reduced to the individual's belonging to the bourgeois public sphere. Since enlightenment presupposes the critique of all unvindicated authorities, it cannot be seen as merely a form of emancipation of civil society from the state. A possible objection to this interpretation would be that the critique of unvindicated authorities is a critique performed by reason, the same reason which is the seat of the very human rights that ground the private/public distinction. In fact, in *The Metaphysics of Morals*, Kant seems to deduce property-ownership as condition for citizenship precisely from the basis of the laws of practical reason.

The question stated above, namely, 'Is enlightenment a concealed form of political emancipation?' needs, therefore, to be reformulated. For Kant, the legal norms which define the citizen's personal freedom are a priori, not derived from experience. Their authority is not based on empirical knowledge but on the practical authority of reason. Hence, the rational critique of the state seems to be performed within the legal constraints established by practical reason. Thus stated, the problem represents a particular case of an even more general question, which Kant has already formulated in this essay.

Recall that, on Kant's account, one is supposed to reject all existing authorities and to try to judge morally what ought to be done in a certain situation on the basis of one's own understanding. Yet, Kant also mentions that the deceitful imperatives which have been imposed on people have become second nature. The question is, therefore, whether it is possible even in principle for a person to question existing authorities in a genuine manner. For it seems impossible to determine whether reason does not assess the validity of existing norms on the basis of those deceitful imperatives which have been internalized and which would only reinforce the imperative under investigation.

This is a problem which will reappear in Chapter 6. We will see that, since it is a problem facing both Kant and Sartre, and since dealing with it will lead too far away from our purpose in this book, I will not discuss it in detail.[7] Nevertheless, in what follows I will briefly mention what I take to be Kant's approach to it and how this approach can successfully deal with it. To begin with, since this is a very general problem of justification, it would be useful to narrow it down and approach a more limited question. I will start with the question of the justification of particular principles on the basis of the Categorical Imperative. In the remainder of this section, I will introduce the conceptual background for this question and will reformulate it by means of these concepts.

According to Christine Korsgaard, there are three ways in which, starting from the Categorical Imperative's formula of the universal law, the justification of practical norms can be understood (Korsgaard 1996). Recall that the formula of the universal law of the categorical imperative is expressed as follows: "*Act only in accordance with that maxim through which you can at the same time will that it become a universal law*" (*GMS*: 4:421, 73).

The three interpretations of the formula of the universal law are the logical, teleological and practical interpretations and, in what follows, I will focus mainly on the first and the third. I focus only on these not because the teleological understanding is any less interesting, but because it would involve a preliminary discussion of the difference between causal and teleological laws, which, for the purpose of this chapter, will be an unnecessary detour; confining my comments to the logical and practical interpretations will suffice for my argument here.

Before presenting these two interpretations, I mention that Korsgaard's points refer to what is sometimes called the 'contradiction-in-conception', rather than the 'contradiction-in-the-will', test. Thus, for Kant, the general criterion for the evaluation of an action is that we "*be able to will* that a maxim of our action become a universal law" (*GMS*: 4:424, 75). But this general criterion can reject two types of immoral actions: some actions have maxims which "cannot even be *thought* without contradiction as a universal law of nature"; for other actions, it is "impossible to *will* that their maxim be raised to the universality of a law of nature because such a will would contradict itself" (*GMS*: 4:424, 75).

So, the focus in the next sections will be on the question of the justification of practical principles, starting from the contradiction-in-conception test as construed on the practical and logical interpretations.

§67. Logical interpretation

In the previous section, I introduced several distinctions in order to narrow down the scope of the question of justification. I have explained the choice of the formula of universal law, the choice of the two interpretations, but I have not mentioned anything about the focus on the contradiction-in-conception test. In fact, the reason is that, as we will see, understanding the contradiction in thought (i.e. in conception) raises already serious problems, so the additional difficulties of understanding the contradiction-in-the-will must be left for discussion elsewhere.

The logical and practical interpretations are ways of understanding how the formula of the universal law can reject immoral maxims by the contradiction-in-conception test. To see how a maxim can be rejected on the logical interpretation, consider the example of false promising:

> Perhaps the clearest way to bring out the logical contradiction is to say that there would be no such thing as a promise [...] in the world of the universalised maxim. The practice of offering and accepting promises would have died out under stress of too many violations.
>
> (Korsgaard, 1996: 82–3)

What Korsgaard suggests here is that the maxim of making false promises cannot be thought as a universal law of nature, since, as universal, the maxim of false promising will destroy the practice of making and accepting promises and, therefore, in a world without promises, we cannot think of making promises. By analogy, how can I think of winning an Olympic medal if the institution of Olympic Games did not to exist? Hence, the contradiction which is supposed to be at stake here is the following: "The non-existence of the practice that results from universalization is contradicted by the existence of it presupposed in the individual maxim" (Korsgaard 1996: 86).

The problem with this interpretation, Korsgaard thinks, is that it cannot reject certain maxims as leading to logical contradictions, although the maxims are clearly wrong. For instance, why would the maxim of "killing children that tend to cry at night more than average, in order to get enough sleep" be rejected by the contradiction-in-conception test? After all, on the logical interpretation of the Categorical Imperative, such a maxim can be thought of without contradiction as a universal law, as, by universalizing it, the practice will not disappear. This will, therefore, be the case of a false positive, that is, a maxim which, although clearly wrong, must be considered on the basis of the universalizability test as morally permissible.

Korsgaard's diagnosis is that the example points to a serious problem for the logical interpretation, namely, that it cannot deal with natural actions, but only with conventional actions. Promising is an institution, a convention, which has a certain purpose to be pursued by following certain rules; once the rules are systematically broken, the purpose is no longer pursued and the practice disappears, being at best replaced by some other practice, which will achieve the required purpose in a different way (i.e. by following different rules). In other words, whereas the practice is conventional, the purpose is natural and, as such, it will have to be pursued in some other way.

Unlike the maxim of making false promises, that of killing does not undermine itself:

> No amount or kind of use of the action of killing is going to make it impossible. And this is because the existence of this kind of action and its efficacy depend only on the laws of nature, not on any conventional practice.
>
> (Korsgaard 1996: 85)

Immoral natural actions cannot be justified as immoral by the logical interpretation, since the contradiction which is specific for the logical interpretation is premised on the disappearance, under conditions of universalization, of the very practices which give meaning to those actions. But the killing of crying babies, no matter how often carried out, can still be performed and, hence, does not undermine itself; or so argues Korsgaard.

So far, I have presented the way in which the logical interpretation is supposed to function and how it can easily lead to false positives. It remains to be seen whether the practical interpretation fares better and whether it does not have problems of its own. In the next section, I will focus on the practical interpretation. I will first present it, then raise some questions concerning its effectiveness as an ethical criterion and, finally, I will compare it with the logical interpretation.

§68. Practical interpretation

The practical interpretation makes use of a different type of contradiction, which Korsgaard calls "practical" (Korsgaard 1996: 93–4). This contradiction would derive from the analyticity of hypothetical imperatives. A hypothetical imperative has the following form: if you will a certain end, then, insofar as you are rational, you ought to will also the best means to the given end. The analytic character of such an imperative is, according to Korsgaard, derived from a relation of "containment":

> Willing is regarding yourself as the cause of the end in question – as the one who will bring it about. This distinguishes willing from mere wanting or wishing or desiring. Conceiving yourself as the cause of the end is conceiving yourself as the setting off of a causal chain that will result in the production of the end. It is conceiving yourself as using the available causal connections. But the available causal connections are, by definition, "means".
>
> (Korsgaard 1996: 94)

Following Korsgaard, by applying this to the maxim of making false promises in order to gain some cash, we are supposed to see that we cannot think of the maxim as a universal law. This is because, in a world in which this maxim was universalized, the making of false promises would not lead us closer to making some cash. Hence, by willing to make money through false promises, I cannot will a state of affairs in which making money through false promises is not possible. But the world in which the maxim of false promises for easy gain is universalized is precisely a state of affairs where making money through false promises is not possible.

This means that I cannot think of acting on the maxim of gaining money by making false promises and, at the same time, will that the maxim becomes a universal law. By willing this maxim as a universal law, I also will that my end cannot be realized and, yet, acting on that maxim implies that I will my end to be realized. Hence, in Korsgaard's own words,

> What the test shows to be forbidden are just those actions whose efficacy in achieving their purposes depends upon their being exceptional. If the action no longer works as a way of achieving the purpose in question when it is universalised, then it is an action of this kind.
>
> (Korsgaard 1996: 92)

To sum up, the difference between the logical and the practical interpretation can be expressed as follows. On the logical interpretation of the Categorical Imperative, an immoral action is the action performed according to a rule that stands under a maxim that the agent cannot at the same time think of as a universal law, since a world in which the maxim would be universalized would be a world without that maxim; the agent would will to act on a maxim which, at the same time, would not exist.

By contrast, on the practical interpretation, an immoral action is given by a rule connected to a maxim which cannot be thought of at the same time as a universal law of nature, since a world in which the maxim would be such a law would be a world in which the maxim could not be realized; the agent would will to realize something which, at the same time, would not be realizable.

Korsgaard suggests that the practical interpretation better captures the moral point of the universalization test than the logical interpretation. Presumably, this is because, in the case of the practical interpretation, there is no assumption that universalization leads to the disappearance and non-existence of certain practices. Therefore, unlike the logical interpretation, the practical interpretation can also deal with duties of omission with respect to natural actions. Such actions, unlike conventional ones, do not become logically impossible through universalization, although they are no longer realizable; one can think of them, but can no longer realize them.

To illustrate this, Korsgaard considers the maxim of dealing with my successful rival by murder. She thinks that the logical interpretation cannot show what is wrong with this action, since "we cannot say that if this sort of action is abused the practice will die out" (Korsgaard 1996: 98). By contrast, if we specify the purpose of the action differently, not simply as that of killing a certain person, but as that of securing the job, my action will undermine this purpose, since, universalized, it will lead to my own death by the hand of the next in line; yet, my life is a condition of my securing the job. As Korsgaard puts it,

> to want something is to want to be secure in the possession of it. The use of violent natural means for achieving ends cannot be universalised because that would leave us insecure in the possession of these goods, and without that security these goods are not good to us at all. So, if we include as part of the purpose that the agent wants to be secure in the possession of the end, we can get a practical contradiction in the universalisation of violent methods.
>
> (Korsgaard 1996: 99)

Again, Korsgaard means here to illustrate the point that the practical interpretation can deal both with natural and with conventional practices, whereas the logical interpretation leaves behind false positives, that is, maxims (in this case, of natural actions), which pass the test although they should not.

Let me sum up the points so far. We have now an account of justification starting from the very formal criterion given by the Categorical Imperative's formula of the universal law. In evaluating a norm (say, a norm about how to distribute jobs in society), we can justify it as permissible or reject it as impermissible on the basis of the contradiction-in-conception test and, more exactly, on the basis of its practical interpretation. As we will see in the next section, everything sounds much simpler than it actually is.

§69. The problem of justification

Barbara Herman objects to the Korsgaardian version of the practical interpretation. She identifies two maxims which, even though intuitively not impermissible, do not pass the practical interpretation of the contradiction-in-conception test. In fact, only one such maxim would be sufficient to demonstrate that the practical interpretation is not an accurate account of the justification provided by the contradiction-in-conception test, and, in what follows, I will focus on her example of a maxim of playing tennis on Sunday morning when all the neighbours are in church.

Thus, if universalized, this maxim would lead to its own disappearance. For, at other times, the courts are crowded and, if everyone acted on the maxim, courts would also get crowded on Sunday morning. The feasibility of the person's action under this maxim is given by the fact that "others do not act as he does" (Herman 1993: 138). Clearly, this seems to be a reason to reject the maxim, since, as we have seen, "what the test shows to be forbidden are just those actions whose efficacy in achieving their purposes depends upon their being exceptional" (Korsgaard 1996: 92).

And, yet, such a maxim is not morally impermissible. There does not seem to be anything wrong with acting under this maxim. What we have here is a case of a false negative, that is, a case of a maxim which is rejected as morally impermissible on the basis of a particular test, although intuitively there is nothing wrong with it. Therefore, for Herman, the logical interpretation is to be preferred, insofar as it does not reject such a maxim. Drawing on a comparison with the maxim of making deceitful promises, she says:

> According to the logical interpretation, under universalisation, the deceitful promise is not intelligible as a deceitful promise, because promising (and so deceitful promising) is not possible in the world of universal deceitful promising. Given universalisation, a "tennis at 10:00" maxim will not achieve its purpose (finding an empty court), but it is not for that reason inconceivable or impossible.
>
> (Herman 1993: 139)

The maxim of playing tennis when all the neighbours are in church is, for Herman, a maxim in a coordination case. The logical interpretation of the contradiction-in-conception test is able to distinguish between cases of coordination and cases of deceit, whereas, she claims, the practical interpretation misses this (Herman 1993: 140). Yet she also acknowledges that the logical interpretation does have difficulties, especially with action descriptions that are not general. For instance, if I decide to ask you for a loan in order to prevent you from gambling the money away and to make it possible for your children to benefit from it later, I deceive you, because I promise I will return your money, while my intention is to give it to your children. For Herman, "the possibility of such a maxim, its coherence, does not depend on others not acting similarly in similar circumstances" (Herman 1993: 141).

Hence, Herman advances the logical interpretation as an accurate one as far as general maxims are concerned. Yet she also makes a further suggestion which is quite surprising. Reflecting on the various debates between supporters of the practical interpretation and supporters of the logical interpretation, she suggests that we are, in fact, in a "permanent fix-it" situation: any new interpretation can in principle again and again be challenged and reformulated. This, however, is not a very good premise for her own defence of this logical interpretation. That this will be challenged is very likely, but that her proposal will have to be tinkered with, rather than simply defended, is worrying. If one puts forward an argument knowing that it has certain problems which need to be addressed, one would be better to address those problems first and then advance the argument.

Why should we think that an argument is worth tinkering with, rather than replacing with an altogether new argument? And how can we conclude, as Herman does, that her version of the logical interpretation is sound for the case of maxims expressed in general terms? For we can see that the contradiction involved in the case of the logical interpretation is a contradiction in conceiving that an action which actually does not make sense be performed, as if it made sense and it could be performed. The contradiction involved in the case of the practical interpretation is a contradiction in conceiving that an action which actually cannot be carried out, nevertheless is carried out.

Yet, while it is indeed contradictory to think at the same time that an action does and does not make sense, and that an action can and cannot be carried out, the reason why these two contradictions arise is that, when the maxims of these actions are universalized, the conditions which are necessary for the actions to make sense or to be carried out are undermined. One problem is that some maxims with this kind of self-undermining nature are not morally impermissible; moreover, the self-undermining character of these maxims depends on certain consequences' obtaining, which means that the test can no longer account for *unconditional* obligations.

The doubt we can raise with regard to the account of justification based on these two interpretations of the contradiction-in-conception test is, therefore, not of an idle kind. It is not simply a matter of saying that it can always be objected to, but it is a doubt raised by pointing to specific problems: both interpretations seem unable to account for specifically *moral* impermissibility and for its unconditional character. Let me try to examine this further by tracing the problem to one of its roots.

§70. The problem of practical judgement

The logical and practical interpretations look at the contradiction-in-conception test and read it as a test for the possibility of acting on a maxim in a world where the maxim is universally followed. So far, so good. The textual ground for this general account of how the Categorical Imperative is supposed to test maxims is given by Kant's comments on the Typic of Pure Practical Judgement, in the *Critique of Practical Reason* (*KpV*: 5: 67–71, 89–94). In the attempt to go further and account for this possibility of acting on a maxim which functions as a law, the logical and practical interpretations misconstrue what Kant says. I will first present what I take to be the accurate interpretation. I will then show where the logical and practical interpretations go wrong.

According to Kant, in the case of practical philosophy, judgement is made more difficult by the kind of normativity moral judgements presuppose. Thus, Kant says:

Whether an action possible for us in sensibility is or is not a case that falls under the rule requires practical power of judgement, by which what was said universally (*in abstracto*) in the rule is applied *in concreto* to an action. However, a practical rule of pure reason, *first*, as *practical*, concerns the existence of an object, and second, as a *practical rule* of pure reason, carries with it necessity with regard to the existence of an action and hence is a practical law, and specifically not a natural law of nature [concerning action] through empirical determining bases but a law of freedom according to which the will is to be determinable independently of everything empirical (merely through the presentation of a law as such and of its form); yet, all occurring cases of possible actions can only be empirical, i.e., can belong only to experience and nature. Therefore it seems paradoxical to want to find in the world of sense a case which, while to this extent it always falls only under the law of nature, nonetheless permits the application of a law of freedom to it, and to which the suprasensible idea of the morally good to be exhibited in that world *in concreto* to be applied.

(KpV: 5:67–8, 90)

This long quotation presents the justificatory problem that confronts Kant's practical philosophy. To judge, for Kant, is to subsume a particular case under a general rule; for instance, I judge this object as round by subsuming it, first, under the general rule which distinguishes between the object and its properties and, secondly and in particular, under a rule which distinguishes between the properties of objects and identifies our object's round shape. Practical judgement is supposed to decide whether or not an action is morally good, so it must subsume an action under the rule which distinguishes between morally good and morally bad actions.

An action which has been performed is an action which is possible in the world. In addition, it is an action which can be accounted for in theoretical, scientific terms: we can explain, on the basis of natural laws, how the action necessarily occurs given the appropriate conditions. But this is something we can do for both morally permissible and impermissible actions, as long as these are actions that have been performed. Hence, the aspect or aspects of an action in virtue of which it is morally permissible, rather than impermissible, cannot simply be an aspect which would be relevant for a scientific account of how the action took place, since what takes place, insofar as we regard it as having taken place, can equally be a morally permissible or a morally impressible action.

Of course, one ought not to perform a morally impermissible action, but, if such an action has been performed, then an account of how this action has been performed need not mention anything about its moral status. Even when we assume that an evil/good person performed such an action precisely because *she thought* the action was morally impermissible/permissible, whether or not the action was actually impermissible/permissible is not relevant for the account of how it was performed.

Similarly, it would be useless to apply practical judgement to actions regarded as phenomena. The features in virtue of which an action was performed (for instance, those which made a person believe it was a wrong/right action) are distinct from those in virtue of which an action ought to be performed. Kant proposes the following solution:

> In the subsumption of an action possible for me in the world of sense under a *pure practical law* the concern is not with the possibility of the *action* as an event in the world of sense; for, this possibility pertains to the judging of the theoretical use of reason according to the law of causality, a pure concept of understanding for which reason has a *schema* in sensible intuition. Physical causality, or the condition under which it takes place, belongs under the concepts of nature, and the schema of these concepts is drafted by the transcendental power of imagination. Here, however, the concern is not with the schema of a case according to laws but with the schema (if this word is fitting here) of a law itself, because the *determination of the will* (not the action in reference to its result) through the law alone and without any other determining basis ties the concept of causality to conditions that are entirely different from those that amount to natural connection.
>
> (*KpV*: 5:68–9, 91)

Hence, according to Kant, it is not the action as a phenomenon which must be judged, since, again, such an action is subsumable under the principle of physical causality and can no longer be seen as determined by the will in accordance with a morally valid law, specifically by the form of a maxim which is morally valid. What must be judged is the action as the determination of the will by a morally valid maxim. The practical and logical interpretations, I argue, go wrong in their interpretation of how practical judgement is supposed to function. In the next section, I will examine the standard view of practical judgement, a view which lies at the basis of the logical and practical interpretations.

§71. The standard view of practical judgement

On Kant's account, practical judgement cannot consist in the connection of sensible intuitions to rules of understanding through the power of imagination which provides schemata of such connections. This is because we cannot have sensible intuitions constituting an action which *ought* to be performed. Practical judgement will consist instead in the connection of a maxim of action to the ideas of practical reason (the ideas of good and evil) through the faculty of the understanding, which connects the maxim to objects of nature through the form of a law of nature.

This form of a law of nature provided by the understanding is called by Kant the "type" of the moral law. Kant concludes that the rule of judgement through which we can judge whether a maxim is morally valid is the following: "ask yourself whether, if the action you propose were to occur according to a law of the nature of which you yourself were a part, you could indeed regard it as possible through your will" (*KpV*: 5:69, 91).

The standard interpretation of Kant's solution is offered by Onora O'Neill. According to her, Kant avoids the problem of practical judgement "by considering the possibility of acts falling not under the universalised maxim, i.e., the practical principle, but under an analogous natural law which he calls the *type* of the (putative) moral law" (O'Neill, 1975: 62). In other words, according to O'Neill, we are supposed to test the maxims of our actions by trying to imagine ourselves in a world in which our maxims functioned as universal laws; if we cannot will to be in such a world, the maxim is morally impossible or impermissible.

Specifically with regard to the contradiction-in-conception test, the interpretation of practical judgement offered by O'Neill is supposed to work in the following way:

> It asks whether we can simultaneously intend to do *x* (assuming that we must intend some set of conditions sufficient for the successful carrying out of our intentions and the normal and predictable results of successful execution) and intend everyone else to do *x* (assuming again that we must intend some conditions sufficient for the successful execution of their intentions and the normal and predictable results of such execution).
>
> (O'Neill 1975: 73)

Applied to the maxim of making false promises, the test is supposed to yield the expected conclusion, namely, that making false promises is forbidden. This is because, first, by making a false promise, the agent must intend the set of conditions for successfully acting in that way and the normal and predictable results of his successful act. Part of the set of conditions necessary for the successful carrying out of this action is that there be a sufficient level of confidence to allow his promise to be believed, rather than immediately questioned.

At the same time, however, to intend that everyone make false promises implies to intend the normal and predictable results of the maxim of making false promises' functioning as a law of nature. Among such results, there would be a constant decrease in public trust which would lead to this institution's dying out sooner or later. But to intend both this and a level of confidence sufficient for one's maxim to be believed, rather than immediately questioned, is contradictory (O'Neill 1975: 78).

It is not difficult to see that Korsgaard's practical and logical interpretations stem from this standard view of the contradiction-in-conception. Recall that, for both these interpretations, the contradiction is supposed to occur between the intention to act in a certain way in a world where the maxim of one's action functions as a universal law and, hence, is universally followed.

The logical interpretation is supposed to judge as morally impermissible that action which is meaningful only within a certain institutional framework, but which destroys this institutional framework when its maxim is regarded as a universal law and acted upon. By contrast, the practical interpretation is supposed to reject as morally impossible that action which can only be successfully performed under conditions which are undermined by the normal and predictable results of following the maxim of that action as a universal law.

One may still try to stick to this standard view by putting forward some other interpretation based on a different type of contradiction, however, I did not rehearse the arguments for and against the logical and practical interpretations of the contradiction-in-conception test with this intention in mind; I have used these arguments as illustrations of what I take to be an inappropriate strategy of approaching practical judgement. More precisely, the problem is in the interpretation of the type. I think that O'Neill's view (namely, that Kant tries to solve the difficulties of practical judgement "by considering the possibility of acts falling not under the universalised maxim, i.e., the practical principle, but under an analogous natural law which he calls the *type* of the (putative) moral law" (O'Neill 1975: 62)) is the root of the problem. I will talk more about this in the next section.

§72. Problem of standard view

O'Neill regards Kant as a philosopher interested in the conditions sufficient for the successful carrying out of our intentions and the normal and predictable results of such execution. Both of these factors, however, regard the actions precisely as events in the phenomenal world, something Kant specifically warned us against. As I have mentioned, Kant's point is that such an interpretation is unable to account for their distinctly moral character and the unconditional necessity of these actions. All we can obtain in this case is an account of a contradiction between intending that X be the case and intending that non-X be the case.

While there is clearly a contradiction in "intention" here, that is, a contradiction between two intentions, by itself this does not seem *morally* impermissible. If I intend that there is a bar of chocolate in my hand and that there is not, then I am certainly contradicting myself, but I am not doing something morally impermissible. Moreover, assuming that there is something morally impermissible in such conflicting intentions, we can still raise a question about the way they arise.

More exactly, on O'Neill's interpretation, conflicting intentions emerge when I consider the sufficient conditions for the performance of my action and the normal and predictable results of everybody's acting on the maxim of my action. Again, looking at the action in this way is precisely what Kant warned us against, since it involves the sensible aspects of the action. This is problematic because the impossibility which obtains from the conflict of intentions is conditional on what is sufficient for performing an action and on actually obtaining the normal and predictable results of everybody's following the maxim of my action. But that which is sufficient for actually performing an action and the normal and predictable results of following the action's maxim is contingent on further conditions. What we need, however, is an unconditional obligation.

What can we do? We obviously need a different interpretation of what Kant says. I have provided an alternative reading elsewhere and I have argued that it is not only more accurate, but also better able to provide an approach to the question of moral judgement.[8] In what follows, for the purpose of the argument in this book, I can only outline the approach and make a comment on why I think contemporary Kantians fail to adopt it.

The type of contradiction one should look for is specific for transcendental logic, where concepts are not only important in their relationships to each other, but also to their objects. In Kant's theoretical philosophy, when a concept or the rule at the basis of such a concept is denied with regard to an experience to the constitution of which the concept or rule is contributing, we do not simply have a logical contradiction or what may be called an empirical contradiction, which is based on a negation of the truth given by an empirical generalization. The necessary character of the concept within that experience is not given by analysis or by reference to the empirical generalization, but by its constitutive role.

By analogy with the theoretical case, a similar type of contradiction is needed in the practical realm. There, we deal with rules which ought to regulate a person's will when the situation concerns herself or herself in relation to others. In Chapter 6, I will say more about what Kant calls the "fact of reason", but, for the moment, I need to note an implication of this notion. Thus, on Kant's view, the fact of reason implies that, as soon we raise the question of how we ought to act in a particular situation, we invoke the moral law or the Categorical Imperative and the valid practical principle for that particular situation.

If we assume that, in that context, we act on the contradictory maxim (say, instead of the maxim of beneficence we act on a maxim of self-interest or, instead of a maxim of truthfulness, we act on a maxim of conditional deception), then willing this action will lead to a contradiction. The assumption that the categorical imperative is constitutive of how a person ought to act in that particular situation implies that whatever maxim is followed, if it is valid, it can be followed universally. This is why we universalize the maxim of the action. At the same time, the valid maxim will also be constitutive of how persons ought to act in that situation, and the assumption that they act on the contradictory maxim will lead to a contradiction.

We universalize the contradictory maxim and ask whether it is valid. The question of validity enacts the moral law and the valid maxims as rules which ought to determine the person's will. Hence, the scenario in which everybody follows the contradictory maxim will be contradictory, since it will assume the valid rule as constitutive and will have to deny it through the action which is performed on the contradictory maxim. Again, the contradiction will obtain because the maxim which determines the will is the contradictory of the valid maxim.

To be sure, the contradiction will not simply arise in this way, since, in this case, we could simply be accused of taking for granted the maxim we consider as valid and rejecting its contradictory in a dogmatic way. The contradiction will emerge between the maxim and some more general condition, which is also grounded in the Categorical Imperative, but is more basic than the maxim. For instance, in a world where everybody lies, a positive response to my lie cannot be taken to indicate a successful lie, since the person who says she believes what I say will also lie. Here, the assumption of lying as the good maxim is in contradiction with a more basic requirement that makes lying possible, namely, the possibility of a truthful commitment to what I say on the part of my interlocutor.

In the next section, I will briefly discuss a particular example and, then, I will move on to the issue of the relevance of this discussion for political or juridical issues and, more generally, for moral issues.

§73. Ethics and politics

To conclude the discussion on the contradiction-in-conception test, consider, for instance, the case where we are interested to know how we ought to act in a situation, like that in Constant's example, where we cannot avoid acting: we must respond to the murderer's question by a 'yes' or 'no'. To raise the problem of how we *ought* to act means to make appeal to a standard of action. Assuming that this is a standard of moral goodness understood as objective, the standard would have to be universalizable. Hence, the problem of the *ought* already invokes the moral criterion given by the Categorical Imperative.

Obviously, depending on the context, the moral law will ground more specific moral principles and, depending on the agent, each principle will ground more specific rules of action. These rules and principle ought to regulate the relationship between persons – they ought to determine their wills to act in accordance with what is morally good. Now, a person who, instead of acting according to the morally valid standard, acts against it, will act on the basis of a principle which will contradict the morally valid principle the moral law would be able to ground in that situation. This is the source of the contradiction which the Categorical Imperative is supposed to make manifest in the case of morally impermissible actions.[9]

Starting from the case of a maxim of lying, I offered a sketch of the activity of practical judgement. Clearly more needs to be said to support these claims – both in working out the idea of a transcendental practical philosophy and in the applications of such an idea to the particular cases for the justification of moral principles. What is clear is that, if an account of the normative force of morally valid principles is to be appropriate, then we need something like this critical approach in practical philosophy.

The type of necessity presupposed by an unconditional obligation cannot be reduced either to a logical contradiction or to a contradiction based on an empirical generalization, so the idea of a maxim that is constitutive of a situation where persons act towards themselves and towards the others on the maxims on which they ought to act is required. Yet, such an idea of a constitutive practical principle suggests a metaphysical commitment to some version of Kant's transcendental idealism, which contemporary moral philosophers, even Kantians, try to avoid.

Although I have mainly referred to Kant's and Sartre's ethical theories, the discussion so far has implications for their moral theories more generally. So far, I have consistently used Kant's distinction between moral theory, ethics and juridical philosophy to indicate the various domains in which normative claims can be made. I have taken 'moral theory' to refer to practical philosophy as a whole and to include juridical philosophy (which we can also call theory of justice or political philosophy) and ethics. Let me now present in more detail this Kantian distinction between ethics and theory of justice.

The main difference between these domains concerns the relationships between their respective incentives and norms.[10] Juridical norms only require that we act in accordance with them or, in other words, they require 'legality'. Ethical norms require legality, but, in addition, also require 'morality'. This means that ethical norms prescribe not only that we perform certain types of action, but also that we perform them with the appropriate motive. The idea here is that, in the case of ethical norms, we need to be prompted in our actions by the norms' rightness.

A related feature of juridical norms is that they can be enforced. This is why commentators can claim that

> juridical laws can only require external behaviour, but not motivation, since external coercion (as the specific incentive connected with juridical laws) does not (reliably) affect the inner attitude or motive.
>
> (Willaschek 2002: 68)

This means that external coercion is unlikely to bring about in the agent the motivation which is appropriate for ethical norms.[11] In other words, by being externally coerced, it is unlikely the agent will get to act on the ethical norm out of respect for the norm's rightness. Perhaps an even stronger argument would be that, no matter how effective a method of bringing about motivation would be, external coercion should still not try to bring this about, since there is no reliable way of publicly monitoring motivations.

Assuming that coercion cannot determine inner attitude or motive, then nor will it be able to determine inner actions. This is why Kant does not see an imperative like the omission of self-deception as a juridical norm, although it may well be performed for other motives than the norm's rightness. It may seem, therefore, that the condition of enforceability excludes as possible candidates for the status of juridical norm all ethical imperatives, because of their requirement for appropriate motivation.

Yet, from the example of the maxim of self-deceit, we can see that some maxims, which do not presuppose that they be performed with a specific motivation, can also be excluded, since they are not publicly accessible actions. Since they are not publicly accessible, or, at any rate, not completely accessible in this way, they cannot be enforced. There are, however, rules which forbid the performance of *publicly accessible* actions, and which, because of specific circumstances, cannot be enforced, since no punishment can be a sufficient source of incentive for the omission of the action.

The case presented by Kant refers to someone in a shipwreck who, in order to save his own life, shoves another, whose life is equally in danger, off a plank on which he had saved himself. According to Kant, there is no legal authorization to do anything which endangers the life of the person on the plank and, if the shoved person dies as a result of the shover's pushing him off the plank, the shover is legally accountable for the consequence of his action. And, yet, the action is not enforceable, since it is not punishable.[12]

Having outlined the difference between ethics and theory of justice, as distinct parts of a moral theory, in the next section I will clarify further the notion of motivation and will explain how considerations pertaining strictly to ethics are nevertheless significant for juridical theory (or theory of justice) and, hence, for moral theory in general.

§74. Intention and motivation

The differences between ethical and juridical norms stem from the requirement that the latter be enforceable. Enforceability requires externality and, hence, legality. We cannot enforce norms where the observance of which is not public or capable of being publicly monitored. Hence, nor can we enforce norms which require that they be observed from a particular motivation. What can publicly be monitored, therefore, is the action, not the motivation with which I perform the action.[13]

Motives make a difference in the understanding of actions only when they also reveal the ends or intentions of actions. Unfortunately, however, there is no way in which motives can be established objectively. Hence, perhaps the main role of motives is personal: motives are relevant ethically and make a difference in the understanding of the actions' and agents' moral worth. Thus, whether I give the right change to my customer because I think this is the right thing to do or because I am risk-adverse and I am too scared I would be caught will make no difference to the police officer who is in the shop (unless she is also the moralist in the area). Yet, depending on my motive for an action, I can conclude that my action is morally worthy (and not *merely* in accordance with the appropriate standard) or morally unworthy (merely in accordance with the appropriate standard).

Similarly, whether I commit murder, because (mistakenly or not) I think this to be (in some sense) for the good of the person will not make a difference to the prosecution. To be sure, if I dispute that it was my intention to commit murder, then, of course, it does make a difference for the prosecution, but then what I dispute is my end or purpose or intention, not my motive. To put it differently: what is juridically important to establish is the end or purpose of the action, because this is what shows which kind of action has been performed. But whether or not this reveals anything about the motive with which the action has been performed is not juridically relevant.

And this is how it should be. The motive with which I perform my action cannot, in principle, be publicly monitored. My intention of killing a person can be doubted, if, for example, the person who sold me mushrooms can testify that I asked her twice whether mushrooms were tested against toxic content and that only then I bought them (the assumption being, of course, that I also took them home and cooked them, rather than going to another shop to buy mushrooms which had not been tested). But my motive is much more difficult, perhaps even impossible, to ascertain with sufficient degree of confidence.

So enforceability of a norm implies externality and legality. Juridical norms have to be enforceable; hence, they cannot require a particular motive. By contrast, ethical norms necessarily require that they be performed for the sake of the norm's rightness, otherwise actions performed on them have no moral worth. Since, for an ethical norm, being acted upon requires a specific motive (I call this 'ethical motive' and I refer by this to the fact that my reason for acting is that this is the right thing to do), acting for the sake of the norm's rightness is an essential part of ethical norms. By contrast, an essential part of juridical norms is the fact that they can be acted upon *either* for the sake of their rightness *or* out of empirical incentives (e.g. fear of punishment).

I have claimed that discussion of ethical theory and, in particular, of the justification of ethical standards is also politically (or juridically) relevant. The examination of the distinction between ethics and juridical theory, in the previous section, as well as the foregoing analysis of the contradiction-in-conception test should make this evident. Thus, while it is clearly the case that, for Kant, maxims which include non-ethical motives cannot be universalized, those which include ethical motives must still be tested.

When a maxim includes an ethical motive, what we test is merely the maxim's legality, since we already know that the motive is ethically good. When the maxim is not only legally valid, but includes also the appropriate motivation, then the action performed on the maxim is ethically worthy or, in Kant's term, has morality. If the action is performed in accordance with the maxim, but out of a non-ethical motive (fear of punishment, interest in the action's consequences and so on), the action has mere legality.

Hence, in testing a maxim, we also test a maxim's legality, not simply its morality. In this sense, the test offered by the Categorical Imperative is also politically (legally or juridically) relevant. Any attempt to understand how the Categorical Imperative is supposed to be applied in the justification of more specific practical principles will also be significant for a theory of justice, at least insofar as this is understood along Kantian lines.

I have started this chapter with Kant's account of the Enlightenment, as the process of questioning existing authorities and, through emancipation, acquiring autonomy. I have continued with an account of Kant's conception of practical justification and judgement, and I have shown how this process, even when it is confined to ethics, is still relevant politically or legally. Before concluding this chapter, I would like to discuss briefly an issue which so far seemed to divide most clearly Kant's and Sartre's practical philosophies, the issue whether a practical philosophy should be principle- or value-based. We will see that, by the end of Chapter 6, although this issue will still stand as marking a difference between their practical philosophies, the difference it will point to will be much subtler than it seems now.

§75. Empirical good

According to Kant, the concept of the good must be derived from the moral law. At least this is how Kant is standardly interpreted.[14] Since this is how Sartre interprets him too, I am not primarily interested in challenging the standard interpretation. I will assume that this interpretation is an accurate construal of Kant's position, but I would like to explore the reasons for this focus on principles in Kant. While, for the sake of the argument, I will accept that Kant offers a principle-centred ethics, my question is whether he has sufficient grounds for doing so.[15]

The thesis of priority appears most clearly in Chapter II of the Analytic of Pure Practical Reason *(KpV*: 5: 62, 84 and 5: 64, 85). Kant stresses that "the concept of good and evil must be determined not prior to the moral law [...] but only after it and by means of it" (*(KpV*: 5:62–3, 84). In other words, the fundamental criterion of morality is the moral law and not the moral value of absolute goodness, which is derived from the moral law. We should not try to establish whether or not an action conforms to the moral law by determining whether or not the action is absolutely good; on the contrary, an action has moral value insofar as it conforms to the moral law.

Not only ancient, but also modern, philosophers have traditionally taken as a starting point a particular conception of the good and have derived from it moral principles *(KpV*: 5:64, 86). For Kant, the situation should be exactly the opposite: one should start from moral principles. He justifies the claim by a *reductio:*

> Suppose, then, that we wanted to start from the concept of the good in order to derive from it the laws of the will; then this concept of an object (as a good object) would at the same time indicate it as the one determining basis of the will. Now, because this concept had no practical a priori law for its standard, the touchstone of good and evil could be posited in nothing other than the agreement of the object with our feeling of pleasure or displeasure. [...] Since what conforms to the feeling of pleasure can be established only through experience, and since the practical law, by stipulation, is after all to be based on this as its condition, the possibility of practical a priori laws would straightforwardly be excluded.
>
> *(KpV*: 5:63, 84–85)

The starting point of a *reductio* is an assumption which contradicts what is to be demonstrated. Kant would like to show that the moral law grounds the good. Hence, he begins by accepting provisionally that the good grounds the moral law. Next, he claims that the good can be based either on the moral law or on feelings of pleasure and displeasure. Since the good is supposed to ground the moral law, it cannot be based on the moral law. Therefore, it must be based on feelings of pleasure and displeasure.

But a good which is based on the feelings of pleasure and displeasure cannot ground the moral law, since the moral law is supposed to be objective. In other words, the moral law prescribes certain actions as unconditionally good, and not only as good for the purpose of promoting pleasure or avoiding displeasure. Hence, contrary to the initial clam, the good cannot ground the moral law and, since this was the assumption of the *reductio,* it follows that the contradictory of the initial assumption is true: the moral law grounds the good.

Let us look more closely at this *reductio.* Apart from the case where the good is indeed based on the moral law, this being the case corresponding to what is to be demonstrated, Kant accepts only a situation where the good is based on experience and, therefore, cannot ground moral a priori principles. The force of what Kant says relies heavily on the assumption that the only alternative to his position is the view that the good is determined in accordance with feelings.

But how can this exclusive disjunction be justified? Up to a certain point, Kant can make appeal to the distinction between the two parts of practical reason or the will, namely, the pure and the empirical part. The pure or rational part of the will is supposed to act in accordance with objective standards, whereas the empirical or sensible part follows subjective standards. Being pure, the rational part is independent from experience; therefore, Kant says, it must find within itself a determining standard of action *(KpV:* 5:19, 29). By contrast, the 'impure' or empirical part is determined to act by the pleasure or displeasure produced in a person by a certain object or state of affairs.

Hence, actions and their outcomes either are the result of the will's being determined a priori by a standard from within itself or are produced by the will's following a posteriori the aim of experiencing the pleasure associated with a certain object. From this, we can deduce the conclusion that actions and their outcomes can be either the result of the will's self-determination on the basis of the moral law (from which objective practical principles are derived) or the effect of the will's following the empirical incentives which it experiences in relation to certain objects.

Once the exclusive disjunction concerning the nature of values is explained in this way, Kant can argue that the concept of the good as the concept of an object of the will cannot ground the moral law, since either it itself is based on the moral law or it is based on the sensible incentives produced by the object of the will. But it is not clear how Kant gets from the claim that the will can be determined a priori by an objective standard from within itself to the conclusion that this objective standard cannot be a concept of the good, but only a moral law from which the concept of the good is to be derived.

I will discuss Kant's assumption, as well as his argument for principles as the privileged forms of normativity which can determine the will a priori, in the next section.

§76. External good

Kant's assumption here seems to be that an independently defined concept of the good is necessarily empirical and, therefore, that the only a priori good depends on the moral law. On the basis of Kant's texts, I cannot see how this assumption can be argued for. Commentators do not usually explore this particular argument of Kant in depth, but take it for granted that the moral law is normatively prior to the good. One exception is John Silber who devotes a section of his article "The Copernican Revolution in Ethics: The Good Re-examined" to the question of "The primacy of the moral law in the determination of the good".[16]

According to Silber, "we may fairly ask why the good, as the object of the will, must be related to the will by means of desire at all" (Silber 1995: 201). For him, the good, as the object of the will, cannot be a priori, because "the traditional concept of the good, defined prior to the moral law, is the concept of an object for which the will is to strive" (Silber 1995: 197), and, Silber adds, either the will's striving will be determined "empirically and contingently, and hence without obligation; or it will be compulsive upon will as the natural cause of the effects of the will, and hence the freedom of the will, and thereby the will itself, will be destroyed" (Silber 1995: 197).

In other words, there is an additional alternative position concerning the nature of the good which Kant would implicitly consider and reject, namely, the view that values determine the will in the manner in which a natural cause determines an effect; this view must be rejected, since it conflicts with the freedom of the will. I think that, while Silber is right to suggest that a compulsive good is incompatible with the freedom of the will, he leaves the question that he himself has raised unanswered. The question was why the good, as the object of the will, must be related to the will by means of desire.

If correct, the assumption that the good can determine the will either compulsively or empirically can justify Kant's first exclusive disjunction, according to which the good is either independent from the law and is empirical, or is a priori and normatively derived from the moral law.

Hence, this second exclusive disjunction would seem to justify the first, which would then justify the priority of the moral law. But the second disjunction also needs a justification. Kant's implicit argument is that the good, as an object of the will, is placed outside the will and can only affect the will either as a natural cause or by means of feelings; the good cannot affect it from within, as the moral law does. Thus, recall that, for Kant, the pure part of the will can only be determined by a standard from within itself, since only in this way can the will be determined independently from experience.

But, it is not clear why, in the same way in which we can accept that pure will takes as self-determining basis the moral law, we cannot also accept that it can take the good as a self-determining basis. Silber must provide an additional justification for why Kant excludes the possibility that the will's self-determining basis be the good.

Indeed, Silber considers this further objection.[17] His answer is that the good, as the concept of an object of the will, cannot function as a motivating cause for the pure or rational will, since the pure will's motivating cause "must determine the will formally and not materially by reference to the previously defined object" (Silber 1995: 203).

The assumption here is, therefore, that the object of the will necessarily determines the will materially. A material principle determines the will to act by a sensible desire for an object (*KpV*: 5:21, 32). But whether something is desired or not depends on how it or things similar to it are perceived by a person. Hence, a material principle determines the will empirically. By contrast, a formal principle would determine the will independently from experience. Thus, Silber says,

> by abstracting from all consideration of the object, [...] the will can be related to the object only by reference to its own idea of law which through the universality of its form is beyond all condition and, hence, can serve as the ground of the determination of the will without conditioning it.
>
> (Silber 1995: 203)[18]

Yet, again, the claim that the will can determine itself autonomously only by reference to a law is unsupported. It is not clear why the will could not have an idea of the good, which would be formal and could serve as the ground of an autonomous determination of the will. In the same way in which the will can be determined to act by a formal law, which commands actions as morally right, it can also be determined by a formal value, which prescribes actions as morally good.

Kant is right to exclude empirical concepts of the good as a starting point or normative ground of morality, but this does not necessarily imply that the moral law is prior to the good in general, that no concept of the good could determine the will formally and, thus, be a motivating cause of moral action.

On the basis of this critical discussion, it follows that Kant's priority of the moral law over the concept of the good is only valid for a particular notion of the good, as an object distinct from the will, which can determine the will only empirically. One implication of this conclusion is that, contrary to Kant's argument, at least on the standard interpretation, the moral law is not necessarily more fundamental than the concept of the good.[19] A second implication is that the centrality of principles in Kant's moral theory is not motivated by practical (in the sense of morally normative) reasons. Therefore, there does not seem to be any reason why an account of the fact of unconditional obligation in terms of principles would be better than one in terms of values.[20]

This concludes the presentation of my reading of Kant. Recall that I started, in Chapter 1, with an account of Kant's Third Paralogism, transcendental unity of apperception and self-choice (or, more accurately, revolution in disposition). I continued, then, in Chapter 3, with a construal of his Third Antinomy and of the Antinomy of Practical Reason. Recall also that the need for a preliminary presentation of my reading of Kant was methodological: if we are to examine comparatively Kant's and Sartre's practical philosophies, then it would be good to have at least one of these theories presented as a reference point for the comparison.

In the next chapter, I will focus on two objections Sartre formulates in relation to these aspects of Kant's ethics – one is an objection to Kant's authoritarianism, the second one, to his dogmatism. Both objections are in fact supported by the same accusation that Kant is unable to justify the normative claims he makes, starting from his strong commitments to freedom and critical philosophy. It remains to be seen to what extent Sartre is right and what the implications are for the comparative study of their practical philosophies.

6
Sartre and Kant

Sartre's *Critique of Dialectical Reason* can be seen as the first step towards the realization of one of his earliest philosophical projects: that of authoring a theory of politics.[1] That Sartre was fully aware of the importance, for ethics and politics, of a conception of the person can be gleaned from his claims concerning the main task of the *Critique of Dialectical Reason*, namely that of developing a conception of the person that could incorporate the historical and social aspects of the human agent.[2] This is also evident from the way in which he dismisses, at 75 (1980), his earlier writings on ethics:

> the new third attempt would have to be based on a new ontology of consciousness as interpenetrating with other consciousnesses, an ontology which would leave "nothing of *Being and Nothingness* and even of the *Critique of Dialectical Reason* standing, leading to an ethics of 'we' in contrast to the earlier ethics of the 'I' ".[3]

In the *Critique*, Sartre further develops his view of the person as articulated in *Being and Nothingness*. This view is not changed but is complemented by an account of those aspects of a person's life which, in *Being and Nothingness*, were mainly considered from the perspective of ontological freedom as potential obstacles to the spontaneity of the individual. Thus, social, economic, cultural and political institutions, as well as the objects in the world which were clear manifestations of the in-itself, were primarily examined in order to establish whether they can limit the individual's ontological freedom and to a lesser extent whether they can potentially advance or hinder the realization of a person's projects.[4]

The conception of freedom in the *Critique* shifts its emphasis from ontological to practical freedom. Without downgrading the crucial role of ontological freedom, and without making freedom dependent on the realization of the goals that a person projects, Sartre attempts to account for the relation between practical freedom, on the one hand, and, on the other, the types of institution that organize a society. For, while the realization of a person's purposes is neither a necessary nor a sufficient condition of a person's practical freedom, it may be a symptom of the degree of practical freedom a person has.

The question is no longer whether a person can freely create her projects and what the good values are which structure those projects, but what type of good projects can be realized in society and how the institutions of the society should be designed in order that citizens be practically free. Hence, the person's action is no longer seen as simply related to the project, but also as linked to those factors which condition the realization of the project. The term used by Sartre now in order to refer to a person's activity is "praxis".[5]

Having presented my reading of Kant's account of the authority of the moral law and of his view of enlightenment, in this chapter I will consider two objections Sartre formulates to Kant. Let me begin, however, with an overview of this chapter.

§77. Practical freedom and history

Although the focus here is on what is usually called Sartre's 'later' work, in this chapter, I will begin with an objection Sartre formulates in the *Notebooks*. There, he portrays Kant's moral theory as authoritarian, because the Categorical Imperative, as an unconditional law, must have practical validity for all rational persons, in all morally relevant situations. Moreover, given the priority of practical reason (which is structured by the Categorical Imperative) over theoretical reason, the entire Kantian philosophy seems to be determined by this Imperative.

Yet, this seems incompatible with a common feature of Kant's and Sartre's practical philosophies, a feature that I identified in Chapter 4, namely their critique of an account of negative (transcendental or ontological) freedom that sets any limits to the spontaneity of the negatively free agent. In this respect, the Categorical Imperative seems to have much more authority than an appropriate account of negative freedom allows and, hence, given the priority of practical reason over theoretical reason in Kant, his philosophy displays an authoritarianism clearly in conflict with existentialism.

One issue which I left open for further exploration in Chapter 4 concerned Sartre's objection to Kant's account of normativity, in particular his view of the essential role of interpersonal relations for moral normativity and the lack of an appropriate account of interpersonal relations in Kant. At the basis of Sartre's claim to the significance of interpersonal relations, I have identified a distinction between imperatives and values, which seems to set actual choice as a sufficient condition for the moral validity of values. I have argued that this distinction is clearly problematic and even goes against some of Sartre's own claims concerning the moral goodness of values. Nevertheless, I have concluded that, from the perspective of this distinction,

Sartre's objection to Kant marks a genuine difference – whether or not we eventually side with Sartre or (as I have shown we should) with Kant.

I will return to this issue in this chapter, since a clarification of Sartre's position from the perspective of his later ethics will also be very helpful for an appropriate understanding of his critique of Kant's authoritarianism. I will argue that, by looking at Sartre's later ethics, we can understand better why and in what sense Sartre could think that values are morally good or valid as soon as they are adopted by a person. In this way, the tension which I identified in Sartre's practical philosophy disappears and his objection to Kant's account of normativity can be better understood. The objection turns out to be an objection to moral realism, which Sartre seems to attribute to Kant, but which Kant himself rejects.

I will then return to Sartre's objection to Kant's authoritarianism and offer a sketch of an argument for the claim that, paradoxically, both Kant and Sartre need to accept a constraint on negative freedom, if this freedom is to be possible. To be sure, this constraint must be self-imposed by the negatively free agent and will make the agent autonomous. What remains of Sartre's objection is at best a critique of the particular way in which Kant formulates this constraint, namely, as an imperative. Yet I think Kant does not deny the possibility, in principle, of better formulations. Moreover, given both Kant's and Sartre's moral anti-realism, their views of this constraint will be that it is a structure of the mind – a law of practical reason, for Kant, or a genuine value or goal for consciousness.

After considering some possible objections to this interpretation, I will turn to Sartre's next objection to Kant, which focuses on Kant's idea of universal history. Interpreted as an idea of reason, this view of universal history does not seem open to Sartre's objection and some further discussion is necessary to capture the force of Sartre's critique. I will first offer a sketch of the background to Sartre's objection, since, although it is initially put forward in the *Notebooks*, the objection is reformulated in the *Critique*. Moreover, it is in the *Critique* that Sartre engages more seriously with the philosophical issues related to Kant's notion of an idea of reason. A discussion of the two volumes of the *Critique* will certainly go beyond the scope of this book, so I will present a few aspects of that work with two specific purposes in mind.

First, I would like to illustrate the changes Sartre makes in his account of a person. The focus now is on praxis, rather than consciousness, and Sartre attempts to offer a much richer account of the relationship between a person and her world. Secondly, I would like to illustrate how, in his account of interpersonal relations, Sartre can now account for various elements of social life which were not the main focus in his early work, in particular social class and economic conditions. In this way, it will become also clearer how Sartre himself can attempt, in the *Critique*, to offer an account of history and its development.

Having offered an overview of the background against which Sartre formulates his objection to Kant's idea of universal history, I will return to this objection in order to clarify Sartre's intended target. The object of the challenge seems to be Kant's inconsistent use of this idea constitutively in predictions concerning the moral progress of human beings, although ideas of reason in general can only function legitimately regulatively. Finally, I will argue that Kant's idea of universal history does not in fact have the status of a regulative idea of reason, but that of a postulate of practical reason. This suggests, again, that Sartre's objection turns out to indicate a structural similarity with Kant, rather than a genuine difference.

§78. The authority of the Categorical Imperative

The first of Sartre's objections to Kant that I will consider in this part of the book is no longer restricted to one particular aspect of Kant's practical philosophy, but aims at questioning his entire thought. We have seen that the normative origin of categorical imperatives is an unconditional and universal obligation, which is expressed by the Categorical Imperative. With Kant's distinction between rules of action, maxims (which, when ethically valid, are practical principles) and the criterion of ethical validity (the Categorical Imperative), we can clearly see that the Categorical Imperative is a more general guide for action than ethically valid rules and maxims. Since maxims are second-order prescriptions which set conditions for the rules of action, the Categorical Imperative is a third-order prescription which sets conditions for maxims.

As we have seen in Chapters 3 and 5, which action or rule is relevant for a particular situation depends on the particular features of the circumstances and of the agent under consideration; moreover, which of the relevant maxims and rules of actions are ethically valid is something tested by the Categorical Imperative. Hence, the Categorical Imperative applies to relevant maxims and is, therefore, valid for moral situations and moral agents in general. It is a universal criterion, since it applies to all moral agents; and it is unconditional, since it applies to all ethical circumstances, irrespective of specific conditions which define those circumstances (whether they refer to the agent or the situation in which the agent finds himself).

Yet, in this case, its universality and unconditional validity suggest that the philosophical system it grounds is fixed once and for all.[6] Kant takes practical reason (the main principle of which is given by the Categorical Imperative) to have primacy over theoretical reason. Hence, this universally and unconditionally valid Categorical Imperative grounds not only Kant's practical philosophy, but his philosophy as a whole. Not surprisingly, Sartre objects to this very strong prescription. Thus, on his account, "for Kant, morality is set forever as is the tenor of reason and the orientation of science" (*CM*: 99, 92).

Is there anything wrong with this? First, such an account is in tension with the view of freedom that existentialism puts forward. Moreover, if our evaluation in Chapter 4 is correct, the imposition of as strong a prescription as that of the Categorical Imperative seems to go against Kant's own account of freedom. After all, there, the claim was that he, too, would reject an account of transcendental freedom as spontaneity, an account which would be limited by constraints, even very general ones, such as the view of the spontaneous agent as a subject which can never be a predicate. We have seen that Sartre's objection to Kant's account of normativity seems to rest, among other things, on a peculiar distinction between values and imperatives. According to this distinction, only values can account for the interpersonal relationship normativity requires.

This distinction between imperatives and values and the corresponding view of values are in stark conflict with an account like Kant's. Moreover, sometimes it seems Sartre himself should reject them, given his other remarks about ethical normativity, for instance, the discussion of impure reflection and bad faith. Nevertheless, although these two elements of Sartre's ethics do not fit well with his ethics as a whole, they fit well with other elements, in particular Sartre's objection to Kant's view of the ontological source of moral standards.

This led us to the conclusion, at the end of Chapter 4, that, in the case of the objection concerning ethical normativity, in particular the objection about the ontological source of moral standards, we seem to deal not so much with a structural similarity between Kant's and Sartre's ethical theories but with a clear disagreement. In this case, Sartre does not seem to object to the same account Kant would object to. On the contrary, Sartre formulates a certain condition for an appropriate account of normativity (that it must make room for interpersonal relations as essential); he does not find it in Kant, but not because his view of Kant's theory is inaccurate.

At the end of Chapter 4, I have mentioned that the situation is in fact much more complex, and the debate which can be reconstructed between Kant and Sartre becomes quite interesting. This is because, in his next attempt to author an ethical theory – the series of lectures Sartre was invited to give at Cornell University (written in 1964–5) – the distinction between imperatives and values and the corresponding view of values I attributed to him in Chapter 4 change significantly. Moreover, further investigation into this will also shed different light on Sartre's distinction between imperatives and values in *Being and Nothingness* and the *Notebooks*, and will lead me to a reinterpretation of his view.

As a result of this further investigation and reinterpretation, the tension I identified in Sartre's theory and the disagreement with Kant evaporate. Furthermore, the additional investigation will also offer a better background for the presentation of Sartre's objection to Kant's view of the authority of the Categorical Imperative. So, before I move on to the discussion of the objection to Kant's alleged authoritarianism, I will present, relatively briefly, Sartre's distinction between values and imperatives in the unpublished and never-delivered Cornell Lectures.

First, in the Lectures, Sartre comes to reject the ethics of values which he announced in *Being and Nothingness* and which he conceived of in a specific form in the *Notebooks for an Ethics*. The moral theory underlying the phenomenological ontology of *Being and Nothingness* goes against an ethics that would aim to deduce a set of moral standards as the principles to be followed by all. The reason why, in spite of this, in the *Notebooks* Sartre aims to put forward such an ethics stems from the difference between values and imperatives, and from Sartre's insufficient attention, in *Being and Nothingness* and the *Notebooks*, to the social dimension of the person's existence in the world.

Imperatives are principles which are formulated so that they take into consideration the specific circumstances in which they are supposed to legislate. This consideration of circumstances is evident in the maxim.[7] Although the same end can be included in various maxims, we can distinguish between these maxims, because they are formulated for different circumstances. Moreover, the various rules of actions under different maxims will vary, since different actions will be able to bring about the end when the agent and circumstances are different. A code of imperatives, therefore, will be much less able to guide action in concrete situations and for specific circumstances than a code of ethically good ends or values would be.

This is because, to say it again, the same end can be included in various maxims and will yield various rules of action, depending on the circumstances and the agent involved; hence, the same end or value will be an appropriate candidate for many situations and circumstances, whereas a maxim will only be appropriate for some circumstances. Consequently, an ethics consisting of a code of values is less likely to lead to an attitude of bad faith than one of imperatives.

However, as I have mentioned, in his Cornell Lectures, written after the publication of the *Critique of Dialectical Reason*, Sartre reformulates the distinction between values and imperatives, and he reconsiders the relation between them by offering a distinct account of ethical normativity.

§79. Ethical experience

Sartre identifies the experience of the unconditional as what is specific for the ethical experience in general.[8] He offers several examples in order to make clear the relation between the conditional and the unconditional, and in order to explain the characteristics of ethical experience. First, he examines the ethical experience as expressed in language (Simont 1987b: 36). He thinks the *sign* of an ethical standard is given by the unconditional "ought". Various formulae of an ethical standard have in common an "ought".

"You ought to vote", for instance,[9] uttered before the elections is for Sartre a good example of an ethical imperative. This formula cannot be reduced to an evaluation of interests, it does not express the result of a deliberation in the form of a hypothetical imperative, such as: "If you want to maintain your privileges, then you ought to sacrifice your plans for Sunday and go to vote" (Simont 1987b: 36). "You ought to vote" does not make reference to any subjective condition, such as interests, inclinations, desires or preferences, but orders an action as unconditional, that is, as to be done in spite of all these conditions.

In this sense, the imperative is "formal", since there is no mention of the concrete singular or particular incentives one may have for voting. Its formal character is relative to the content of particular incentives; however, Sartre claims that this "ethical purity" of the formal imperative is in fact deceptive: "'You ought to vote' is an unconditional imperative only under the strict conditions that the vote is in those circumstances a defence of some factual privileges" (Simont 1987b: 37). Hence, conditions specified by such a contextual element hide behind the imperative.

Another example used by Sartre in order to identify the specificity of the ethical experience comes from politics. Thus, the political victory of Kennedy in Wisconsin[10] was, on Sartre's account, the result of his proposing the ethical as a motive for a political choice. Kennedy had not prepared any political programme or concrete policy, but advanced "tolerance" as a prime goal of his political project (Simont 1987b: 37–8). In this way, Sartre suggests, Kennedy's message was that "it is impossible that the Protestant citizens of Wisconsin refuse to vote for Kennedy under the pretext that he is a Catholic" (Simont 1987b: 37).

The impossibility Sartre refers to here must be associated with a contradiction. Presumably, the point is that, when citizens intend to vote for another candidate on the grounds that Kennedy is a Catholic, religious tolerance seems to be taken for granted as an assumption of a free election process and, at the same time, to be rejected by a vote which does not go to Kennedy on religious grounds. The implication seems to be that "it is in the name of a purely ethical appeal to tolerance that Kennedy is elected" (Simont 1987b: 38).

Yet, on Sartre's account, even in this example, tolerance is not purely unconditional. True, he rejects the claim that, in fact, Kennedy's campaign was based on political calculation. He does not think that, in this case, tolerance was merely valid conditionally, as a means to the end of willing the elections. Nevertheless, he maintains that it was a political action, with concrete political consequences. The value of tolerance is proposed as a political ideal and this has certain political consequences. Such consequences cannot entirely be attributed to the ethical worth of the voters. Some voters will act in virtue of already internalized particular normative structures, which make an appeal to tolerance as a recognizable motive for action.

After all, Sartre says, "tolerance is always a conservative value"; only revolutionary epochs are intolerant. Furthermore, Kennedy does not only advocate tolerance and morality, he is at the same time supporting capitalism (Simont 1987b: 38). Nevertheless, according to Sartre, this does not mean that Kennedy's action is not moral; even though his political decisions take place within a context in which he represents the "dominant class", he nonetheless brings about a change: "the established order cracks", and he can introduce antiracist policies (Simont 1987b: 39).

We have here only a few claims, but they are quite rich and complex in content. First, by distinguishing between values and the consequences of the actions which are supposed to realize these values, Sartre indicates clearly that his ethics will not be a form of consequentialism, which takes as criterion of morality some mark of the worth of actual consequences – whether consequences of actions or of following higher-order standards under which various rules of action might fall.

Secondly, by noting that a particular value, such as tolerance, may be more likely to occur in certain kinds of contexts (in this case, non-revolutionary contexts), Sartre makes a first step towards the separation of values from the purposes people tend to have as a matter of course in specific circumstances. So, we can read here an implicit critique of an ethics of values, understood as a theory which offers a list or code of appropriate values to be followed. This may be a surprising claim, since the view that a particular value is more likely to occur in a certain type of situation suggests precisely an ethics that attempts to match values and paradigmatic situations.

The point here is, however, that the ends people tend to have as a matter of course in specific circumstances may be the result of the conditions specific for those circumstances but need not be ethically good. Hence, values are to be followed upon consideration of the situation and there may be no list which can exhaustively present the ethically good ends for all possible situations. In addition, by following a certain value (say, promoting tolerance), the actions performed may go against certain other ethical standards (for instance, that of equality). What is more, Sartre goes even further and claims that non-ethical results necessarily happen: "The ethical does not necessarily exhaust itself in its result, but it necessarily produces non-ethical results" (Simont 1987b: 39).[11] In this way, Sartre reasserts his non-consequentialist leanings and also underscores the ambiguous and paradoxical nature of values.

So far, we have seen that Sartre offers an account of ethical experience that suggests a more complex view of ethical normativity than that presented in the *Notebooks* and announced in *Being and Nothingness*. This conclusion is confirmed by other claims in the Cornell Lectures, as we will see in the next section. These will also clarify further the nature of the values, with regard to which Sartre talks in terms of an ethical paradox.

§80. Values and imperatives

By criticizing an ethical theory understood in terms of a code of values, Sartre advances an account which is closer to Kant than his own view in the *Notebooks*. A major difference, however, survives: his emphasis on values, as opposed to Kant's emphasis on imperatives. An even more careful look at Kant's and Sartre's accounts will, however, lead to additional surprising conclusions.

For Sartre, the ethical in general is "a manner of regulating human relations" (Simont 1987b: 40). For instance, it is a way of establishing a "normative reciprocity" between the electors and the person whom they vote for. But there are different forms in which the ethical manifests itself. He distinguishes between institutions and morals, and takes the imperatives to be institutionalized standards, which are enforced by political power (Simont 1987b: 40). By contrast, morals are not imposed by direct and strictly defined sanctions, but by standards which are more diffusely enforceable.

Sartre distinguishes several types of morals: values, goods, examples and ideals (Simont 1987b: 41). He illustrates the category of values with the example of "sincerity" (Simont 1987b: 41). Such a standard is conceived as "invention"; it is not "positively constraining" but it allows every person to realize it as an end, that is, as a situation which is desired. In other words, Sartre seems here to contrast an enforced standard (presumably an imperative which is positively constraining) with a value that can be freely adopted in virtue of its ethical validity. To the extent that it is an invitation for each person to project herself towards her own ends and in this way to acquire sincerity, this value is liberating; on the other hand, however, this is Sartre's ethical paradox to which both Simont and Verstraeten refer,[12] value is alienating.

It is precisely because every particular value is socially determined in its meaning that a person's proposal of a value is ethical only if it is considered one-sidedly. Sartre's suggestion here is that values are often adopted as a result of constraints which are not "positive", that is, presented explicitly in the manner in which, say, political power is enforced through explicitly formulated laws. If they are adopted without a commitment to their ethical validity, but as given and to be followed irrespective of their justification, then they are followed in bad faith. Hence, the other aspect of value is inauthenticity, it is the attempt to posit or to take a particular value as given absolutely, and, hence, as to be merely accepted as such, rather than adopted in virtue of its rightness.

With this revised account of values, it becomes now possible for Sartre to claim that values and imperatives are two aspects of the same phenomenon: moral *normativity* (Verstraeten 1987: 69). The same ethical "object" may become a value or an imperative, depending on the way it is regarded. The example used by Sartre is that of "virginity" (Verstraeten 1987: 69–70).

Virginity may appear to the young woman as an imperative, as an order imposed by others which has to be unconditionally observed; but it may also be seen as a value, when she interprets virginity as "culture and power, that is, as conserved nature and power of getting married" (Verstraeten 1987: 69). It is because of this common root in ethical normativity that imperative and values can be regarded as definable in the same way: "They propose determined ends to the human conduct and give as unconditional the possibility of realising them" (Simont 1987b: 43).

However, Sartre seems to deem imperatives as a more appropriate expression of freedom, because values lead to a higher degree of inauthenticity. From the perspective of Sartre's revised account of values and of the distinction between values and imperatives, this is not surprising. It represents an implication of his new account of normativity in the Cornell Lectures:

> If value is lived internally whereas the imperative is lived externally, this is because value is a more profound and deceptive internalisation of the practico-inert [in-itself], in fact so thoroughly internalised that it is no longer felt as constraint. The imperative, on the other hand, because of its relative externality, is conflictual; to obey it is subjectively problematical since not to obey it is an ever present possibility. Hence, the imperative is closer to liberty than is the value.
>
> (Simont 1992: 203)

This distinction between value and imperative strongly resembles Kant's distinction between juridical and ethical imperatives, presented in Chapter 5. Recall that, on Kant's account, given that juridical imperatives have to be enforceable, it must be possible to monitor the extent to which persons comply with them. Hence, one conclusion is that juridical imperatives have to be in the form of maxims or rules of actions, which describe the action or actions that ought to be performed.

But, in order to be monitored, the performance of actions in accordance with juridical imperatives must only imply conformity of the action with the principle or rule, it cannot presuppose, as it does in the case of ethical imperatives, that the action be performed with a certain motivation. Motivations cannot be monitored, cannot be controlled and cannot be enforced.[13] Several further points can be made in relation to this quotation and to the ethical paradox. They not only point to further implications of Sartre's revised ethical account, but also shed light on his early ethics.

§81. Radical ethics

Let me start by noting that, in the Cornell Lectures, Sartre makes one important step towards a solution to the classical conflict between principle and value, between the right and the good. He regards principles and values as different aspects of the same ethical phenomenon, namely, that of normativity. Starting from this common element, they acquire specific and distinct functions. Values are standards which persons follow in their actions; imperatives are standards with which persons conform. Following from this, a priority can be established for imperatives over values in their relation to the agent.

More exactly, for Sartre, the priority is in terms of authenticity, since he deems imperatives more authentic, less alienating. He does not make this prioritization in order to find a starting point for an ethics of imperatives, that is, an ethics conceived as a code of imperatives; this is because, as we have seen, both an ethics regarded as a code of imperatives and one conceived of as a code of values are problematic on his account.

A second point we can note is that Sartre is able to make this rapprochement between imperatives and values by moving values and imperatives on what I would call, for the sake of simplicity, the 'juridical' plane. Thus, Sartre regards values as normative standards adopted and followed as a result of internalization, rather than because they are ethically good and recognized as such by the agent. I have said that I use 'juridical' for the sake of simplicity, because standards can be enforced through various forms of power, not all of which are reducible to the political power through which laws are enforced in society.

Thirdly and as an implication, Sartre conceives of imperatives as closer to liberty than values. This may seem to suggest an ethical position similar to Kant's. Note, however, the reason why Sartre makes this claim about imperatives. He argues that, since imperatives are explicitly enforced, they cannot be taken as expressions of an authentic choice of possibilities in the way in which values can. Values, being sometimes internalized and enforced less visibly than imperatives, may mislead us into thinking they express authentic possibilities.

It follows that Sartre's claim is not as strong as it might have seemed at the beginning. He does not simply endorse imperatives and reject values. In fact, given that he now takes imperatives and values to be expressions of moral normativity, any preference for one over the other must be related to some aspect which is morally relevant only indirectly. That is, if imperatives are endorsed over values, given that both values and imperatives express the same ethical normativity, the advantage imperatives have must be in virtue of some feature which is not directly related to moral normativity. As we have seen, in Sartre's Lectures, imperatives are regarded as less alienating and less likely to affect a person's freedom negatively: this is because they express moral normativity through enforceable means, whereas values cannot be directly enforced and may give the impression that they are freely adopted.

As I have mentioned, Sartre can now relate values and imperatives more easily, since he regards them as juridical; however, if we focus on *ethically* valid standards (principles and values), which were adopted by critical consideration and solely in virtue of being valid, rather than as a result of being more or less explicitly enforced, then Sartre's preference for what he calls "imperatives" (i.e. juridical, as opposed to ethical norms or principles) cannot be transferred to ethical norms. Since ethical principles cannot be externally enforced, they share the fate of values, which may seem to be freely adopted in virtue of their validity, but may turn out to be adopted because they mesh with other internalized principles and values.

Still, we can see that, in the same way in which Sartre would now reject an ethics understood as a code of values, he would also reject an ethics conceived as a code of ethical norms, although he regards the effect of imperatives on the agents as more conducive to freedom than the effect of values. This attitude towards ethical codes is due to the fact that the problem of an ethics understood as a code (the problem of a lack of guiding force in concrete circumstances) remains – whether we talk about values or imperatives.

Sartre tries to advance a radical position in ethics, something we can call ethical radicalism or radical ethics. On this view, ethics is not to be seen as

the unconditional conditioning of freedom by value or by some inert and stationary end, but it is the unconditional deconditioning of those conditions that are obstacles to the reproduction of the end – that is, of the relation to the world in which freedom has been freely engaged.

(Simont 1992: 207)

Sartre suggests here more clearly than in his early ethical writings that his radical ethics is an ethical system (i.e. an ethics which has a criterion for the evaluation of standards of action). To be sure, an ethical system was already at work in *Being and Nothingness*. Thus, as we have seen in Chapter 4, in a manner similar to Kant's, Sartre excludes two types of value as impermissible. First, there are those values which, when adopted, limit the freedom of the agent herself; these are all those values that are adopted in virtue of an authority (social, political, religious) the agent simply assumes (whether or not reflectively) as legitimate. Secondly, there are all those values that give pride of place to the agent or her group over other agents.

This suggests that Sartre's value of authenticity in his early writings functions in a similar way to Kant's Categorical Imperative. And, yet, other claims Sartre makes suggest sometimes, as we have seen, that he is convinced any projection (and hence) adoption of *values* (as opposed to *imperatives*) is ethically valid. Such an account resonates with the standard view of existentialism as the proponent of an ethics of absolute freedom and of an ethics of free creation of values, where 'everything goes'.

I have said that Sartre's revised account of the distinction between imperatives and values, and his revised conception of values in the later ethics of the Cornell Lectures shed new light on the discussion of values and imperatives from his early writings. In this way, I have suggested, we might be able to account for the apparent tension between Sartre's view of values and his account of authenticity in the early writings. So, before I go back to the objection to Kant's alleged authoritarianism, in the next section I would like to draw the implications of this shift in Sartre's view for his objection to Kant's account of normativity (in particular the objection concerning the lack of an appropriate account of interpersonal relations) presented in Part II.

§82. The role of interpersonal relations

Recall that, on Sartre's account, in the *Notebooks*, imperatives are considered as prescriptive even when a person does not choose to act on them, whereas a value can only be prescriptive when it is actually pursued by the agent. On the basis of this distinction between, and understanding of, imperatives and values, Sartre claims that intersubjectivity is required for values. He goes on to add that Kant allows imperatives to be self-legislated and self-imposed, and that, to compensate for the lack of interpersonal relations, he introduces a split in the person between a rational and a sensible part. These two parts, quite radically separated, are supposed to replicate intrapersonally the interpersonal relation that Sartre thinks ethical normativity requires. Thus, in the same way in which a person puts forward a value and invites the other person to adopt it and pursue it freely, reason, as constituted by the Categorical Imperative, invites the sensible part of the person to comply with this Imperative.

To understand why Sartre requires the existence of interpersonal relations, in Chapter 4, §62, I linked this requirement to his account of values. Insofar as values have prescriptivity only when they are freely chosen and pursued by the agent, they exist for the agent as values when they are proposed as such by other agents who have adopted them or when the agent actually adopted them. The first alternative requires interpersonal relations. The second alternative raises two problems: first, how agents come to adopt a value without the split between two parts of the person; secondly, once adopted, how an agent knows that she is following the chosen value and not some other one. Both problems can be answered if interpersonal relations are introduced.

Nevertheless, as I have argued, although interpersonal relations answer these problems, they give rise to further problems. We can answer that an agent comes to adopt a value when she is invited by another agent to adopt it freely. We can also say that a person knows she is pursuing the value she initially chose, because, when in doubt, she can refer back to the person who initially invited her to adopt that value and check that this is the value she adopted.

But, of course, we can then raise the same problems for the initial person – how she came to adopt the value she is now proposing and how she knows she is pursuing this value, rather than some other one. Ultimately, the question which needs to be resolved here is a question concerning objectivity. It is not possible here to pursue an argument for the advantage of the Kantian solution to this problem, although my claim is that Kant's transcendental idealism is the most convincing account to date. What I would like to suggest here is only that Sartre also follows the Kantian approach in this respect.

My claim is not that Sartre advances a version of transcendental idealism; I think he does not, although I tend to think there might be reasons why he should have. My point is that he adopts a view on objectivity that ascribes the same ontological status to moral standards and criteria as Kant does. From the perspective of the question I raised at the beginning of this book (the question of the relation of a moral theory to metaphysics), this is the question which is of primary concern here. So, going back to my evaluation of Sartre's objection to Kant's account of normativity, consider now the shift in Sartre's view of normativity. As I have mentioned, it might have seemed that the major difference in Sartre's position now is the positive character of his comments on imperatives, but I have argued in the previous section that this is not crucial.

One very significant change is the realization that imperatives and values have a similar normative status. But perhaps an even more important change is Sartre's emphasis on the unconditional as the specific feature of ethical experience. That Sartre now regards the 'ought' as characteristic for ethical normativity means that he thinks it is also a feature of ethical values. However, I have suggested in Chapter 4 that his requirement of interpersonal relationships for ethical normativity relies on his account of values as prescriptive when actually adopted and pursued. The acknowledgement that an 'ought' is involved in good values means that he no longer subscribes to this account, for, in principle, a value which implies an 'ought' can be prescriptive even when it is not actually adopted and followed, and, in addition, a value which is actually adopted and pursued need not be the value the agent ought to have adopted and pursued. This is why, as we have seen in Chapter 4, Sartre needs something like a split in the person.

My purpose here is to point to the fact that, from the perspective of this new account of values, Sartre's objection to Kant dissolves. While Kant would not deny that interpersonal relations are essential for the development of a person, he would disagree that norms cannot correctly be identified, adopted and pursued by individuals and, hence, he would disagree that self-legislation is an illusion. Interpersonal relations are certainly essential for the existence of moral standards, but they are essential whether these standards are right or wrong; hence, for the justification of right standards, interpersonal relations are only indirectly significant. Thus reformulated, Sartre's objection would be directed against a position to which

Kant would also object. Consequently, this points to a further structural similarity between their practical philosophies.

I think there is one further surprising result that the discussion of Sartre's radical ethics and his new position of values and imperatives brings about. I will focus on this in the next section.

§83. Values

Having looked closer at Sartre's position and his interpretation of Kant in *Being and Nothingness* and the *Notebooks*, there emerges an objection to Kant which is much more subtle than it seemed at the beginning. Moreover, we can also answer some questions one can immediately raise against my reinterpretation, in the previous section, of the evaluation of Sartre's objection to Kant's account of normativity that I initially offered in Chapter 4. Thus, in the previous section, I suggested that Sartre's objection is not in fact an objection to Kant, but to a position that would deny the role of interpersonal relations for the development of individuals and the existence of moral standards. Kant himself, I concluded, would have argued against this too.

This similarity may look implausible. After all, it seems clear that Sartre objects to Kant's view of autonomy and criticizes the Kantian split between the rational and sensible parts of a person. Besides, one may add, to argue (as I suggested Kant and Sartre would) against a position that claims that interpersonal relations are not important for the development of a person is to argue against a straw man – who would deny this?

I have already argued that Sartre, too, needs to introduce a split in the person to be able to explain how the ends we sometimes follow are not those we ought to follow. Moreover, recall that my claim was not simply that Kant and Sartre can be understood as arguing against the view that interpersonal relations have no essential role to play in the development of the individuals; in addition, I made the stronger claim that they argue against the view that interpersonal relations are not essential for the existence of moral standards. Some realist theorists in ethics would be happy to affirm this, so Kant and Sartre would have real and strong opponents – both in the history of philosophy and among contemporary ethicists.

Furthermore, Sartre also talks about autonomy and seems to regard this as the best account of a person's freedom. Even his account of self-choice is, as we have seen in Chapter 2, similar to Kant and indicates Sartre's attempt to account for the possibility of self-governance or self-legislation. It would, therefore, seem strange to take issue with this in Kant. Nevertheless, one could still reply that Sartre might have a notion of autonomy distinct from Kant's notion and that his objection is to the particular Kantian understanding of autonomy. Consider, however, Sartre's claim which I quoted above:

> If value is lived internally whereas the imperative is lived externally, this is because value is a more profound and deceptive internalisation of the

practico-inert [in-itself], in fact so thoroughly internalised that it is no longer felt as constraint.

(Simont 1992: 203)

In this quotation, we have the source of the change in Sartre's view of the relation between imperatives and values. As we have seen, in the Cornell Lectures, Sartre realizes that values may also be adopted through force and need not be adopted freely, in virtue of their ethical goodness. In the *Notebooks*, values can only be adopted freely, since only rules of action and principles can be enforced. When one tries to enforce a value, what one can do is merely enforce the actions and principles which seem to lead to the realization of the value; the value itself cannot be directly enforced. Hence, in the *Notebooks*, Sartre regarded values as the result of authentic choices in virtue of their nature.

Later on, he came to acknowledge that one might adopt a certain value and follow it without feeling a constraint, because the value had already been internalized. Of course, the point here is not that values will be adopted or internalized critically and in virtue of their validity, which is unproblematic; the idea is that they are internalized values through enforced or simply unquestioned practices (principles and rules), but since values and principles are aspects of the same phenomenon (moral normativity), through the enforcement of practices one will also end up with some values enforced. For instance, practices of tolerance will eventually be internalized around the value of tolerance, which may be followed without any feeling of constraint, although it has not been adopted merely out of the value's ethical goodness.

This means that Sartre's talk of imperatives as prescriptive, even when they have not been adopted, and of values as prescriptive only when they have been adopted, need not mean that Sartre confuses a distinction in metaethics between a descriptive and a prescriptive account of action. It might mean that Sartre talks about values from the perspective of an agent who has not yet internalized norms and who finds himself in a situation in which he must choose freely his values. By contrast, imperatives are, in principle, enforceable and, if power is used to constrain a person to conform to them, whether or not a person adopts them freely is a secondary issue.

From the perspective of this discussion of Sartre's revised view of the relation between values and imperatives, in the next section I will conclude briefly on Sartre's objection to Kant's account of ethical normativity and I will then return to the objection with which I started this chapter.

§84. Negative freedom and autonomy

The analysis, in the last four sections, of Sartre's view of values and imperatives confirms that, with his objection to Kant's account of ethical normativity, Sartre does not simply make a mistake, that is, he does not simply formulate a critique which misses its target; on the contrary, he offers a strong objection to the position he wants to challenge. Yet, as we have seen, this position turns out not to be Kant's, but the same position against which Kant would also argue. Sartre's problem here is therefore interpretative: he attributes to Kant a position Kant does not hold. Both Kant and Sartre suggest that ethical standards of action (imperatives, for Kant, and values, for Sartre) should not be regarded as standards which exist independently from the agent and which can be imposed, in virtue of their validity, on the agent.

After all, if the agent cannot adopt them in virtue of their being considered as ethically valid, rather than because they correspond to contingent factors, such as inclinations, sensible desires, preferences, internalized ideals or unquestioned authorities, then it is unclear in what way these standards are valid; moreover, it is not clear in what sense the agent can be autonomous, especially from the perspective of Kant's and Sartre's views of the free person as a spontaneous agent. The spontaneous agent is beyond constraints, but while an action which is performed when one is beyond constraints is in a sense free (namely, in the negative sense that it is free from constraints), it can only be performed if an end is adopted by the agent.[14]

As we have seen in Chapter 5, this is an implication of Kant's Incorporation Thesis. Sartre seems also to agree to a version of this thesis, namely, that an agent cannot act without choosing to act in that way. Recall Sartre's analysis of action presented in Chapter 4. On Sartre's account, an action is caused by a state of affairs, which is perceived as having to be changed and is motivated by the agent's ensemble of desires, emotions and passions that urge her to perform an action. Yet, in order for a state of affairs to be revealed to the agent as a cause of her action, it is necessary for her to posit an end. Similarly, the motive depends on the cause and on the end, and it represents the non-positional consciousness of self, insofar as consciousness posits the cause, and

> experiences itself non-thetically as a project, more or less keen, more or less passionate, toward an end at the very moment at which it is constituted as a revealing consciousness of the organisation of the world into causes.
>
> (*EN*: 503, 471)

But, if action presupposes choice of an end, this end is either regarded as good in itself or as good for further purposes. The latter alternative presupposes a further purpose as given and, hence, as constraining action. It is only the former alternative that is compatible with negative freedom, but it requires some criterion for the evaluation of the action and its end. Hence, free action is action on this law, the criterion of goodness, which can only yield free action if it is self-legislated and, hence, autonomous.

Now, let me go back to Sartre's objection to Kant's authoritarianism, with which I began this chapter. Sartre is right that Kant's Categorical Imperative formulates a universal and unconditional obligation for all limited rational beings. The universality and unconditionality of this obligation is absolute in comparison with the more specific obligations expressed by morally valid maxims and rules of action. Thus, as I have noted, a maxim is universal (and, hence, it is a principle or imperative and not merely a maxim) in the sense that *all* persons ought to act according to it when they are in the type of situation that this maxim appropriately regulates; or, in other words, the fact that, in the relevant situation, actions ought to be performed according to that maxim holds for *all*, whether they are agents in that situation and, hence, obligated by the maxim or agents in other circumstances, who simply judge the case.

It would, therefore, be useful to distinguish here between two types of validity and obligation. We can first talk about the 'practical' validity of a standard and mean that this is the right standard to be followed by all agents who are in the appropriate circumstances and have the appropriate features. This standard will only impose an obligation on the relevant agents, that is, those moral agents who are in the appropriate circumstances and with the relevant features. This obligation, which I call 'practical' as corresponding to the standard's practical validity, will require that these agents act on the standard.

By contrast, a standard will impose a 'cognitive' obligation on all rational agents, that is, all agents who can judge a situation from the ethical perspective, whether or not they are in the appropriate circumstances or have the appropriate features to fall under the incidence of that obligation. This cognitive obligation will only require that rational agents acknowledge the rightness of the standard. In other words, the cognitive obligation will require that any rational agent acknowledge that the agent, who is under the appropriate circumstances and has the appropriate features, ought to act on the standard.

Some agents may be cognitively and practically obligated by a standard, whereas others may be obligated only cognitively. If an agent is obligated practically, she must also be obligated cognitively. Otherwise, for an ethics where motivation is important, as it is the case for Kant and Sartre, this would be contradictory, since it would presuppose that the agent ought to act according to a standard and act on the ethical motive, but that she need not acknowledge the standard as an obligation; without acknowledging the standard as an obligation, however, she would not be able to act on it from an ethical motive. Having seen how the negative freedom of the spontaneous agent is related to autonomy, in both Kant and Sartre, and having discussed the normative status of the Categorical Imperative as the self-legislating criterion of Kant's moral theory, it is now time to approach head-on Sartre's objection to Kant's so-called 'authoritarianism'.

§85. The law of freedom

Now let us consider the distinction between rules of action, standards (maxims or values) and the ethical criterion (say, the Categorical Imperative). We can see that the ethical criterion is practically valid without restriction for accountable agents, a particular standard is practically valid for all those rational agents who are in the appropriate circumstances, and a specific rule of action is practically valid for those agents who are in the appropriate circumstances and have the ethically relevant features.

Recall now the discussion of Sartre's distinction between imperatives and values in the previous sections. One aspect which seems to survive changes in his opinion and reinterpretations is the view of imperatives as enforceable. On this account, therefore, the Categorical Imperative would be enforceable and, since it formulates a practical obligation for all human beings, they should follow it. Sartre seems, therefore, to be right in his claim that, for Kant, morality is set forever, as is the tenor of reason and the orientation of science.

Now, on Kant's account, as we have seen, *any* practical principle pre-supposes a purpose or end. Sometimes, however, he is unclear about what exactly he takes this purpose to be in the case of ethically valid imperatives.[15] One place where he is more specific about the purpose or object of practical reason is in the "Dialectic of pure practical reason", more exactly in the chapter "On the concept of an object of pure practical reason". As we have seen, for him, the only object of pure practical reason is what is morally good (*KpV*: 5:58, 78). This object cannot be defined starting from what is pleasant, since that would mean to make what is morally good dependent on experience, and hence, to present moral goodness as relative to the subjective and contingent experience of a person (*KpV*: 5:58, 78–9).

Let's assume moral goodness was defined as starting from elements that depend on contingent factors, such as what I happen to find pleasant in the circumstances and the state of mind I find myself in, and given the sensory-perceptive apparatus I happen to be born with. In that case, moral goodness could not be cognitively and, hence, practically universal, as its validity would depend on those (not ethically relevant) factors obtaining. Since the Categorical Imperative expresses the necessary condition for a standard to be ethically good or valid, the notion of the good is to be defined starting from the Categorical Imperative.

In this way, the action of a will determined by an ethically valid standard will be good in itself (*KpV*: 5:62, 84). The conclusion is that one has to determine first the Categorical Imperative, and only after that and by means of it, should one define the concept of the good (*KpV*: 5:62–3, 84). As we have seen in Chapter 3, for Kant, ancient philosophers committed the conceptual fallacy of defining first the good, and then the moral law. They placed this value either in happiness, or in perfection, or in moral feeling or in the will of God. The principle derived from this value, as a principle of action which contributes to its realization, places the origin of moral goodness in something which cannot be objectively valid, since it depends on the contingent experiences or beliefs of a person (*KpV*: 5:64, 85–6).

In this way, they confused two distinct notions – the good, as a principle of virtue, and the pleasant, as a principle of happiness. Recall that, in the "Antinomy of Practical Reason", Kant excludes a merely analytic connection between virtue and happiness: happiness is not merely part of virtue and virtue does not necessarily imply happiness (*KpV*: 5:112–13, 144). Both virtue and happiness are relatively independent parts which contribute to the whole, or perfect good (*summum bonum*). This whole or perfect good is an even stronger requirement than the universal and unconditional purpose that is posited by the Categorical Imperative (what Kant calls the "supreme good") and to which Sartre refers in his critique of Kant's 'authoritarian' moral system.

Consider, however, the function of the Categorical Imperative: it is meant to define moral goodness, the fundamental notion of an ethical theory. One answer to Sartre's objection would, therefore, be to say that the Categorical Imperative does not introduce any other constraint on the action of human beings than the very general and uncontroversial one that those who would like to act ethically must do what is ethically good. There does not seem to be anything authoritarian about this. The further suggestion that Kant would authorize coercion for the imposition of the Categorical Imperative can easily be shown to be a misreading of Kant. We have already seen that Sartre seems to attribute to Kant a view of imperatives as principles enforceable through power – political, social, economic or other types. An imperative will be obeyed if the threat is sufficiently strong. Sartre seems to claim in the *Notebooks* and in *Being and Nothingness* that all imperatives are principles which are (as a matter of fact) imposed by power, whereas values are adopted in virtue of their ethical goodness.

If this were correct, then the Categorical Imperative would also have to be imposed through power. Yet, in Chapter 5, we have seen how Kant distinguishes between ethical and juridical imperatives and how he regards ethical imperatives as principles the agent ought to follow in virtue of their rightness. The issue is not simply that ethical imperatives *can* be pursued out of duty, for they can in fact be pursued *only* out of duty. Recall that ethical imperatives or principles are those ethical maxims which prove to be permissible. Ethical maxims, however, include in their formulation the motive of the action, and only those maxims which make reference to the ethical motive of duty can be permissible. Performing an action on an ethical imperative necessarily implies acting on the ethical motivation, rather than on some other incentive (for instance, fear generated by threat).

The Categorical Imperative seems to be a formal principle, and sometimes this is taken to mean that it cannot make any substantive normative claims.

In fact, in a certain sense, the more formal such a principle is, the stronger is the force of its normative claims. Thus, the Categorical Imperative is a principle with full authority over agents, when it expresses a condition which holds for all the ends that are ethically or unconditionally good or good in themselves. The process of internalization which Sartre discusses in the *Critique* and in the Cornell Lectures generates some problems for an account of unconditional obligation. I will discuss this briefly in the next section.

§86. Internalization

In addition, certain ethical imperatives, even when they are formulated without specifying the motive of action, *cannot* be enforced by power. For instance, there is no way of enforcing by, say, political power, the imperative of being truthful with oneself. It is interesting to point out here that, by referring to the internalization of the practico-inert in the Cornell Lectures, Sartre raises a serious question. One can argue that a person who internalized a particular criterion of moral goodness will adopt a certain imperative and will act on it out of duty. But this notion of duty depends on the internalized criterion, and if it is possible to argue that an agent can be determined effectively to internalize such a criterion through political power, then the claim that ethical imperatives can only be acted upon out of duty is not incompatible with Sartre's claim that imperatives are enforced through power.

Note, however, that Kant's point is not to deny the possibility of enforced internalization or the possibility that human beings have an inappropriate notion of duty. On the contrary, as we have seen in Chapter 5, questioning such internalized criteria is one of the main topics of his essay on the Enlightenment. The process of questioning and vindicating one's assumptions is necessary precisely because these may be the result of internalization of morally impermissible principles or criteria. Kant's point is the following: if an action is ethically worthy when it both conforms to the moral criterion and was performed with the ethical motive, then the ethically worthy action cannot be enforced.

Enforcing an action means exerting power until the action is performed. But if an action means not only performing certain controllable acts, but also acting with a certain motivation, then the action cannot be controlled. Even if I can reliably make an agent through power to internalize a certain moral criterion, all I have done is to make sure that the agent may consider a certain standard as right, because she will judge the standard on the basis of the internalized criterion. But whether she will act on the criterion because she thinks it is right is something that I cannot control and, hence, I cannot enforce. Even if I hypnotise an agent and command her to act out of duty only, how can I reliably verify this? After all, on Kant's account, the agent herself cannot be sure about her motivation.[16]

The issue of internalization raises a further very important question: any attempt an agent makes to question her standards of action and even the criterion on the basis of which she judges these actions must rely on some further criterion on the basis of which the standards and criterion can be evaluated; but, if the further criterion is also the result of internalization, there seems to be no objective guide for this process. However, this will be a problem not only for Kant, but also for Sartre and, in fact, as far as the comparative analysis undertaken here is concerned, we need not go further with the investigation of this problem, since it raises the same difficulties for both Kant and Sartre.[17]

Hence, in general, insofar as an imperative is taken to include the motive with which it is enacted, it cannot be enforced by power. There are two rejoinders we need to consider here, however. First, it may be said that Sartre's objection is not directed against the contention that the agent who acts ethically must do what is ethically good, but to the way in which Kant interprets ethical goodness and defines it starting from the Categorical Imperative; Kant's approach does not only imply giving priority to principles over values, but also bringing into the notion of moral goodness all the problems of Kant's particular formulation of the Categorical Imperative.

Concerning the priority of principles, in particular the Categorical Imperative, we have seen in Chapter 5 that the issue is not altogether clear: Kant seems sometimes to suggest a relation of mutual dependence between the value of ethical goodness and the Categorical Imperative. Besides, one can grant to Kant an epistemic priority for principles over values, insofar as values can only be realized through actions and, hence, by acting on the corresponding principles.

Concerning the potential problems of Kant's formulation of the Categorical Imperative as a definition of moral goodness, it can first be said that the Categorical Imperative is a very formal criterion, which seems quite uncontroversial as far as its formulation is concerned. If anything, its very formal character raises questions concerning its capacity to guide action. We have seen, however, in Chapter 5, a possible answer to this problem.

The second rejoinder to consider at this point has to do with Kant's argument for the existence of freedom. Recall that, as discussed in Chapter 3, in the Third Antinomy, Kant only shows that freedom is possible. In the *Critique of Practical Reason*, he claims that he is able to demonstrate what he takes to be "the *keystone* of the whole edifice of a system of pure reason", namely, "freedom's being actual" (*KpV*: 5:4, 5). For Kant, the idea of freedom "reveals itself through the moral law" (*KpV*: 5:4, 5), hence to prove the existence of the moral law becomes the main aim of the second *Critique*.

The reason why this turns out to be a problem is that the moral law is demonstrated on the basis of a "fact of reason". As we have seen, this represents the "consciousness of this basic law" which "one cannot reason [...] out from antecedent data of reason [...] because, rather, it thrusts itself upon us on its own as a synthetic a priori proposition not based on any intuition" (*KpV*: 5:31, 46). This adds force to Sartre's interpretation and critique of Kant's moral system as an authoritarian theory that not only posits an universal and unconditional purpose, but justifies its reality by a putative "fact" that appears to be an unjustified datum, the authority for the imposition of which Kant seems to arrogate too easily. As Henry Allison notes, the appeal to this "fact"

> has struck the many students of Kant as an act of desperation, a lapse into a dogmatism that is hopelessly at odds with the whole spirit of the "critical" philosophy.
>
> (Allison 1989: 116)

I will discuss this problem in the next section.

§87. The fact of reason

According to Kant, the fact of reason does not only prove the existence of the Categorical Imperative, but also the practical force of pure reason, its capacity to command an action on the basis of the form of moral imperatives alone.[18] For Kant,

> one need only dissect the judgement which human beings make about the lawfulness of their actions: one will always find that, whatever [their] inclination may interject, their reason, incorruptible and self-constrained, nonetheless always holds the will's maxim in an action up to the pure will, i.e., to itself inasmuch as it regards itself as practical a priori.
>
> (*KpV*: 5:32, 46–7)[19]

Kant's suggestion is that the very process of ethical evaluation presupposes as constitutive the Categorical Imperative; the fact of reason is the fact that *any* ethical evaluation, insofar as it tries to determine whether an action is ethically good, will make reference to the law of pure practical reason. Kant is far from simply dictating the moral law and grounding it in something called a "fact of reason". The fact that is supposed to ground the moral law is given by the judgement of claims, actions, attitudes, a judgement which relies on a questioning of their rightness.

However, this means that, insofar as a person questions the ends of his actions and tries to determine how he *ought* to act, he has already assumed implicitly the validity of the Categorical Imperative. We have seen that to adopt the perspective of a moral agent in order to judge the moral worth of the empirical agent's ends is to assume that it is possible to determine which actions and principles of action are right and ought to be followed. But a morally valid principle or rule of action is valid for *all*; hence at the same time, both that agent and all rational agents should be able to will and follow it. But the latter is exactly the condition imposed by the Categorical Imperative.

This argument starts precisely from the distinction between the descriptive and the prescriptive approaches to action that Sartre also accepts and that he explicitly acknowledges in the Cornell Lectures by reference to the unconditional "ought".[20] Moreover, Sartre himself talks about a "fact of mind [*esprit*]", as "an original fact of wrenching away from self", in *Being and Nothingness* (*EN*: 348, 325).[21] Kant does not dogmatically assume the validity of the Categorical Imperative, he puts forward an argument for it. To be sure, this implies that the argument may be challenged and, together with it, the supreme good Kant thinks the moral law defines as practically valid for all rational agents. However, this very challenge presupposes a distinction between a right and a wrong argument; in other words, the validity of the unconditional and universal law and purpose is compatible with the freedom of the limited rational person.

As Kant says in the *Critique of Pure Reason*:

> But putting the investigating as well as the examining reason in a state of complete freedom – so that it can attend unhindered to its own interest – is always and without any doubt beneficial. Reason furthers this interest just as much by setting limits to its own insight as it does by expanding them; and this interest always suffers when outside hands intervene to lead reason – against its natural course – in accordance with forced aims.
>
> (*KrV*: A744/B772, 691)

This quotation confirms two claims I have made. It confirms, first, the claim concerning the structural similarities between Kant's and Sartre's views of the free person as a spontaneous agent, for Kant and Sartre reject the attempt to set limits to the form this spontaneity may take; even when we assume that spontaneity is guided by some self-imposed limits (for instance, that given by the Categorical Imperative or that given by the value of authenticity), they still encourage a self-critical attitude that would probe the extent to which the guiding criteria are indeed those intended. Secondly, the quotation confirms the constitutive role of a guiding yardstick, such as the Categorical Imperative, which is necessary to distinguish between right and wrong, good and evil, truth and falsehood. Any attempt to question such a benchmark must rely on some further point of reference on the basis of which one is able to decide whether or not the criticism is successful.

It follows that such a benchmark is a limit of the inquiry, although its particular *formulation* is open to challenge and change, as Kant himself seems to admit by setting no limits to the critical and self-critical power of reason. Hence, in questioning the unconditionally valid and universally applicable status of the Categorical Imperative, Sartre challenges a type of account Kant himself would challenge – the authoritarian ethical theory which would posit particular standards, standards appropriate under particular conditions, as practically universal and unconditional. For Sartre regards any principle, including the higher-order principle represented by the Categorical Imperative as appropriate under specific conditions and, hence, to be challenged as a universally applicable principle.

In the *Notebooks*, Sartre's objection to Kant's authoritarianism goes even further. He does not only argue against a general principle set by Kant as the ground of morality, science and reason, he also argues against what he takes to be Kant's illegitimate optimism concerning the moral progress of human beings and institutions. For Sartre, all "true" philosophy should put an end to History, since it discovers what it is, what is possible, what is impossible (*CM*: 99, 92). Yet,

> Existentialism does not give itself out to be the end of History, or even as a form of progress. It simply wants to give an account through discourse of the absolute that each man is for himself within the relative.
>
> (*CM*: 99, 92).

Initially seen as the mark of a true philosophy, the capacity to formulate an absolute end is transformed from the perspective of existentialism into a deficiency. Thus, Sartre claims that the sadness of all philosophy is that it declares itself in its own way as the end of history. Moreover, Sartre adds, every human being feels repugnance for an end of history, since every human being wants to make himself and to make his world in creative ignorance (*CM*: 99, 92). As we will see, these comments echo an objection Sartre raises also in the *Critique of Dialectical Reason*, the final objection I will consider in this book and to which I now turn.

§88. Universal history

In Chapter 3, I presented Kant's account of the Antinomy of Practical Reason and his solution to the Antinomy. We have seen that, for him, the complete good involves actual happiness in proportion to worthiness to be happy (i.e. in proportion to virtue). Kant justifies faith in God and the immortality of the soul as necessary conditions for the possibility of the complete good. Yet, in his writings on the philosophy of history, he suggests that moral progress of human beings or, more exactly, of human species will take place sooner or later.

Thus, Kant's idea of universal history presupposes that "*all the natural capacities of a creature are destined sooner or later to be developed completely and in conformity with their end*" (*IaG*: 8:18, 42). This end is that of "*attaining a civil society which can administer justice universally*" (*IaG*: 8:22, 45), a society which regulates not only the relations between individual persons, but also between states; the realization of which Kant already discerns in history:

> Nature has thus again employed the unsociableness of men, and even of the large societies and states which human being construct, as a means of arriving at a condition of calm and security through their inevitable *antagonism.*
>
> (*IaG*: 8:24, 47)

The final end of history is also "the highest purpose of nature" (*IaG*: 8:22, 45). By antagonism (a propensity which is "obviously rooted in human nature" (*IaG*, 8:20, 44) –

> the first true steps are taken from barbarism to culture, which in fact consists in the social worthiness of man. All man's talents are now gradually developed, his taste cultivated, and by a continuous process of enlightenment, a beginning is made towards establishing a way of thinking which can with time transform the primitive natural capacity for moral discrimination into definite practical principles; and thus a *pathologically* enforced social union is transformed into a *moral* whole.
>
> (*IaG*: 8:21, 44–5)

Hence "*the hidden plan of nature*" (*IaG*: 8:27, 50) is that of bringing all human beings into a moral community, organized as a "universal *cosmopolitan existence*" (*IaG*: 8:28, 51). Nature develops the qualities and talents of individuals by setting them into an antagonism. Even if they try to reach a state of harmony, nature brings them again into discord. Like in the *Critique of Practical Reason*, where God is postulated as a guarantee that morality will lead to happiness, here again the plan of nature would "seem to indicate the design of a wise creator – not, as it might seem, the hand of a malicious spirit" (*IaG*: 8:22, 45).

Kant's idea for a universal history serves not only "as a guide to us in representing an otherwise planless *aggregate* of human actions as conforming, at least when considered as a whole, to a *system*" (*IaG*: 8:29, 52); in addition, it is useful in "explaining the thoroughly confused interplay of human affairs and in prophesying future political change" (*IaG*: 8:30, 52). Hence, what may at first sight appear as a hypothesis that is useful as a means to the giving of unity to an aggregate of historical data from a particular standpoint proves to be effective for providing explanations and predictions too. In Kant's terms, what first appears as a regulative idea of reason seems to become a category of understanding on the basis of which historical data are constituted, and the cognition of the laws of history is possible.[22]

It must be noted here that the two postulates of practical reason, introduced by Kant in the discussion of the Practical Antinomy, refer to the possibility of an individual's reaching *summum bonum*. The postulate of the immortality of the soul explains how the person has the necessary time to become virtuous, whereas the postulate of the existence of God explains how the virtuous person will become happy in proportion to her virtue. In his writings on history, Kant seems interested in explaining how the human species will become virtuous and how institutions run by virtuous persons will distribute benefits and burdens in accordance with virtue. In this way, the *summum bonum* becomes realizable in this life for the human species as a whole and without divine intervention. This seems, therefore, to become a matter of natural forces, the effects of which can be predicted.

This interpretation of Kant informs the background of Sartre's criticism of Kant's view of moral progress in the *Notebooks* and the *Critique*. Thus, when Sartre claims that Kant's critical philosophy gives itself out to be the end of history, he does not simply criticize Kant for having established a moral law which could justify particular principles of action as the universal standards of acting, he also alludes to Kant's contention concerning the progress of human race towards a perfect cosmopolitan society. However, we can note straight away that if what Kant does with his view of moral progress and his account of an end of history is to put forward a regulative idea, then Sartre's critique turns out to be misdirected.

We have first, therefore, a difficulty in understanding what Sartre's objection really is; however, I have presented as a background for Sartre's objection his interpretation of Kant and I have introduced this objection. So, to further clarify this objection, it is now time to focus on the regulative role of ideas and to present Sartre's own account of a person's relation to the world in his later *Critique of Dialectical Reason*.

§89. Ideas of reason

Kant's idea of an end of history is that of a cosmopolitan order, in which individuals will have developed all their abilities and will have started to live moral lives. As an idea of reason, this view of history would have to share the two main features of the other ideas of reason Kant discusses in the first *Critique*. Thus, it would have to be a priori and regulative. For Kant, unlike concepts of the understanding, under which sensible intuitions can be subsumed, and which are therefore constitutive of phenomena, ideas of reason refer directly only to concepts of the understanding and only indirectly to intuitions. They do not constitute experience but give it an order and regulate it under the hypothesis that the various phenomena we experience have a unity.

Yet, being a priori, the unity presupposed by an idea of reason will refer to all possible phenomena, despite the fact that all we can have access to is a limited set. Thus, under the three ideas of reason presented by Kant in the first *Critique*, we have: the totality of the subjective conditions of all presentations in general; the totality of the temporal, causal and other series, which provide the objective conditions of all appearances; and the totality of the conditions under which objects in general can be thought (Gardner 1999: 218). But, since we cannot have intuitions of such totalities, the ideas will not have a corresponding object, and they only refer to concepts of the understanding. Ideas, Kant says, are heuristic devices, which offer a perspective on the world *as if* the world were ordered and constituted as a unitary whole.

Now, if we think of Kant's idea of a universal history as a regulative idea of reason, then Sartre cannot object that Kant is using it constitutively. Here we have a problem first in understanding Sartre's objection. It is clear that Sartre argues against such regulative elements of the mind. After all, as Juliette Simont argues, in the *Notebooks for an Ethics* Sartre makes critical references specifically to all the three ideas of pure reason that Kant presents in the first *Critique* (1987a: 131–2). Nevertheless, Sartre is well aware of the qualification introduced by Kant in the epistemic claims of pure reason, namely the qualification that cognitions about totalities are to be seen as relative claims, for instance, as claims about the world seen *as if* it was caused by a supreme intelligence.[23]

Nevertheless, it seems that Sartre criticizes precisely this *"as if"*, this Kantian way of advancing epistemic claims, which cannot lead to cognition. From Simont's article, however, the reason why Sartre deems the Kantian "as if" problematic is not clear. The only account advanced by Simont concerns the fact that Kant's use of the "as if" betrays a double optimism (1987a: 138–9). On the one hand, Kant would be "ontologically optimistic", to the extent that he takes pure reason to be naturally inclined to speculate about totalities (of the world, of the soul, of the perfect being), and that he considers any natural inclination as intrinsically good (Simont 1987a: 138–9). On the other hand, Kant would be epistemologically optimistic inasmuch as, even when pure reason abandons its speculative function, it can still restrict itself to an empirical use without causing any "damage" (Simont 1987a: 139).

By contrast, Sartre develops his notion of a "totalization of envelopment" by acknowledging the "ineluctable loss" to which human praxis is subject in its action (Simont 1987a: 139). Before moving on with this discussion of Sartre's objection, we need to pause and consider his conception of totalization in the *Critique of Dialectical Reason*.

For Sartre, every praxis is at the same time comprehension, and each process of comprehension is a praxis. The comprehending praxis is called "totalization", and Sartre sees it as a process of "internalization" and "externalization". Thus, the worker who uses certain tools in order to transform a raw material into a product realizes an activity which totalizes the world. To see this, a few obvious things must be mentioned.

First, the activity of the worker is complex. Each action, even a simple one, presupposes several other acts. For instance, the worker must differentiate between different tools (as useful or useless for that activity); this differentiation must take place on the basis of an understanding of the functional differences between various tools. Furthermore, the activity presupposes a plan that is guided by the goal of the activity (the product to be externalized or realized); finally, it also presupposes that the product accomplishes another function within a larger project and that worker understands the limits imposed by the tools, by the material to be transformed and by his own capacities.

This only suggests that an agent must be aware of the larger context of agency. Why does Sartre use the motif of totality and totalization? We can look at the understanding the worker manifests in the process of producing an object as a process of internalization of the various rules and features of the various tools and contexts. But, unless this internalization is regarded as a process of totalization, it cannot start from the assumption of a relatively reliable control the worker has over the world. For any action is the result of some cause or set of causes taking place under certain conditions and each of these causes and conditions can be seen as effects occurring in some way. Similarly, every action will have certain effects under specific conditions, and the effects will produce further effects.

For Sartre, the product is a totality, as distinct from the totalization implied in the praxis that brings about the product. The distinction between the in-itself and the for-itself is thus replaced by that between totality and totalization. Since the notion of an absolute totality is only an ideal, objects are partial totalities. The internalizing praxis externalizes itself in the form of the product. Since every activity is a relation between the human being and the world, human beings are singular totalizations:

> Since the individual worker is just such a totalisation, he can only understand himself in his acts, and in his relation to Nature (and indeed, as we shall see, in his relations to others) if he interprets every partial totality in terms of the overall totalisation, and all their internal relations in terms of their relations to the developing unification, the means in terms of the end and the present in terms of the relation which links the future to the past.
>
> (*CRDI*: 92, 205)

Here, Sartre points to the various aspects which contribute to the understanding a person can acquire of himself. This is the starting point for his distinction between dialectical and analytic reason, which I will pursue in the next section.

§90. Analytic and dialectical

In the quotation with which I closed the previous section, Sartre re-emphasises the significance of the context and of the various relations between person and world. Current and future actions depend on past actions, and each action depends on the various acts through which the action is performed. The acts can be seen as the means to the end, the action, or simply as constitutive elements of the action. These, in their turn, can be regarded as a means to further ends. In short, the individual's inextricable relation to the world becomes even more evident, since the very reflective process of self-understanding[24] is mediated by the individual's relation to the world.

This way of understanding the individual's relation to the world represents one of the most important differences between dialectical and analytical reason. Whereas the latter approaches the object as if between the knowing subject and the object there were only a relation of exteriority, the former finds itself already related to the object. The presupposition from which analytical reason starts is that the process of understanding an object is neutral with regard to the object:

> The stance of the de-situated experimenter, however, tends to perpetuate analytical Reason as the model of intelligibility; the scientist's passivity in relation to the system will tend to reveal to him a passivity of the system in relation to himself. The dialectic reveals itself only to an observer situated in interiority, that is to say, to an investigation both as a possible contribution to the ideology of the entire epoch and as the particular praxis of an individual defined by his historical and personal career within the wider history which conditions it.
>
> (*CRDI*: 38, 156)

The last statement in the quoted passage defines the individual as universal-singular, that is, as conditioned at the same time by various general determinations characterizing an epoch and by singular circumstances, that is, circumstances which are irreducible to the general features of the epoch, and which are specific for a particular and concrete person. In the first moment of totalization, a person is surrounded by various objects. The elements of the totality represented by each object are related to each other and at the same time related to the totality which they form. Tools, objects of desire, obstacles are all organized by relation to the person's totalizing outlook; even an object that has no immediately visible use can only have this negative designation from the perspective of the person's interest.

The mutual relationships between the parts of a totality and between the parts and the totality itself ensure that every part of the totality contains through its relations the totality as a whole. From this perspective, even the stance of the de-situated experimenter can be understood as a way of unifying the world through relationships which deny the links between various totalities, while at the same time and on a deeper level affirming the relationship between them in a negative way. The experimenter is not related to the world, is detached and is not in a particular situation, is de-situated and the totalities are not regarded as means or ends, since he is a neutral observer. On Sartre's account, the totalization obtained by the person's totalizing praxis is not a way of enacting already existing relations. Relations are created by the praxis and, without this totalizing activity, a totality sinks into dispersion and its parts become a multiplicity:

> Within a totality (whether completed or developing), each partial totality, as a determination of the whole, contains the whole as its fundamental meaning and, consequently, also contains the other partial totalities; the secret of each part therefore lies in the others.

> (*CRDI*: 92, 205)

> If, indeed, anything is to appear as the synthetic unity of the diverse, it must be a developing unification, that is to say, an activity. The synthetic unification of a habitat is not merely the labour which has produced it, but also the activity of inhabiting it; reduced to itself, it reverts to the multiplicity of inertia. Thus totalization has the same statute as the totality, for, through the multiplicities, it continues that synthetic labour which makes each part an expression of the whole and which relates the whole to itself through the mediation of the parts. But it is a *developing* activity, which cannot cease without the multiplicity reverting to its original statute.

> (*CRDI*: 46, 162–3)

The relationships between the parts and the whole are dialectical,[25] since they are established by praxis. Therefore, if dialectical reason exists, then a particular totalization as praxis should be accessible to a dialectical epistemic process. This epistemic process is itself totalizing. Since the epistemic process as totalizing knowledge cannot be conceived of as a process that recreates its object (the particular totalization) in its totalizing process (this would mean to be an "ontological totalization"), the dialectical, totalizing knowledge becomes a moment of the totalization which created the object. Thus, the "method" at work in the totalizing process – dialectic – is also a totalization.[26]

Having presented Sartre's view of the distinction between analytic and dialectical reason, as well as his view of praxis as universal-singular, in the next two sections I will discuss his objection to traditional Marxism and his account of interpersonal relations.

§91. Social structures

On Sartre's account, the dialectical process involved in the activities of the praxis do not follow some pre-established laws. His view of praxis contains an implicit critique of traditional Marxism, against which he argues in writing the *Critique*. Thus, for Sartre, dogmatic Marxism sees the laws of dialectics as fixed laws, which are universally applicable in the understanding of any process. By contrast, according to Sartre, the laws of dialectics are themselves the result of a totalizing activity, only this time the praxis is an epistemic activity reflecting on the totalizing processes that are in its purview. The result will be a totalization, which may be linked in various relations by another praxis:[27]

> The failure of dialectical dogmatism has shown us that the dialectic as rationality must be open to direct, everyday investigation, both as the objective connection between facts and as the method for knowing and fixing this connection.
>
> (*CRDI*: 34–5, 153)

> So we must take up the problem once again, and explore the limits, the validity and the extent of dialectical Reason. We cannot deny that a *critique* (in the Kantian sense) of dialectical Reason can be made only by dialectical Reason itself; and indeed it must be allowed to ground itself and to develop itself as a free critique of itself, at the same time as being the movement of History and of knowledge.
>
> (*CRDI*: 21, 141)

The reason why Sartre calls the totalizing process of a praxis dialectical is that, once the totalization is obtained, the praxis separates itself from the totalization, which becomes now a totality. This separation presupposes a negation whereby the totalization is no longer part of the praxis' process of externalization. If reappropriated, this totality will become an element within a new totalizing process. The process may of course be merely a process of internalization or may include any kind of spatial activity related to the world or to the praxis itself.

What is the situation in the case of interpersonal relations? One implication is that, in their interactions, persons are no longer regarded by Sartre as determined in their activities and relations by some rigid social structure. Rigid social structures play certainly an important role, but they cannot determine a person's actions and thoughts.

Let us consider one of the examples that Sartre gives in order to illustrate the way in which dialectics function in the process of the formation of interpersonal social relations. The example shows us an intellectual in a small hotel, looking through the window. He sees two workers, a gardener and a road-mender, who are separated by a wall. He can see them, but they cannot see each other and cannot see him. Whereas the intellectual has come to the hotel on a holiday, the workers are there performing their daily jobs. For Sartre, the first moment of the comprehending process of dialectic is given by the intellectual's identification of the workers as two different beings in the world.

This identification of two people as merely two objects among the other objects of attention in the world is accompanied by an identification of them as human beings performing a particular type of activity, an activity which the intellectual would not be able to do. As such, two types of understanding function at the same time: the first is the perception of the world as an object and it is characterized by a relationship from the part to the whole, according to the past functions of the parts (the functions of the workers are presumably part of the institutional settings of society); the second comprehends the conscious beings and is a movement from the whole to the part, a movement starting from those human beings' projects for their future, and determining the role of their particular activities in relation to those projects. Thus, Sartre says,

> my perception provides me first with a multiplicity of tools and apparatuses, produced by the labour of Others (the wall, the road, the garden, the fields, etc.) and it unifies them according both to their objective meaning and to my own project. Every *thing* maintains with all its inertia the particular unity which a long forgotten action imposed upon it; things in general are indifferent to the living, but ideal act of unification which I perform in perception. But I see the *two people* both as objects situated among other objects in the *visual field* and as prospects of escape, as outflow-points of reality. In so far as I understand them on the basis of their work, I perceive their gestures in terms of the aims they set themselves, and so on the basis of the future which they project. The movement of intra-perceptual comprehension, then, is achieved by reversing the simple perception of the inanimate: the present is explained by the future, particular movements by the overall operation, the detail in terms of the totality.
>
> (*CRDI*: 101–2, 214)

The workers' different activities evoke their different world, a world comprising past experiences, future plans and present abilities. This perception of the workers as subjects, and not simply as subject-objects, marks the second dialectical movement, which is similar to the process provoked by "the look" in *Being and Nothingness*:

> Each of the two men is re-conceived and located in the perceptual field by my act of comprehension; but with each of them, through the weeding, pruning and digging hands, or through the measuring, calculating eyes, through the entire body as a lived instrument, I am robbed of an aspect of the real. Their work reveals this to them and in observing their work, I feel it as a lack of being. Thus their negative relation to my own existence

constitutes me, at the deepest level of myself, as definite ignorance, as inadequacy. I *sense* myself as an intellectual through the limits which they prescribe to my perception.

(*CRDI*: 102, 214–15)

What happens at this point is that, once understood in light of their roles and projects, the two praxes observed by the intellectual are perceived as engaged in activities that reveal their freedom and the possibility of changing their projects and thus escaping the totalizing understanding of the intellectual. At this point, the intellectual perceives himself differently, as ignorant of their activities and their world and with a limit to his understanding and freedom.

Having examined Sartre's account of dialectical reason and his view of the first two moments in the formation of interpersonal relations, in the next section I will conclude the discussion on interpersonal relations and I will draw some implications from freedom.

§92. Freedom in the social world

Finally, the "synthesis"[28] of these two moments occurs when the intellectual realizes that the difference between the activities of the workers is less important than the difference between his activity and theirs. This final moment of the dialectical sequence is nothing but another moment of negation: the complicity of the workers against the intellectual.

> The mere fact, for each of them, of seeing what the Other does not see, of exposing the object through a special kind of work, establishes a relation of reciprocity in my perceptual field which transcends my perception: each of them constitutes the ignorance of the Other. [...] [M]y perception makes me a real and objective mediation between these two molecules: if I can, in effect, constitute them in a reciprocity of ignorance, it is because their activities jointly affect me and because my perception defines my limits by revealing the duality of my internal negations. Even my subjectivity is objectively designated by them as Other (another class, another profession, etc.), and in interiorising this designation, I become the objective milieu in which these two people realise their mutual dependence *outside* me.

(*CRDI*: 102–3, 215–16)

Sartre mentions here first a complicity between workers, which is constituted in virtue of the fact that each ignores the intellectual and each ignores one another. This complicity, which affects now the way the intellectual perceives himself, takes on a more concrete form as complicity in virtue of belonging to the same social class and type of profession. Recall that, in

Being and Nothingness, Sartre describes being-for-others as the result of the transformation of being-for-itself (the person looking through the keyhole) in the presence of another person or of the thought of another person (the unexpected witness, who turns out in fact to be merely an impression of the first person, who hears a noise and thinks someone is approaching). Although the second person does not eventually show up, Sartre is still keen to emphasize the reality of being-for-others as a distinct type of being.

A similar claim is made here:

> It is important not to reduce this mediation to a subjective impression: we should not say that *for me* the two labourers are ignorant of one another. They are ignorant of one another *through me* to the extent that I become what I am *through them*. [...] They differ from each other less than they differ from me and, in the last analysis, their reciprocal negation is, for me, a kind of deep complicity. A complicity against me.
>
> (*CRDI*: 102–3, 215–16)

Sartre's analysis of the situation in the example shows that, as part of a society, a person cannot be understood independently from her society, or community. Every project of a person and every action by which that person attempts to change the world are conditioned by the past and present activities and the projects of the others. In her actions, every person interiorizes all these conditionings by totalizing them, and then exteriorizes them as totalized outcomes of her action.

The knowledge that individuals can achieve with regard to these phenomena must not be seen as a particular actualization of a totalizing faculty similar to the Hegelian Spirit. Sartre criticizes this conception and grounds dialectical reason on the particular totalization of the particular persons' praxes. Thus, Sartre writes:

> If there are individuals, *who*, or *what*, totalizes?
>
> [...] *The entire historical dialectic rests on individual* praxis *in so far as it is already dialectical*, that is to say, to the extent that action is itself the negating transcendence of contradiction, the determination of a present totalisation in the name of a future totality, and the real effective working of matter.
>
> (*CRDI*: 80, 194)

The intersubjectivity that can be achieved, even in the case of a radical conflict, is not based on some features which are taken to be shared by all individuals, like particular values or ideals. On the contrary, Sartre's conception of interpersonal relations makes intersubjectivity dependent only on the person's freedom. Whether or not several persons can find a general interest, on the basis of which they could accept the questioning of their particular and singular interests, for Sartre a person already questions her singular, particular and general interests, and it is this capacity that makes intersubjectivity possible. This basis of intersubjectivity was conceived by Sartre in *Being and Nothingness* as the pre-reflective cogito. Now Sartre discovers the same notion of freedom as autonomy in praxis.[29]

Hence, in the *Critique*, Sartre is still maintaining the position that human beings are individually free, but he is also trying to account for the obvious lack of effectiveness of the individual's actions. The social, cultural and political ties that condition the individual make it more plausible to advocate the "realization" of a person *together with others*.

For Sartre, dialectic is "the living logic of action". Since both action and knowledge are praxes, dialectic is immanent both in one's theoretical and practical activities. In fact, the very distinction between theoretical and practical is dissolved, or reduced to a useful convention. This distinction, however, is not the Kantian one, namely, that between an investigation with regard to what actually happens as opposed to an investigation concerning what ought to happen. In the second part of this chapter, we will see that the Kantian distinction is maintained by Sartre. What is dissolved is the distinction between theory as a disinterested contemplation of an object and practice as an activity that aims to change the object.[30]

Having set up the background of Sartre's objection in the *Critique*, let me go back to the objection and the evaluation of its merits.

§93. Kantian optimism

As we have seen in §91, for Sartre the externalization of praxis in the process of production leads to a simultaneous separation of the praxis from its product. Any productive activity is, therefore, at the same time in the product (as that which generates the product) and outside the product, as the transcendent praxis which separates itself from its products after having created them. Insofar as the emphasis is on their distinct character, rather than on their internal relation, the productive activity results in an object, which, once created, exists in the world. The totalization the praxis had to undertake to create the object turns now into a totality, which is transcended by the praxis in other totalizations. Hence, the praxis retains freedom through a separation from itself, that is, from that part of itself it has invested in the object through the productive, totalizing activity (Sartre, 1991: 316–7, 305–6).

Sartre also attempts to cast the epistemic process in terms of internalization and externalization, and to view these as constitutive for an epistemic activity of finding the totality of conditions of cognition (whether subjective, objective or a synthesis). Compared with the approach in *Being and Nothingness*, his approach in the *Critique* focuses much more on the various social, economic, political and cultural conditions that can be involved in such a process, although, of course, cognition is conceived of here in much broader terms than in his early work.

The charge of epistemological optimism that Simont thinks Sartre attributes to Kant consists in the view that the latter takes theoretical cognition to be necessarily progressive. Any attempt to identify the totality of conditions of cognition and to cognize, in this way, the object which corresponds to the unity introduced by reason leads in Kant's philosophy to an expansion of cognition, although never to the realization of a complete totalization and, hence, of cognition of the object corresponding to the unity of all conditions. Moreover, the charge of ontological optimism presupposes that Kant not only regards the natural tendency to the totalizing activity as leading to more knowledge, but takes this natural tendency to be good, to progress towards a morally good end. Hence, insofar as reason limits its use to the regulative role, there is no loss, but only cognitive progress.

Why does Simont claim that, on Sartre's account, the process of totalization is accompanied by "ineluctable loss" and "damage"? The suggestion is that Sartre regards the result of the praxis' externalization as generated by freedom and, yet, as deprived of freedom once the praxis transcends this result. The types of freedom relevant here are the ontological and practical freedom introduced in Chapter 4; the latter enables the praxis to overcome obstacles in the process of totalization and the former is presupposed by the unity that is involved in any totalizing activity. Insofar as the process of totalization necessarily results in failure, because the result becomes separated from the praxis and transforms itself into a mere totality, there is "loss" and perhaps "damage".

Yet, this does not seem much less optimistic than Kant's own account, where any attempt to determine the totality of conditions of experience and cognition is bound to achieve only a partial totalization, rather than a complete totality, and any attempt to claim knowledge of the whole set of conditions necessarily leads to contradictions and illegitimately drawn conclusions. For instance, in Chapters 1 and 3, we have seen that Kant deems the radical empiricist view as problematic, precisely because it cannot account for the person's identity and freedom, but turns the presupposition of numerical identity into a set of unrelated and fleeting impressions and transforms her into an object.[31] This is the problem Kant attempts to address, in the Third Paralogism, in order to save a person's numerical identity while avoiding the rationalist stance. This was also the source of Kant's attempt, in the Third Antinomy, to reconcile natural causality with freedom.

To see a person merely as part of the phenomenal world is to contemplate her (to use Kant's term) "theoretically" as an object. Besides, construed in this way, it becomes difficult to account for the moral connotations of Sartre's critical remarks on Kant. Indeed, not only in the *Notebooks* but also in the *Critique of Dialectical Reason*, Sartre claims that regulative ideas lead to alienation (Sartre 1991: 422), and he draws a parallel between this use of "alienation" and the use of "inauthenticity" or "bad faith" in *Being and Nothingness* (Sartre 1991: 421–2). So, if we stick to the non-moral charge of (epistemological and ontological) optimism, then we do not seem to go very far, since Sartre, like Kant, deems the "teleological" (guiding, heuristic) use of reason as essential for cognition.

By contrast, if we take the twofold charge of optimism as advanced from a moral perspective, then there are more chances of making sense of Sartre's objection. Thus, by itself, accumulation of cognition is neither good nor bad from a moral point of view: it may be used to morally good or bad purposes. It is when progress is also regarded as leading towards good ends that the moral perspective becomes relevant. I think, therefore, that the sense of Sartre's critique of the notion of a regulative idea has not so much to do with Kant's theoretical philosophy as with his practical philosophy and, more precisely, with his "Idea for a Universal History".

This direction of interpretation seems quite promising and, in the next section, I will follow it in discussing further Sartre's objection.

§94. Moral progress

Indeed, as we have seen, Kant's claims concerning the end of history seemed ambiguous as to the status of the idea for a universal history. The latter apparently has, at the same time, a regulative role and a constitutive function. Kant's assumption is that, by looking at historical events from the perspective given by the hidden plan of nature, one could anticipate political events and contribute to the advent of the perfect cosmopolitan community. It is true that, in a later essay, Kant seems less optimistic about the possibility of precipitating the arrival of the end of history by a study of historical events and by predictions about its future course:

> If we now ask by what means this unending progress toward the better can be maintained and even accelerated, it is soon seen that this immeasurably distant success will depend not so much upon what *we* do [...] and by what methods we should proceed in order to bring it about, but instead upon what human *nature* will do in and with us to *force* us onto a track we would readily take of our own accord.
>
> (Kant 1996: 8:310, 307)

Here, Kant claims that progress is not a matter of what we do, but a matter of what nature does through us and in us. In spite of this distinct view, Kant still regards the idea of a universal history from a cosmopolitan viewpoint as related to a claim concerning the moral, that is, ethical and political progress of human beings. This may suggest that, for Kant, the idea for a universal history has not only a regulative function but also a constitutive one. For otherwise it is not clear how the unity of history would be determined by the morally good purpose of a perfectly moral cosmopolitan community.

In this case, the end of history would not only be a "mere thought", as the concepts corresponding to regulative ideas should always be, but it could also be an object absolutely.[32] Moreover, if the ideas of reason are various aspects of one and the same unity, then the direction of progress in the attempt to determine the conditions of experience in accordance with the three ideas of reason presented in the first *Critique* is morally determined by the idea of the unity of history. The cognitive progress, which obtains by using these ideas heuristically, is also moral progress. The hidden plan of nature is not simply a heuristic device that helps historians to unify various events from a particular standpoint, but it is a phenomenon which can be studied like any other phenomena.

On the basis of this hypothesis, one can read Kant's defence of the rightness of particular norms (for instance, the necessity of owning property in order to have the right to vote) as an epistemic contention that they are the laws which govern the perfect cosmopolitan society. Kant seems to hold at the same time that there is a sharp distinction between constitutive ideas, which belong to the understanding, on the one hand, and regulative ideas, which belong to reason, on the other, as well as that the idea for universal history is regulative and constitutive.

This reading of Kant's idea for a universal history suggests the reason why Sartre criticizes Kant's practical philosophy in moral terms. Indeed, it is only to the extent that the *summum bonum* is posited as a universal value that Kant can, at the same time, explain why this is the value towards which history is directed and why it is not yet realized.[33] However, for Sartre, to make this type of contradictory claim means to act in bad faith. We have seen[34] that a project is authentic when it is carried out with the conscience of being freely assumed and not on the assumption that it is based on a given value. Similarly, particular legal norms are authentic just to the extent that the members of a community can freely and authentically adopt them, and not if they are imposed by the theorist who has a privileged access to the perfect constitution of a moral community.

But is Kant's idea of a universal history a regulative idea, which claims at the same time to be a constitutive category? After all Kant explicitly says that

> It would be a misinterpretation of my intention to contend that I meant this idea of a universal history, which to some extent follows an *a priori* rule, to supersede the task of history proper, that of *empirical* composition. My idea is only a notion of what a philosophical mind, well acquainted with history, might be able to attempt from a different angle.
>
> (*IaG*: 8:30, 53)

If the study of history from the angle provided by the idea for a universal history is not replacing the theoretical (empirical) approach to history, then presumably Kant talks in the mode of the "as if" about the prophecies which the philosopher can make. Hence, the perfect moral community is only a regulative idea. But Kant does not claim anywhere that his idea of universal law is regulative. At this point, it becomes necessary to question whether the whole approach to this issue, in terms of regulative and constitutive functions of ideas, is not misleading. Perhaps there is a distinct status that can be attributed to the idea of universal history.

In this section, I have argued that Sartre's objection to the Kantian "as if" can be understood by looking at Kant's idea of universal history as the history of the moral progress of human beings. This idea, Kant claims, is not constitutive; yet, Sartre thinks that, inconsistently, Kant uses it in a constitutive manner to make predictions about future states of affairs and the end of history, the perfect moral community. In the next section, I will present a different interpretation of this idea of Kant.

§95. A third practical postulate

David Lindstedt argues precisely for the distinct status of the idea of universal history. On his account, this should be understood as a middle ground between a constitutive and a regulative idea. According to Lindstedt, this middle ground is represented by the postulate of practical reason. Hence, the idea of universal history is not meant to expand the understanding's cognition of history as if the latter were simply the hidden plan of nature; moreover, this idea of universal history is more than an empirical exercise in finding some unity in history.

One thing that can immediately be noted in support of this interpretation is that the idea of moral progress, which Kant associates with his view of universal history from a cosmopolitan standpoint, cannot be realized from the theoretical perspective of an idea, even when this idea is considered (illicitly) as having a constitutive role to play. So Lindstedt's suggestion that we abandon this approach and adopt a new one seems not only interesting but is also required if we want to explain the moral connotations of Kant's claims. Lindstedt's alternative is to read Kant as talking about the cosmopolitan purpose of history as a presupposition of the moral law. In other words, if the moral law is accepted, then the idea of a cosmopolitan society should be accepted too:

> Kant does not appeal primarily to nature, regulative ideas, or empirical history in order to justify his position. Rather, time and time again he makes an appeal to morality, and to the futility which would result from the rejection of the idea of progress of human beings. [...] It is important for Kant's system to posit a progression so that persons may pursue the

highest good for this world. It is only after such justification has been made that Kant attempts to spell out how a progression might occur, after which he maintains that such a description is mere hypothesis.

(Lindstedt 1999: 147)

Hence, on Lindstedt's account, Kant does not regard the idea of universal history with a cosmopolitan purpose as a regulative, let alone as a constitutive, idea. Nor does he hope to reach such a conclusion about the moral progress of human species by an empirical investigation of history. What Kant tries to do, on Lindstedt's account, is to derive this idea as a postulate of practical reason from the moral law. The assumption here is that persons may not try to become virtuous in this world if the possibility of moral progress is not demonstrated at least in principle.

I think this assumption is problematic. First of all, on Kant's account, the sufficient incentive for acting virtuously is given by the moral law itself, more exactly, by respect for the moral law. To act in a particular way because that action is right, is to act on the motive of respect. Agents need not stop acting in this way because they don't know whether human species will become virtuous in this world. In other worlds, persons may well pursue the highest good, whether or not human species makes moral progress.

Secondly, in discussing the possibility of the complete good in the Antinomy of Practical Reason, Kant does not make it a requirement that individuals progress morally in this life. He only sets some conditions for the possibility of reaching the complete good in general. Moreover, the possibility of reaching the highest good by individuals is demonstrated by appeal to the claim concerning the immortality of the soul, which clearly places the moment of becoming virtuous in afterlife. So it is unclear on what basis Kant would need, as Lindstedt claims, to demonstrate the possibility for the human species to reach the highest good in this life.

A possible reply here, however, is that, for the idea of universal history with a cosmopolitan purpose Kant need not start from such a requirement. Given the general function of pure reason (that of organizing and unifying phenomena), as a first step one can claim that the unity presupposed by any idea of reason imposes an approach to history as progressing towards some end. The second argumentative step will *not* try to determine whether this end is a good or an evil end; the point here is *not* to offer some argument as to why persons will necessarily act morally, since this is a contradiction in terms. The second argumentative step will try to explain how, *in case* there is moral progress, this is compatible with the necessary freedom persons must have in order to reach the highest good (virtue).

One way to explain this is to identify the end of this moral progress and to show how this is an end where all persons can be morally virtuous. Hence, this will have to be some international political order. If such an order were not possible, moral progress would not be possible and we would have to accept that the end which unifies history is necessarily evil. Kant's reference to the unsociable sociability of persons is also a way to explain how moral progress is possible and how it would look for those engaged in the empirical study of history. This need not be in tension with, or contradict, the freedom required for virtuous action, given the conclusions of the discussion of the Third Antinomy.

It would be beyond the scope of the argument here to pursue these points further. For the purpose of the comparison between Kant and Sartre, and, in particular, for the purpose of the discussion of Sartre's objection to Kant's idea of moral progress, a first conclusion is that Kant does not take regulative ideas of reason and use them constitutively. Secondly, the argument concerning the end of history is not an argument that claims to provide cognition of this end. The claim of an end of history is only a presupposition of the function of pure reason in general, namely to order and unify various phenomena we experience, and such claim of an end is a heuristic device.

Thirdly, the actual universal history provided from Kant is, as the title of the short essay says, a narrative from the perspective of a good end, an international order which makes it possible for all persons to act and live in accordance with the highest good. The conclusion of the argument is not that this end will be reached or that we make progress towards it – not even as a postulate of practical reason, in the manner in which Lindstedt suggests; by contrast, moral progress is the starting point and the narrative tries to show how this would be possible. Were this to be impossible, the attempt to act on the moral law would indeed be futile, just like it would be futile to act in such a way as to realize a concept which is contradictory.

§96. Dialectical a priori

In the previous section, I have argued that Kant's argument is not vulnerable to the objection that he is using regulative ideas constitutively, nor is it open to the objection that it postulates a particular end as the end of history. Kant's claim is not that we have either theoretical or practical cognition that we make moral progress towards the cosmopolitan end of history, his argument is that, *if* we make moral progress, then this progress would be possible in certain ways which he describes. But this is only a conditional claim.

Now, at this point, one could still object in the following way: let's assume that we do make moral progress (although we cannot be sure about this); one reason why it is useful to present how this is possible (apart from making sure that it is not impossible and, hence, not an alternative worth considering) is that, in this way, we offer suggestions of how moral progress can be pursued and realized. However, if one mistakenly tries to describe such a possible path from the perspective of an end of history which is not good, but evil, then one sets persons on an evil path with the misleading justification that this will bring about moral progress.

Is this a relevant objection to Kant's theory? Could Sartre be interpreted as raising such an objection? And, perhaps independently, can a similar argument be formulated against Sartre himself?

It is very noticeable that Sartre thinks Kant's account of experience is much too narrow and rigid. First, Sartre talks about a unity corresponding to the unity that Kant links to transcendental apperception, but he claims that this can only be conceived in relation to that of multiplicity. As an implication, he claims that the action of the organism or of the human praxis can create a unity only in relation to the dispersion of matter into a multiplicity. But, insofar as this unity is the result of human praxis, it cannot be determined in advance with respect to its content, in the manner in which, he thinks, Kant determines the transcendental unity of apperception. Hence, on Sartre's account, it is "the practical regulation of the organism by matter, of the matter by the organism, which produces the idea of unity, which invents it" (Simont 1987a: 148).

Moreover, Sartre rejects not only the Kantian conception of unity, but also the a priori categories of the understanding, and he takes the a priori of the laws of dialectics to be based on the very praxis by which individuals encounter the world:

> The *"a priori"*, here, has nothing to do with any sort of constitutive principles which are prior to experience. It relates to a universality and necessity contained in every experience but which go beyond each experience.
>
> (*CRDI*: 35, 153)[35]

And further:

> there is no *one* dialectic which imposes itself upon the facts, as Kant's categories impose themselves upon phenomena; but the dialectic, if it exists, is the individual career of its object. There can be no pre-established schema imposed on individual developments, neither in someone's head, nor in an intelligible heaven; if the dialectic exists, it is because certain regions of materiality are *structured* in such a way that it cannot not exist. In other words, the dialectical movement is not some powerful unitary force revealing itself behind History like the will of God.
>
> (*CRDI*: 37, 155)[36]

These quotations suggest that Sartre regards Kant's a priori conditions for the possibility of experience as substantive and narrow principles, which not only make possible experience, but also are "imposed" on individual activities. From Chapters 1, 3 and 5, we know, however, that all these claims Sartre makes against Kant are, in fact, claims Kant himself would support. He would agree that the a priori is the universality and necessity which is within each experience and which goes beyond each particular experience;

he would agree that there is no pre-established schema imposed on individual developments either in a person's head or in an intelligible heaven; and he would also agree that the structures which make possible experience are those without which experience would not be possible; finally, he would agree that principles of understanding and of reason are not unitary forces which reveal themselves behind history as the will of God.

Kant's structures of the mind (pure intuitions, categories and a priori principles of understanding and ideas of reason) are not imposed on our actions or development. Kant conceives them precisely as necessary conditions of experience, conditions without which experience would not be possible. An imposed structure, by contrast, is a structure which constrains an already existing action or activity.[37]

As we have seen, on Kant's account, the unity that ideas of reason bring to the phenomena are only heuristic devices for the organization of disperse knowledge, they are not cognitive principles that enable predictions. In fact, by his reference to history, Sartre makes it clear that his reading of Kant as imposing some narrow structure on the world refers not only to the transcendental unity of apperception and the a priori concepts and principles of understanding, but also to the ideas of reason.[38]

In this respect, however, like Kant's *Critique of Pure Reason*, Sartre's *Critique of Dialectical Reason* makes sometimes claims that invite misinterpretation. I will discuss these in the next section.

§97. If and as if

Thus Sartre can be found talking about the "Truth of History", and about the way in which human praxes are led to this truth of history without their being aware of it.[39] Such claims echo Kant's contention in "Theory and Practice" and "Idea of Universal History" that human nature works so that it would force us to take the course which furthers the moral plan of history irrespective of our actions. For instance:

> A critique of dialectical Reason must concern itself with the field of application and the limits of this reason. If there is to be any such thing as the Truth of History (rather than *several* truths, even if they are organised into a system) our investigation must show that the kind of dialectical intelligibility which we have described above applies to the process of human history as a whole, or, in other words, that there is a totalising temporalisation of our practical multiplicity and that it is intelligible, even though this totalisation does not involve a grand totaliser. It is one thing to claim that individuals (possibly "social atoms") totalise dispersals through their very existence (but individually and each within the private region of his work), and it is quite another to show that they totalise

themselves, intelligibly, without for the most part showing any concern about it.

(CRDI: 64, 178–9)

Here, Sartre seems to reject the idea of "*several* truths" and opts for that of one Truth. According to Andrew Dobson, Sartre would maintain "that his method – the 'dialectical method' which provides for History's intelligibility – is singular and unsurpassable in that it 'applies to the process of human history as a whole'" (Dobson 1993: 182). He then remarks that Sartre's method rejects relativism and that, contrary to his claim that human beings are free and that they make history, he

castigates relativism for not allowing for syntheses – and it is not just *any* synthesis that Sartre is recommending, but a synthesis which is the dialectical unity of history with all its bonds of interiority.

(Dobson 1993: 182)

If Sartre is indeed convinced that he puts forward a method of finding the truth that cannot be surpassed, and by means of which one could discover the "Truth of History", then he seems to do precisely what he rejects in Kant. He seems to claim that it is possible to know the meaning of historical events, and hence to prescribe the values which are to be pursued by human beings. One could thus interpret Sartre's defence of the particular values of the Algerian War of Liberation as a claim that these are the right values, which should be pursued.[40] When he claims that the Algerians' killing of a European leaves us with one oppressor less and one more free human being, is he not saying that the values for which the Algerian people fight are the morally good values?

However, caution is necessary in the interpretation of the passage about the Truth of History, since Sartre does not invoke it unconditionally. He rejects indeed the Kantian "as if", but he constantly employs a conditional "if" when he talks about the "Truth of History". For instance, "if we are to ground it [dialectical Reason] as the rationality of *praxis*, of totalisation, and of society's future [...], then we must realise the situated experience of its apodicticity *through ourselves*" (*CRDI*: 39, 157), or "if History is a totalisation which temporalises itself, culture is itself a temporalising and temporalised totalisation" (*CRDI*: 54, 169), or "If History is totalisation and if individual practices are the sole ground of totalising temporalisation, it is not enough to reveal the totalisation developing in everyone" (*CRDI*: 64, 179).

To be sure, Sartre does not simply attempt to deduce the logical consequences of the hypothesis concerning the existence of one truth of one history. In the second volume of the *Critique*, he attempts "to establish that there is *one* human history, with *one* truth and *one* intelligibility" (*CRDI*: 64, 179); however, Sartre states explicitly that he is not concerned with a truth of history in the sense of a goal or end that everybody ought to follow. His claim here seems to be similar to Kant's claim concerning the necessary unity from the perspective of which history must be approached. The idea is not to determine that unity and the corresponding end of history, but to give order to the cognition of past events and to suggest a direction for the investigation of further events as they happen.

Sartre is not engaged in the same Kantian process of identifying the possibility of a moral end of history and, hence, he is probably not concerned about the specific features of the political order to which the moral progress of human species would lead. Nevertheless, he is concerned about the specific way in which Kant articulates his theoretical and practical philosophy, in particular the rule-centred character of the Kantian approach. The objection to its constraining character is a standard accusation Sartre raises against Kant. Hence, eventually Sartre's objection to Kant's idea of moral progress turns out to rely on his view of morality as value-centred, a view which the Cornell Lectures show Sartre starts to refine.

In fact, Sartre objects to a morality which postulates particular values and imperatives as universal. But Kant's moral theory could also support a similar criticism. If Sartre had realized that Kant distinguishes between imperative and maxim, then he would have understood that Kant's ethics also rejects any attempt of positing a set of universal standards. Moreover, we have seen that Kant's account of normativity rejects moral realism, but goes beyond the attempt of moral constructivism to rely only on experience or the rules of logic. For Kant, the criterion of morality is not formulated by the moral theorist in terms of procedures but represents a condition of the possibility of asserting a normative claim.

Indeed, every person's claim concerning the validity of a standard implies a claim concerning the criterion of morality. Hence, by the very fact of making a validity claim when choosing a standard of action as valid, a person also chooses the moral criterion on the basis of which she acts. It is on the basis of this conception of the Categorical Imperative (as criterion of morality) that Kant could provide a sound solution to the moral conflict between the liberty of the ancients and that of the moderns. If the criterion of morality presupposes a choice that the person makes with every normative claim, then it is possible to offer an appropriate account of self-realization and to reconcile the two types of liberty.

§98. Closing remarks

I began this chapter with an objection Sartre formulates in the *Notebooks*, where he portrays Kant's moral theory as authoritarian. I have shown, however, that both this objection and the objection to Kant's account of interpersonal relations presented in Chapter 3 are better considered from the perspective of Sartre's changed view of the relation between values and imperatives in the Cornell Lectures. Whereas he seemed to regard a commitment to values as a commitment which can only be made in virtue of the value's ethical goodness, in his later work he realizes the important role that internalization of norms plays in our life. From this perspective, his objection to Kant's account of interpersonal relationships becomes an issue of identity of standards, rather than of normative validity.

The issue of the standards' identity can, in principle, be solved by a split introduced in the person. Kant distinguishes, for instance, between a human being as a rational person and a human being as a sentient being. As a rational person, a human being has a pure reason which is practical, that is, on its own has the capacity to motivate her to act. The idea is that we are motivated to perform certain actions, because we can see that performing those actions means acting on morally valid maxims, that is, on practical principles which can be laws. Hence, the criterion of morality enables us to determine morally valid principles and their moral validity can motivate us.

By contrast, as a sentient being, we are motivated to act by countless contingent incentives. We know we are acting on a practical law because we can distinguish between the way we are acting and the way we ought to be acting on the basis of the moral law or the Categorical Imperative. Hence, the problem of identity need not be solved in Kant by appeal to interpersonal relations, although interpersonal relations are, of course, very important too. It is not surprising, therefore, that Sartre would also need to introduce a split in the person, a split which makes possible for a person to distinguish between the way she acts and the way she ought to act.

I should mention, however, that the split introduced by Sartre is not able to play the role it is meant to play. The pre-reflective cogito is, of course, able to bring about consciousness (of) self, that is, a consciousness which is non-positionally conscious of itself through reflexivity. We have, therefore, a consciousness which, in this respect (as reflected by the reflexive consciousness), is in-itself and a consciousness which, as non-positionally conscious of the first, is for-itself. But Sartre needs to introduce the ideal of the in-itself-for-itself or the notion of a value, as presupposed by the pre-reflective cogito, in order to be able to make room for the difference between what happens in the world and what ought to happen in the world.

What Sartre therefore does, is to say that the pre-reflective cogito is always in search for the ideal of the complete self. Yet, as we have seen, this can merely describe how it is possible for a person to project something as to be desired, but not yet how a person can take the object of a desire to be desirable or undesirable. As long as Sartre thinks all actual choices of values are choices of values that are ethically good, he needs no additional criterion of morality, although he misses the important metaethical distinction between a descriptive and a prescriptive account of action. The ideal of authenticity plays, therefore, only the role of criticizing certain attitudes which make morality impossible – for instance, those attitudes which are the result of impure reflection, and which regard persons as determined by their circumstances or which conceive of moral standards as given once and for all or which mistakenly deal with other persons as if they were objects.

Once Sartre realizes that a choice of values may be a choice of bad values, he no longer draws a sharp distinction between imperatives and values, and he attempts to formulate an ethics which can lead to a choice of valid standards of action. We have seen that his objection to Kant's account of interpersonal relations becomes an objection to moral realism, to a view of moral norms as given independently from the person who acts. Moreover, we have seen that his objection to Kant's authoritarianism is directed against an account of autonomy where self-legislation is understood as following the principle that structures practical reason, rather than authentic self-projection.

I have shown that both these objections reveal, in fact, structural similarities between Kant's and Sartre's critique of moral realism and their rejection of a lawless or valueless freedom. Moreover, we have seen that Sartre's objection to Kant's claim concerning the moral progress of humankind is also evidence of a structural similarity between their critical reactions to an illegitimate use of regulative ideas.

One difference seems to remain: Sartre's emphasis on values and Kant's focus on principles. Yet, we have seen that Sartre proposes in his later ethical writings an account of values and imperatives as aspects of the same normative claims, and we have also seen that Kant can be seen as arguing for a similar relationship, although he is primarily concerned to resist attempts to formulate principles starting from empirical notions of the good.

In the final part of this monograph, I will bring together the results of the comparative analysis and raise again the question of an ethical theory able to account for unconditional obligation without dogmatic presuppositions.

Conclusion

In Conclusion, I would first like to go back to Constant's example presented in the Introduction and to show the similarity between Constant's view of conditional obligations through representation and the view of what is currently called 'Kantian constructivism'.[1] I will present some problems of this approach and, after a summary of the argument so far, I will examine the answers a critical ethics can give to the problems I raised, starting from Constant's example: the problem of justification, of normativity and of the conflict of liberties. I will then go back once again to Constant's example and examine some unpalatable implications of the idea of an unconditional obligation to avoid untruthfulness.

§99. How to account for unconditional obligations

Imagine an oppressive regime in which citizens are arrested and sent to certain death in forced labour camps because of their political affiliations; imagine your friend is pursued by the police and hides in your house. Intuitively, it seems that, to be truthful in this situation would be wrong. Why? Because being truthful contributes to something *wrong* taking place.

Imagine now a democratic regime in which citizens are arrested when they are suspected of having broken the law. Laws are, there, the result of legitimate political processes. Imagine further that your friend has done something wrong (for instance, murder) and is pursued by police. He hides in your house. In this case, being truthful seems the *right* thing to do. Why? Because being truthful in this situation contributes to something *right* being done and, one could say, discourages other wrong actions.

This suggests that truthfulness is a conditional standard.[2] When being truthful has a morally good purpose, then it is the right thing to do; when it has a morally dubious purpose, it is wrong.

According to Kant and, it would seem, to Sartre too, not being untruthful in statements is an unconditional duty.[3] By contrast, for Constant, being untruthful is right or wrong depending on what the representatives of the citizens decide. Representatives are supposed to decide by taking into consideration the good of the community, rather than the particular interests of some groups. Hence, in principle, a law may go against certain citizens' moral intuitions and interests. Yet laws do not simply follow some abstract standards set in stone, they depend on the common interests of the citizens, and this is reflected in the fact that representatives are chosen by the citizens themselves.

This is precisely the way in which constructivism tries to avoid the scepticism of a non-cognitivist position and the realist version of cognitivism. Take, for instance, Rawls's version of constructivism. In *A Theory of Justice*, in a discussion concerning the concept of liberty (1994: 201–5), he mentions Constant's distinction between the liberty of the moderns and the liberty of the ancients[4] and acknowledges the fact that the question concerning the relationship between these two kinds of liberty "is clearly one of substantive political philosophy, and *a theory of right* and justice is required to answer it" (Rawls 1994: 202).

In the John Dewey Lectures (1980), he sees contemporary political philosophy as leading to an "impasse" generated in "the course of democratic thought over the past two centuries" by the disagreement on "the way basic social institutions should be arranged if they are to conform to the freedom and equality of citizens as moral persons" (Rawls 1980: 517). The conflict between civic liberties (freedom of thought and conscience, the basic rights of the person, of property and association), on the one hand, and public values (the equal political liberties and the values of public life), on the other, stems from the different prioritizations that they are given in "two traditions of democratic thought, one associated with Locke, the other with Rousseau" (Rawls 1980: 519).

According to Rawls's reading, Locke would give priority to the liberties of civic life (the liberties of the moderns), whereas Rousseau would opt for those of public life (the liberties of the ancients). The goal of a conception of justice becomes that of resolving this conflict (Rawls 1980: 517). Rawls's starting point is the intuitive idea that a disagreement between two parties over a particular issue can be solved by finding a basis of agreement concerning that issue, and by working out the implications which can be drawn from this common benchmark under conditions that would be accepted by both parties as fair.

In the dispute between the proponents of the liberty of the ancients and those of the liberty of the moderns, the issue to be "adjudicated" by Rawls's conception of justice is that of the organization of the basic institutions of society (Rawls 1985: 227). There are three main topics of disagreement between the conflicting parties: society, the person and the conditions on which the conflict is to be solved. The political theorist attends to them and tries to find some deeper basis of agreement. The result is a set of three "model-conceptions", namely that of a "well-ordered society", that of a "moral person" and that of the "original position", respectively, where the third has a mediating role between the first two (Rawls 1980: 520).

The model conception of a well-ordered society is that of a polity in which basic institutions are regulated by principles of justice which everyone accepts because they are "founded on *reasonable* beliefs as established by the society's generally accepted methods of inquiry" (Rawls 1980: 521).[5] The well-ordered society is related to the original position and the model conception of a moral person insofar as the first principles of justice are chosen by hypothetical moral agents in the original position. The original position is conceived of as a device of representation, whereby hypothetical agents that are defined according to the model conception of the person are imagined as choosing the right principles of justice on the basis of some criteria of rightness.

It is this strategy of solving political conflicts that Rawls calls "Kantian constructivism".[6] In the next two sections, I will examine further this position and the possibility of accounting for unconditional obligations from the perspective of Kantian constructivism.

§100. Kantian constructivism

Rawls defines the model conception of the person by means of three characteristics: persons are moral, equal and free (Rawls 1980: 521). The moral aspect of a person is essentially given by two moral powers and two corresponding interests. Thus, the first moral power is "the capacity to understand, to apply, and to act from (and not merely in accordance with) the principles of justice" (Rawls 1980: 525). The second moral power is "the capacity to form and revise and rationally to pursue a conception of the good" (Rawls 1980: 525).

The corresponding interests are those of realizing these powers; they are complemented by a third interest, namely that of "protecting and advancing their [the citizens'] conception of the good as best as they can" (Rawls 1980: 525). Persons are equal in the sense that each has an equal right to participate in the deliberations concerning the principles of justice, and they are free in that they can argue for or against a particular design of their institutions from the perspective of their own interests and they can change these interests (Rawls 1980: 521).

In order to obtain the *just* solution to the problems raised by a situation of conflict, Rawls constructs the "original position" as a set of procedures, whereby principles of justice are to be chosen. This is "a purely hypothetical situation" and not an actual framework of deliberations (Rawls 1994: 12). Once chosen, the principles of justice arbitrate in cases of conflict. Rawls assumes that "there is a broad measure of agreement that principles of justice should be chosen under certain conditions" (Rawls 1994: 18). He tries to work out these conditions on the basis of some "commonly shared presumptions" (Rawls 1994: 18).

If the conditions cannot yield principles of justice, then the conditions are redefined by adding further "equally reasonable premises". If the conditions thus obtained lead to principles of justice, then the latter are tested against our considered judgements concerning justice (Rawls 1994: 20). If the conditions do provide principles but there are discrepancies between them and our considered judgements, we either modify the account of the conditions or we modify our judgements.

Rawls assumes that "eventually we shall find a description of the initial situation that both expresses reasonable conditions and yields principles which match our considered judgements, duly pruned and adjusted" (Rawls 1994: 20). He calls this state of affairs a "reflective equilibrium". Actually, Rawls does not deal in detail with the process that aims at reflective equilibrium; he simply assumes that the original position is the result of this type of process. One important point here is that, on the basis of his account of the original position and the principles of justice, Rawls claims that the justification of a conception of justice "is a matter of the mutual support of many considerations, of everything fitting together into one coherent view", and not one of truth (Rawls 1994: 21).

Nevertheless, the principles of justice are considered as justified by their being agreed to in the original position because the conditions which constitute it "are ones that we do in fact accept" (Rawls 1994: 21). Hence he rejects the moral realism of a theory for which there are legal norms which are true independently of a view of human agency. The principles of justice are constructed, and they depend essentially on Rawls's conception of the person.

As an element of the original position, the "veil of ignorance" stands for a set of restrictions imposed on the parties that deliberate in the hypothetical situation and is a direct consequence of the way in which the conception of the person is defined:

> In order to ensure that the original position is fair between individuals regarded solely as free and equal moral persons, we require that, when adopting principles for the basic structure, the parties be deprived of certain information; that is, they are behind what I shall call a "veil of ignorance". For example, they do not know their place in society, their class position, or social status, nor do they know their fortune in the distribution of natural talents and abilities.
>
> (Rawls 1980: 522–3)

After having applied the procedures which constitute the veil of ignorance, every individual becomes a person in the original position, that is, she comes to be a free and equal moral being. The moral deliberations on issues of justice presuppose that those who deliberate be persons. Apart from being free and endowed with moral powers, individuals are equal: the parties have to be situated "symmetrically" in their discussions (Ralws 1980: 529). The symmetry condition is given by the fact that the citizens are required to adopt a *public* conception of justice (Rawls 1980: 529); they are equally situated in the original position in the sense that they have an equal right to express their conception of justice and to argue for it. This also presupposes that they have equal access to all relevant information (Rawls 1980: 529).

Rawls's Kantian constructivism seems able to account for the problem of justification, insofar as it is able to avoid moral scepticism by supporting moral cognitivism and, yet, without being committed to a form of moral realism. Is this account of justification able to answer Constant's problem of the conflict of liberties, one of the problems with which we began this book in the Introduction?

§101. Problems for constructivism

On Rawls's Kantian constructivism, as a citizen in the original position and situated behind the veil of ignorance, a person is rationally autonomous. This means that she deliberates as a self-interested individual who tries to find the best principles of justice for given "ends" (Rawls 1980: 529). Behind the veil of ignorance, however, persons do not know their particular conceptions of the good. Nevertheless, they are driven in their deliberations by certain general ends or conceptions of the good that Rawls calls "primary goods". These are "social conditions and all-purpose means to enable human beings to realise and exercise their moral powers and to pursue their final ends", and they are to be distributed by the principles of justice (Rawls 1980: 526).

The sense in which a person is to be viewed as autonomous in the original position is, therefore, first given by his being driven by interests formally defined by means of the restrictions imposed by the veil of ignorance, and not by particular conceptions of the good. Since, for Rawls, the person's freedom implies the possibility of changing one's conception of the good, he has to eliminate from the original position any information concerning one's conception of the good. Hence, the individual's moral identity is not given by his standards of morality, but by his being a person capable of choosing his conception of the good. In the original position, this rational autonomy of the person ("the Rational") makes possible the *rational* agreement on the organization of the basic institutions of society.

As a citizen in the well-ordered society, a person is fully autonomous (Rawls 1980: 521). This means that not only does she advance her conception of the good – by choosing principles of justice which maximize her share in the primary goods – but she also cooperates with other persons on the basis of fair terms, "that is, terms each participant may reasonably be expected to accept, provided that everyone else likewise accepts them" (Rawls 1980: 528). When a person is cooperating fairly with other citizens, she is "reasonable" (her attitude belongs to "the Reasonable"[7]). Full autonomy is also incorporated into the original position as a constraint that frames the discussions between the parties. Hence, the conditions which are required in order for an individual to become a person in the original position are supplemented with a procedure or criterion of justice.

After having achieved the reflective equilibrium, the procedures which define the original position are justified and the principles of justice can be used for the purpose of solving moral conflicts. In particular, it should be possible to use the principles of justice to solve the dispute between the proponents of Constant's two types of liberty. These liberties are, according to Rawls, equally represented in the original position and, hence, appear in the principles of justice without one having priority over the other.

In this way, Rawls's constructivist cognitivism seems to be able to solve both the ethical and the political conflicts between the liberty of the moderns and that of the ancients. Rawls does not advocate moral non-cognitivism, but adopts a moral cognitivism and a notion of self-realization that are based on an unconditional criterion of morality (the condition of reasonableness). Moreover, Rawls seems to be able to solve the political problems raised by the conflict between "moderns" and "ancients" since he gives no priority to the public or to the private rights: these appear in the first principle on an equal footing.[8]

In fact, despite the complex conceptual framework, Rawls's theory of justice fails to steer a path between the sceptical position of the non-cognitivist and the realist version of cognitivism. This suggests that his solution to Constant's problem of the conflict of liberties is also problematic. For one thing, the process of achieving a reflective equilibrium between citizens' deeply held moral intuitions and the principles of justice remains normatively underdetermined.

One wonders on what basis the moral theorist decides whether to change the procedures of the hypothetical agreement, that is, the principles of justice, or to leave the principles of justice as they are and change the citizens' moral intuitions. In general, constructivism implies that it is the moral legislator, that is, the representative of citizens or the moral theorist, who is entitled to establish the circumstances in which being untruthful is morally right or wrong.

Recall the problem of the conflict of liberties as presented in the Introduction; recall, in particular, the distinction between the ethical and the political versions of this problem. I have said that the ethical version refers to a conflict between negative freedom and self-realization, which seems to be solved by the idea of autonomy. I have also mentioned that the political version pertains to a conflict between freedom from political power and interference by other persons, within the equal area of external freedom each person is supposed to have, and self-determination, as the freedom of the person to participate to the legislation of the rights which define this equal area of external freedom. I have suggested that the notion of political autonomy seems able to answer this problem.

The focus of the comparative discussion of Kant and Sartre has mainly been on their ethical theories. I have claimed that, on the basis of the similarities between their views, we can outline a critical ethics which is able to answer the problems of justification and conflict of liberties and, in this way, offer a better account of normativity than that offered by contemporary versions of constructivism. To be sure, what we can expect here is that critical ethics will offer an approach to the questions of ethical justification and to the ethical version of the problem of the conflict of liberties.

But, of course, if this proves to be the case, further examination of the possibility of extending this critical ethical theory into a critical moral theory dealing also with political–legal issues will be the natural step to take. So let me summarize the results of the discussion so far and attempt to present the main elements of a critical ethics.

§102. Kant and Sartre: Similarities

I have examined six objections to Kant that Sartre formulates in his early and later writings. I have started with the objection, noted by Sartre in the *Transcendence of the Ego*, that the formal I of the transcendental unity of apperception is not in fact purely formal and must be placed outside consciousness, in the world. Through an examination of Kant's Third Paralogism and Sartre's account of consciousness in *Being and Nothingness*, we have seen that both Kant and Sartre criticize the rationalist and empiricist positions concerning personal identity. By contrast, they talk about the identity of the moral agent in terms of a unity which makes possible self-identification throughout time and, hence, makes possible moral judgement.

I have then investigated the Sartrean objection in *Being and Nothingness* concerning Kant's view of self-choice (or, to use Kant's own terms, the revolution in disposition), as presented in his *Religion within the Bounds of Mere Reason*. We have seen that both Kant and Sartre argue, in fact, against a model of agency as ultimately based on deliberation. While both Kant and Sartre agree that decisions may be taken on the basis of deliberation, they reject the view of freedom as ultimately grounded on deliberation. What enables the agent to choose or adopt her fundamental project or disposition is not some process of deliberation, of weighing reasons for alternatives and deciding in favour of whatever course of action is indicated by this symbolic scale; rather, self-choice is only a necessary condition of empirical freedom and makes no assumption concerning a privileged way of making choices.

In Part II, I have started with Sartre's objection to Kant's account of freedom as spontaneous agency. I have shown that, in fact, both Kant and Sartre argue against an account of negative freedom that limits the negative freedom the person can have, that is her freedom from the conditions which constitute her circumstances and situation. An account which assumes that freedom takes a particular form is an account which mistakenly limits the freedom and spontaneity of the agent. In this sense, Kant's and Sartre's objections to the deliberative model of moral agency can be seen as a particular case of this more general objection.

The forth objection considered (the second discussed in Part II) represents, in fact, a set of critiques of Kant's account of normativity that Sartre presents in the *Notebooks for an Ethics*. The first critique concerns the possibility, for a Kantian ethical system, of guiding action in concrete situations. I considered two interpretations of this critique. According to one interpretation, Sartre regards Kant's ethical system as a code of rules of action, whereas the second assumes that Kant puts forward a more flexible ethics, this time understood as code of ethical standards. Whereas the second is a more accurate interpretation, both of them support the same critique, namely, a critique of an ethical system conceived as an ethical code. This is a view of ethics that Kant himself rejects.

In fact, both Kant and Sartre rely on a threefold structure of agency, which starts from actions (to which correspond rules of action), higher-order standards (principles of action or projects, which ground rules of action) and a second-order criterion (the Categorical Imperative or value of authenticity, which imposes constraints on the second-order standards). Furthermore, Sartre objects to Kant's account of the ontological ground of moral standards. Whereas Kant suggests this is given by the person's practical reason, as structured by the Categorical Imperative and distinct from the person's sentient or empirical self, Sartre claims that standards are free choices of another person's proposal and the interpersonal relation is essential as a basis for ethical standards.

I have examined this objection both in Part II and in Part III. I have explained on what grounds Sartre has formulated this objection in the *Notebooks* and how he eventually came to change his view concerning these grounds in the Cornell Lectures. From the perspective of these lectures, Sartre's objection can survive either as an objection to a split in the person or as an objection to an ethics of imperatives. I have shown that Sartre's early distinction between the in-itself and the for-itself also introduces a split in the person, and such an argument can be made also about Sartre's later distinction between internalization and externalization. Yet, I have said that the target of Sartre's objection is, in fact, moral realism and I have argued that this is a position Kant himself rejects.

I have also argued that both Kant and Sartre problematize the distinction between values and imperatives, although Kant does so only implicitly and although both continue to put more emphasis on one of them – Kant on imperatives, Sartre on values. So we have here a genuine difference between Kant's and Sartre's ethical theories, but it is a difference of emphasis rather than a matter of excluding one element to the advantage of the other. Sartre does not simply argue for an ethics of values to the exclusion of an ethics of imperatives, and Kant does not simply argue for an ethics of imperatives to the exclusion of an ethics of values.

In Part III, I have first looked at the accusation that Kant's ethical system is authoritarian. On Sartre's account, Kant's practical philosophy imposes absolute constraints which are incompatible with the freedom of the person. In fact, however, both Kant and Sartre would argue against an ethical theory which would posit unjustified standards of action; such standards would indeed limit the freedom of moral agents. For Kant, however, the claim that the Categorical Imperative has *absolute* authority must be qualified: first, we do not deal with an absolute authority in the sense of a normative fact which is given independently from our mind; secondly, although we do not create this law (since, as moral agents, we cannot exist independently from it), it is the law of *our* practical reason and we must legislate on its basis if we are to commit ourselves to ethically valid standards; finally, since this is the law of our practical reason, in legislating and acting on it, we are free: we are not determined by natural causality, but we commit ourselves to moral necessity, and this moral necessity is our own.

§103. Critical ethics

This notion of freedom is called by both Kant and Sartre autonomy and it represents, in fact, the answer they can both give to the problems of justification and conflict of liberties. As we have seen, if we regard the ethical criterion as constitutive of ethical judgement and the standards which are grounded in the criterion as constitutive of ethical judgement in a specific situation, we can make sense of the contradiction which arises when we imagine that, in the same situation, action is guided by the contradictory of the appropriate standard.

We can make sense of this contradiction without reducing it to a logical contradiction or to the negation of an empirical generalization. Hence, we have also an adequate approach to ethical justification and an appropriate account of the necessity presupposed by ethical normativity or, in other words, of unconditional obligation. This also enables us to make sense of the idea of self-realization. Insofar as we act on other grounds than natural causality, we are negatively free. Since the grounds of our actions are given by an ethical criterion, we act rightly and, hence, we can talk about self-*realization*. At the same time, since this action is autonomous, we can talk about it in terms of freedom and more exactly in terms of *self*-realization.

The ethical version of the problem of the conflict of liberties requires us to choose between negative freedom and positive freedom. As presented by Constant, the solution to this conflict seems to be a matter of choosing sometimes negatively free and sometimes positively free actions. What we have in the case of a critical ethics similar to that of Kant and Sartre is a solution of principle: the two types of freedom are reconciled and are both shown to be necessary for a genuinely free action. Sartre's objection to Kant's authoritarianism may still hold as an objection to the particular way in which Kant conceives of the ethical criterion, as a categorical imperative, and to the particular formulation of this imperative. Such an objection, however, is not very serious given Sartre's discussion of the relation between imperatives and values in the Cornell Lectures; but it does, however, point to the main difference I identified here between their ethical theories.

The final objection I considered raised an interesting question concerning Kant's account of history as a unitary process making progress towards a specific moral end. Although figuring prominently in the *Critique of Dialectical Reason*, this objection is also reflected by some of Sartre's claims in the *Notebooks*. Sartre's objection is not directed to an account of history which would claim unity and progress, since Sartre himself claims that history is unitary and has a meaning; the objection seems rather to challenge a theory which also posits this end and makes predictions concerning the realization of this end. We have, however, seen that Kant would also argue against such an account. His claim is a moral postulate, rather than a prediction, the possibility of which he explicitly rejects.

So far, I have presented an outline of the results of the comparative analysis undertaken in this book. I should mention, however, that similarities have been presented without distinguishing between structural and substantive similarities. As I have said, when Sartre formulates an objection to Kant, which is based on an inaccurate reading of Kant, we end up with a structural similarity, that is, a similarity in virtue of the fact that both argue against the same position and are committed to avoiding it. Through the investigation of Sartre's objections, I have also identified, however, several substantive similarities, that is, several similarities between the positions Kant and Sartre do not simply attempt to avoid, but intend to support. We have seen, for instance, that there are similarities between their accounts of personal identity (transcendental unity of apperception and the non-reflective self-consciousness), between their accounts of freedom (three types of freedom, similar solutions to the antinomy), of agency (threefold structure, similarity in the functions of each of the three elements in relation to the other elements), of the ethical criterion (autonomy and the relation to negative freedom and ethical standards) and of history.

One further question needs to be considered: even if we grant the ensuing critical ethics outlined above – the capacity to answer the problems of justification, normativity and conflict of liberties – we still need to examine the extent to which the kind of argument put forward in this answer is non-dogmatic. I have already argued that the presuppositions of Kant's and Sartre's accounts of personal identity are quite weak and I have suggested the same for their views on self-choice, freedom, normativity and moral progress.

As I have said, one reason why I think the comparison with Sartre can lead us to this type of ethical theory, which is quite distinct from the contemporary Kantian theories currently influential in the literature is Sartre's phenomenological background. Although Sartre is concerned about Kant's distinction between phenomena and noumena, and hopes to do without noumena, he is not concerned about synthetic a priori elements of consciousness which make possible (in the sense of constituting) phenomena. Yet, it is precisely this which enables an answer to the problems of justification, normativity and conflict of liberties.

I have said that Sartre hopes to keep this constitutiveness as important for his account, but without the Kantian metaphysical baggage of a noumenal realm. Whether or not this is possible is an important question which I could not consider here. The only worrying alternative would be if constitutiveness would require the distinction between phenomena and things in themselves. But even if it turned out that Sartre would have to commit himself to this distinction, it would still be a question whether this distinction is indeed dogmatic or would lead to a dogmatic attitude. These, however, are questions to be pursued elsewhere. Assuming Kant's and Sartre's practical philosophies can in this way account appropriately for unconditional obligations and, hence, answer the problems formulated in the Introduction, the question still remains concerning the counterintuitive answer they have to give in the situation described by Constant's example. Let me turn to this final issue now.

§104. Conflicting duties

Both Kant and Sartre seem to argue against a conditional right to lie even in an "authoritarian" (or "totalitarian") society. The same would be the case for the supporter of a critical ethics, since the standard of truthfulness would be the right standard in such a situation. Yet, to begin with, in section 99 above, we have seen that truthfulness seems to be a conditional standard: When being truthful has an ethically good purpose, then it is the right thing to do; when it has ethically dubious purposes, it is wrong. This seems to endorse Constant's view and undermine Kant's and Sartre's accounts, as well as the account formulated from the perspective of the critical ethics outlined in the previous section.

Nevertheless, the argument here is misleading. The initial question is whether we can enforce a principle of avoiding untruthfulness as an unconditional obligation or whether the principle is conditional; and, of course, the question is not whether the principle is conditional on being ethically good or evil. In this sense, whatever principle one considers, it is going to be an obligation, if it is ethically good, and it is going to be ethically impermissible, if it is evil. The question is whether the principle is an obligation independently from factors, such as philanthropy or the nature of the political regime.

The second question, however, is that the initial scenario seems to indicate compellingly that the principle of avoiding untruthfulness cannot be unconditional: we have an oppressive (for instance, Communist or Nazi) regime in which citizens are arrested and sent to certain death in forced labour camps because of their political affiliations; imagine your friend is pursued by the police and hides in your house. Intuitively, it seems that, to be truthful in this situation would be wrong, since being truthful contributes to something *wrong* taking place.

But, here, the force of the example is given by the claim that being truthful contributes to something which is ethically wrong. What this claim does is to place the action we consider (uttering the words in a truthful manner) under a maxim of doing something wrong, more exactly, causing the death of an innocent person. Hence, being truthful is an obligation under the maxim of avoiding untruthfulness and in a situation in which, as Kant says, we cannot avoid giving an answer while, at the same time, it is an action which is morally forbidden under the maxim of not committing murder. Similarly, the action of being untruthful is an obligation under the maxim of not committing (or assisting someone in committing) murder and, at the same time, it is morally forbidden under the maxim of avoiding untruthfulness.

And, yet, Kant thinks that precisely this kind of conflict of duties is not possible. Thus, for him,

> A *conflict of duties* [...] would be a relation between them in which one of them would cancel the other (wholly or in part). – But since duty and obligation are concepts that express the objective practical *necessity* of certain actions and two rules opposed to each other cannot be necessary at the same time, if it is a duty to act in accordance with one rule, to act in accordance with the opposite rule is not a duty but even contrary to duty.
>
> (*MM*: 6:224, 378–9)

If it is indeed impossible to have such a conflict of duties, it is impossible also to place the action of uttering certain words under two maxims and two obligations. I cannot regard my action of uttering certain words described at the same time as condemning an innocent person to death and being truthful. What a supporter of a critical ethics would need to work out would be which obligation is appropriate to consider as valid in the situation presented in Constant's example. Questions concerning Kant's claim that "a *collision of duties* and obligations is inconceivable" (*MM* 6:224, 379) also need to be answered. These will, of course, all be tasks belonging to the project of a critical ethics, but will have to be pursued elsewhere.

Notes

Introduction

1. As noted in the "Bibliographical Note" to Constant's speech "The Liberty of the Ancients Compared with That of the Moderns", the text was delivered in 1819, and draws on ideas already published by Constant in the *Spirit of Conquest and Usurpation* and in the *Principles of Politics* (1988: 310).
2. See esp. ch. 8. The text was first published in April 1797, and not in 1796 as the editor of Kant's *Practical Philosophy* claims (1996: 607).
3. This interpretation of Sartre's story is presented by Kevin Sweeney in "Lying to the Murderer: Sartre's Use of Kant in 'The Wall' " (1985). Serge Zenkin acknowledges earlier attempts to draw the parallel between Sartre's story and Kant's "On a Supposed Right to Lie" (1985: 225 n2), and challenges Sweeney's interpretation by an attack on the very premise of Sweeney's study, namely the relation between philosophy and literature.
4. There is no evidence that Sartre intended to get involved in the debate between Kant and Constant. As Sweeney notes, examples similar to Constant's can be found in works as early as Plato's *Republic*, and Sartre could have taken inspiration also from Victor Hugo's *Les Misérables* (Sweeney 1985: 16 n7). This may go some way towards explaining why Sartre does not consider the two conditions set by Kant's discussion of Constant's example.
5. I have here in mind those who claim to put forward their own theories, such as John Rawls, Jürgen Habermas or Karl-Otto Apel, but also those who claim to stay close to Kant's texts and improve on Kant's ideas, such as Onora O'Neill, Henry Allison, Christine Korsgaard, Barbara Herman and Paul Guyer; the list can easily continue. I have discussed in more detail Rawls's and Habermas's accounts of justification by comparison to those of Kant and Sartre in my doctoral dissertation, 'Persons and Politics in Kant and Sartre' (2001). A very recent discussion of Kant, Rawls and Korsgaard is offered by Paul Guyer, who concludes that, given Kant's and Korsgaard's unsuccessful attempts to vindicate the ambitious Kantian project of justification, one should perhaps settle with the more modest Rawlsian account (Guyer 2011).
6. In what follows, I will use 'moral' to include both ethical principles that individuals are expected to adopt, because they are the right principles, and political principles, which are enforced through the threat of political power and which need not be observed from a specific motivation.
7. The most famous representative is Rawls, who interprets his early theory of justice as a version of Kantian constructivism (1980).
8. We can find it formulated almost in the same words by Wilhelm von Humboldt, in his *The Limits of State Action*, a book written in the period 1791–2, and published for the first time posthumously in 1852 (1993). For instance, Humboldt says: "As to those limitations of freedom, however, which do not so much affect the State as the individuals who compose it, we are led to notice a vast difference between ancient and modern governments. The ancients devoted their attention

more exclusively to the harmonious development of the individual man, as man; the moderns are chiefly solicitous about his comfort, his prosperity, his productiveness. The former looked to virtue; the latter seek for happiness. And hence it follows that the restrictions imposed on freedom in the ancient States were, in some important respects, more oppressive and dangerous than those which characterise our times" (1993: 7). The book greatly influenced Mill in his writing of *On Liberty*. However, concern for the difference between ancient virtues and modern happiness can be also found in Machiavelli's *The Prince* and *Discourses*, as well as in Locke's *Second Treatise*.

9. For instance, we can find it expressed in Aristotle's *Nicomachean Ethics*, where the suggestion is that ethics is a subdivision of political morality (1998: 1094a–b, 2).

10. Isaiah Berlin is one exponent of this unilateral defence (Berlin 1997).

11. Taylor defends a notion of freedom as self-realization, which includes also the concept of freedom as liberty from constraints, but he thinks the question concerning the political implications of the concept of freedom represents a different question from that at issue in the debate between freedom as self-realization and freedom as absence of constraints. Thus, he says: "Whether we must also take the second step, to a view of freedom which sees it as realizable only within a certain form of society; and whether in taking a step of this kind one is necessarily committed to justifying the excesses of totalitarian oppression in the name of liberty; these are questions which now must be addressed" (1997: 428).

12. "Once we admit that the agent himself is not the final authority on his own freedom, do we not open the way to totalitarian manipulation? Do we not legitimate others, supposedly wiser about his purposes than himself, redirecting his feet on the right path, perhaps even by force, and all this in the name of freedom? The answer is that of course we don't" (Taylor 1997: 421).

13. Note, however, that it is in principle possible to say that an ethically valid principle of action is that which has been chosen arbitrarily. The implication is that there is no other condition for the ethical validity of a principle apart from its having been chosen. As we will see, this is sometimes a view attributed to Sartre and is also taken to be an implication of the constructivist interpretation of Kant. See, for instance, Robert Stern's "Kant, Moral Obligation and the Holy Will" (2011). The problem with this 'account' of normativity is that, because an arbitrary choice can be any choice, moral normativity is reduced to the idea of actual choice, and this makes the supporter of such a view unable to account for the distinction between a descriptive claim, like 'Person A has chosen value V', and a normative claim, such as 'Person A ought to have chosen value V.'

14. I make haste to add that I use here 'political' in a narrow sense. I agree that there are many factors in a society, apart from politically enforced laws, which influence the way in which society is organized. I should also mention that I take this broader notion of politics, which includes all factors affecting the organization of society, to be limited to those factors that exert their influence through some form of power: peer pressure, social structures, tradition, culture and many others. I contrast this with factors that are effective in virtue of their being considered morally right.

15. Habermas is currently one of the most prominent defenders of this notion. A possible implication of Habermas's defence of political autonomy is the presupposition that a person's "greatest good" lies "in the activities of political life" (Rawls 1995: esp. 150–70). In turn, Habermas challenges Rawls's position

as privileging the "modern", "liberal" rights of political freedom (Habermas 1995: 128).

16. Sometimes it may seem that intuitions stand for those spontaneous reactions a person has when she is presented with an issue and asked her opinion. In this case, my intuition about abortion would be whatever happens to cross my mind when the problem of abortion is presented to me. Rawls qualifies this view, however, by referring to "considered convictions of justice" (1994: 20). Rawls's *A Theory of Justice* was revised in 1999; I use here the pagination of the edition listed in the bibliography.

17. On Rawls's account of justification, see Scanlon (1992).

18. Some of the most interesting accounts of justification are put forward by Karl-Otto Apel (e.g. 1988), Habermas (e.g. 1993), O'Neill (e.g. 1989), Rawls (e.g., 1994 and 1980) and Scanlon (e.g. 1998). I argue against Apel's and Habermas's solutions in "Phenomenology and the Ethical Possibility of Differences: A Recent Answer to an Old Question" (2004). See also my "Dealing Morally with Religious Differences" (2011).

19. In fact, one of the reasons why he eventually disowns his lecture "Existentialism is a Humanism" (1948; delivered in 1945) seems to be precisely because it would show him to be too Kantian. In what follows, I will not draw on this lecture in my comparison of Kant and Sartre.

20. According to Sweeney, in the first place Sartre's story represents a critique of Husserl's phenomenological method of *epoché*, which preoccupied Sartre ever since 1933–4 when he was studying Husserl's philosophy in Berlin. The *epoché* effects "the bracketing or setting aside of one's natural attitude toward the existence of things in the world so as to reduce the objects of one's experience to a presentation of phenomena. This reduction, according to Husserl, allows one to perceive the world objectively" (Sweeney 1985: 7). To be sure, it is not at all clear that Husserl actually viewed the phenomenological *epoché* in this way, and that Sartre's critique is not a critique of an inappropriate interpretation of Husserl. James Edie, for instance, argues that, "stripped of its pseudo-polemic and reduced to its bare bones, to its ultimate meaning, Sartre's surface disagreement with Husserl is merely factitious, a purely verbal and not a substantial dispute" (1993: 105).

21. George Kerner's introductory book, *Mill, Kant, and Sartre: An Introduction to Ethics* (1990), provides valuable insights into certain aspects of the relation between Kant's and Sartre's philosophies, but goes over some of the most important features of Kant's and Sartre's moral theories. He takes Kant's formulations of the Categorical Imperative to be principles of action, and pits Sartre against Kant along the lines of Sartre's critique of fixed standards of action (1990: 194). Moreover, Kerner interprets Sartre's conception of the original choice as an attempt to give an ultimate foundation to morality (1990: 162). He takes, therefore, Sartre's notion of authenticity for a value that shares the same status as Kant's Categorical Imperative (in Kerner's interpretation). Even if Kerner realized that authenticity and the Categorical Imperative are criteria of morality and not standards of action, he would still misinterpret these criteria as foundations or "unchallengeable starting-point[s]" (1990: 162), while, in fact, they represent formulations of the way in which persons freely reason about moral issues, and they are as much open to criticism as any standard or rule of action.

22. See, for instance, Jonathan Webber's series of texts on Sartre's character-centred ethics (2006, 2007, 2009; cf. also Morris 1976: chs 4 and 5; esp. 112–27).

23. By an ethical system I mean an ethics which claims to be able to guide a person in his prescriptive attitudes, that is, in his attempts to act morally. This presupposes an ethical criterion, on the basis of which the moral worth of an action can be judged. For Kant this criterion is, of course, the Categorical Imperative. But other ethical systems, such as those of Mill or Aristotle, will have other ethical criteria. I contrast an ethical system primarily with an ethics understood as a reflection on the nature of moral terms, of moral virtues, of freedom, of personal identity or of any other aspects related to an ethical system. Such a reflection is presupposed by any ethical system and may even have implications for the way a person ought to act, but the implications are only *indirect*.

24. See, for instance, Habermas's attempt, in *Between Facts and Norms*, to counter the interpretation of rights as values (1996: esp. 253–67). See also David Strauss's review of Dworkin's *Freedom's Law: The Moral Reading of the American Constitution* (1997).

25. Rules of action, like saving a drowning child or helping a blind person to cross the street, stand under maxims or values, like that of being considerate or that of helpfulness. The criterion of morality, that is, Kant's Categorical Imperative or Sartre's ideal of authenticity test the validity of maxims or values, and not that of the rules. There is, however, a difference between maxims and values, and between the ideal of authenticity and the Categorical Imperative. Thus, a maxim expresses in the form of a sentence the requirement presupposed by a value; for instance, the value of helpfulness can be expressed as the maxim: always help those in need. Since values can be differently interpreted, a value's expression in the form of a maxim goes some way towards reducing the polysemous character of the value. It is for this reason that principles or norms are more appropriate guides for regulating interpersonal relations. The problem with the maxim or principle is that it can quickly become a rigid interpretation of a value. By acknowledging the complementarity between principles and values, the polysemy of values and the rigidity of principles can be compensated for.

26. Examples of such an approach can be found in Baldwin (1980), Jopling (1986), Beavers (1990) and Lieberman (1997).

27. An exception may seem to be found in Gillett's "The Subject of Experience" (1990). He draws several parallels between Sartre's and Kant's accounts of personal identity, but subsequently does not try to offer an account of the differences between them. However, this is mainly because the purpose of his paper is not primarily that of providing a comparative analysis of the relationship between Kant's and Sartre's philosophies; he attempts to use Sartre's and Kant's arguments in order to defend a certain position in metaphysics.

28. The same approach is employed by Juliette Simont (1987a); however, she adds an interesting preliminary stage, where she highlights several superficially contrasting aspects of Sartre's and Kant's views (on regulative ideas) (1987a: 131–3). However, then she shows that they are underpinned by 'argumentative similarities' (1987a: 133–7). A similar version of the standard approach is used also by Pierre Verstraeten (1995). Nevertheless, once the argumentative similarities are surveyed, it becomes necessary to account for dissimilarities and both Simont and Verstraeten conclude their studies with remarks on the divergences between the two philosophers. Verstraeten's final conclusion is that Sartre moved from Platonism to a Kantian position, but by 'Kantian' he does not mean 'Kant's'.

29. Other reasons for this lack of interest in the comparison of Sartre's and Kant's works, in particular their moral and political writings, include, as I will also specify further in the text, the mentioned link between Kant's philosophy

and Rawls's 'Kantian' constructivism, which tends to emphasize the opposition between a politics of principles (i.e. of justice), on the one hand, and Sartre's seemingly 'postmodern', radical scepticism about universal norms, on the other; or the fact that Habermas's 'Hegelian' discourse ethics adopts the constructivist criticism of metaphysics and moral scepticism, and combines it with an attack on 'individualism' – perhaps the only label that Sartre's and Kant's works share in the huge non-comparative secondary literature; or the disagreement between some of their views on political morality, a disagreement that is so stark that any likeness tends to dwindle into insignificance.

30. See, for instance, Mary Warnock (1970), Herbert Spiegelberg (1987), Robert Misrahi (1990), Leo Fretz (1992), David Jopling (1992) and Andrew Dobson (1993). Those who claim that the ethics that can be found in Sartre is not an ethical system refer to some sort of meta-ethical reflection of the type presented in n. 23 above.

31. In "Sartre's Critique of Kant", Dennis Rohatyn (1975) starts from Sartre's critique of Kant's account of personal identity. Yet he does not raise the question whether what Sartre tries to challenge is actually Kant's position. The conclusion of the study is that Kant's position is correct, whereas Sartre's "empirical" account is not.

32. See n. 28 above.

33. I first came across this interpretation of Plato in Noica (1991). In her *The Fragility of Goodness*, Martha Nussbaum puts forward an interpretation of Aristotle as a transcendental philosopher (1986). Michelle Darnell's conclusion that Sartre is a transcendental philosopher seems to me to rely on a similar strategy (2006).

34. Although I am sympathetic to the Cambridge School, in particular to the theory offered by John G. A. Pocock, it would lead me too far away from the issues discussed here to try to defend such a theory and to apply it (see, for instance, Pocock 1972, 1981 and 2009).

35. Husserl, however, did write on ethics (1988). On Husserl's discussion of Kantian ethics, see Peucker (2007).

36. For instance, de Beauvoir (1976) and Schutz (1964).

1 Kant

1. The issues of practical normativity, of freedom and identity are in fact necessary conditions of constitutive aspects of Kant's theory of responsibility. Thus, identity is required for performance-ascription, freedom is necessary for practical relevance and normativity, for practical judgement. For a discussion on Kant's theory of responsibility, see Suzanne Uniacke (2005). For a critical approach to Kant's theory of responsibility, see Garrath Williams (2007). I focus on these necessary conditions, since it is on these issues that Sartre engages with Kant.

2. Here, following Graham Bird, I assume that the versions of the Third Paralogism in the two editions of the *Critique of Pure Reason* are not significantly different. On Bird's account, the reason why Kant rewrote the whole section on paralogisms has to do with the Fourth Paralogism (2006: 627).

3. See Graham Bird's illuminating account of the differences between Kant's and Descartes's projects (2006: esp. 366–9).

4. The apodictic certainty of the judgement 'I think' is given by the impossibility of doubting it, since in order to doubt it I have to think; hence, by the very process of doubting, I am re-asserting what I doubt. Of course, the fact that *I* cannot

doubt something does not mean that it is true. I may be unable to doubt the fact that I see a river in this desert, but I am still wrong about it. Of course, the indubitability of the judgement 'I think' does not depend on special conditions, like the presence of a desert and of my delusion or my being unable at that moment to doubt what I see; the judgement is indubitable not because my epistemic powers function appropriately, it is sufficient that they function: it is because I have to think in order to doubt something that I cannot doubt that I am thinking. Or rather, to put it more precisely, I can of course doubt that I am thinking, but this doubt raises no objection to the fact that I am thinking. On the contrary, my doubting the fact that I am thinking will reinforce the truth of this fact (See, for instance, Descartes 1996: 25, 16–17.).

5. "Psychology [...] may be called rational psychology if I demand to know nothing more about the soul than what can be inferred from this concept *I*, insofar as it occurs in all thought, independently of all experience" (Kant, *KrV*: A342/B400, 383).

6. There is, of course, at least another problem for an account of action, namely, how all the various acts performed by the same person can be seen as constituting the same action. A discussion of this issue will lead to further discussions of Kant's first paralogism, of the Analogies of Experience and of his investigation of the empirical criterion of the necessary permanence of subject as author of action (See *KrV*: A204/B249ff, 271ff.). On Kant's account of action, see also Piper (2009).

7. Bird distinguishes between two possible meanings of this phrase: it may refer to identity *at* those different times or identity *over* the whole range of times. For him, the first meaning might be all that can be established by the obvious truth that "In my consciousness I am always the same" (Bird 2006: 638). Hence, on Bird's account, when Kant claims that this sense of identity is indubitable for me, he must have in mind an identity *at* a particular time. The reason why I take Kant to have in mind an identity *over* time is that the claim 'In my consciousness I am always the same' will not make sense *at* a particular time – in my consciousness, I can only present myself in time and, hence, were there to be any difference, which alone could make it the case that I would not be the same, that would be over at least two moments in time. There is, of course, the possibility that I consist of various parts and that, at a particular time, I can be said to be those distinct parts and, hence, not to be numerical identical. But, since my inner sense forms intuitions in time, and my various parts are supposed to coexist at the same moment, they must be distinguishable in some other way. In this case, I must abandon the limitation to inner sense and make reference to the outer sense or perhaps talk about things in themselves. Both alternatives would not be legitimate.

8. 'Numerical identity' is similarly explained by Dieter Henrich (1989).

9. Kant makes this argument by reference to time as the necessary condition of experience: the "external observer considers *me* first of all *in time*, for in apperception *time* is in fact presented only *in me*. Hence although he thus grants the *I* that in *my* consciousness accompanies at all time – and with full identity – all presentations, he will not yet infer from it the objective permanence of myself. For here the time wherein the observer posits me is not the time found in my own but the time found in his sensibility, and hence the identity that is necessarily linked with my consciousness is not therefore linked with his, i.e., with his outer intuition of myself as subject" (*KrV*: A362–3, 397). Here Kant does not question the assumption that an external observer can say something about my states of

mind, since we can start with the presupposition that I am the external observer – I regard myself as an object of study. Hence, Kant grants that an external observer will notice that there is an *I* that accompanies all my states of mind; nevertheless, what he cannot grant is that there is indeed a permanent element in me of which I am aware as of my *I*.

10. See §§12–13 below.

11. A qualification must be introduced here. Of course, on Kant's account, the fact that a concept is not related to empirical intuitions does not immediately make it an ideal, that is, a concept that *cannot* be related to empirical intuitions and which, in Kant's terms, is regulative, rather than constitutive, of experience. A priori concepts of the understanding are concepts that are not immediately related to sensible intuitions, precisely because they are a priori. Nevertheless, they can be schematised and they necessarily play a constitutive role in experience. Empirical concepts are immediately related to empirical intuitions, but this makes them a posteriori and, hence, they cannot be necessary conditions of cognition. The difference between the concept of a thinking I and the a priori concepts of the understanding is that the former is even more general than the latter; it is meant to "bring forward [*aufführen*] all thought as belonging to consciousness" (*KrV*: A341/B400, 382–3). Or, as Kant says, it refers to "the mere apperception *I think* that makes even all transcendental concepts possible" (*KrV*: A343/B401, 383). This makes the I one of the ideas of pure reason, which can only refer to experience through the concepts of the understanding. I will discuss in more detail Kant's view on ideas of reason in Chapter 6.

12. We can equally well regard the equivocation as occurring over 'person'. In the major premise, 'person' is defined by reference to a necessary condition of cognition (consciousness of the identity of a formal concept that accompanies states of mind). 'Person' therefore cannot refer to an object in the world, since any claim about such an object requires as necessary this consciousness of identity. By contrast, in the conclusion of the syllogism, 'person' refers to such an object or entity, otherwise the rational psychologist would not be able to demonstrate what she intended.

13. This need not mean that the individual should not be judged and punished. If a person can no longer be conscious of being the author of some past actions, because of short memory, he does not seem less accountable for those actions. Think, for instance, of Thomas Reid's (1788: 333–4) objection to John Locke (1759: II, xxviii, 9).

14. That this is what Kant has mind when he refers to a condition sufficient for practical use is evident from the way he spells out the sense of 'person' that is legitimate. Thus, for him, this is a concept that is "merely transcendental, i.e., insofar as it concerns the unity of the subject with which we are otherwise unacquainted but in whose determinations there is a thoroughgoing connection through apperception" (*KrV*: A365, 399). I will say more about Kant's account of apperception in the following sections.

15. Numerical identity would not be sufficient either. Numerical identity, as conceived by the rational psychologist, would refer to the same entity corresponding to the thinking I, an entity that would be the same whether or not consciousness of identity was experienced. Hence, numerical identity cannot even be a sufficient condition of the person's accepting the status of moral subject and, hence, of her accepting accountability.

16. Note, however, that Kant does not ignore the situation of an individual who is merely *affected* by the world around. By making use only of his senses, such an individual may be affected differently by different stimuli, but she could not perceive the difference between different affects; to perceive differences, one must perceive differences between two entities and, to compare these entities, one must consider them together and establish a relationship between them – not merely be affected by them: "The [uncombined] manifold of presentations can be given in an intuition that is merely sensible, i.e., nothing but receptivity; and the form of this intuition can lie a priori in our power of presentation without being anything but the way in which the subject is affected. But a manifold's combination (*coniunctio*) as such can never come to us through the sense; nor therefore, can it already be part of what is contained in the pure form of sensible intuition" (*KrV*: B129–30, 175–6).

17. Again, one may use the phrase 'sensation of red' to refer to a sensation that is the result of being affected, but that is not perceived as red, since no synthesis of sensations has been performed. An analogy might help: if something/someone touches my shoulder, I look back and I see my friend who wants to draw my attention to something. I can retrospectively relate this by saying 'I felt her hand on my shoulder', although, of course, what I had was only an indistinct sensation.

18. These, of course, are mutually dependent types of pre-reflective awareness. For, in order for me to have a pre-reflective consciousness of self, I must be able to identify myself with that of which I am pre-reflectively aware; and, in order for me to be the same across different times, I need to be able to be pre-reflectively conscious of myself at these times. This relationship of mutual dependence is, in fact, an implication of a similar relationship between the synthesis and analysis of apperception.

19. One famous definition occurs in section 4 of his *Principles of Nature and Grace* (1969). However, the exact meaning of the term in Leibniz is disputed, especially when one also takes into account occurrences in some of his other works.

20. Kant leaves some terms unspecified, and I think there is no point in expecting precise and clear-cut definitions of them. He says, for instance, that "there is, in inner perception, consciousness of oneself in terms of the determinations of one's state. [...] It is usually called *inner sense*, or *empirical apperception*" (*KrV*: A107, 158). Later on, however, he distinguishes, on the one hand, between sense and apperception, and, on the other, between an empirical and a transcendental consideration of each of them (*KrV*: A115, 164). It seems to me that we cannot even regard what he calls empirical apperception in the first context as the same as what he calls apperception considered as empirical in the second context. An implicit distinction seems to be at work between apperception as self-consciousness in general (first context) and apperception as a specific form of self-consciousness that explains the identity of certain determinations of one's state with the presentations that imagination reproduces on the basis of the initial determinations (second context). The significance of all this will become apparent later on in the comparative discussion of Kant and Sartre.

21. He also makes this point later on: "... synthetic unity of the manifold of intuitions, as given a priori, is the basis of the identity itself of apperception, which precedes a priori all *my* determinate thought" (*KrV*: B134, 179).

22. That all necessary conditions of cognition take place in experience seems to be unwarranted. Yet, on Kant's account, experience is a technical term and is equivalent with cognition and, hence, the conditions of cognition will also be

conditions of experience. Therefore, they should take place in order for the experience to occur.

23. *KrV*: B140–3, 183–5. When I said that Kant's claim in §19 will clarify what he says about the empirical unity of apperception, I said it with great hesitation. Usually, when Kant says something, new problems arise and old problems remain – they don't disappear. §19 raises a host of interpretative questions, which I cannot even begin to formulate properly here, let alone discuss, investigate and solve. See, for instance, Béatrice Longuenesse's discussion of this section in her *Kant and the Capacity to Judge* (1998: 180–8). This is part of a chapter that was not eventually published in the French edition (1993). This is what Longuenesse says on the meaning of §19: "The *Critique* does not make use of the *Prolegomena* because it opposes not two types of empirical judgements [judgement of perception and judgement of experience], but two origins of judgement. One origin would result in the fact that judgement is the expression of mere association according to laws of imagination (= Humean reduction of judgement, which indeed would oblige us to consider all our judgements as mere judgements of perception; it may explain the proximity in formulation between the two texts.) The other origin, the one Kant argues for, relates judgement back to the original function of judging. It alone can explain the possibility for us to obtain those empirically objective judgements that Kant calls, in the *Prolegomena*, 'judgement of experience' " (1998: 188).

24. Kant uses a different example, but comes to the same conclusions (*KrV*: B142, 185).

25. Hence, the claim about the necessity and universal validity of an objective judgement is not a claim about its truth, but about "*the necessary unity* of apperception in the synthesis of intuitions" (*KrV*: B142, 184).

2 Sartre and Kant

1. Opinions seem, in this respect, to be divided. Michelle Darnell (2006) claims that, in the past, authors have either taken for granted that Sartre's critique of Kant is unsuccessful or have applauded Sartre for an accurate interpretation of Kant (Darnell 2006: 5–6). These two positions are not, in fact, incompatible. Stephen Priest (2000) adopts a view that supports precisely both these positions. A detailed account of Sartre's critique of Kant is also offered by Vincent de Coorebyter (2000: 177–187).

2. I have been using 'presentation' to stand for Kant's *Vorstellung*. I follow here Pluhar's translation; he changes the traditional rendering of the term by '*re*presentation'. For his reasons for introducing this change, see his note in: Kant (1996: 22 n73).

3. The problem, of course, is not that I have no additional access to the tree *as it exists independently from my consciousness*. This would make the argument circular; the problem is that I don't have *additional* access to the tree, apart from my sensible perception of the tree.

4. In principle, it should be possible to distinguish between the way a thing is and the way we know it. In principle, therefore, it should be possible to say that epistemology is a study of the latter topic, whereas metaphysics or ontology, of the former. Kant introduces a fundamental change in this respect, when he claims that we have no knowledge of the way things are in themselves, and our knowledge of how they are depends on how we know them. Phenomenologists,

including Sartre, reject the claim that we cannot know the way things are in themselves, but agree that our knowledge of how things are depends on how we know them. Knowledge of the conditions that make experience possible becomes both part of epistemology and ontology. These conditions establish the limits of our knowledge and are constitutive of the things we know. In Heidegger's account, with which Sartre was well acquainted, "the question of Being aims therefore at ascertaining the *a priori* conditions not only for the possibility of the sciences which examine entities as entities of such and such a type, [...] but also for the possibility of those ontologies themselves which are prior to the ontical sciences and which provide their foundations" (1997: 11, 31).

5. This is a feature Kathleen Wider identifies as distinct for Sartre position when compared with Descartes's (1997: 14).

6. In this respect, Sartre often refers critically to Husserl's *Cartesian Meditations* (1988).

7. In *Being and Nothingness*, he formulates this as a methodological requirement: "The first procedure of a philosophy ought to be to expel things from consciousness and to reestablish its true connection with the world, to know that consciousness is a positional consciousness *of* the world" (*EN*: li, 18).

8. For a detailed analysis of these differences, including also those of lesser importance brought about by the *Critique of Dialectical Reason*, see Leo Fretz (1992).

9. In his article, Fretz discusses the *implications* of this shift of perspective for the problem of solipsism tackled by Sartre in both works. For Fretz, the fact that pre-reflective consciousness becomes personal makes the problem of solipsism emerge again: "At the very moment when transcendent consciousness is provided with a 'selfness', solipsism presents itself again with undiminished force" (1992: 83–4). The question is, however: why does Sartre change his conception of the person in the first place? Here, Sylvie Le Bon's comment on the notion of freedom in *The Transcendence of the Ego* hints, I think, at a good answer to this question: "At the time when Sartre was writing the *Essay on the Ego* (1934), he did not accord to the concept of freedom the large scope which he would accord it in *Being and Nothingness*. [...] Freedom is here [in the *Transcendence...*] restricted to the transcendent sphere of the ethical" (*TE*: 80 n73).

10. This is also Wider's (1997) suggestion. For her, the difference between positional and non-positional consciousness is the difference between a focused and a non-focused consciousness (Wider 1997: 40–41). Since, according to Sartre, "there is no consciousness which is not a *positing* of a transcendent object" (*EN*: 17, 7), it follows that what we call non-positional consciousness is simply an indistinct consciousness of something distinct from consciousness. As soon as this distinctness is specified, it is possible to pass judgements on the object and, hence, we no longer have an immediate or non-positional consciousness.

11. Joseph Catalano's (1985) distinction between Sartre's ideas of pure and impure reflection suggests that I can have a form of self-consciousness and, hence, reflection, which does not posit its object (that is, the consciousness reflected on). This is the result of pure reflection. Yet, he adds, "for Sartre (pure) reflection is not, strictly speaking, a 'knowledge', since it does not posit (self-)consciousness as a clearly defined object separated from other objects" (Catalano 1985: 129). So he seems to suggest that those who are positionally aware of something, cannot at the same time be also positionally aware of positing that thing. What he says in fact is that the object of pure reflection is not a "clearly defined object separated from other objects". Yet, I can still be positionally aware of an object that is

not clearly defined and separated from other objects. Even when I am perceiving something that I cannot distinguish from other objects, I am still perceiving something that is different from me. However, the distinction between myself and an undifferentiated world will still have to take place spatially. (Recall Sartre's description of the world, in *IFP* as "essentially external to consciousness".) Hence, the undifferentiated world would be posited, even if not clearly defined. At this point, Catalano could argue that, in the case of reflection, we do not deal with objects of the world but with our own consciousness. So I could have an object that is not clearly defined, is not distinguishable from other objects, is distinguishable from me only to the extent to which it enables reflection, but is not different from me in the way in which a world is (spatially). But, in this case, it is unclear why this would be anything else than non-positional self-consciousness. To make the distinction Catalano attempts to present clearer, consider his example: "if I am now reflecting on my playing tennis, I am aware of myself as playing tennis; I am certain that the self-that-is-playing tennis is the self reflecting on my tennis playing. Nevertheless, I am also aware of the difficulty of continuing to play tennis while reflecting" (Catalano 1985: 129). In this way, he tries to steer a path between non-positional self-consciousness and positional reflection in the form of a non-positional reflection. Yet, in the example he gives, what happens is that I change the object of my focus from the performance of the activity to myself as performing the activity. Insofar as this is not simply a non-positional consciousness of myself (since I could not distinguish myself as paying tennis), it must be a form of reflection. This explains why I find it difficult to continue to play tennis while reflecting, namely, because I am focused on something else. The fact that I continue to play tennis is not a sign of my being focused on the performing the activity, but of the fact that it is an acquired skill that I can perform mechanically up to a certain point. That this is what is hidden behind Catalano's description seems to me confirmed by the following description he provides in the same context: "We can reflect on the naturalness and ease with which we perform a certain acquired skill. I can thus momentarily become aware of myself as one-who-swims easily and naturally. But if I continue in such reflection and try to unite my explicit awareness of myself with myself as swimming, I interfere with the naturalness of my swimming" (Catalano 1985: 129 n15). Here it is quite clear that what I am doing when I am reflecting on the way I swim is to change the focus of my attention from the world (the water, the distance from the edge of the pool, other people in the pool, etc.) to what I am doing and, hence, swimming happens insofar as it is an automatically exercised acquired skills, rather than an activity in which I am engaged. The activity in which I am engaged is reflection, and this is a positing activity that captures my whole attention (as long as I am engaged in this activity).

12. At the beginning of *Being and Nothingness* (up to *EN*: liv, 20), Sartre uses the particle "of" from the expression "non-positional consciousness of itself" like in the expression "positional or knowing consciousness of something". Then, he replaces the particle with "(of)", because in the expression "consciousness (of) itself" the particle put between parentheses would mark the non-positional consciousness and thus would preclude its being confused with a positional consciousness.

13. In principle, a non-positional, immediate consciousness of X must also be non-positionally conscious of itself. But, if all consciousness, positional or non-positional, is at the same time non-positionally conscious of itself, then

a non-positional self-consciousness must also be non-positionally conscious of itself and we end up with an infinite regress. It is perhaps in order to break this infinite regress that Sartre stipulates that first-order consciousness (of) self is a consciousness (of) itself as consciousness of something, an *X*. But, then, a second-order consciousness (of) self is at best a consciousness (of) itself as consciousness (of) *itself*, not of *X*. Hence, *pace* Wider, I do not think this marks an important difference between Kant's transcendental unity of apperception and Sartre's consciousness (of) self (see Wider 1997: 38).

14. It is easy to observe that Sartre's conception of the person does not regard desires, beliefs and emotions as given entities that exhaust the scope of personal phenomena. On the contrary, they are possible only to the extent that other phenomena – especially those related to various conscious processes – constitute them. As we have already seen and will see further on, this proves to have significant implications for the way in which Sartre conceives of personal identity, and for the manner in which he avoids the errors of the empiricist view of identity, non-cognitivism, as well as those of a rationalist position. Concerning the way reflection destroys pre-reflective consciousness, consider again the case of belief; believing something is a consciousness that something is the case, and it is accompanied by a consciousness (of) self as believing that that is the case. The attempt to reflect on oneself as believing such-and-such a thing modifies the object of consciousness from belief to myself-as-believing. But, if I posit myself as believing something, then the only pre-reflective consciousness there can be is of myself as positing myself, and this is already a distinct consciousness from the initial pre-reflective consciousness.

15. This is Alain's claim that "to know is to know that one knows" (*EN*: lii–liii, 18–19).

16. "The reduction of consciousness to knowledge in fact involves our introducing into consciousness the subject-object dualism which is typical of knowledge. But if we accept the law of the knower-known dyad, then a third term will be necessary in order for the knower to become known in turn" (*EN*: lii, 18–19).

17. The argument here is of course circular: if X is a necessary condition of knowledge, X cannot be challenged, since any challenge must rely on X; but to claim that any challenge must rely on X is to assume that X is a necessary condition of knowledge. However, the aim here is to understand Sartre's claim concerning the absolute character of this condition of knowledge, it is not to justify its status.

18. See also Schroeder 1984: 174. There is a complication here, insofar as it is plausible to claim that there are many conscious beings that are not persons. My cat is conscious of the world around him and of many of his 'states of mind' – for instance, pain. Yet, he is not a person, at least not in the standard sense. In what follows, rather than trying to adjudicate on a debate that has attracted huge interest, namely, that concerning the concept of the person, I will simply follow and try to clarify what Kant and Sartre have to say about this. One interesting feature of Sartre's account is that, for him, self-consciousness makes possible not only the knowing consciousness of the world, but also the perceiving consciousness of the world. This is the way in which Sartre translates Husserl's formula "Consciousness is consciousness *of* something": "This means that transcendence is the constitutive structure of consciousness; that is, that consciousness is born *supported by* a being which is not itself." He calls this "the ontological proof", that is the proof for the existence of a being outside consciousness (*EN*: lxi, 28). Furthermore, as the mode of existence of any consciousness of something (*EN*: liv, 20),

pre-reflective consciousness or consciousness (of) self is also constitutive of perceptive consciousness (*EN*: liii, 19). Finally, the positional consciousness of an object is at the same time an immediate consciousness of itself, because positional consciousness is the result of an immediate consciousness, which *perceives* the immediate consciousness of the object, and in this way posits the object and reflects on it. But what makes possible the perception of an immediate consciousness of an object is the fact that the immediate consciousness of the object is also a pre-reflective consciousness of itself. In other words, the immediate consciousness of an object is a *reflecting* and *reflexive* process. As Hazel Barnes notes, "the translator encounters a difficulty here owing to the fact that the English word 'reflection' has two different meanings which are perfectly distinct in French. In discussing the dyad 'reflection-reflecting' [specific to self-consciousness], Sartre uses *reflet-reflétant*. Here 'reflection' means that which is reflected – like an image – and easily suggests to Sartre the idea of a game with mirrors. In the present section [Part 2, ch. 2, III: 'Original Temporality and Psychic Temporality: Reflection'], however, the subject of discussion is *reflexion*, which means the process of mental reflection in general and in particular introspection" (*EN*: 151 n8). So far, I have used "reflexive" to describe the process of mirroring that takes place at the level of self-consciousness, and "reflectivity" to talk about the positional activity of reflection that appears at the level of consciousness. I will do the same in what follows. In particular, I will use "reflection" for the process whereby consciousness reflects something as immediate consciousness of that thing. Since immediate consciousness is bound up with self-consciousness, I will sometimes use "reflection" to designate the reflexive movement of self-consciousness too. However, it will be clear from the context which type of consciousness I refer to.

19. "Identity is the ideal of 'one', and 'one' comes into the world by human reality" (*EN*: 74, 116). We deal in fact with a twofold ideal – the identity of the in-itself, which needs the idea of separation (even if used negatively) in order to make sense of an "identity without immanent separation", and the identity of the person, who is identical with herself only at the limit, where the self is simply a notion necessary to make sense of the claim that the person is identical with herself and of the fact that we deal with a for-itself, rather than an in-itself.

20. "The term in-itself, which we have borrowed from the tradition to designate the transcending being, is inaccurate. At the limit of coincidence with itself, in fact, the self vanishes to give place to identical being. The *self* cannot be a property of being-in-itself" (*EN*: 76, 118).

21. Sartre's example is "il s'ennui".

22. Sartre calls this mode of being of a person "presence to self" (*EN*: 77, 199).

23. "Thus the reflective consciousness of man-in-the-world in his daily existence is found in the face of psychic objects which are what they are, which appear in the continuous woof of our temporality like the designs and motifs on a tapestry, and which succeed each other in the manner of things in the world in universal time; that is, by replacing each other without entering into any relation other than the purely external relations of succession" (*EN*: 158, 205).

24. "By Psyche we understand the *Ego*, its states, its qualities, and its acts. The *Ego* with the double grammatical form of 'I' and 'Me' represents our *person* as a transcendent psychic unity. [...] It is as the *Ego* that we are subjects in fact and subjects in theory, active and passive, voluntary agents, possible objects of a judgement concerning value or responsibility" (*EN*: 162, 209 – translation slightly amended).

25. To be sure, "moment" here does not represent a specific point in time, but a logical starting point for a for-itself.
26. "Thus from its first arising, consciousness by the pure nihilating movement of reflection [the *reflexive* movement] makes itself *personal*; for what confers personal existence on a being is not the possession of an Ego – which is only *the sign* of the personality – but it is the fact that the being exists for itself as presence to itself" (*EN*: 103, 148).
27. My suggestion, here, starts from Habermas's interpretation (1963) of the early Hegel (1986), as taking intersubjectivity as more fundamental than individuated subjectivity. This is what Sartre seems to endorse in *The Transcendence*. The impersonal transcendental field of consciousness is the ground for the formation of personal, individuated features. For a comparative study of Sartre and Hegel, see Pierre Verstraeten (1992).
28. See, for instance, Wider (1997: 37–9, 184 n88).
29. Here the discussion could be qualified in light of my analysis of Kant's notion of character in Chapter 1, §16. As we have seen, intelligible character refers to the rule that determines the causality of reason in my performance of actions. Hence, Sartre is right to view his fundamental project as the Kantian disposition, since the fundamental project is Sartre's term for that which gives reasons for actions.
30. Of course, the weight of this claim depends on how one understands 'freedom'. In certain accounts, in particular the so-called "compatibilist" accounts, one is free when one's actions are not determined by external obstacles or when one has the possibility of forming second-order desires, although one is at the same time completely determined. On the difference between Kant's account of freedom and compatibilism, see Flikschuh (2000, esp. ch. 2). For an evaluation of current accounts of freedom and a critical examination of their attempt to do without metaphysics, see her *Freedom: Contemporary Liberal Perspectives* (2007).
31. He discusses this example at *EN*: 453–4, 530–1.
32. "This way of yielding to fatigue and of letting myself down at the side of the road expresses a certain initial stiffening against my body and the inanimate in-itself. It is placed within the compass of a certain view of the world in which difficulties can appear not worth the trouble of being tolerated" (*EN*: 464, 542).
33. Six theses are offered as common for Kant and Sartre, two related to action and the other four to project:

> T1. (*Action Comprehension*) A person's actions are comprehensible only in the light of his disposition/fundamental project.
>
> T2. (*Project Identity*) The identity of a person's disposition/fundamental project is a condition of his identity.
>
> T3. (*Project Choice*) The disposition/fundamental project is chosen in an original act of choice.
>
> T4. (*Project Change*) No transformation of a person's disposition/fundamental project can be voluntary.
>
> T5. (*Project Comprehension*) A person has no knowledge of his disposition/fundamental project.
>
> T6. (*Action Freedom*) What makes a person's actions free is that they derive from his disposition/fundamental project.

To be sure, there is a certain sense of freedom involved here, an idea of empirical freedom, which may take the form of a relative notion of freedom from external constraints. In this sense, I am free and you are not, when I am not constrained by the external obstacle that is in your way, although in all other respects we are equally free from constraints. This empirical freedom may take another form, namely, that of acting against certain obstacles and incentives (Baldwin 1980: 31–2 and 35). It is important to note that T2 is regarded as formulating a necessary and sufficient condition in Sartre's philosophy, but only a necessary condition in Kant, who, moreover, at least in *Religion*, takes this condition to be restricted to *moral* identity. Baldwin provides textual evidence for his claims, but, since he thinks Kant's and Sartre's accounts are plagued by some inconsistencies, he proposes a conception of agency in terms of only four of the six similar aspects: theses 1, 3, 5 and 6. In other words, he keeps the two theses about action and, in addition, two about project – those concerning comprehension and choice. He proposes a different interpretation of the idea of original choice/revolution in disposition, in order to bring consistency between as many of the original theses as possible.

34. This is Merleau-Ponty's objection to the concept of original choice, an objection that Baldwin deems directed at Sartre. I think it is debatable whether Merleau-Ponty intended this as an objection to Sartre. He rather seems interested to criticize a possible interpretation of Sartre along the lines of the deliberative model (2006: 504–30, esp. 505–7).

35. In fact, as we will see below, Sartre does not talk of a painting in this context, but he claims that "there are certain lines which I can add to or subtract from a given figure without altering its specific character" (*EN*: 470, 548). By this, he tries to provide an analogy for the way in which, even though I choose a fundamental project, I can still make free choices within the framework of that *determinate* fundamental project.

36. The other analogy of Sartre's used by Baldwin is that between "the relation between project and particular action" and the "physical object and its sensible aspects on a Husserlian view of the latter" (1980: 40). In fact, by this analogy Sartre compares "the abstract, ontological 'desire to be'" and "the fundamental, *human* structure of the individual" (*EN*: 567, 655), and not the fundamental project and the particular action.

37. I think that Baldwin correctly identifies propositions T1, T3, T4 and T6 as similar aspects of Kant's and Sartre's conceptions of human agency. But I think he is mistaken in claiming that Kant and Sartre hold T2 and T5. Thus I would claim that Kant's and Sartre's accounts of human agency do not establish a relationship between a person's identity and her original choice and do not maintain that she has no knowledge of her disposition or fundamental project. I will show that, with regard to the problem of a person's identity, similarities between the two philosophers can be found in Sartre's idea of the unity of self-consciousness and in Kant's doctrine of the unity of pure apperception. Concerning the question whether a person knows her fundamental project/intelligible character, I will demonstrate that Sartre's account of the method for identifying the fundamental project (existential psychoanalysis) and Kant's conception of practical cognition offer positive answers to the question. Moreover, I think Baldwin wrongly attributes to Kant and Sartre the view that a person's disposition/fundamental project is determinant, and he misleadingly associates this with their claims that the original choice is not deliberate. A special note needs to be made here: Baldwin does not claim that, for Kant, the person's disposition is a condition of a person's identity *simpliciter*, but of a person's *moral* identity – see n. 33 above.

38. It is worth mentioning that Kant does not talk about a "choice" of disposition, but about a "revolution" in disposition, and that Sartre uses the expressions "radical choice" or "original choice", and not simply "choice". Both Kant and Sartre do, however, talk about "choice" *simpliciter*, but this happens when they refer to a choice of a particular end or of a particular maxim, and in that case "choice" may presuppose deliberation. It is probably for this reason that Baldwin does not confine his criticism to the use of the term "choice" in relation to a person's deeper project, but extends it to Kant's and Sartre's second use of the term.

39. This might be what Sartre has in mind when he says we sometimes decide simply by action, rather than by voluntary deliberation or passion.

40. Moreover, on this point Baldwin seems to agree with them. Thus, Baldwin deems inappropriate Sartre's and de Beauvoir's interpretation of Kant's revolution in disposition as a choice "achieved in the intelligible world by a purely rational will" (De Beauvoir 1976: 33). Thus Baldwin says "this is, I think, to ascribe transcendent metaphysics to Kant, and it seems better to aim to interpret his view in terms of an *a priori* condition for the imputability of action" (Baldwin 1980: 37). Similarly, when discussing Merleau-Ponty's critique of Sartre, he rejects the same interpretation this time applied to Sartre: "Merleau-Ponty is not here attacking the view that there is some timeless original choice of self which is distinct from our ordinary choices; for he knew as well as anyone that this was not Sartre's view" (Baldwin 1980: 42).

41. Emphasis in original.

42. For the purpose of the comparison between Kant's and Sartre's non-moral conceptions of agency, it is sufficient to note that both philosophers consider that a person's deeper project can be the "object" of knowledge, and that both set the investigation of this project as a condition of morality. Baldwin then is wrong when he claims that the deeper project cannot be known for Kant and Sartre. What cannot be known is the way in which a deeper project is replaced by another one. For Kant, for instance, the adoption of a disposition is the result of a free choice, "but there cannot be any further cognition of the subjective ground or the cause of this adoption" (*RGV*: 6:25, 74). Similarly, for Sartre one cannot determine the ground for the original choice, since it is by this original choice that the idea of grounding begins to make sense for a person. Finally, since the fundamental project/disposition is determinate and can be investigated, Kant and Sartre would reject the claim that its identity provides the identity of the person. On the contrary, it is the synthesizing act of pure apperception in Kant, and of self-consciousness in Sartre, which unify the various deeper projects of a person, and it is the experience of the unity as such that represents the person's identity.

43. Baldwin confines the task of his article to bringing these similarities to the fore. He does not claim "to have uncovered a Kantian 'source' for Sartre's views" since "Sartre never openly refers to Kant's *Religion*" (Baldwin 1980: 31).

44. This is confirmed in the very text in which Sartre criticizes Kant's notion. Thus he later offers his interpretation of the Kantian concept. For Sartre, the choice of intelligible character should be seen as the person's choice of the fundamental project: "A jealousy of a particular date in which a subject historicises himself in relation to a certain woman, signifies for the one who knows how to interpret it, the total relation to the world by which the subject constitutes himself as a self. In other words this *empirical* attitude is by itself the expression of the 'choice of an intelligible character' " (*BN*: 563, 650).

45. "Although much may be done *in conformity with* what *duty* commands, still it is always doubtful whether it is really done *from duty* and therefore has moral worth. [...] In fact, it is absolutely impossible by means of experience to make out with complete certainty a single case in which the maxim of an action otherwise in conformity with duty rested simply on moral grounds and on the representation of one's duty" (*GMS*: 4:406–7, 61).
46. Emphasis added.
47. Verstraeten's article also compares Kant and Sartre with regard to the issue of how it is possible to maintain a moral character (Verstraeten 1995: 221–3). But again, in relation to Kant, he treats the question as a theological question; the distinctions between Kant's and Sartre's conceptions of moral action are blurred when the comparison is placed on a moral plane.

3 Kant

1. One of the few to advance the second reading is Thomas Anderson (1993); for him, the ethics of the early Sartre (and perhaps even that of the later Sartre (Anderson, 1993: 148)) is one based on the value of freedom. I think that this is correct, insofar as we understand freedom as autonomy, a notion which includes the other two notions I will distinguish in Sartre's practical philosophy. In places, Anderson points to the need for such a notion of freedom. See also his *Foundation and Structure of Sartrean Ethics* (1979). Such an interpretation would answer also some of the objections formulated by David Detmer (1986).
2. As Kant puts it, "since [...] no absolute totality of conditions in the causal relation can be obtained, reason creates for itself the idea of a spontaneity that can, on its own, start to act – without, i.e., needing to be preceded by another cause by means of which it is determined to action in turn, according to the law of causal connection" (*KrV*: A533/B562, 535–6).
3. As I have mentioned in the Introduction, my main concern here is to present a view of Kant which is reasonably recognizable as Kantian. To present it also as the best interpretation of Kant, I would need at least, first, to make an excursus into various theories of interpretation and to choose the most appropriate one; secondly, I would need to show why, from the perspective of this best theory of interpretation, the interpretation I offer is the best. To argue, as sometimes interpreters do, that my presentation of Kant might not be the most accurate interpretation, but it would philosophically be the most cogent one, while still being based on Kant's texts, would require me to argue against the various critique of the elements of Kant's position that I present here. I cannot engage in any of these two debates, if I am to be able to say anything about Kant and Sartre. For a recent interpretation of Kant's Third Antinomy that claims to be accurate, see Allison (1990: ch. 1); for a recent presentation of Kant's position, which claims to be the most philosophically compelling view of Kant available, see Korsgaard's recent *Self-constitution: Agency, Identity, and Integrity* (2009).
4. Kant also talks about a "speculative interest" and "an advantage of *popularity*" of dogmatism (*KrV*: A466–7/B494–6, 489–90). Since this chapter focuses on Kant's account of the person and agency, I will refer only to the practical interest.
5. As regard the speculative interest, empiricism offers "advantages that are very enticing and that far surpass what advantages the dogmatic teacher of ideas of reason may promise" (*KrV*: A468/B496, 490). Empiricism may in fact only try "to subdue the inquisitiveness and presumption of reason", but if it becomes

dogmatic and *denies* reason, then it "itself commits the mistake of immodesty, which is all the more censurable here because it causes irreparable detriment to reason's practical interest" (*KrV*: A471/B499, 492).

6. "Here the question is only whether, if in the entire series of all events we acknowledge nothing but natural necessity, it is still possible to regard the same event, which on the one hand is a mere natural effect, as yet being on the other hand an effect arising from freedom" (*KrV*: A543/B571, 542).

7. I have said that, on Kant's account, the arguments of the empiricist and dogmatist are compatible. This is by no means a suggestion that Kant's view would be 'compatibilist', in the sense usually employed in the debates between free-will theorists and determinists. Unlike other commentators, however, I do not think that attributing such a view to Kant is a very serious interpretative mistake. This is because I think Kant *is* a compatibilist when we consider his view of practical freedom; yet, I agree that he is not advancing such a view, as far as his view of theoretical or transcendental freedom is concerned.

8. Translation slightly amended.

9. See the discussion of character in Chapter 1, §16.

10. The assumption here is that we do not consider other non-moral evaluative claims which may require, for instance, that one ought to act in a particular way for aesthetic considerations. Freedom might, in such a case, be connected with the obligatory character of laws, although not of moral laws.

11. The definition of practical freedom is formulated by Kant on the basis of a contrast between a pathologically necessitated and a pathologically affected will, that is, between the animal power of choice (*arbitrium brutum*) and the human power of choice (*arbitrium liberum*) (*KrV*: A534/B562, 536).

12. "All actions of a human being are determined in appearance on the basis of his empirical character and the other contributing causes according to the order of nature" (*KrV*: A549/B577, 546). Also, according to Kant, without this law, the cause "would not be cause at all" (*KrV*: A539/B567, 539).

13. I distinguish between a compatibilist and an incompatibilist view, unlike Allison – see his *Kant's Theory of Freedom*, chs 3 and 11. In order for my actions to be considered as practically free, I do not need to show that transcendental freedom exists. My action, as the result of introducing (choosing) an incentive of action which causes the effect (action), is free if I can conceive myself as free to choose an incentive of action which would lead to a change of my empirical character. This is the solution offered by the compatibilist. The *possibility* of transcendental freedom has been proven by the solution to the Third Antinomy. In this sense, I am free, since I act as a result of choosing my (incentive for) action. This choice is based on the possibility of choosing my action in accordance with the obligatory laws of my intelligible character. See, however, Flikschuh's critique of Allison's account (in *Kant's Transcendental Idealism*) in her *Kant and Modern Political Philosophy* (2000: ch. 2).

14. Kant uses "reason" in several ways, from the specific sense of a faculty distinct from understanding and sensibility to the general sense of mind as including all conscious processes.

15. I am trying at this point to provide a way of describing the distinction independently from the so-called Two-Aspect View *versus* Two-World View debate concerning the nature of things in themselves.

16. This is the name given by Allison (1990: 189) to Kant's claim, in *Religion*, that "freedom of the power of choice has the characteristic, entirely peculiar to it,

that it cannot be determined to action through any incentive *except insofar as the human being has incorporated it into his maxim"* (*RGV*: 6:23–4, 72–3). As McCarty (2008) recently argued, Kant's claim was noticed as important already 50 years ago by John Silber (1960). Ralws called it, approximately 40 years ago, the "Principle of Election" (2000: 294). Very recently, Westphal (2011) suggests that the Incorporation Thesis is a particular case of a more general principle that he calls the "Principle of Autonomous Judgement".

17. For instance, Otfried Höffe makes this point in his *Immanuel Kant* (1994: 141). Felicitas Munzel identifies a new direction in Kant scholarship, which maintains that, in Kant, "practical rationality and the practice of moral judgement, not duty, are central" (1999: 3). Munzel's discussion of Kant's conception of moral character is intended as a further development along this direction.

18. See also Stephen Engström's recent *The Form of Practical Knowledge* (2009).

19. There is a growing body of literature on idealization and real world ethics. I only refer here to one of the first contemporary authors to deal with the problems of ideal and non-ideal theory in ethics, namely, Onora O'Neill. See, for instance, her *Towards Justice and Virtue* (1996). The distinction between ideal and non-ideal theory is, of course, Rawls's, in *A Theory of Justice* (1994).

20. See, for instance, Julia Annas's comparative analysis (1996). See also Introduction, n. 33.

21. Moral intuitions handed down by tradition or claims based on the will of God seem the exception. Yet, they are asserted as providing moral guidance either because they correspond to some inclination or they satisfy some type of desire or they fulfil some (longer- or shorter-term) interests, on the one hand, or, on the other, because they can be shown to be good in some rational way.

22. In *Groundwork*, Kant formulates what Allison calls the "Reciprocity Thesis" as follows: "A free will and a will under moral laws are one and the same" (*GMS*: 4:447, 95). For discussion on the reciprocity thesis, see Allison (1986 and 1990: 201–13).

23. On maxims, see also O'Neill (1989: 83–9). A distinct interpretation of Kant's notion of maxim is offered by Adrian Moore in his "Maxims and Thick Ethical Concepts" (2006).

24. The process by which one passes from maxims to particular actions is mediated in Höffe's view by a process of outline- or contour-knowledge (*Umriß- oder Grundriß-Wissen*). Thus, this notion of outline-knowledge incorporates both the conceptually precisely determined structure of moral action and the historical and individual particularities. The first element is compared by Höffe with Aristotelian virtues, whereas the second is supposed to take into account various changes of ethos or of circumstances and conditions of life (Höffe 1977: 364).

25. Kant explains the role of the sections under "Casuistical Questions" as attempting to determine which maxims particular actions fall under. These are actions which can be regarded under more than one maxim and, depending on the maxim, the action will appear as morally permissible or impermissible. See, for instance, the examples in the 'Doctrine of Virtue' in relation to the maxim of lying (*MS*: 6:431, 554).

26. §§36–37.

27. This consciousness of the moral law is Kant's famous "fact of reason". Commentators continue to debate the meaning, role and cogency of this notion, but for the classical views on this, see Beck (1960) and Allison (1989). See also the discussion below.

28. As Kant puts it, "whereas freedom is indeed the *ratio essendi* of the moral law, the moral law is the *ratio cognoscendi* of freedom. For if the moral law were no *previously* thought distinctly in our reason, we would never consider ourselves entitled to *assume* such a thing as freedom (even though freedom is not self-contradictory). But if there were no freedom, then the moral law *could not be encountered* in us at all" (*KpV*: 5:4, 5 n25).

4 Sartre and Kant

1. "While I must *play at being* a café waiter in order to be one, still it would be in vain for me to play at being a diplomat or a sailor, for I would not be one. This inapprehensible *fact* of my condition, this impalpable difference which distinguishes this drama of realisation from drama pure and simple is what causes the for-itself, while choosing the *meaning* of its situation and while constituting itself as the foundation of itself in situation, *not to choose* its position" (*EN*: 121, 107).
2. This first personalizing movement of reflection also involves a second reflection that Sartre terms "selfness". Thus, "in selfness my possible is reflected on my consciousness and determines it as what it is. Selfness represents a degree of nihilation carried further than the pure presence to itself of the pre-reflective *cogito* – in the sense that the possible which I am is not pure presence to the for-itself as reflection to reflecting, but that it is *absent-presence*" (*EN*: 143, 127–8). It is at this level that intentionality as the structure of consciousness becomes manifest. At the level of self-consciousness, the for-itself simply exists as appearance to itself. At the level of selfness, the for-itself is an immediate consciousness of the world and a consciousness (of) itself as immediate consciousness (of) the world.
3. While selfness brings my possibilities to the level of intentionality, it does not transform them into the object of a positional consciousness (*EN*: 103, 149).
4. As is obvious from Sartre's conceptions of intentionality and selfness, the conscious being as being-for-itself cannot exist without a world. Conversely, the world necessarily presupposes a person, as can be seen from Sartre's definition of the world: "We shall use the expression [...] 'world' for the totality of being in so far as it is traversed by the circuit of selfness" (*EN*: 141, 126).
5. As already mentioned, in his article on Sartre's conception of individuality, Fretz sees as one of the changes in Sartre's philosophy from the *Transcendence* to *Being and Nothingness*, the existence in the latter of only two types of consciousness, instead of the three which appear in the former (Fretz 1992). In fact, the situation is more complicated than Fretz's account portrays it. Thus, we have seen that the self implies a type of reflection, and that selfness implies a second-type reflection, both different from the reflective impure consciousness. Therefore, it seems that the threefold distinction of consciousnesses still holds in *Being and Nothingness*, even though it is differently drawn.
6. Sartre's claim concerning the failure of the person's attempt to recover her identity is very significant, because it is this failure which lies behind his claim that the person is a de-totalized totality or "a totality in perpetual incompletion" (*EN*: 179, 196), a view of the person which proves to be central in Sartre's later writings too – see Chapter 6.
7. "Thus reflection or the attempt to recover the for-itself by a turning back on itself results in the appearance of the for-itself for the for-itself. The being which wants to find a foundation in being is itself the foundation only of its own nothingness

[…]. This turning back upon the self is a wrenching away from self in order to return to it" (*EN*: 193, 177).

8. Selfness is the second essential aspect of the person. The relation of the for-itself to its possibilities is called by Sartre a "circuit of selfness" (*EN*: 141, 126). Sartre characterizes the relationship between the world and selfness as a relation of mutual dependency: "Without the world there is no selfness, no person; without selfness, without the person, there is no world" (*EN*: 144, 128).

9. Another aspect on which the transcendent psychic unity depends is selfness. See note 8 above.

10. As an illustration, this interpretation underpins Gary Jones's objection in his "Sartre, Consciousness and Responsibility" (1981).

11. Taylor (1997) makes a case for this.

12. Sartre defines the *négatités* as follows: "There is an infinite number of realities which are not only objects of judgements, but which are experienced, opposed, feared, etc., by the human being and which in their inner structure are inhabited by negation, as by a necessary condition of their existence. We shall call them *négatités*" (*EN*: 56, 45). The surpassed situation is an example of *négatité*, and is a condition of action: "Every action has for its express condition […] the discovery of a state of affairs as 'lacking in ____', *i.e.* as a *négatité*" (*EN*: 490, 458).

13. "Freedom is originally *a relation to the given*. But what is this relation to the given? […] The given does not cause freedom (since it can produce only the given) nor is it the *reason* of freedom (since all 'reason' comes into the world through freedom). Neither is it the *necessary condition* of freedom since we are on the level of pure contingency [and freedom is contingent in the sense that it is not able not to exist]. Neither is it an *indispensable matter* on which freedom must exercise itself, for this would be to suppose that freedom exists ready-made […]. The given in no way enters into the constitution of freedom since freedom is interiorised as the internal negation of the given […]. The given is freedom itself in so far as freedom *exists*; and whatever it does, freedom can not escape its existence" (*EN*: 543–4, 508).

14. "It is strange that philosophers have been able to argue endlessly about determinism and free-will, to cite examples in favour of one or the other thesis without ever attempting first to make explicit the structures contained in the very idea of *action*" (*EN*: 487, 453).

15. "The motive (*mobile*) […] is generally considered as a subjective fact. It is the ensemble of desires, emotions, and passions which urge me to accomplish a certain act" (*EN*: 501, 468).

16. "Generally by cause (*motif*) we mean the *reason* for the act; that is, the ensemble of rational considerations which justify it. […] One will note here that the cause is characterised as an objective appreciation of the situation" (*EN*: 500, 468).

17. Sartre's term for "cause" is *motif*, which does not provide the sense of scientific determinacy usually suggested by "cause".

18. "Nevertheless this objective appreciation can be made only in the light of a presupposed end and within the limits of a project of the for-itself toward this end" (*EN*: 501, 468).

19. "Thus cause and motive are correlative, exactly as the non-thetic self-consciousness is the ontological correlate of the thetic consciousness *of* the object. Just as the consciousness *of* something is self-consciousness, so the motive is nothing other than the apprehension of the cause in so far as this apprehension is self-consciousness. But it follows obviously that the cause, the

motive, and the end are the three indissoluble terms of the thrust of a free and living consciousness which projects itself toward its possibilities and makes itself defined by these possibilities" (*EN*: 504, 471).

20. One possible source for this view is that Kant fails to consider the possibility that features of appearances or phenomena are features of things in themselves, and, hence, that his argument in the Transcendental Aesthetic is not valid. This is one interpretation of the so-called "neglected alternative", which led to a heated dispute among neo-Kantian German philosophers. My reason for scepticism concerning the phenomenological assumption is also supported by Graham Bird's recent evaluation of the dispute (2006b). See also Bird (2006a: Section 9.1.2.).

21. See §§79–83.

22. By a moral system, I mean a moral theory, which claims to be able to guide a person in his attempts to act morally. See also 253 n23 for a definition of an ethical system.

23. "Apparently, in a demand there is some information from one free consciousness to another free consciousness touching upon a duty. I communicate a *categorical imperative* to the Other" (*NE*: 237; *CM*: 248). Sartre aims to show that, in fact, a morally valid imperative expressing a duty or an obligation is grounded in a demand, and not the demand in an imperative.

24. More exactly, in §47.

25. *EN*: 721, 626–7.

26. See §47.

27. This mode of being of the for-itself, where she is simply her possibility, is called by Sartre "selfness". Together with the world, selfness forms a "circuit of selfness", for instance: "I am a pure consciousness of things, and things caught up in the circuit of my selfness, offer me their potentialities as the proof of my non-thetic consciousness (of) my own possibilities" (*EN*: 305, 283).

28. See n31 below.

29. "Shame motivates the reaction which surpasses and overcomes the shame inasmuch as the reaction encloses within it an implicit and non-thematised comprehension of being-able-to-be-an-object on the part of the subject for whom I am an object. This implicit comprehension is nothing other than the consciousness (of) my 'being-myself'; that is, of my selfness reinforced" (*EN*: 336–7, 313).

30. In discussing Sartre's *Notebooks for an Ethics*, William L. McBride points out that it is this relation between authenticity and solidarity with others which marks "a decisive departure from (or, if one prefers, transcendence of) the much more individualistic intellectual and ethical climate of *Being and Nothingness*" (1991: 64). I think that the major difference between Sartre's *Being and Nothingness* and *Notebooks for an Ethics* is that whereas the former is a study of phenomenological ontology (which, according to Sartre, cannot yield an ethics), the latter is an attempt (as we will see, a failed one) to elaborate an ethical system, in the sense of a set of normative standards. Hence, the outcome is a constructivist moral theory where the person is assumed to have the freedom to construct her moral standards on the basis of already given prescriptions, in Sartre's case a hierarchy of values. In order to elaborate this ethical theory, Sartre appeals to the notion of authenticity presented in *Being and Nothingness*. In the latter book, Sartre claims, the for-others was described from the perspective of impure reflection; in the *Notebooks*, the conflictive interpersonal relations can lead to solidarity if the person undergoes a conversion (*CM*: 514–15, 480).

31. "In short there are two authentic attitudes: that by which I recognise the Other as the subject through whom I get my object-ness – this is shame; and that by which I apprehend myself as the free object by which the Other gets his being-other – this is self-pride or the affirmation of my freedom confronting the Other-as-object" (*EN*: 337, 314). Translation has here been slightly amended – I have followed McBride's suggestion (1991: 217–18 n49) of changing Barnes' rendition of "*orgueil*" as "arrogance". McBride suggests, as a better translation, that of "pride". However, Barnes has already translated with "pride" the French "*fierté*". From McBride's analysis of the meaning of these words, it seems to me that "self-pride" is a more appropriate term for "*orgueil*": "Sartre's suggestion of 'vanity' (*la vanité*) as an equivalent of '*fierté*' goes a long way toward explaining the subtle distinction that he is trying to make here: 'vanity' does imply, in English as in French, an uneasy, unstable type of attitude – an effort to impress others, based on small details of one's behaviour, dress, etc., that is always in danger of faltering; by contrast a certain self-confident pride, in the sense of "*orgueil*", may be more stable and more global" (McBride 1991: 218).

32. Whereas psychological states represent the result of a description of the consciousness reflected-on that is regarded as an object (a state), ontological structures are the result of a description of the relations between the levels of consciousness which are manifested by the various projects of the for-itself. Whereas psychological states are posited as objects, ontological structures, even when they presuppose the level of reflective consciousness, are accounted for in relation to the non-reflective levels of consciousness, and hence in relation to freedom.

33. In pride, "I attempt in my capacity as Object to act upon the Other. I take this beauty or this strength or this intelligence which he confers upon me – in so far as he constitutes me as an object – and I attempt to make use of it in a return shock so as to affect him passively with a feeling of admiration or of love. But at the same time I demand that this feeling as the sanction of my being-as-object should be entertained by the Other in his capacity as subject – *i.e.*, as freedom. This is, in fact, the only way of conferring an absolute object-ness on my strength or on my beauty. Thus the feeling which I demand from the other carries within itself its own contradiction since I must affect the other with it in so far as he is free" (*EN*: 338, 314 – translation amended).

34. Sartre gives this example as an instance of a principle, but not in this imperatival form (*CM*: 14, 7).

35. Strictly speaking, one could say the imperative is actually conditioned by the purpose of doing the right thing. Yet, as we have seen in Chapter 3, this purpose does not make the maxim any less objective or unconditional.

36. Of course, Sartre has reasons to endorse this interpretation. Kant's *Metaphysics of Morals*, for instance, displays his confidence in the possibility of deriving the main principles of ethics and political morality from the moral law. However, for Kant this work does not belong among his "critical" writings, but is a "doctrinal" text, and its aim is to "expand the cognitions" provided by the "Critiques" (*KrV*: A11–12/B25–6, 64). The "unconditionality" of the principles thus derived by Kant is relative to the situations he considers in the *Metaphysics of Morals*.

37. It should be noted here that, in fact, Sartre does not criticize abstraction *per se*. Any concept is in fact an abstraction, in the sense that it refers to only some (the significant) characteristics of a thing. Sartre's critique cannot be simply aimed at

whatever is abstract, unless he advocates the exclusive use of proper names. So, in fact, the abstraction that is being criticized by Sartre is one which is arrived at without a prior study of the features from which something is to be abstracted. In other words, Sartre's critique of abstraction refers to potentially distorting abstract principles and rules.

38. For instance, still in Höffe's example, different maxims are relevant depending on where the person lives, and different imperatival rules of action result depending on the capacity of the person to sing.

39. That Kant's moral theory is sometimes perceived (without sufficiently good reasons) as a morality of imperatives, in the manner in which Sartre sees it, may also be one of the reasons why comparative analyses of Kant's and Sartre's practical philosophies are not undertaken, or are concluded with the claim that, despite some similarities, the difference between Kant and Sartre is that Kant hopes to provide a code of imperatives, whereas Sartre rejects a morality of imperatives – for instance, Beavers says: "Kant is much more of a moralist than Sartre and, consequently, needs to bring the possibility of ethics into a prescriptive domain and formulate a code of action. At the same time, however, he would never want to maintain that a moral code is the source of moral action; and that the satisfaction of such a code cannot [*sic*] be the sole cause of the moral life. The code is a necessary but not sufficient condition of morality. Sartre, on the other hand, is unable and unwilling to present a moral code..." (1990: 166). However, not only does Kant not advance a morality of imperatives, but in fact Sartre is the one who hopes to provide an ethics of values, a hierarchic code of values, in the *Notebooks for an Ethics* (CM: 16, 12); see also Juliette Simont (1992: esp. 191–3).

40. Sartre's critiques of the abstract character of Kant's ethical theory are based on what Harold Bloom would call a "clinamen" (1973: 14). Bloom borrows this term from Lucretius, where it stands for a swerve of atoms that makes change possible. Paraphrasing Bloom, a "philosopher swerves away from his precursor, by so reading his precursor's philosophy so as to execute a *clinamen* in relation to it. This appears as a corrective movement in his own philosophy, which implies that the precursor's philosophy went accurately up to a certain point, but then should have swerved, precisely in the direction that the new philosophy moves" (1973: 14). (Here and in what follows, I use 'paraphrase' and not 'quote' since I slightly alter Bloom's text: I replace "poetic" with "philosophical", "poetry" and "poem" with "philosophy", and "poet" with "philosopher".)

41. The distinction is drawn in the *Critique of Practical Reason* (e.g., *KpV*: 5:43, 174–5), but commentators generally agree that it no longer plays the important justificatory role that Kant intended for it in *Groundwork* (see, for instance, Allison 1990: esp. 221–31).

42. Sartre's claims might rely here on considerations similar to Habermas's, in his interpretation of Wittgenstein's account of rule-following (1987: esp. 17–22).

43. As I have already mentioned, I have in mind here the distinction between phenomena and things in themselves, which is defining for the Kantian position. See also Allen Wood's *Kant* (2005: ch. 4). See also my review of this book (Baiasu 2006).

44. This second critique of Kant's account of ethical normativity is based on what Harold Bloom would call a "tessera", that is, the search for completion and antithesis. Bloom takes this term from the ancient mystery cults, where it meant a token of recognition which, with other pieces of the same kind, would

reconstitute an object (1973: 14). Paraphrasing him, one could define tessera as a relation in which "a philosopher antithetically 'completes' his precursor, by so reading the parent-philosophy as to retain its terms but to mean them in another sense, as though the precursor had failed to go far enough" (Bloom 1973: 14).

45. This means that, in their temporality, the subjective changes in a person (changes in desires, feelings, inclinations) cannot affect the validity of a moral principle, which is a law of freedom.

46. The same scenario is at work in Sartre's redefinition of the Kantian distinction between autonomy and heteronomy. For instance, he says: "We need to invert the terms of the Kantian problem and say that there is never heteronomy when one is on the plane of psychological determinism. If this determinism were to exist, there would be neither heteronomy nor autonomy but only the necessary unity of interconnected processes" (*CM*: 266, 255).

47. This sentence may suggest that Sartre's inaccurate reading of Kant is a cause of his anxiety of influence. In discussing Sartre's objections to Kant, I do not try to claim or to prove that, in his reading of Kant, Sartre was affected, consciously or unconsciously, by some psychological factor. I only claim that Sartre's texts reveal a *textual* anxiety of influence; in other words, I only claim that the reader of Sartre and of Kant can clearly perceive that Sartre's reading of Kant conflicts with Kant's own claims, and that this conflict follows certain patterns, namely, those identified by Bloom as "revisionary ratios". I am grateful to Andy Leak for correspondence on this point.

48. The further distinguishing characteristic (an imperative transforms me into a means to an other's end, whereas the value transforms the world into a means to my end) is a consequence of this difference of normative force.

49. The other dualities Sartre refers to here are those generated by the divide between freedom and sensible desires. According to Sartre, at the basis of the distinction between freedom and desire lies the distinction between the normativity of the value and that of the imperative.

50. One may see Sartre here foreshadowing one aspect of J. L. Mackie's argument from queerness. Thus, as presented by Richard Garner, "it is hard to believe in objective prescriptivity because it is hard to make sense of a demand without a demander, and hard to find a place for demand and demandingness apart from human interests and cognition" (1990: 143).

51. This account of moral realism, as given by the thesis of the independence of values from the agent, is presented in more detail in the Introduction.

52. Thus, according to Jeanson, the two aspects of the person provide "[a] perfect definition [...] of an essentialist grasping of human ambiguity: 'by one look [...] with both its terms'. We could place the perspective [...] which refuses to distinguish the two terms on the one side of this standpoint, and all metaphysical dualism which effects in principle their separation, and which afterwards shows itself incapable of placing them back in connection – unless through an arbitrary move towards a monism of Matter or Spirit – on the other side. In both cases, it seems that the possibility of a Morality is compromised. Indeed, if it is true [...] that the moral attitude is as such only at the expense of not being continuous with a natural attitude – that is to say, if it requires a revolution beyond all evolution; and if it is equally true that, in order for its value to be preserved, this revolution must be accomplished by the very subject who is in evolution – then only an ontology which maintains the ambiguity in the very heart of the action performed by the subject, and which refuses to reabsorb it in some artificial unity

as well as to separate it in a duality of independent substances, can provide a start-ing point for Morality, a starting point which would not be an illusion" (1965: 259 – my translation). As we have seen, Sartre rejects the notion of self-identity precisely because of the ambiguous character of the self, which at the same time refers to itself and to something else.

5 Kant

1. See Neiman (1994: ch. 3).
2. It might have seemed more appropriate to have used the term 'definition', but Kant contends that in philosophy it is more appropriate to speak about the exposition of concepts, rather than about their definition (*KrV*: A728–9/B756–7, 680).
3. For Kant, practical reason functions as guidance for the will, but not by sug-gesting actions for some purpose: "the true vocation must be to produce a will that is good, not perhaps *as a means* to other purposes, but good *in itself*" (*GMS*: 4:396, 52).
4. "There can be no doubt that all our cognition begins with experience" (*KrV*: B1, 43). In the first edition of the *Critique*, Kant says: "Experience is, without doubt, the first product to which our understanding gives rise, by working on the raw material of sense impressions. That is precisely why experience is our first instruc-tion, and why, as it progresses, it is so inexhaustible in new information – so much so that if the lives of all future generations are strung together, they will never be lacking in new knowledge that can be gathered on that soil" (*KrV*: A1, 43–4).
5. "There is more chance of an entire public enlightening itself. This is indeed almost inevitable, if only the public concerned is left in freedom. For there will always be a few who think for themselves, even among those appointed as guardians of the common mass. Such guardians, once they have themselves thrown off the yoke of immaturity, will disseminate the spirit of rational respect for personal value and for the duty of all men to think for themselves" (Kant 1970: 8:36, 55).
6. Bruno Bauer, "The Jewish Question", 66 (quoted in Marx 1979: 89).
7. A more detailed discussion can be found in my "Dealing Morally with Religious Differences" (2011).
8. See Baiasu (2011).
9. One question would be how we know whether to adopt the maxim or its contra-dictory, but I think Kant's answer would be that the universalization of the maxim of truthfulness will not lead to any contradiction, whereas that of the maxim of lying will do.
10. I draw here on Marcus Willaschek's account of the distinction (2002). There are a few points where I disagree with his account and which I mention either in the text or in endnotes. I talk about *norms*, rather than laws or imperatives, because Willaschek argues that the expressions 'juridical imperative' and 'imperative of right' are misnomers (Willaschek 2002: 71 n.11). He argues against Otfried Höffe's use of the notion of a categorical imperative of right, and he himself prefers to talk about juridical laws. Given Kant's distinction between law and imperative, I avoid the use of 'law'. Instead of 'law' (which seems to me inappropriate) or 'imperative' (which Willaschek regards as a misnomer), I use 'norm'.

11. This, however, is not altogether unproblematic. One could perhaps reliably condition persons to form motivations through some form of brainwashing or by similar methods. See Newey (2008).
12. For discussion of this case, see Uniacke (1996) and (2005).
13. Here I disagree with Willaschek's claim that "we often can tell what kind of action has been done only by considering its motivation" (Willaschek 2002: 68). He illustrates this with the following example: "whether something is a successful murder or a mistaken attempt at cooking a nice mushroom dinner depends, among other things, on what the agent wanted to achieve" (Willaschek 2002: 68 n6). I agree that "what the agent wanted to achieve" is necessary in order for us to understand which action has been performed by the agent, but I think it refers to the purpose or end of the action, not to its motive. I take the motive of the action to be the reason with which the agent tries to achieve her purpose, and I think it reveals a goal an agent finds attractive for its own sake. In Willaschek's example, what the agent wanted to achieve by cooking a mushroom dinner was to kill or treat the guest. Either of these will be a motive, if the agent finds killing or treating guests as valuable for its own sake. Some may do, but some may also want to kill or treat because they hate/love the guest or because they love/hate the guest's partner or for some other motives.
14. See, for instance: Beck (1960), Paton (1970), Pieper (2002), Silber (1995). The standard interpretation is also implicitly maintained by Reath (1995). This interpretation is not challenged even by Herman (1993). She aims to be "leaving deontology behind" (this is the title of ch. 10, 208–40) in her interpretations of Kant, but the question she is in fact dealing with is whether there is a conception of value in Kant, that is, whether the moral principles Kant talks about can form a conception of value: "Rules or principles or laws can be used as a basis of assessment independent of any conception of value they contain. (That is, after all, what canonical deontology asserts.) It is thus necessary to ask for the sense in which the formal constraints of rationality could be said to introduce a standard of value" (Herman 1993: 215). This does not challenge the standard prioritization of the moral law over the good. For interpretations which challenge the standard view, see Ward (1971) and Wood (2005).
15. Two qualifications must be added at this point. First, the fact that I am not challenging the accuracy of the standard interpretation should not be taken to imply that I find it satisfactory. Yet, what I take to be its main problem is not that it would make any obvious mistakes in ascribing to Kant the view that the moral law is prior to the good: after all, Kant repeatedly makes claims which suggest this interpretation; rather, I think that its main problem is that it does not offer a construal sufficiently subtle to account for claims by which Kant seems to deny this priority. For instance, for Kant, "if [...] there is to be a supreme practical principle [...], it must be one such that, from the representation of what is necessarily an end for everyone because it is an end in itself, it constitutes [ausmacht] an objective principle of the will and thus can serve as a universal practical law" (*GMS*: 4: 428, 79). This suggests that the objective principle of the will requires the representation of a universal end from which the moral law constitutes the principle. This suggests that it is possible to conceive of a notion of the good, as a universal end, which is at least independent from the moral law. The second qualification I would like to add is that I am not trying to show simply that the priority of the moral law in Kant is ultimately unjustified; my claim is that the moral law's priority does not have a moral justification. This is compatible with there being

non-moral justifications for adopting this priority, for instance, pragmatic reasons or reasons of consistency. In fact, I think that there are such reasons; however, the aim of these sections is only to consider some possible moral justifications and to argue that they are not sufficient.

16. This article was first published in *Kant Studien* in 1959. Since then, it has been reprinted in several collections. More recently, it appeared in the third volume of Ruth Chadwick's collection, *Immanuel Kant: Critical Assessments* (1993/1995).

17. He says: "If the good so defined [that is, as an object of the will which is not a causal determinant of the will] is to be related to the will at all, without destroying the freedom of the will, it can be related only by the agency of the will itself. That is, the will must freely elect the good as its object" (Silber 1995: 202). Yet, it eventually turns out that Silber only considers the case where the will is to elect an object distinct from itself, rather than the good as a concept or an idea of practical reason.

18. A similar argument is suggested by Beck, for whom, "if there is a law which expresses an absolute obligation, it must do so in virtue of its form and not its object. Since every principle of volition, however, has a material or an object, this is to say that the form of the principle, which is one of categorical obligation, must determine the concept of the good" (1960: 133).

19. My view, which I can only formulate here, is that the moral law and the concept of the good as a formal concept of a self-determining standard of the will are correlated, mutually grounding. The suggestion is made, but not developed, by Paton: "A rational will and goodness may be definable only in relation to one another, like 'right'and 'left', or 'above' and 'below'. This view is clearly worthy of exploration [...]; but even this view he [Kant] would probably consider a mistake since it treats goodness as co-ordinate with a rational will instead of subordinate to it and derived from it" (1970: 111–12). This suggestion can, I think, also improve on the standard interpretation of Kant by better accounting for his claims concerning the absolute good in the *Groundwork*. (see n. 15 above).

20. I think, but, again, I can only advance this as a suggestion, that the main reason for the centrality of principles in Kant's moral theory is given by Kant's conception of causation in his theoretical philosophy and by his view of freedom as a special type of causation. But I do not see any specifically practical or moral reason why Kant's ethics should be principle-centred, rather than value-centred.

6   Sartre and Kant

1. Sartre's first published theoretical work is one on the theory of the state ("The Theory of the State in Modern French Thought" 1974). The *Transcendence* points to the possibility of constructing a political theory on the basis of his critique of the later Husserl's phenomenology. Hence, his writings on imagination and his ontological approach to "human reality" could be read as the groundwork for a moral and political philosophy that he was intending to develop later. Sartre's drama "Dirty Hands" (Sartre 1948) names today a particular field within moral philosophy, where the idea of a separation between a private and a public morality is in place. However, taking a critical public position with regard to various political and social issues, Sartre makes always use of ideas that belong to – in the

terms of the theoreticians of "dirty hands" – a private morality: respect for the human being's dignity and for his rights, and rejection of violence, torture and discrimination. For him, morality seems to be 'of one piece'.

2. Thus, Sartre says, "my intention is to raise one question, and only one: do we now possess the materials for constituting a structural, historical anthropology?" And a little further on: "I came to feel that I ought to tackle the fundamental problem – whether there is any such thing as a Truth of Humanity (*une Vérité de l'homme*)?" (*CDRI*: 14, 822).

3. Spiegelberg (1987: 41). Here Spiegelberg is quoting from an interview with Sartre, published in *Obliques* (nos 18–19, 1978: 15).

4. Here I slightly disagree with those commentators who claim that the main change in Sartre's later work is a decision to acknowledge the power of circumstances – for instance, Anderson (1993: 87). I think the main difference is given by a decision to focus more on practical or empirical freedom, rather than on ontological freedom. Of course, this will lead to a more detailed treatment and examination of circumstances, but this is not due to a change in Sartre's view of ontology and of human reality (Anderson 1993: 4). Important changes occur, to be sure, but, as I have shown, not only between *Being and Nothingness* and the *Critique*, but also between the *Transcendence* and *Being and Nothingness*.

5. In the "Glossary" of the *Critique* "praxis" is defined as follows: "the activity of an individual or group of organising conditions in the light of some end" (1960: 829). This definition strongly resembles Sartre's definition of the project in *Being and Nothingness* (see Chapter 4).

6. One may wonder how Sartre's critique of the alleged incompatibility between the unconditional and universal character of the Categorical Imperative, on the one hand, and the freedom of the person who is under the obligation formulated by the Categorical Imperative, on the other, can lead to a questioning of Kant's entire thought. But Sartre is right to include here Kant's theoretical philosophy or epistemology, since for Kant practical reason has priority over theoretical reason (see, for instance, *KpV*: 5:119–21, 152–5).

7. I follow Timmons (2005) in taking the general form of the maxim to be: If/whenever _____ I will _____ in order to _____. Blanks stand for, respectively, a description of the circumstances of action, a description of the action and of the end.

8. Sartre prepared two sets of lectures on ethics after the publication of the *Critique*. The first was given in 1964, in Rome, to the conference at the Gramsci Institute organized by the Italian Communist Party. The second was supposed to be given at the conference organized by Cornell University in 1965, but Sartre refused to go as a result of the American bombardment of North Vietnam. Both these lectures are still unpublished, but a few Sartrean scholars had access to them and offered an account of their structures and main ideas. In what follows I will refer to Sartre's Cornell Lectures, where he developed more fully the relation between value and imperative, as it is presented in the texts of Simont (1987b) and Verstraeten (1987). For the Rome Lectures, see Anderson (1993: esp. ch. 7).

9. Sartre uses some titles of articles published in newspapers in order to make manifest what stands behind this "ought".

10. As McBride points out, Sartre misidentifies the place where the election contest between Robert Kennedy and Hubert Humphrey took place in 1964; it was not Wisconsin but West Virginia (McBride 1991: 212 n19).

11. A good example of an unexpected non-ethical consequence would be the American bombardment of Vietman. Sartre's critique of an ethics of values may seem so far-reaching as to make him appear an advocate of an ethics of imperatives. For instance, he reads even the appeal to tolerance as a categorical imperative, which he formulates as "You ought to vote for tolerance"; however, Sartre's critique of an ethics of values also holds for an ethics of imperatives. Indeed, the imperative "you ought to vote for tolerance" can also be seen as conditioned by circumstances like the fact that Kennedy is white and that he addresses mainly white people, even though it is an unconditional demand to the extent that it does not make reference to any of those circumstances (Simont 1987: 39).

12. "Even though value is that force of nihilating wrenching away in relation to the given, it is no less true that it has an immediate content, that everyone knows from the start what is means 'to be sincere', and that finally this wrenching away is mobilised only in view of an illusory coincidence of the sincere self with itself, hence in view to a repose of all nihilating activity" (Simont 1987b: 41). See also Verstraeten (1987b: 61–8).

13. As I have mentioned, the claim is not as undisputable as it might seem. See, for instance, Newey (2008).

14. In recent Kantian scholarship, a distinction has been introduced between the content of morality (what is right/wrong) and the obligatoriness of morality. The former is not created by rational beings, not even by the supreme rational being, God. The latter is created by rational beings, but only by those limited rational beings, like us. We legislate on the basis of the moral law or, rather, Categorical Imperative, what we ought to do. See Stern (2011).

15. Thus, he says: "A practical rule is always a product of reason, because it prescribes action as a means to an effect that is the aim. [...] [Practical laws or moral imperatives] must sufficiently determine the will as will even before I ask whether I so perhaps have the ability required for a desired effect, or what I am to do in order to produce it" (*KpV*: 5:20, 30–1). Also he asserts that "it is indeed undeniable that every volition must also have an object and hence a matter. But the matter is not, just because of this, the determining basis and condition of the maxim" (*KpV*: 5:34, 50). From these two claims a distinction between the object of volition (the purpose of a practical principle) and the determining ground of the will emerges. This suggests that the moral imperative does posit a purpose, but this is not the determining ground of the will.

16. This is the famous problem of opacity formulated by Kant in *Groundwork* (*GMS*: 4:406–7, 61).

17. I have discussed this in Baiasu (2010).

18. As far as I can see, there is a distinction between an argument which shows that the Categorical Imperative exists and one which shows that pure reason is practical. To demonstrate that the Categorical Imperative exists is to show that it is morally valid, hence it ought to be followed by all (limited) rational beings. However, that it ought to be followed by all does not mean that pure reason *is* practical, that is, that pure reason *does* indeed command actions only on the basis of the Categorical Imperative. Here I am interested only in the first argument, since this is the focus of Sartre's criticism.

19. Here it is worth highlighting an aspect of Kant's moral theory which can also be found in Sartre's ethical thought, and which is sometimes misunderstood by commentators. This is what might be called the 'democratic' character of Kant's

ethics, for which any rational person has the authority to judge morally a situation and act on his judgement. This is reiterated, for instance, in the second *"Critique"* (5:36, 54; 5:43–4, 62–3). In *Being and Nothingness*, Sartre makes a similar point when he presents the "Ethical implications" of his phenomenological ontology; shortly after having claimed that "existential psychoanalysis is *moral description*" (*EN*: 690, 645), Sartre says: "In truth there are many men who have practiced this psychoanalysis on themselves and who have not waited to learn its principles in order to make use of them as a means of deliverance and salvation" (*EN*: 691, 646). However, it is precisely on account of a difference in this respect that they are sometimes contrasted. For instance, Lieberman says: "Kant thus differs from Sartre in at least two important aspects: first, Sartre lacks the world view that accepts common (and perhaps unquestionable) knowledge of the moral law; and second, Sartre lacks the theoretical orientation in which an a priori awareness of the moral law is possible – in which a fact about our essence as rational beings precedes, or is at least independent of, our existence – thereby reversing the existentialist canon that existence precedes essence" (1997: 215). As we have seen, the moral law is only an implication of the difference between a descriptive and a prescriptive approach to action; as we will see, the fact of reason is "a fact about our essence as rational beings" only if by "essence" one understands with Sartre a mode of being, and, in that case, this fact by no means goes against the "existentialist canon".

20. In *Being and Nothingness*, the clearest expression of this distinction is introduced by Sartre through the notion of *négatité*. As we have seen, however, he seems to reduce the significance of the distinction when he contrasts imperatives and values.

21. I have explored the relationship between these facts in my "From self to other: Kant's fact of reason and Sartre's fact of mind" (1998).

22. According to David Lindstedt, these are the two most influential interpretations of Kant's idea for a universal history. It is either seen as a fourth regulative idea of reason (along with the ideas of God, immortal soul and whole world), or as an attempt to give account of the dialectical laws of history, an attempt which will be later developed by Hegel (1999: 133–5).

23. In the second volume of the *Critique of Dialectical Reason*, Sartre ironically pastiches Kant's use of the "as if", by using thought-experiments in which we would imagine how an extraterrestrial being would regard the earth, or an amphibian would encounter our form of life (Simont 1987a: 136–7).

24. See Chapter 4, §47.

25. In the "Glossary" of the *Critique*, "dialectic" is defined as "the intelligibility of the *praxis* at every level" (Sartre 1976: 828). Sartre relates, therefore, dialectic to the *praxis*, that is, to the person. Hence, dialectic is a process of creating relationships between two entities on the basis of an internal negation ("Every negation is a relation of interiority. By this I mean that the reality of *the Other* affects me in the depth of my being to the extent that it *is not* my reality" (*CRDI*: 101, 214)); precisely because there is an internal negation at stake, that is, a negation which affects the very being of the entities which are connected, I cannot understand those entities independently of their individual relations to the world and of their relation to one another.

26. "If dialectical Reason exists, then, from the ontological point of view, it can only be a developing totalisation, occurring where the totalisation occurs, and, from the epistemological point of view, it can only be the accessibility of

that totalisation to a knowledge which is itself, in principle, totalising in its procedures. But since totalising knowledge cannot be thought of as attaining ontological totalisation as a new totalisation of it, dialectical knowledge must itself be a moment of the totalisation, or, in other words, totalisation must include within itself its own reflexive re-totalisation as an essential structure and as a totalising process within the process as a whole" (*CRDI*: 47, 163).

27. This remark echoes Kant's idea of the critique of pure reason, and aims at offering a better account of the way in which Kant overcomes the difficulties of beginning implicit in reason's free self-critical activity. See Chapter 5, Sections 64–66.

28. This is not really a synthesis to the extent that the previous negation presupposed by the difference between the two workers is not only negated in order to harmonize the relation between them; the result of the negated negation is the conflict between the intellectual and the workers. This transforms Sartre's dialectic into a *sui generis* process, which cannot easily be identified with the Hegelian or Marxist dialectic. Yirmiahu Yovel deems it "a dualistic theory of correlation" (1977: 175). It is this type of negation that Sartre defends in *Being and Nothingness* against Hegel's "dialectical" nothingness (*EN*: 46–51, 36–40) and Heidegger's "phenomenological" negation (*EN*: 51–6, 40–5). For some of the similarities between Kant's and Sartre's conceptions of negation (which Sartre also acknowledges (*EN*: 40–1, 30)), see Simont (1998: 39–49).

29. Sartre defines freedom as "that small movement which makes of a totally conditioned social being a person who does not give back entirely what he has received from his conditioning" (1970: 101–2).

30. For Sartre, a theoretical approach that attempts to understand an object is an activity, a totalization, and hence it is practical. The interests or values which guide this activity are conditioned by the situation in which the praxis takes place and by the object which the praxis includes in its totalization. However, this epistemic activity does not, by any means, ask the Kantian practical question as to what *ought* to be the values or interests of an action.

31. See especially §9.

32. "It makes a great difference whether something is given to my reason as an *object absolutely* or only as an *object in my idea*. In the second case there is actually only a schema. No object is directly added to this schema, not even hypothetically; rather, the schema serves only for presenting, by means of the reference to this idea, other objects according to their systematic unity, and hence for presenting them indirectly" (*KrV*: A670/B698, 639).

33. As we have seen in Chapter 5, Habermas considers that Kant's idea of a continual progress of the human race also provides the solution for the dilemma concerning how a perfectly just society can be brought about. But this is a solution only to the extent to which Kant can see that idea as at the same time constitutive and regulative.

34. Chapter 4, especially §53.

35. Translation slightly amended.

36. Translation slightly amended.

37. One could, of course, claim that Kant does not succeed in identifying accurately the necessary conditions of experience, but Sartre makes no attempt to show we can have experience without the category of, say, cause/effect or that of substance/accident; on the contrary, he uses these in his account of experience.

38. With these comments, Sartre seems to continue a direction of thought that Kant himself initiated and which attempts to locate reason in the world. Thus, according to Howard Williams, after Kant, Hegel made an even more radical attempt, particularly with respect to the possibility of virtuous action: "Kant accepts that in our practice we cannot be fully moral [...]. Hegel, of course, affords an important contrast to Kant in this respect. He believes that reason can be fulfilled in practice, and this is done in the activity of the loyal citizen within the modern state" (1983: 57).

39. These claims are central to the *Critique of Dialectical Reason*.

40. Written between March 1956 and September 1961, Sartre's writings on the Algerian War, especially the preface to Frantz Fanon's book *Les Damnés de la terre* (2001), seem to be written by a fanatic supporter of the cause of the Algerian people. Thus, David Drake draws attention not only to the "irresolvable" existential contradiction in which Sartre found himself during those years – French against France – but also to the contradiction in which he found himself as a philosopher, as a result of his strong commitment to the liberation of Algeria: "In his preface to Fanon's *Les Damnés de la terre*, Sartre wholeheartedly endorsed the revolutionary violence of the anti-colonial movements. [...] [S]uch was Sartre's rage, frustration and guilt at European colonialism in general and French colonialism in Algeria in particular, that he made no attempt to develop any philosophical, moral or political guiding principles for the practical application of the violence of the colonised peoples, nor did he attempt to theorise any limits to the violence of the oppressed" (Drake 1999: 27). How can one, on the one hand, advocate and justify violence and, on the other hand, claim to theorize and argue against "inhumanity"? Thus, in *Search for a Method* and the *Critique of Dialectical Reason*, Sartre criticizes the inhumanism of traditional Marxism, as well as the anti-humanism of "bourgeois humanism" (see, for instance, *CRDI*: 799, 876).

Conclusion

1. For Constant's example, see the beginning of the Introduction.

2. For Jens Timmermann, for instance, Kant is wrong to consider as unconditional the duty not to be untruthful. For him, Kant is right to claim that lying is unconditionally wrong, but lying is not the same as being untruthful. Lying is being untruthful for morally dubious reasons (Timmermann 2001).

3. Kant is discussing this example under certain conditions, namely that one "cannot evade an answer of 'yes' or 'no'" (*VRML*: 8:426, 611) to the question of the would-be murderer, and that truthfulness in that situation is not looked at from an ethical point of view, but as "a duty of right" (i.e. as a legal duty) (*VRML*: 8:426, 612). Sartre's story changes Kant's proviso: Pablo's response does not have to be a "Yes" or "No" reply: he can choose to remain silent; and the issue raised by Sartre is moral, not legal. Nevertheless, both of them reject a conditional right to lie, be it for moral or political reasons.

4. See the Introduction.

5. Since commentators generally agree on the continuity between Rawls's first book and the Dewey Lectures (see, for instance, Baynes 1992: esp. 18–24), and since the Dewey Lectures thematize the distinction between the rational and the reasonable that is important for my purposes here, I will mainly follow the latter.

6. Constructivism consists in two fundamental conceptions of justice as fairness, namely the original position and the reflective equilibrium.

7. In subsequent writings, Rawls adds, as an element of the Reasonable, the acceptance of a "fact of pluralism", which consists in the existence of a plurality of conceptions of the good. This plurality is not to be regarded as reducible to a monism centred on a single and overarching conception of the good (Rawls 1993, 2001).

8. The formulation of the first principle of justice makes this plain: "Each person is to have an equal right to the most extensive basic liberty compatible with a similar liberty for others" (Rawls 1994: 60).

Bibliography

Primary Literature

Kant

Kant, I. ([1st edn 1781; 2nd edn 1787]1996) *Critique of Pure Reason*. Trs. W. S. Pluhar. Indianapolis: Hackett.

——([1784]1970) "An Answer to the Question: 'What Is Enlightenment?' ", in H. Reiss (ed.) *Kant's Political Writings*. Trs. H. B. Nisbet. Cambridge: Cambridge University Press.

——([1784]1970) "Idea for a Universal History with a Cosmopolitan Purpose", in H. Reiss (ed.) *Kant's Political Writings*. Trs. H. B. Nisbet. Cambridge: Cambridge University Press.

——([1785]1996) "Groundwork of The metaphysics of morals", in M. J. Gregor (ed.) *Practical Philosophy*. Trs. M. J. Gregor. Cambridge: Cambridge University Press.

——([1788]2002) *Critique of Practical Reason*. Trs. W. S. Pluhar. Indianapolis, IN: Hackett.

——([1790]1987) *Critique of Judgement*. Trs. W. S. Pluhar. Indianapolis, IN: Hackett.

——([1793]2001) "Religion within the boundaries of mere reason", in A. Wood and G. di Giovanni (eds) *Religion and Rational Theology*. Trs. G. di Giovanni. 1st edn 1996. Cambridge: Cambridge University Press.

——([1793]1996) "On the common saying: That may be correct in theory, but it is of no use in practice", in M. J. Gregor (ed.) *Practical Philosophy*. Trs. M. J. Gregor. Cambridge: Cambridge University Press.

——([1797]1996) "The metaphysics of morals", in M. J. Gregor (ed.) *Practical Philosophy*. Trs. M. J. Gregor. Cambridge: Cambridge University Press.

——([1797]1996) "On a supposed right to lie from philanthropy", in M. J. Gregor (ed.) *Practical Philosophy*. Trs. M. J. Gregor. Cambridge: Cambridge University Press.

——([1798]2001), "The contest of the faculties", in A. Wood and G. di Giovanni (eds) *Religion and Rational Theology*. Trs. M. J. Gregor and R. Anchor. 1st edn 1996. Cambridge: Cambridge University Press.

——(1900ff.) *Gesammelte Schriften*. Berlin: vols 1–22 Preussische Akademie der Wissenschaften; vol. 23 Deutsche Akademie der Wissenschaften zu Berlin; vols 24- Akademie der Wissenschaften zu Göttingen.

Sartre

Sartre, J.-P. ([1927]1970) "La Théorie de l'État dans la pensée française contemporaine", in M. Contat and M. Rybalka (eds) *Les Écrits de Sartre: Chronologie, Bibliographie Commentée*. Paris: Gallimard.

——([1927]1974) "The Theory of the State in Modern French Thought", in M. Contat and M. Rybalka (eds) *The Writings of Jean-Paul Sartre*. Trs. R. McCleary. Vol. 2: *Selected Prose*. Evanston, IL: Northwestern University Press.

——([1936–7]1985) *La Transcendance de l'Ego: Esquisse d'une Description Phénomènologique*. Ed. Sylvie le Bon. Paris: Vrin.

——([1936–7]2004) *The Transcendence of the Ego: A Sketch for a Phenomenological Description.* Trs. A. Brown. London: Routledge.
——([1937]1939) *Le Mur.* Paris: Gallimard.
——([1937]1969) *The Wall.* Trs. L. Alexander. New York: New Directions.
——([1939]1990) "Une idée fondamentale de la phénomènologie de Husserl: l'intentionalité", *Situations Philosophiques.* Paris: Gallimard.
——([1939]1970), "Intentionality: A Fundamental Idea of Husserl's Phenomenology", *The Journal of British Society for Phenomenology* 1(2): 4–5. Trs. J. P. Fell.
——(1938) *Esquisse d'une Théorie des Émotions.* Paris: Hermann.
——([1938]1962) *Sketch for a Theory of the Emotions.* Trs. P. Mairet. London: Methuen.
——([1943]1973) *L'Être et le néant: Essaie d'ontologie phénomènologique.* Paris: Gallimard.
——([1943]1956) *Being and Nothingness: An Essay on Phenomenological Ontology.* Trs. H. E. Barnes. New York: Philosophical Library.
——([1943]1967) *L'Existentialisme est un Humanisme.* Paris: Nagel.
——([1945]1948) *Existentialism and Humanism.* Trs. Philip Mairet. London: Methuen.
——([written 1947]1983) *Cahiers pour une Morale.* Paris: Gallimard.
——([written 1947; 1983]1992) *Notebooks for an Ethics.* Trs. David Pellauer. Chicago: University of Chicago Press.
——(1948) *Les Mains Sales.* Paris: Gallimard.
——(1948) *Les Mains Sales.* Trs. K. Black. London: Methuen.
——([1956]1964) "Le colonialisme est un système", *Situations, V.* Paris: Gallimard.
——([1957]1964), " 'Portrait du colonisé' précédé du 'Portrait du colonisateur' par Albert Memmi", *Situations, V.* Paris: Gallimard.
——([1958]1964) "Nous sommes tous des assassins", in *Situations, V.* Paris: Gallimard.
——([1960]1985) *Critique de la Raison Dialectique.* Tome I: *Théorie des Ensembles Pratiques.* Paris: Gallimard.
——([1960]1976), *Critique of Dialectical Reason.* Vol. I: *Theory of Practical Ensembles.* Trs. A. Sheridan-Smith. London: Verso.
——([1961]1964) "Les Damnés de la terre", in *Situations, V.* Paris: Gallimard.
——([1964]2001) *Colonialism and Neocolonialism.* Trs. A. Haddour, S. Brewer and T. McWilliams. London: Routledge.
——(1970) "Sartre par Sartre", in *Situations, IX.* Paris: Gallimard.
——([1972]1976) "Justice et État", in *Situations, X.* Paris: Gallimard.
——([1973]1976) "Élections, piège à cons", in *Situations, X.* Paris: Gallimard.
——([1975]1976), "Autoportrait à soixante-dix ans", in *Situations, X.* Paris: Gallimard.
——(1985, unfinished) *Critique de la Raison Dialectique.* Tome II: *L'Intelligibilité de l'Histoire.* Paris: Gallimard.
——([1985, unfinished]1991) *Critique of Dialectical Reason.* Vol. 2: *The Intelligibility of History.* Trs. Q. Hoare. London: Verso.

Secondary Literature

Allison, H. E. (2004) *Kant's Transcendental Idealism: An Interpretation and Defense.* Revised and enlarged edn. New Haven and London: Yale University Press.
——(1990) *Kant's Theory of Freedom.* Cambridge: Cambridge University Press.

———(1989) "Justification and Freedom in the *Critique of Practical Reason*", in E. Förster (ed.) *Kant's Transcendental Deductions: The Three 'Critiques' and the 'Opus Postumum'*. Stanford, CA: Stanford University Press.

———(1986) "Morality and Freedom: Kant's Reciprocity Thesis", *Philosophical Review* 95(3): 393–425.

———(1983) *Kant's Transcendental Idealism: An Interpretation and Defense*. New Haven and London: Yale University Press.

Ameriks, K. ([1982]2000) *Kant's Theory of Mind: An Analysis of the Paralogisms of Pure Reason*. New edn. Oxford: Clarendon Press.

Anderson, T. C. (1993) *Sartre's Two Ethics: From Authenticity to Integral Humanity*. Chicago: Open Court.

———(1979) *Foundation and Structure of Sartrean Ethics*. Lawrence, KS: University Press of Kansas.

Annas, J. (1996) "Aristotle and Kant on Morality and Practical Judgement", in S. Engstrom and J. Whiting (eds) *Aristotle, Kant, and the Stoics: Rethinking Happiness and Duty*. Cambridge: Cambridge University Press.

Apel, K.-O. (1988) *Diskurs und Verantwortung: das Problem des Übergangs zur postkonventionellen Moral*. Frankfurt am Main: Suhrkamp.

Aristotle (1998) *The Nicomachean Ethics*. Trs. D. Ross, revised J. L. Ackrill and J. O. Urmson. Oxford: Oxford University Press.

Baiasu, S. (2011a) "Metaphysics and Moral Judgement", in S. Baiasu, S. Pihlström and H. Williams (eds) *Politics and Metaphysics in Kant*. Cardiff: Wales University Press. Forthcoming.

———(2011b) "Dealing Morally with Religious Differences", in M. Mookherjee (ed.) *Democracy, Religious Pluralism and the Liberal Dilemma of Accomodation*. New York: Springer.

———(2006) "Allen Wood's *Kant*", *Philosophical Books* 47(2): 162–3.

———(2004) "Phenomenology and the Ethical Possibility of Differences", *International Journal of Philosophical Studies* 12(2): 204–18.

———(2003) "Sartre's Search for an Ethics and Kant's Moral Theory", *Sartre Studies International* 9(1): 21–53.

———(2001) "Persons and Politics in Kant and Sartre". PhD Dissertation. Manchester: Manchester University.

———(1999) "Kant and the Difficulties of Beginning: Freedom and Emancipation", *The MANCEPT Working Paper Series* 1: 1–27.

———(1998) "From Self to Other: Kant's Fact of Reason and Sartre's Fact of Mind". Unpublished manuscript.

Baldwin, T. (1980) "The Original Choice in Sartre and Kant", *Proceedings of the Aristotelian Society*. New series 80(1): 31–44.

Baynes, K. (1992) "Constructivism and Practical Reason in Rawls", *Analyse & Kritik* 14 (1): 18–32.

De Beauvoir, S. ([1948]1976) *The Ethics of Ambiguity*. Trs. B. Frechtman. New York: Philosophical Library.

Beavers, A. (1990) "Freedom and Autonomy: The Kantian Analytic and a Sartrean Critique", *Philosophy and Theology* 5(2): 151–68.

Beck, L. W. (1960) *A Commentary on Kant's 'Critique of Practical Reason'*. Chicago: Chicago University Press.

Berlin, I. ([1958]1997) "Two Concepts of Liberty", in R. E. Goodin and P. Pettit (eds) *Contemporary Political Philosophy: An Anthology*. Oxford: Blackwell.

Bird, G. (2006a) *The Revolutionary Kant: A Commentary on the 'Critique of Pure Reason'*. Chicago: Open Court.

——(2006b) "The Neglected Alternative: Trendelenburg, Fischer, and Kant", in G. Bird (ed.) *A Companion to Kant*. Oxford: Blackwell.

Bloom, H. (1973) *The Anxiety of Influence: A Theory of Poetry*. Oxford: Oxford University Press.

Catalano, J. (1985) *A Commentary on Jean-Paul Sartre's "Being and Nothingness"*. Chicago: University of Chicago Press.

Constant, B. ([1797]1998) "Des réactions politiques", in L. Omacini and J.-D. Candaux (eds) *Écrits de jeunesse (1774–1799)*. Tübingen: Max Niemeyer Verlag.

——([1819]1988) "The Liberty of the Ancients Compared with That of the Moderns", in B. Fontana (Trs. and ed.) *Political Writings*. Cambridge: Cambridge University Press.

De Coorebyter (2000) *Sartre face à la Phenomenology: Autour de "L'intentionalité" et de "La transcendence de l'Ego"*. Bruxelles: Éditions OUSIA.

Darnell, M. (2006) *Self in the Theoretical Writings of Sartre and Kant: A Revisionist Study*. Lewiston: The Edwin Mellen Press.

Darwall, S., Gibbard, A. and Railton, P. (1992) "Toward Fin de siecle Ethics: Some Trends", *Philosophical Review* 101(1): 115–89.

Descartes, R. (1996) *Meditations on First Philosophy: With Selections from the Objections and Replies*. Ed. John Cottingham. Cambridge: Cambridge University Press, Cambridge.

Detmer, D. (1986) *Freedom as Value: A Critique of the Ethical Theory of Jean-Paul Sartre*. Chicago: Open Court.

Dobson, A. (1993) *Jean-Paul Sartre and the Politics of Reason: A Theory of History*. Cambridge: Cambridge University Press.

Drake, D. (1999) "Sartre, Camus and the Algerian War", *Sartre Studies International* 5(1): 16–32.

Edie, J. (1993) "The Question of the Transcendental Ego: Sartre's Critique of Husserl", *The Journal of the British Society for Phenomenology* 24(2): 104–20.

Engstrom, S. (2009) *The Form of Practical Knowledge: A Study of the Categorical Imperative*. Cambridge, MA: Harvard University Press.

Flikschuh, K. (2007) *Freedom: Contemporary Liberal Perspectives*. Oxford: Polity.

——(2000) *Kant and Modern Political Philosophy*. Cambridge: Cambridge University Press.

Fretz, L. (1992) "Individuality in Sartre's Philosophy", in C. Howells (ed.) *The Cambridge Companion to Sartre*. Cambridge: Cambridge University Press.

Gardner, S. (1999) *Kant and 'The Critique of Pure Reason'*. London: Routledge.

Garner, R. (1990) "On the Genuine Queerness of Moral Properties and Facts", *Australasian Journal of Philosophy* 68(2): 137–46.

Gillett, G. (1990) "The Subject of Experience", *Logos* 11(2): 93–109.

Guyer, P. (2011) "Constructivism and Self-constitution", in M. Timmons and S. Baiasu (eds) *Kant on Practical Justification: Interpretative Essays*. Oxford: Oxford University Press. Forthcoming.

Habermas, J. ([1992]1996), *Between Facts and Norms*. Trs. W. Rehg. Oxford: Polity Press.

——(1995) "Reconciliation through the Public Use of Reason: Remarks on John Rawls's Political Liberalism", *The Journal of Philosophy* 92(3): 109–31.

——([1990–1]1993) *Justification and Application*. Trs. C. Cronin. Cambridge: Polity Press.

——([1962]1989) *The Structural Transformation of the Public Sphere: An Inquiry into a Category of Bourgeois Society*. Trs. T. Burger with the assistance of F. Lawrence. Cambridge: Polity Press.

———([1981]1987) *The Theory of Communicative Action*. Vol. II: *Lifeworld and System*. Trs. T. McCarthy. Boston: Beacon.

———([1963–71]1973) *Theory and Practice*. Trs. J. Viertel. Boston, MA: Beacon Press.

Hegel, G. W. F. ([1804–5]1986) *The Jena System, 1804–5: Logic and Metaphysics*. J. W. Burbidge and G. di Giovanni (eds). Montreal: McGill-Queen's University Press.Heidegger, M. ([1926]1997) *Being and Time*. Trs. J. Macquarrie and E. Robinson. 1st edn 1962. Oxford: Blackwell.

Heidegger, M. (1997) Being and Time. Trs J. Macquarrie and E. Robinson. Oxford: Blackwell.

Henrich, D. (1989) "The Identity of the Subject in the Transcendental Deduction", in E. Schaper and W. Vossenkuhl (eds) *Reading Kant: New Perspectives on Transcendental Arguments and Critical Philosophy*. Oxford: Blackwell.

Herman, B. (1993) *The Practice of Moral Judgement*. Cambridge, MA: Harvard University Press.

Höffe, O. ([1992]1994) *Immanuel Kant*. Trs. M. Farrier. Albany, NY: State University of New York Press.

———(1977) "Kants kategorischer Imperativ als Kriterium des Sittlichen", *Zeitschrift für Philosophische Forschung* 31(3): 354–84.

Howells, C. (1988) *Sartre: The Necessity of Freedom*. Cambridge: Cambridge University Press.

Humboldt, W. v. ([1852]1993) *The Limits of State Action*. Trs. and ed. J. W. Burrow. Indianapolis, IN: Liberty Fund, Inc.

Husserl, E. ([1931]1988) *Cartesian Meditations*. Trs. D. Cairns. 1st edn 1950. Dordrecht: Kluwer.

———(1988) *Vorlesungen über Ethic und Wertlehre, 1908–1914*. Vol. 28: *Husserliana*. Ed. U. Melle. Dordrecht: Kluwer.

Jeanson, F. (1965) *Le Problème Moral et la Pensée de Sartre*. Paris: Éditions du Seuil.

Jones, G. E. (1981) "Sartre, Consciousness, and Responsibility", *Philosophy and Phenomenological Research* 81(1/2): 234–7.

Jopling, D. (1992) "Sartre's Moral Psychology", in C. Howells (ed.) *The Cambridge Companion to Sartre*. Cambridge: Cambridge University Press.

———(1986) "Kant and Sartre on self-knowledge", *Man and World* 19(1): 79–93.

Kerner, G. (1990) *Mill, Kant, and Sartre: An Introduction to Ethics*. Oxford: Clarendon Press.

Korsgaard, C. (2009) *Self-constitution: Agency, Identity, and Integrity*. Oxford: Oxford University Press.

Leibniz, G. W. ([1714]1969) "Principle of Nature and Grace", in L. Loemker (ed.) *Leibniz: Philosophical Papers and Letters*. 2 vols. Dordrecht: Reidel.

Lieberman, M. (1997) "The Limits of Comparison: Kant and Sartre on the Fundamental Project", *History of Philosophy Quarterly* 14(2): 207–17.

Lindstedt, D. (1999) "Kant: Progress in Universal History as a Postulate of Practical Reason", *Kant-Studien* 90(2): 129–47.

Locke, J. ([1690]1759) *An Essay Concerning Human Understanding*. New ed. Glasgow: Printed by Robert Urie.

Longuenesse, B. (1998) *Kant and the Capacity to Judge: Sensibility and Discursivity in the Transcendental Analytic of the 'Critique of Pure Reason'*. Trs. C. T. Wolfe. Princeton, NJ: Princeton University Press.

———(1993) *Kant et le pouvoir de juger: Sensibilité et discursivité dans l'Analytique transcendentale de la 'Critique de la raison pure'*. Paris: Presses Universitaires de France.

McBride, W. L. (1991) *Sartre's Political Theory*. Bloomington, IN: Indiana University Press.

McCarty, R. (2008) "Kant's Incorporation Requirement: Freedom and Character in the Empirical World", *Canadian Journal of Philosophy* 38(3): 425–52.

Marx, K. ([1844]1979) "On the Jewish Question", in D. McLellan (ed.) *Early Texts*. Trs. D. McLellan. Oxford: Blackwells.

Merleau-Ponty, M. ([1945]2002) *The Phenomenology of Perception*. Trs. C. Smith. 1st edn 1962. London: Routledge.

Misrahi, R. (1990) "L'inachèvement pratique de la philosophie de Sartre", *Études sartriennes*, IV: 9–24.

Moore, A. W. (2006) "Maxims and Thick Ethical Concepts", *Ratio* 19(2): 129–47.

Morris, P. S. (1976) *Sartre's Conception of a Person: An Analytic Approach*. Amherst: University of Massachusetts Press.

Munzel, G. F. (1999) *Kant's Conception of Moral Character: The "Critical" Link of Morality, Anthropology, and Reflective Judgement*. Chicago: University of Chicago Press.

Neiman, S. (1994) *The Unity of Reason: Rereading Kant*. Oxford: Oxford University Press.

Newey, Glen (2008) "How Not to Tolerate Religion". Paper presented to the ESRC Workshop on "Toleration, Recognition and Religious Diversity", Keele University. Published in (2011) M. Mookherjee (ed.) *Democracy, Religious Pluralism and the Liberal Dilemma of Accomodation*. New York: Springer.

Noica, C. (1991) *Jurnal de idei*. Bucharest: Humanitas.

Nussbaum, M. (1986) *The Fragility of Goodness: Luck and Ethics in Greek Tragedy and Philosophy*. Cambridge: Cambridge University Press.

Olafson, F. (1967) *Principles and Persons: An Ethical Interpretation of Existentialism*. London: The John Hopkins Press.

O'Neill, O. (1996) *Towards Justice and Virtue: A Constructive Account of Practical Reasoning*. Cambridge: Cambridge University Press.

——(1989) *Constructions of Reason. Explorations of Kant's Practical Philosophy*. Cambridge: Cambridge University Press.

Paton, H. J. ([1947]1970) *The Categorical Imperative: A Study in Kant's Moral Philosophy*. London: Hutchinson.

Peucker, H. (2007) "Husserl's Critique of Kant's Ethics", *Journal of the History of Philosophy* 45(2): 309–19.

Pieper, A. (2002) "Zweites Hauptstück (57–71)", in O. Höffe (ed.) *Kritik der praktischen Vernunft*. Berlin: Akademie Verlag.

Piper, A. M. S. (2009) "Kant's Transcendental Analysis of Action", in *Kant's Metaethics: First 'Critique' Foundations* (in progress). Delivered at the *Transcendental Philosophy* Conference, Manchester Metropolitan University. Unpublished excerpt.

Pocock, J. G. A. (2009) *Political Thought and History: Essays on Theory and Method*. Cambridge: Cambridge University Press.

——(1981) "Virtues, Rights and Manners: A Model for Historians of Political Thought", *Political Theory* 9(3): 353–68.

——(1972) "Languages and Their Implications: The Transformation of the Study of Political Thought", *Politics, Language and Time*. New edn 1989. London: Methuen.

Priest, S. (2000) *The Subject in Question: Sartre's Critique of Husserl in 'The Transcendence of the Ego'*. London: Routledge.

Rawls, J. (2001) *Justice as Fairness: A Restatement*. Ed. E. Kelly. Cambridge, MA: Harvard University Press.

——(2000) *Lectures in the History of Moral Philosophy*. Ed. Barbara Herman. Cambridge, MA: Harvard University Press.

———(1995) "Reply to Habermas", *The Journal of Philosophy* 92(3): 132–80.

———([1971]1994) *A Theory of Justice*. Rev. edn 1999. Oxford University Press, Oxford.

———(1993) *Political Liberalism*. 2nd rev. edn 2005. New York: Columbia University Press.

———(1985) "Justice as Fairness: Political not Metaphysical", *Philosophy and Public Affairs* 14(3): 223–51.

———(1980) "Kantian Constructivism in Moral Theory", *Journal of Philosophy* 77(9): 515–72.

Reath, A. ([1984])1995) "Two Conceptions of the Highest Good in Kant", in R. F. Chadwick (ed.) *Immanuel Kant: Critical Assessments*. Vol. III. London: Routledge.

Reid, T. ([1785]1788) *Essays on the Active Powers of Man*. Edinburgh: printed for John Bell and G. G. J. & J. Robinson.

Rohatyn, D. (1975) "Sartre's Critique of Kant", *Indian Philosophical Quarterly* 2(2): 171–6.

Scanlon, T. M. (1998) *What We Owe to Each Other*. Cambridge, MA: Harvard University Press.

———(1992) "Rawls on Justification", in S. R. Freeman (ed.) *Cambridge Companion to Rawls*. Cambridge: Cambridge University Press.

Schroeder, W. R. (1984) *Sartre and his Predecessors: The Self and the Other*. London: Routledge & Kegan Paul.

Schutz, A. ([1955]1964) "Equality and the Meaning Structure of the Social World", in A. Brodersen (ed.) *Collected Papers II: Studies in Social Theory*. The Hague: Martinus Nijhoff.

Silber, J. ([1959]1995) "The Copernican Revolution in Ethics: The Good Re-examined", in R. F. Chadwick (ed.) *Immanuel Kant: Critical Assessments*. Vol. III, 196–214. London: Routledge.

———(1960) "The Ethical Significance of Kant's *Religion*", in Immanuel Kant (ed.) *Religion Within the Limits of Reason Alone*. Trs. Theodore M. Greene and Hoyt H. Hudson. New York: Harper & Row.

Simont, J. (1998) "La conception sartrienne du néant est-elle classique? (à propos de la simultanéité et de l'action-réciproque chez Kant et Sartre)", *Études Sartriennes* VII: 39–49.

———(1992) "Sartrean ethics", in C. Howells (ed.) *The Cambridge Companion to Sartre*. Trs. Oreste F. Pucciani. Cambridge: Cambridge University Press.

———(1987a) "La problèmatique de 'l'idée régulatrice' de Kant chez Sartre", in P. Verstraeten (ed.) *Sur les Écrits Posthumes de Sartre; Annales de l'Institut de Philosophie et de Sciences Morales*. Bruxelles: Éditions de l'Université de Bruxelles.

———(1987b) "Autour des conferences de Sartre à Cornell", in P. Verstraeten (ed.) *Sur les Écrits Posthumes de Sartre; Annales de l'Institut de Philosophie et de Sciences Morales*. Bruxelles: Éditions de l'Université de Bruxelles.

Solomon, R. C. (1989) *From Hegel to Existentialism*. Oxford: Oxford University Press.

Spiegelberg, H. (1987) "Sartre's Last Word on Ethics in Phenomenological Perspective", in Simon Glynn (ed.) *Sartre: An Introduction of Some Major Themes*. Aldershot: Avebury.

Stern, R. (2011) "Kant, Moral Obligation and the Holy Will", in M. Timmons and S. Baiasu (eds) *Kant on Practical Justification: Interpretative Essays*. Oxford: Oxford University Press. Forthcoming.

Strauss, D. (1997) "Principle and Its Perils", *The University of Chicago Law Review* 64(3): 373–87.

Sweeney, K. (1985) "Lying to the Murderer: Sartre's Use of Kant in 'The Wall' ", *Mosaic* 18(2): 1–16.

Taylor, C. ([1979]1997) "What's Wrong with Negative Liberty?", in R. E. Goodin and P. Pettit (eds.) *Contemporary Political Philosophy: An Anthology*. Oxford: Blackwell.

Timmermann, J. (2001) "The Dutiful Lie: Kantian Approaches to Moral Dilemmas", in V. Gerhardt, R.-P. Horstmann and R. Schumacher (eds) *Kant und die Berliner Aufklärung: Akten des IX. Internationalen Kant-Kongresses*. Band III: Sektionen VI-X. Berlin: Walter de Gruyter.

Timmons, M. (2005) "Decisions Procedures, Moral Criteria, and the Problem of Relevant Descriptions in Kant's Ethics", *Jahrbuch für Recht und Ethik* 13: 313–33.

Uniacke, S. (2005) "Responsibility and Obligation: Some Kantian Direction", *International Journal of Philosophical Studies* 13(4): 461–75.

——(1996) "The Limits of Criminality: Kant on the Plank", in H. Tam (ed.) *Punishment, Excuses and Moral Development*. Aldershot: Avebury.

Verstraeten, P. (1995) "Le Mythe d'Er (du platonisme de Sartre à son kantisme)", *Études Sartriennes* 6: 193–224.

——(1992) "Appendix: Hegel and Sartre", in C. Howells (ed.) *The Cambridge Companion to Sartre*. Cambridge: Cambridge University Press.

——(1987) "Imperatifs et Valeurs", *Sur les Écrits Posthume de Sartre: Annales de l'Institut de Philosophie et de Sciences Morales*. P. Verstraeten (ed.) Bruxelles: Éditions de l'Université de Bruxelles.

Ward, K. (1971) "Kant's Teleological Ethics", *The Philosophical Quarterly* 21(85): 337–51.

Warnock, M. (1970) *Existentialist Ethics*. London and Basingstoke: Macmilllan.

Webber, J. (2009) *The Existentialism of Jean-Paul Sartre*. London: Routledge.

——(2007) "Character, Common-Sense, and Expertise", *Ethical Theory and Moral Practice* 10(1): 89–104.

——(2006) "Virtue, Character and Situation", *Journal of Moral Philosophy* 3(2): 195–216.

Westphal, K. (2011) "Kant's Constructivism and Rational Justification", in S. Baiasu, S. Pihlstrom and H. Williams (eds) *Politics and Metaphysics in Kant*. Cardiff: University of Wales Press. Forthcoming.

Wider, K. V. (1997) *The Bodily Nature of Consciousness: Sartre and Contemporary Philosophy of Mind*. Ithaca, NY: Cornell University Press.

Willaschek, M. (2002) "Which Imperatives for Right? On the Non-Prescriptive Character of Juridical Laws in Kant's *Metaphysics of Morals*", in M. Timmons (ed.) *Kant's Metaphysics of Morals: Interpretative Essays*. Cambridge: Cambridge University Press.

Williams, G. (2007) "Judges in Our Own Case: Kantian Legislation and Responsibility Attribution", *Politics and Ethics Review* 3(1): 8–23.

Williams, H. (1983) *Kant's Political Philosophy*. Oxford: Blackwell.

Wood, A. (2005) *Kant*. Oxford: Blackwell.

Yovel, Y. (1977) "Dialectic without Mediation: On Sartre's Variety of Marxism and Dialectic", in S. Avineri (ed.) *Varieties of Marxism*. The Hague: Martinus Nijhoff.

Zenkin, S. (1995) "Les forces de l'absurde: Une relecture du *Mur*", *Études Sartriennes*, VI: 225–42.

Index

Note: The letter 'n' followed by the locators refers to notes cited in the text.

accountability, 17–19, 26, 36, 38, 42, 59, 70–1, 77, 83, 103, 172, 198, 247 n13, n15
action-guiding, 140, 236
see also guiding force
alienation, 131–2, 135, 217
see also bad faith, inauthenticity
Allison, Henry E., 202, 241 n5, 257 n3, 258 n13, n16, 259 n22, n27, 264 n41
Ameriks, Karl, 19
analyticity
of ethics, 121–3
of hypothetical imperative, 160
of judgement, 23–4
of reason, 208–10; *see also* dialectical, reason
of relation between happiness and virtue, 94–6, 199
Anderson, Thomas C., 257 n1, 269 n4, n8
Annas, Julia, 259 n20
antinomies, 84, 86
practical, 92–8, 103, 178, 199, 204–5, 220
third, 84–91, 101–2, 105–6, 116, 118, 139, 145, 178, 201, 216, 221, 257 n3, 278 n13
anxiety
of free choice, 140–1
of influence, 8, 265 n47
Apel, Karl-Otto, 241 n5, 243 n18
apperception, 30, 246 n9, 247 n11, n14, 248 n18
empirical, 30, 33, 248 n20, 249 n23
transcendental, 29–31, 33–4, 36, 43, 49, 56–8, 83, 178, 222–3, 234, 247, 248 n21, 249 n25, 252 n13, 255 n37, 256 n42

Aristotle, 7, 92, 242 n9, 244 n23, 245 n33, 259 n24
Aron, Raymond, 75
as if, 207, 219, 223–4, 271 n23
authenticity, 12, 74–6, 131, 133–4, 136, 147, 178, 189, 191–2, 195, 203, 218, 226–7, 235, 243 n21, 244 n25, 262 n30, 263 n31
see also bad faith; inauthenticity
authoritarianism, 135, 155, 179, 181, 182, 185, 192, 197, 204, 227, 237
autonomy, 12, 92–3, 114, 123, 125, 136, 140–1, 153–5, 174, 178, 182, 194, 196–7, 215, 227, 232–3, 236–7, 265 n46
personal, 4–5
political, 4–5, 157, 234, 242 n15, 257 n1; *see also* heteronomy; self-governance; self-legislation

bad faith, 74–6, 123–9, 131, 133–5, 141, 143, 146, 185, 188, 217–18
see also inauthenticity *and* good faith
Baiasu, Sorin, 264 n43, 266 n8, 270 n17
Baldwin, Thomas, 62–5, 67–8, 70, 72, 75–6, 244 n26, 255 n33, 256 n38, n40, n42–3
Bauer, Bruno, 155–6
Baynes, Kenneth, 273 n5
De Beauvoir, Simone, 145, 245 n36, 256 n40
Beavers, Anthony, 244 n26, 264 n39
Beck, Lewis White, 259 n27, 267 n14, 268 n18
Berlin, Isaiah, 242 n10
Bird, Graham, 245 n2, n3, 246 n7, 262 n20
Bloom, Harold, 8, 264 n40, 265 n44, n47

Catalano, Joseph, 250–1 n11
Categorical Imperative, 12, 82, 86, 97–8,
    100–4, 138–9, 141, 145–6, 151,
    158–9, 161–2, 164, 169–71, 174,
    181, 183–4, 191–2, 197–204, 225–6,
    235–6, 243 n21, 244 n6, 270 n14,
    n18
    see also authenticity; criterion
Character, 37–8, 41, 58–9, 67, 69, 74–5,
    89–90, 254 n29, 255 n37, 256 n44,
    258 n9, n12, n13
choice, 4, 5, 18, 38–41, 58, 60, 62–4,
    67–71, 89–90, 109, 114, 116, 117,
    120, 124–5, 128, 140–1, 143–4, 155,
    186, 196, 225, 227, 235, 242 n13,
    254 n33, 256 n38, n40, n42, 258
    n11, n13
    actual, 4, 142–4, 146, 181
    deliberative, 67
    original *or* self-choice *or* of disposition,
        4, 12, 15–17, 41–2, 58–65, 67,
        68–72, 74–7, 81, 125, 128–9,
        149–50, 178, 194, 234, 238, 243
        n21, 253 n33, 255 n35, n37, 256
        n40, n42, n44
    power of, 40, 89–92
civil society, 157, 204
code, 122–3, 136–9, 146–7, 185, 187–8,
    190–1, 235, 264 n39
cognitivism, 2–3, 6, 229, 232–3, 252 n14
concreteness, 7, 12, 101, 105, 111,
    121–3, 136–8, 140, 145–6, 185–6,
    191, 235
condition *v.* determination, 89, 109,
    113, 119, 181, 191, 205, 214, 260
    n1, 272 n29
    see also facticity
De Coorbeyter, Vincent, 249 n1
consciousness
    immediate *or* non-positional, 50–1,
        109–10, 129–30, 133, 196, 226,
        250 n10, 251 n11–13, 253 n18,
        260 n2
    positional, 50–3, 109, 127, 132, 250
        n7, 250–1 n11, 251 n12–13, 253
        n18, 260 n3; *see also*
        self-consciousness
consciousness of the moral law, 102,
    140, 259 n27
    see also fact of reason

consequentialism, 10, 187
Constant, Benjamin, 1–6, 15–16, 38, 79,
    81, 105, 108, 138, 170, 228–9,
    232–3, 237–8, 240, 241 n1, n4,
    273 n1
constitutiveness, 6, 47, 74, 86, 108–9,
    147, 192, 207, 213, 238, 256 n44
constitutive, 23, 30, 32, 53, 56, 86–7,
    91, 110, 151, 170–1, 202–3, 206–7,
    217–22, 236, 247 n11, 250 n4, 252
    n18, 253 n18, 272 n33
constructivism, 10–11, 225, 228–30,
    232–4, 241 n7, 245 n29, 274 n6
contingency, 31, 34–5, 48, 93–7, 103,
    128, 137, 146, 156, 169, 177, 196,
    198–9, 226, 261 n13
conventional v. natural, 159–62
conversion, 76, 134, 262 n30
    see also revolution in disposition
cosmopolitanism, 150–1, 205–6, 217–21
criterion, 4–5, 7, 79, 81–2, 100–4, 128,
    135, 138–9, 141, 147, 149, 150–1,
    158, 160, 162, 170, 183, 187, 191,
    196–8, 200, 201, 225–6, 233, 235–7
critical ethics, 6, 11–13, 50, 108, 145,
    147, 228, 234, 236–40

Darnell, Michelle, 245 n33, 259 n1
Darwall, Stephen, 11
deliberative model of agency, 48, 58–61,
    65–9, 116, 234–5, 255 n34, 256 n39
Descartes, René, 7, 19, 62, 245 n3, 246
    n4, 250 n5
determinism, 84, 108, 115–16, 118, 120,
    126–7, 145, 261 n14, 265 n46
    see also free will
Detmer, David, 257 n1
dialectical
    dogmatism, 211
    process, 211–14, 222–3, 271 n22
    reason, 208–11, 213–14, 223–4,
        272 n26
differences between Kant and Sartre,
    5–11, 16, 37, 72–3, 75–7, 82, 105,
    125, 135–6, 142, 147, 149, 172,
    182–3, 188, 227, 236–7, 243 n27,
    252 n13, 264 n39, 265 n48, 271 n19
    see also similarities between Kant and
        Sartre
Dobson, Andrew, 224, 245 n30

dogmatism, 2, 15, 80, 87, 106, 108, 147, 150, 170, 179, 202–3, 211, 225, 238, 257 n4–5
non-dogmatic, 2, 11–14, 15, 82, 238
Drake, David, 273 n40
duty, 1, 6, 92, 96, 101, 124, 135, 199–200, 228, 239, 257 n45, 259 n16, 262 n23, 266 n5, 273 n2, n3

Edie, James, 243 n20
ego, 51, 56–7, 130–1, 253 n24
see also (the) I
emancipation, 151, 153–4, 156, 176
human, 155–7
political, 155–7
religious, 156
empiricism, 87, 100, 257 n4, n5
enforceability, 160, 171–3, 188–91, 195, 198–201, 205, 238, 241 n6, 242 n14
Engstrom, Stephen, 289 n18
enlightenment, 151–5, 157, 200, 205
Epicureanism, 94, 96–7
equality, 121, 187, 274 n8
ethical demand, 122–5, 134–6, 141, 262 n23, 265 n50, 270 n11
ethical paradox, 187–9
ethical worth, 96, 125, 173–4, 186, 200, 202, 244 n23, 262 n22
see also morality *and* legality
ethics, 8–9, 81, 123, 133, 135, 149, 180, 245 n35, 262 n30
of ambiguity, 145
analytic, 121–3
character-centred, 243 n22
Kantian, 8, 10, 82, 92, 100, 122–4, 137, 179, 225, 245 n35, 263 n36, 270–1 n19
meta–, 195
of principles/values, 7, 10, 135, 174, 185, 190, 227, 235–6, 265 n39, 268 n20, 270 n11
radical, 135, 182, 189, 191, 194
of rules, 122
of unconditional standards, 81–2, 236
v. political (legal) philosophy, 170–6, 242 n9
see also system *and* code *and* critical ethics
existentialism, 1, 7, 112–13, 124, 145, 181, 184, 204

externalisation (of praxis), 207–8, 211, 215–16, 235
see also internalisation
externality (of law), 171–3, 191

facticity, 109–10, 130
see also condition *v.* determination
fact of reason, 169, 201–2, 259 n27, 271 n19, n21
see also consciousness of the moral law
false positives, 159–60, 162
first cause, 85
prime mover, 85–6
uncaused cause, 86–7, 107, 116, 118
Flikschuh, Katrin, 254 n30, 258 n13
formula of the universal law, 158–9, 161–2, 167–8
for-others, 111, 127–9, 131, 133–4, 136, 214, 263 n30
freedom, 18, 22, 36–7, 42, 50, 58–9, 68, 76–7, 79–80, 82, 102, 105–6, 112–14, 117–18, 120, 122–3, 126–8, 130–5, 140–1, 144–5, 147, 149–50, 153, 155, 189–201, 194, 198, 201, 203, 213–16, 220–1, 227, 229, 232, 234, 237–9, 241–2 n8, 242 n11, n12, 245 n23, 245 n1, 250 n9, 254 n30, n33, 257 n1, 258 n6, n10, 260 n28, 261 n13, 262 n22, n30, 263 n30, n32, n33, 265 n45, n49, 266 n5, 268 n17, n20, 269 n6, 272 n29
in choice of disposition, 39, 59, 61, 63, 68, 70–2
as generosity, 123
negative, 196–7, 234, 237, 238, 242 n11
popular, 114–15
practical *or* empirical, 89–91, 103, 114–16, 118–19, 146, 180–2, 216, 255 n33, 258 n7, n11, n16, 269 n4
theoretical *or* transcendental *or* ontological, 73, 84–8, 90–1, 102–3, 115, 118–20, 125, 128, 139, 145–6, 149, 180, 184, 216, 217, 258 n7, n13, 269 n4
see also liberties of the ancients *v.* moderns *and* autonomy

free will theory, 108, 116, 118, 145, 259
    n7, 261 n14
    see also determinism
Fretz, Leo, 245 n30, 251 n8, n9, 261 n5
Freud, Sigmund, 62

Gardner, Sebastian, 19, 30, 207
Garner, Richard, 265 n50
Gibbard, Alan, 11, 278
Gillett, Grant, 244 n27
God, 69, 76, 80, 93, 97, 102, 199, 204–6,
    222–3, 259 n21, 270 n14, 271 n22
(the) good, 4, 76, 79, 82, 92–4, 128, 152,
    162, 165–6, 170, 174–8, 188–9, 195,
    198, 201, 219–21, 230, 233, 243
    n15, 267 n14, n15, 268 n17, n18,
    n19, 274 n7
    common, 3, 218, 230
    compulsive, 177
    empirical, 94, 174–6, 178, 199, 227
    external, 176–88
    highest as complete *or* summum
        bonum, 92–5, 97, 121, 199, 204,
        220
    highest as supreme, 94, 97–8, 203
    unconditional *or* absolute *or* in itself,
        92, 94, 101, 104, 175–6, 196, 198,
        200, 266 n3, 268 n19
good faith, 76, 134
    see also authenticity
guiding force, 138, 191
    see also action-guiding
Guyer, Paul, 241 n5

Habermas, Jürgen, 11, 155–6, 241 n5,
    243 n18, 244 n24, 245 n29, 252–3
    n15, 254 n27, 264 n42, 272 n33
happiness *v.* virtue, 92–7, 103, 121, 199,
    204–5, 242 n8
    see also virtue
Hegel, Georg Wilhelm Friedrich, 59, 62,
    214, 245 n29, 254 n27, 271 n22, 272
    n28, 273 n38
Heidegger, Martin, 62, 120, 250 n4, 272
    n28
Henrich, Dieter, 246 n8
Herman, Barbara, 162–6, 241 n5, 267
    n14
heteronomy, 92–3, 139, 265 n46
    see also autonomy

history, 12, 149–51, 181–3, 204–7, 209,
    211, 218–25, 237, 256 n44, 271 n22
Höffe, Otfried, 92, 100–1, 138, 259 n17,
    n24, 264 n38, 266 n10
Howells, Christina, 8
Von Humboldt, Wilhelm, 241 n8
Husserl, Edmund, 7, 10–11, 44–5, 47–68,
    64, 120, 243 n20, 243 n18, 245 n35,
    250 n6, 255 n36, 268 n1

(the) I, 19–25, 27–9, 30–1, 42–3, 48–50,
    57, 83, 130, 247 n5, 248 n24
(the) me, 49, 130–5, 240 n24, 253 n24;
    see also ego *and* self
idealism, 11, 44–8
    see also transcendental idealism
idea of reason, 84, 86–7, 92, 97, 107,
    146, 165, 178, 182–3, 201, 205–7,
    212–20, 271 n22, 272 n33
identity, 54–6, 73, 76–7, 80, 82–3, 103,
    110, 144, 149, 226, 245 n1, 246 n7,
    247 n12, 248 n20, n21, 253 n19,
    266 n53
    numerical, 19–15, 27, 30–1, 33, 49, 57,
        72, 83, 111, 216, 246 n8, 247 n15
    personal, 12, 15–20, 22–7, 29–31, 36,
        42, 48–9, 53–7, 72–3, 77, 81, 83,
        103, 127, 216, 237–8, 245 n23,
        n27, 246 n31, 247 n9, 253 n14,
        255 n33, 256 n37, 257 n42, 261
        n6; moral, 82, 232, 255 n33, n37;
        psychological, 82–3
imperative
    Categorical, 12, 82, 97–8, 100–4,
        138–9, 141, 146–7, 151, 158–9,
        164, 169–71, 174, 181, 183, 189,
        191–2, 197–214, 225–6, 243 n21,
        244 n23, n25, 269 n6, 270 n14,
        n18
    hypothetical, 98, 137, 160, 186
impersonal, 42–4, 48–50, 56–68, 257 n27
inauthenticity, 76, 133, 135, 188–90, 217
    see also authenticity
incentive, 60, 66, 74, 92, 117, 146,
    171–2, 186, 226, 255 n33, 258–60
    n13
intelligible, 40–1, 68, 199, 220
sensible, 38, 40–1, 68, 74, 89, 91–2,
    95–8, 101–2, 137, 140, 173, 176

incorporation, 28, 40, 62, 74, 82, 196, 259 n16
individualism, 11, 124, 245 n29
in-itself-for-itself, 74–5, 110, 145
intentionality, 44, 46–8, 50, 260 n2, n3, n4
intention *v.* motive, 79, 113–14, 116–18, 167–9, 172–3, 218
internalisation, 157, 186, 189–91, 194–6, 200–1, 207–8, 211, 215, 226, 235
intuition
   moral, 5, 93, 230, 234, 243 n16, 259 n21
   sensible, 6, 23–4, 30–2, 35, 83, 85–6, 166, 202, 206–7, 223, 246 n7, n9, 247 n11, 248 n16, n21, 250 n25
intuitionism, 10
I think *or* cogito, 19, 27, 42–3, 48–9, 57, 82–6, 180, 245 n4
   pre-reflective, 49, 50, 53–5, 110–11, 129–30, 215, 226, 260 n2
   reflective, 49, 53

Jeanson, Francis, 145, 265 n52
Jones, Gary, 261 n10
Jopling, David, 244 n26, 246 n30
judgement, 19, 22–3, 27, 44–6, 50, 54, 56, 83, 101, 131, 139, 164, 231, 245–6 n4, 250 n10, 259 n16, 261 n12
   empirical, 30, 249 n23
   moral, 3, 14, 25, 26, 42, 59, 63–4, 69, 77, 100–1, 103, 108, 134, 138–9, 147, 164–9, 171, 174, 202, 235, 237, 245 n1, 253 n24, 259 n17, 271 n19
   objective, 33–6, 249 n23, n25
   reflective, 37
   subjective, 33–4, 36
justification, 6, 11–13, 25, 81–2, 102–4, 138, 141, 151, 158, 162, 164, 171, 173–4, 177, 188, 193, 220–1, 229, 235, 236, 238, 239–40, 241 n5, 243 n17, n18, 268 n15

Kant and Sartre, 5–12, 16–18, 32, 57, 58–9, 63–9, 72, 74–6, 79–80, 82, 100, 104–6, 123, 128, 135, 145–7, 149, 157, 182, 194, 196–7, 201, 203, 221, 235–9, 242 n18, 243 n19, n21,

248 n20, 254 n32, 255 n37, 256 n38, n42, 257 n47, n3, 264 n39
Kerner, George, 243 n21
Korsgaard, Christine, 158–63, 178, 241 n5, 257 n3

legality, 96, 171–4
   see also morality
Leibniz, Gottfried Wilhelm, 19, 30, 248 n19
liberties of the ancients *v.* moderns, 4–6, 11–13, 225, 229–30, 233–5, 236–8, 241–2
Lieberman, Marcel, 244 n26, 271 n19
Lindstedt, David, 219–21, 271 n22
Locke, John, 230, 242 n8, 247 n13
logic, 19, 34, 138, 158, 169, 171, 236
   transcendental, 169, 215, 225
logical interpretation, 158–64, 166, 168
Longuenesse, Béatrice, 249 n23

Marx, Karl, 155–7, 266 n6
Marxism, 210–11, 243 n40
maxim, 7, 24, n25, 36, 38–41, 65, 67–9, 72, 74, 76–7, 92, 98–102, 124–5, 135–8, 145–6, 158–72, 173, 174, 175, 189, 197–9, 202, 225–7, 239, 244 n25, 256 n38, 257 n45, 259 n16, n23, 263 n35, 264 n38, 266 n9, 269 n7, 270 n15
McBride, William L., 262 n30, 266 n31, 269 n10
McCarty, Richard, 259 n16
Merleau-Ponty, Maurice, 255 n34, 256 n40
metaphysics, 6, 11–12, 37, 46, 79–80, 103, 120, 127, 147, 151, 183, 244 n27, 245 n29, 249 n4, 254 n30, 265 n52
   dogmatic, 15, 44, 106, 108, 150, 256 n40
   Kantian, 80, 82, 147, 150, 171, 238
   see also ontology
methodology, 7, 9, 11, 17, 42, 58, 72, 76, 82, 178
Misrahi, Robert, 245 n30
Moore, Adrian W., 259 n23
moral cognition/knowledge, 2–3, 10–11, 72, 82, 101, 141, 221, 255 n37, 271 n19

morality, 68, 96, 171, 173
Morris, Phyllis Sutton, 243 n22
motivation, 60, 96–7, 99, 116–17, 171–4,
    186, 189, 196–7, 199–201, 220, 241
    n6, 261 n15, n19, 262 n29, 267
    n11, n13
Munzel, Felicitas G., 259 n17

necessity, 3–4, 21–3, 25–31, 33–5, 40,
    42–3, 47, 49, 52–3, 57–8, 70, 72,
    80–1, 83, 85, 90–1, 93–7, 102, 110,
    112, 114, 117, 123–5, 132, 140,
    142–3, 164–5, 167–9, 171, 176–9,
    181, 187, 198–9, 203–4, 216, 218,
    220–3, 225, 234, 236–7, 245 n1, 246
    n6, n9, 247 n11, n12, 248 n22, 249,
    249 n25, 252 n17, 253 n19, 255
    n33, 258 n6, n11, 260 n4, 261 n12,
    n13, 264 n39, 265 n46, 272 n37
Neiman, Susan, 266 n1
Newey, Glen, 267 n11, 270 n13
Nietzsche, Friedrich, 62
Noica, Constantin, 245 n33
normativity, 2–3, 5–6, 9–13, 15–17, 38,
    42, 60, 76, 79–80, 82, 91–3, 102,
    123–5, 128, 135, 137–45, 147,
    149–52, 164, 171, 176–9, 181–90,
    192–5, 197, 199–200, 225–7, 229,
    233–7, 238, 242 n13, 245 n1, 262
    n30, 264 n44, 265 n48, n49
prescriptivity, 10, 88, 142, 192–3, 195,
    203, 225, 244 n23, 264 n39, 265
    n50, 271 n19
noumenon, 6, 11, 40, 69–73, 97, 125,
    139–40, 165, 238
    see also phenomenon
Nussbaum, Martha, 243 n33

obligation, 1–2, 15, 16, 79, 82, 88–91,
    108, 124–5, 141–3, 164, 169, 171,
    177–8, 183, 197–8, 200, 227, 231,
    235, 237, 238–40, 242 n13, 249 n23,
    259 n10, n13, 262 n23, 268 n18,
    269 n6, 270 n14
Olafson, Frederick, 7
O'Neill, Onora, 167–9, 241 n5, 243 n18,
    259 n19, n23
ontology, 2, 11, 46, 54, 56, 69, 73, 106,
    111–12, 115, 117–18, 123, 126–9,
    134–6, 139–40, 143, 145–6, 149–50,

180–1, 184–5, 193, 207, 210,
    216–17, 236, 249–50 n2, 252 n18,
    255 n36, 260 n32, 261 n19, 262
    n30, 265 n52, 267 n14, 268 n1, 269
    n4, 271 n19, 271 n26
optimism, 204, 207, 215–17

paralogism, 19–20, 22–7, 29, 31, 48, 57,
    73–4, 103, 178, 215, 234, 245 n2,
    246 n6
Paton, Herbert James, 267 n14, 268 n19
self, 17, 28, 42, 48, 51, 53–6, 62, 64,
    73–4, 87, 108–10, 119, 131, 196,
    203, 226, 235, 248 n18, n20, 251
    n11, 253 n18, n19, n20, 256 n40,
    n44, 260 n5, 261 n7, 270 n12, 271
    n21
personality, 18–20, 23–9, 40, 48, 50, 56,
    73, 143, 254 n26
practical *or* moral, 83, 93, 102–3
psychological, 83, 102–3
Peucker, Henning, 243 n35
phenomenology, 6, 10, 15, 44–6, 48, 72,
    139, 150, 185, 239, 243 n18, n20,
    249 n4, 262 n20, n30, 268 n1, 271
    n19, 272 n28
phenomenon, 11, 17, 41, 59–60, 62,
    69–71, 85–7, 97, 100, 118–20, 130,
    139, 141, 145–7, 166, 168, 188,
    190–1, 190, 195, 206, 214, 216, 218,
    220–3, 238, 243 n20, 252 n14, 262
    n20, 264 n43
    see also noumenon
Pieper, Annemarie, 267 n14
Piper, Adrian M. S., 245 n6
Plato, 21–2, 52, 87, 243 n33, 254 n4,
    257 n28
pleasant (the), 92–3, 298–9
pleasure, 3, 92, 95–6, 137, 175–6
pluralism, 80, 82, 274 n7
Pocock, John G. A., 243 n34
possibility (as ontological structure), 61,
    74, 108–11, 124, 130, 133, 143,
    262 n27
practical interpretation of the CI,
    158–64, 166, 168
presence, 109, 261 n2
    of another person, 131–2, 214
    presence to the world, 109
    to self, 109, 253 n22, 254 n26, 260 n2

Priest, Stephen, 249 n1
private sphere, 3, 155–7, 223, 235,
    269 n1
progress, 12, 80, 104, 149–51, 181, 183,
    204, 206, 216–21, 227, 237, 245, 272
    n33
project (Sartrean), 61, 65–8, 70–1, 74,
    76–7, 108, 111, 113–14, 117, 121,
    124–5, 129–30, 134–5, 140, 146–7,
    180–1, 186, 188, 191, 196, 208,
    212–14, 218, 226–7, 235, 254 n33,
    256 n38, n42, 261 n18, 262 n19,
    263 n32
  fundamental, 58–78, 70–2, 74–5, 109,
    112, 121, 125, 128, 131, 140, 234,
    254 n29, n33, 255 n35, n36, n37,
    n44
  global, 58, 70–1, 74, 147
psychoanalysis, 68, 128, 255 n37, 271
    n19
public sphere, 3, 155, 157, 167, 230,
    234, 269 n1
  see also private sphere

Railton, Peter, 11
rationalism, 20, 48, 55, 81, 216, 252 n14
Rawls, John, 11, 15, 230–4, 241 n5, n7,
    242 n15, 243 n16, n17, n18, 243
    n29, 259 n19, 273 n5, 274 n7, n8
realism, 2–3, 6, 44–8, 81, 144, 147, 182,
    194, 225, 227, 230, 232, 235, 265
    n51
  see also idealism
Reath, Andrews, 267 n14
reflection, *see* self-consciousness,
    reflective
reflexion, 53–8, 62, 109, 111, 119,
    129–30, 214, 226, 253 n18, 254 n26,
    259 n26
  see also self-consciousness,
    pre-reflective *or* reflexive
regulativeness, 32, 86, 183, 205–7,
    216–21, 222, 244 n28, 247 n11, 271
    n22, 272 n33
  see also constitutiveness
Reid, Thomas, 247 n13
revolution in disposition, 39, 40–1,
    58–9, 62–3, 65–9, 71–2, 75, 178,
    234, 254–5 n33, 256 n38, n40, n42
  see also original choice *and* conversion

right to lie, 1–2, 15, 17–18, 20, 38,
    77, 79, 82, 105, 170–1, 238,
    241 n3, 259 n25, 266 n9,
    273 n2, n3
Rohatyn, Dennis, 243 n31

Scanlon, Thomas M., 243 n17, n18
scepticism, 2–3, 11, 110, 230, 233–4, 245
    n29
Schroeder, Ralph W., 252 n18
Schutz, Alfred, 245 n36
self, 17, 28, 42, 48, 51, 53–6, 62, 64, 87,
    93, 108–10, 131, 203, 226, 236, 253
    n20, 256 n40, n44, 258 n21
  see also (the) I
self-choice, 10, 13, 48, 77, 79, 83, 90, 91,
    92, 94, 95, 97, 100, 171, 199, 200,
    238, 261, 317, 322
self-consciousness
  pre-reflective *or* reflexive, 29–31,
    49–55, 110–12, 130–1, 133, 215,
    226, 237, 248 n18, 252 n14, 253
    n18, n23, 260 n2, n5
  reflected-on, 110–12, 116, 117, 129,
    134, 141, 263 n32; *see also*
    reflexion
  reflective, 27–8, 42, 49–53, 56–7,
    110–11, 126–30, 209, 263 n32;
    impure, 73, 112, 123, 125–9,
    134–5, 141, 146, 227, 250 n11,
    262 n30; pure, 126, 128,
    250 n11
self-governance, 80, 194
self-legislation, 123, 193–4, 227
  see also autonomy
sensibility, 31–2, 37, 85–6, 90, 92, 165,
    245 n9, 258 n14
shame, 131–4, 262 n29, 263 n31
Silber, John, 176–8, 260 n16, 267 n14,
    268 n17
similarities between Kant and Sartre,
    5–8, 11–13, 15–16, 75, 77, 79, 82,
    147, 234, 244 n28, 255 n37, 256
    n43, 264 n39, 272 n28
  structural, 9–10, 42, 53, 58, 72, 76,
    105–6, 120, 135, 145–6, 149,
    183–4, 194, 203, 227, 237
  substantive, 72–3, 237
  see also differences between Kant and
    Sartre

Simont, Juliette, 185–9, 191, 195, 207,
216, 222, 244 n28, 264 n39, 269 n8,
270 n11, n12, 271 n23, 272 n28
singularity, 3, 9, 121–3, 138, 186,
208–10, 215, 224
social life, 3, 123, 153, 170, 172, 175,
188, 191, 199, 205, 210–11, 213,
215–16, 223, 230, 232–3, 243 n14,
268 n1, 272 n29
Solomon, Robert, 7
speculation, 219, 257 n4, n5
Spiegelberg, Herbert, 245 n30, 269 n3
spontaneity, 22, 26, 57, 74, 87, 98,
105–7, 113, 119–20, 145–6, 149,
180–1, 184, 196–7, 203, 235, 243
n16, 257 n2
standard, 4–7, 12, 15–17, 36, 59–60, 77,
79, 81–2, 89, 92–3, 103, 105, 135–6,
139–40, 143–4, 146, 151, 170–1,
173, 175–7, 185, 187–8, 189–91,
193–4, 196–8, 200–1, 204, 206,
225–7, 229–30, 233, 235–51, 244
n21, 262 n30, 267 n14, 268 n19
end, 4, 58, 60–1, 65, 67–8, 70, 73–4,
77, 96–7, 112–17, 124, 126, 130,
137, 140, 146, 150–1, 160–2, 173,
185–9, 191, 194, 196, 198, 200,
202, 204–6, 208–9, 210, 216–18,
220–1, 233, 237, 257 n38, 261
n18, 262 n19, 265 n48, 267 n13,
n15, 269 n5, n7
goal, 89, 97, 108, 113, 114, 122, 180,
182, 186, 208, 225, 230, 267 n13
norm, 2–4, 6–7, 17, 77, 93, 124, 126–7,
138, 142, 144, 151, 157, 158, 162,
171–3, 193, 195, 218, 231, 244
n24, n25, 245 n29, 266 n10
principle, 2, 4–5, 38–9, 71, 79, 85,
89–90, 92–3, 97–9, 122–3, 136–9,
142, 147, 151, 158, 167–71,
174–8, 183, 185, 189–91, 195,
197–202, 204, 206, 222, 226–7,
231–4, 236, 237–9, 241 n6, 242,
n13, 243 n21, 244 n25, 245 n29,
263 n36, 264 n37, 265 n45, 267
n14, n15, 268 n18, n20, 270 n15,
271 n19, 273 n40, 274 n8
purpose, 61, 66, 93, 100–1, 113, 122,
124–5, 137, 140–3, 147, 159,
161–3, 173, 181, 187, 196, 198–9,

202–3, 205, 217–20, 228, 238,
242, 263 n35, 266 n3, 267 n13,
270 n15
value, 109–16, 198–9, 201, 203, 214,
218, 224–7, 230, 235–7, 242 n13,
243 n21, 244 n24, n25, 253 n24,
257 n1, 262 n30, 264 n39, 265
n48, n49, n51, 266 n5, n52, 267
n14, 268 n20, 269 n8, 270 n11,
n12, 271 n20, 272 n30
see also maxim
state (political), 4–5, 155–7, 205, 241–2,
n8, , 252 n18, 268 n1
Stern, Robert, 242 n13, 270 n14
Stoicism, 94, 96–7
Strauss, David, 244 n24
summum bonum, *see* (the) good
Sweeney, Kevin, 241 n3, n4, 243 n20
system, 205, 209, 223
ethical, 7–8, 13, 121, 123, 141, 191,
236–7, 244 n23, 245 n30, 262 n30
moral, 8, 79, 199, 202, 262 n22
philosophical, 183, 201, 219
political (representative), 3, 5

Taylor, Charles, 242 n11, n12, 261 n11
teleology, 7, 76, 135, 158, 217
things themselves (the), 12, 120
things in themselves, 6, 11, 45, 48, 82,
85, 87, 90–1, 118–20, 139, 141, 240,
246 n7, 249–60 n4, 258 n15, 262
n20, 264 n43
time, 19, 21–4, 26–30, 32–3, 35, 57–60,
62, 69–71, 77, 82–3, 85–6, 90, 107,
144, 211, 234, 246 n7, n9, 253 n23,
254 n25, 257 n40, 258 n18
Timmermann, Jens, 273 n2
Timmons, Mark, 269 n7
totalisation, 87, 207–11, 213–16, 223–6,
272 n26, n30
totality, 70, 74, 84, 121, 206–12, 214–16,
257 n2, 260 n6
Transcendental Aesthetic, 32, 262 n20
transcendental idealism, 11, 14, 79–80,
91, 120, 139, 141, 144, 145, 150,
171, 193, 258
truthfulness, 1, 6, 15, 79, 81, 108, 138,
169–70, 200, 228, 239–40, 266 n9,
273 n2, n3

unconditionality (moral), 1–2, 5–6, 15,
    17, 77, 79–82, 89, 92–3, 99–102,
    108, 122, 137–8, 164, 168–9, 171,
    175, 178, 181, 183, 185–6, 189, 191,
    193, 197, 199–200, 202–6, 225, 227,
    229, 231, 233, 236, 239, 263 n35,
    n36, 269 n6
conditionality, 1–2, 5–6, 41, 89, 98,
    101, 136–7, 169, 185–6, 191, 221,
    224, 238–9, 239, 242 n13, 244–5,
    270 n11, 272 n30
understanding (the), 31–6, 85–7, 91, 102,
    119–20, 154, 166–7, 205–7, 218–19,
    222–3, 247 n11, 258 n14, 266 n4
Uniacke, Suzanne, 245 n1, 267 n12
unity, 32–4, 43, 54–7, 73, 84, 86–7,
    111–12, 127, 140, 206–7, 210, 212,
    216, 218, 222, 235, 247 n14, n21,
    251 n11, 253 n24, 255 n37, 256
    n42, 261 n9, 265 n46, 265–6 n52,
    272 n32
  of apperception, transcendental,
    29–34, 43, 49, 56, 73, 178, 222–3,
    234, 237, 249 n25, 252 n13, 255
    n37
  empirical, 33, 249 n23
  of history, 12, 205, 218–20, 222–4, 237
  objective, 31, 33, 35
  of projects, 71, 74
  subjective, 31, 35

value of authenticity, *see* authenticity
value, *see* (the) good

Verstraeten, Pierre, 75–6, 188–9, 243
    n28, 253 n27, 257 n47, 269 n8, 270
    n12
virtue, 3, 92, 94–6, 121, 199, 204, 206,
    220, 242 n8, 244 n23, 259 n19, n24,
    n25
  see also happiness *v.* virtue
virtue ethics, 10

Ward, Keith, 267 n14
Warnock, Mary, 245 n30
Webber, Jonathan, 243 n22
Westphal, Kenneth, 259 n16
Wider, Kathleen V., 250 n5, n10, 252
    n13, 254 n28
will, 10, 66, 68, 76, 91, 93, 96, 98–9,
    116–18, 125, 136–9, 142, 145,
    158–60, 165, 166, 169–70, 175–8,
    197, 198, 203, 222–3, 256 n40,
    258 n7, n11, 259 n21, n22, 261
    n14, 266 n3, 267 n15, 268 n17,
    n19, 270 n15
  pure, 102, 142, 202
Willaschek, Marcus, 171, 266 n10, 267
    n13
Williams, Garrath, 245 n1
Williams, Howard, 273 n38
Wolff, Christian, 19
Wood, Allen, 264 n43, 267 n14
world whole, 84, 97, 207

Yovel, Yirmiahu, 272 n28

Zenkin, Serge, 241 n3